NECK DEEP

Also by Robert Parry

Fooling America
Trick or Treason
October Surprise X-Files
Lost History
Secrecy & Privilege

NECK DEEP

※

The Disastrous Presidency
of George W. Bush

Robert Parry, Sam Parry & Nat Parry

•••

The Media Consortium
Arlington, Virginia

To Josie and Drew and their generation

Grateful acknowledgement is made to Diane Duston for her support
and assistance in pre-paration of this book.-

Parry, Robert, 1949-
Parry, Samuel, 1973-
Parry, Nathaniel, 1976-

Neck Deep: The Disastrous Presidency of George W. Bush

Included index.

ISBN 978-1-893517-02-8 (hardcover)
ISBN 978-1-893517-03-5 (paperback)

Printed in the United States of America

CONTENTS

"We were neck deep in the Big Muddy,
and the big fool said to push on."

Pete Seeger

Introduction

It may become one of the great historical mysteries, leaving future scholars to scratch their heads over how someone with as few qualifications as George W. Bush came to lead the world's most powerful nation at the start of the 21st century.

Historians may ponder why so many Americans thought that an enterprise as vast and complicated as the U.S. government could be guided by a person who had failed at nearly every job he ever had. Why did so many voters believe that a little-traveled, incurious and inarticulate man of privilege could lead the planet's only superpower in a world of daunting challenges, shifting dangers and sharpening competition?

The historians may wonder, too, how George W. Bush, born with a shiny silver spoon in his mouth, managed to sell himself as a populist everyman, and why so many Americans rejected Al Gore in Election 2000 despite his record of leadership on difficult issues like alternative energy sources, advanced technology and arms control? Even taking into account the controversial outcome of Election 2000 – which saw Gore win more votes than Bush – why was the margin so close that Bush could snatch the White House away?

After the nation was attacked on September 11, 2001, historians may ask further, why did the American people allow Bush to assume such sweeping and unprecedented presidential powers? Why did the institutions designed to protect the Republic crumble so readily, especially the press and Congress? How was it that Bush was granted so much authority that he could entangle the United States in an aggressive – and disastrous – war in Iraq with few questions asked? Why hadn't the system of checks and balances worked better?

One goal of this book is to explain this historical mystery, how a combination of factors converged to bring the United States to this dangerous moment.

Part of the answer to the mystery can be found in the complex relationship between the American people and mass media. The multi-billion-dollar stakes involved in selling commercial products to the world's richest market have made the American people the most analyzed and dissected population on earth. Controlling their perceptions of reality and tapping their emotions are more than just art forms; they are economic imperatives.

Successful advertising techniques can bring vast fortunes to corporations selling products through television or other media. It logically followed that with so much power and money riding on control of the federal government, those lessons inevitably would seep into the U.S. political process. Just as Madison Avenue ad executives got rich selling products to American consumers, K Street political consultants earned tidy sums by using the false intimacy of TV to make their candidates appear more "down-to-earth" or "authentic" and their opponents seem "weird" or "dirty."

By 2000, the Republicans also had pulled far ahead of the Democrats in the machinery of political messaging, both in the technological sophistication of the party apparatus and the emergence of an overtly conservative media that stretched from print forms of newspapers, magazines and books to electronic outlets of radio, TV and the Internet.

Nothing remotely as advanced existed on the left side of American political spectrum. Conservatives liked to call the mainstream news media "liberal," but in reality, its outlook was either corporate with a strong sympathy for many Republican positions or consciously "centrist" with a goal of positioning the news content somewhere in the "middle."*

In Campaign 2000, the Republican advantages in media guaranteed a rosier glow around George W. Bush's attributes and a harsher light on Al Gore's shortcomings. Many voters said they found Bush more likable – "a regular guy" – while viewing Gore as a wonky know-it-all, who "thinks he's smarter than we are." That was, at least in part, a reflection of how the two candidates were presented by the dominant news media outlets, from Fox News to *The New York Times*. For his part, Bush exploited the anti-intellectualism of many Americans to his political advantage, even disparaging his former classmates at Yale as "so intellectually superior and so righteous."[1]

Many Americans also came to view Bush as that natural leader they often encounter in their everyday lives. He was, in a sense, the alpha male on the cruise ship, who would lead the pack from the elevator to the all-you-can-eat buffet bar, the guy who would keep everyone tittering with jokes at the expense of others. Blessed with a full head of hair himself, Bush especially enjoyed poking fun at bald

---

* For details on the evolution of this modern U.S. news media, see Robert Parry's *Secrecy & Privilege*.

men, sometimes playfully rubbing their bald pates in public or making their baldness the butt of his jokes.[*]

The talented Republican image-makers turned Bush's banter into proof that he was a "politically incorrect" politician who didn't play by conventional rules. He was, they said, a refreshing alternative to the endless parade of consultant-driven, poll-tested candidates – though, in reality, Bush's image was as consultant-driven and poll-tested as anybody's, down to his purchase of a 1,600-acre ranch in Crawford, Texas, in 1999, just before running for the White House.

Then, after the terrorist attacks on New York and Washington, less than nine months into Bush's presidency, the American people invested their hopes in Bush's natural leadership skills. The U.S. news media and the opposition Democrats also granted Bush extraordinary deference.

Bush's political advisers, his neoconservative foreign policy aides, and his allies in the right-wing media saw the 9/11 crisis as an opportunity to strengthen their ideological grip on power. They could use it to demonize their remaining liberal critics, settle some old scores in the Middle East, and possibly lock in permanent Republican control of the U.S. government.

It was in that climate of both voluntary and enforced unity that Bush sought a fundamental transformation of the U.S. constitutional system, asserting what his legal advisers called the "plenary" – or unlimited – powers of Commander in Chief at a time of war.

Under Bush's post-9/11 presidential theories, he could ignore laws passed by Congress. He simply attached a "signing statement" declaring that he would not be bound by any restrictions on his authority. As for laws enacted before his presidency, those, too, could be cast aside if they infringed on his view of his own power.

Bush could override constitutional provisions that protected the rights of citizens. He could deny the ancient right of *habeas corpus* guaranteeing due process and a fair trial – if he designated someone an "enemy combatant." He could order warrantless wiretaps, waiving the Fourth Amendment's requirement for court-approved search warrants based on "probable cause."

He could authorize CIA and U.S. military interrogators to abuse and torture captives if he thought that was necessary to make them

---

[*]For instance, at a press conference on August 24, 2001, Bush called on a Texas reporter who had covered Bush as Texas governor. "A fine lad, fine lad," Bush joshed. "A little short on hair, but a fine lad." Amid the laughter of his colleagues, the reporter acknowledged meekly, "I am losing some hair."

talk. He could order assassinations of anyone he deemed a "terrorist" or somehow linked to "terrorism." He could take the nation to war with or without congressional consent.

Also, Bush's "war on terror" was unique in American history because it knew no limits either in time or space. It was, by definition, an indefinite conflict fought against a vague enemy on a global battlefield, including the American homeland.

After reviewing Bush's broad assertions of powers, former Vice President Al Gore asked in a 2006 speech: "Can it be true that any President really has such powers under our Constitution? If the answer is 'yes,' then under the theory by which these acts are committed, are there any acts that can on their face be prohibited?"

The answer to Gore's rhetorical question was clearly, "no." Theoretically, at least, there were no boundaries for Bush's "plenary" powers. In the President's opinion, his powers were constrained only by his own judgment. He was as Bush called himself the nation's "war president," "the decider," "the unitary executive."

Indeed, looking at Bush's arrogation of powers in total, the troubling conclusion was that the nation's treasured "unalienable rights," which were proclaimed in the Declaration of Independence and enshrined in the U.S. Constitution, no longer applied, at least not as something guaranteed or "unalienable." They were now optional. They belonged not to each American citizen as a birthright, but to George W. Bush as Commander in Chief who got to decide how those rights would be parceled out.

Under Bush's theory of his boundless powers, the only safeguard left for American citizens – and for people around the world – was Bush's assurance that his limitless authority would be used to stop "bad guys" and to protect the homeland.

Patriotic Americans would not feel any change, he promised. They could still go to their jobs, to the shopping mall or to baseball games. Only those who were judged threats to the national security would find themselves in trouble. That list kept growing, however, to include terrorist "affiliates," "any person" who aids a terrorist, and government "leakers" who might divulge Bush's secret decisions.

To comfort Americans who feared that Bush was accumulating powers more fitting a King than a President, Bush's supporters cited previous examples of presidents suspending parts of the Constitution, as Abraham Lincoln did with *habeas corpus* during the Civil War and Franklin Delano Roosevelt did in incarcerating thousands of Japanese-Americans after Japan attacked Pearl Harbor at the start of American involvement in World War II.

But a major difference was that those conflicts were traditional wars, definable in length and with endings marked by surrenders or treaties. By contrast, the "war on terror" was a global struggle against a tactic – terrorism – that had been employed by armies and irregular forces throughout history.

Administration officials acknowledged that there would be no precise moment when the struggle would be won, no clear-cut surrender ceremony on the deck of a U.S. aircraft carrier. Defense Secretary Donald Rumsfeld had called the conflict the "long war," but it had the look of an "endless war," a struggle against elusive and ill-defined enemies. At times, Bush expanded the scope of the conflict beyond defeating terrorism to eliminating "evil" from the world.

Yet, since there was no reason to think the "war on terror" would ever end, a logical corollary was that the American political system – as redefined by Bush – had changed permanently.

If the war would last forever, so too would the "plenary" powers of the Commander in Chief. With the President's emergency powers established as routine, the *de facto* suspension of American constitutional rights also would become permanent. The democratic Republic with its constitutional checks and balances – as envisioned by the Founders – would be no more.

Not only had the first six-plus years of George W. Bush's reign marked an unprecedented assault on America's constitutional system, but Bush and his advisers often waged war against reason itself. Bush resisted scientific judgments on global warming much as he rejected contrary intelligence on Iraq and cautionary advice about his tax cuts driving the nation back into budget deficits.

But this emergence of an imperial presidency operating in a non-empirical world did provoke some resistance. Despite residual fears about another 9/11, many rank-and-file Americans, both liberals and traditional conservatives, grew uneasy over Bush's power grab.

Then, in 2005, the administration's incompetence in handling Hurricane Katrina's devastation of New Orleans awakened more Americans to the emptiness of Bush's promises about protecting the nation. With Bush's Iraq War also going badly, his approval ratings sank below 50 percent and stayed there.

In November 2006, American voters brushed aside Bush's renewed alarms about terrorism and returned control of Congress to the opposition Democrats. In early 2007, the Democrats tentatively began challenging the Iraq War and the President's authority.

Yet, as we completed this book in June 2007, the United States was still at a dangerous crossroads – or perhaps a better image would be that the nation was at a stoplight that permits U-turns. Ahead lay the route that the country had followed for almost six years since 9/11. It was a road toward a future in which a frightened people would rely on a powerful Executive who promised them safety in exchange for their liberties.

It was unclear whether the American people would make the U-turn away from fear and authoritarianism and back toward a Republic with "unalienable rights" restored for "posterity," as the Founders intended. Yet, even as Americans wondered whether to go forward or turn back, many remained confused over how they had gotten to that place on that dark road.

◆◆◆

This book draws from reporting and writing that we have done for a Web site, *Consortiumnews.com*, founded in 1995 as a way to bring important historical, investigative and political stories to the American people. Unexpectedly, the Web site also gave us a front seat to the profound changes occurring in the United States. In many cases, we addressed the emerging crisis in democracy as it was happening, even as major U.S. media outlets looked the other way.

The book also represents the second part of a planned trilogy on the rise – and possible fall – of the Bush family dynasty. The first book of this trilogy was Robert Parry's *Secrecy & Privilege: Rise of the Bush Dynasty from Watergate to Iraq*, which focused on the role of George H.W. Bush in laying the groundwork for his family's emergence as America's leading political family. *Neck Deep* examines how George W. Bush regained the White House and expanded his presidential powers. The planned third book will concentrate on the end game of George W. Bush's presidency.

Neck Deep also is a book that spans two generations in another way. It marks a collaboration between investigative reporter Robert Parry, who broke many of the Iran-Contra stories in the 1980s for *The Associated Press* and *Newsweek*, and two of his sons, Sam and Nat, who brought their own insights and priorities to this project.

1

A Cold Rain

The rain pelted down in icy-cold droplets, chilling both the protesters in soaked parkas and the well-dressed celebrants bent behind umbrellas to shield their furs and cashmere overcoats. Drawn to this historic moment – a time of triumph for some and fury for others – the two opposing groups jostled and pushed their way through security checkpoints, joining the tens of thousands pressing against rows of riot police lining Pennsylvania Avenue.

After taking the subway from Arlington, Virginia, the three of us joined the crowd crammed into a block of 13th Street, on the north side of Pennsylvania Avenue, near the point where Inaugural parades bend in their grand procession from the U.S. Capitol, turn right at the foot of the U.S. Treasury and then veer left before passing in front of the White House.

To our right was a stone expanse called Freedom Plaza, where temporary viewing stands had been erected for invited guests. That corner is marked by a statue of Brigadier General Casimir Pulaski, a Polish cavalryman and freedom fighter who joined the American Revolution and died at the battle of Savannah in 1779. To our left stood a twelve-story building, with the red awnings of a CVS pharmacy on the ground level and rounded balconies of corporate offices on the floors above.

The elegantly attired Republicans squeezed their way through the angry crowd of drenched protesters to the VIP stands or to those rounded balconies, which offered protection from the rain and an unobstructed view of Pennsylvania Avenue below. The Republicans had come to cheer the new U.S. President, George W. Bush, the privileged eldest son of a powerful political family who nonetheless ended his gerunds by dropping the "g" to convey the populist image of a Texas wildcatter.

Bush was replacing President Bill Clinton, a Democrat who had survived an impeachment battle over a sexual dalliance with a former

White House intern. To Bush supporters, the new President would bring back the warmly remembered propriety of his father, President George H.W. Bush. One of George W. Bush's biggest applause lines of Campaign 2000 was his vow to restore "honor and dignity" to the Oval Office.

But other Americans believed January 20, 2001, was a day of infamy for the American Republic. It was the first time in 112 years that a popular-vote loser was to be installed as President of the United States – and then only after he engineered an unprecedented intervention by political allies on the U.S. Supreme Court. Five Republican justices had stopped the vote count in the swing state of Florida, where Bush's younger brother, Jeb, was governor and other Bush loyalists oversaw the election, which then was awarded to Bush by 537 votes out of six million ballots cast.

So, on that cold January day, tens of thousands of protesters poured into the streets of Washington, D.C., shouting angry slogans and waving handwritten anti-Bush signs. The protesters were convinced that Bush had stolen the presidential election and, in so doing, had disenfranchised the plurality of citizens who had cast their ballots for Democrat Al Gore.

Some signs were addressed directly to Bush. "You're not my President," read one. "I know you lost," said another. One sign had just two large letters, "NO." To these Americans, Bush's ascension to the nation's highest office was a travesty of democracy.

Where we stood, the protesters, many in dark-colored parkas and ski or baseball caps, outnumbered the elegantly attired Republicans. Some Republicans in the balconies shouted "Sore Loserman!" down at the crowd, reprising a taunt that right-wing activists had coined to bait supporters of the Democratic ticket of Al Gore and Joe Lieberman during the Florida recount battle.

But the bullying tone, which had characterized the Republicans during those bitter days of November and December, was gone. They seemed taken aback by the size and ferocity of the anti-Bush crowd. Some protesters shouted back up to the balconies, "Jump! Jump!"

The anti-Bush protesters pulsated with the fury of a people who had been robbed of something irreplaceable, like some precious heirloom handed down reverentially through generations and which was now gone. It was as if the protesters sensed they represented the "posterity" that the Founders had envisioned when they laid the cornerstones of a democratic Republic almost 225 years earlier.

Many in the crowd – like the three of us – had gone into the streets that rainy day to bear witness against a violation of the most basic covenant of democracy, that the choice of leaders must be left in the hands of the voters, even when the margins are as narrow as they were in Election 2000.

Though few protesters could have seriously thought they had any chance of reclaiming the nation's democratic legacy that day, they acted as if their presence could at least negate the nodding capitulation of the wise heads of Washington. That acquiescence to a Bush restoration had crossed party lines to include senior Democrats in Congress and extended into the editorial offices of major American news organizations. Many pundits and politicians acted as if it were a quaint notion that the candidate with the most votes was the one who was supposed to win.

That bemused complacency of the elites contrasted with an uncompromising anger in the streets. As Bush took the oath of office, becoming the 43rd President and completing his extraordinary power grab, the growing fury of the crowd built toward a crescendo. Rather than cheers for the new President, the capital echoed with resounding chants of "Hail to the Thief!"

As Bush's limousine began the traditional slow-moving ride down Pennsylvania Avenue, some protesters mocked Bush with a chant of, "Oh, no! Gore's ahead, I better call my brother Jeb," and the more succinct slogan, "Gore got more!"

Though the size and intensity of this protest against an incoming President were unprecedented at least since the Vietnam War, little of the chaos and drama along Pennsylvania Avenue found its way into the mainstream coverage of Bush's inauguration. The major news media approached the event mostly with the hackneyed template of a new President taking office amid a celebration of democracy.

There was little said about Bush losing the national popular vote by more than a half million ballots or how he had clung to his narrow victory in Florida only by the grace of tortured legal logic from five Republicans on the U.S. Supreme Court. Nor was there much commentary about how the anti-democratic election outcome – and the heavy police presence to prevent anti-Bush rioting in Washington – gave the inauguration the feel of an American state of siege.

Instead, Washington's "conventional wisdom" was all about the need for healing, for rallying around the new President and for putting the national bitterness – of both Election 2000 and the eight years of Bill Clinton's presidency – in the past.

Many Washington insiders felt private satisfaction with the outcome. They had despised Clinton and were pleased by the defeat of his sidekick Gore. Clinton was admired for his speaking skills and political acumen, but was hated for his slick style and boorish conduct in the White House; Gore became the whipping boy who suffered for Clinton's sins and for Clinton's survival to the end of his term.

At pre-Inaugural dinner parties around Washington, there was open nostalgia for the "good ol' days" of Ronald Reagan and George H.W. Bush, when integrity and honesty supposedly ruled. A favorite Washington comment in anticipation of George W. Bush's inauguration was that it would "put the adults back in charge."

So, there was little tolerance for the full-throated complaints of the thousands of demonstrators waving protest signs and shaking their fists at the Inaugural parade. TV anchors and political commentators treated the protests as a tasteless nuisance, when the demonstrations were mentioned at all.

It would take more than three years for the fuller historic picture to be put into focus by Michael Moore's documentary, "Fahrenheit 9/11." Moore highlighted dramatic Inauguration Day scenes of protesters surging through the streets, scuffling with police and egging Bush's limousine as it descended from Capitol Hill toward the White House.

"The plan to have Bush get out of the limo for the traditional walk to the White House was scrapped," Moore said in narrating the footage of masses of Americans decrying Bush's tainted victory. "Bush's limo hit the gas to prevent an even larger riot. No President had ever witnessed such a thing on his Inauguration Day."

From our cramped vantage point on 13th Street, we couldn't see the egg-throwing incident which occurred several blocks to our left. But we did notice the presidential limousine and security vehicles speed up, hurrying past both those Americans who came to honor Bush and those who stood in the rain to heckle him. After the limousine rushed past, the crowd experienced a few moments of confusion as the facts of Bush's hasty passage rippled back through the protesters.

Soon, the reality of Bush's presidency began to sink in bringing with it a pang of disappointment to many demonstrators. What many of them saw as an American *coup d'etat* was a *fait accompli*. The bedraggled protesters shouted a few more choruses of "Hail to the Thief!" and slowly began to disperse.

◆ ◆ ◆

As a shaken George W. Bush slipped into the White House on that cold gray day, a divided America was already rushing down two separate paths. The press and the pundits – along with a majority of Americans, as measured by polls – hoped that the second Bush administration would succeed for the good of the country.

But a significant percentage of the population was furious that the institutions of American democracy had performed so badly during the campaign and then during the drawn-out recount battle. This group felt deep animosity toward the Supreme Court's partisan majority and toward the press corps' sudden eagerness to show deference to a new President.

The anti-Bush Americans recalled the relentless attacks on Clinton – from both the Republicans and the news media – during his eight years in the White House, beginning before he took the oath. Where was the deference then? Where was the demand for unity?

Clinton was denied even the semblance of a "honeymoon" from a press corps sensitive to longtime criticism of its supposed "liberal" bias and determined to show that it would be tougher on a Democrat than any Republican. Plus, Washington's insider community judged the Arkansas-born Clinton an interloper, a pretender, a hick who had gotten too big for his britches, an unwelcome guest who quickly overstayed what little welcome he had.

In 1998, after the Monica Lewinsky sex scandal broke, *Washington Post* society columnist (and Georgetown doyenne) Sally Quinn explained this hostility in a column that traced the contempt for Clinton back to his Inaugural Address in 1993. Quinn wrote that Clinton had insulted the Washington Establishment when he described the capital as "a place of intrigue and calculation [where] powerful people maneuver for position and worry endlessly about who is in and who is out, who is up and who is down, forgetting those people whose toil and sweat sends us here and pays our way." [1]

This perceived slight to the Establishment deepened into a burning contempt over the next several years as Republicans and the media kept up a steady drumbeat of accusations challenging the ethics of the Clintons and their associates. When Clinton's sexual dalliance with Monica Lewinsky surfaced in 1998, Quinn wrote that the insider community wanted Clinton to pack up immediately and leave town.

"Privately, many in Establishment Washington would like to see Bill Clinton resign and spare the country, the Presidency and the city any more humiliation," Quinn wrote. [2]

When Clinton survived the Republican impeachment effort in 1999, the Washington press corps and the capital's insiders transferred their unrequited anti-Clinton hostility onto Gore. As the new presidential campaign began, journalists acted as if they had *carte blanche* to misquote Gore or otherwise distort his positions.

For instance, the media eagerly adopted a Republican-invented quote for Gore about him claiming that he "invented the Internet," an apocryphal phrase that became a running punch line used both to deny Gore credit for his farsighted early work as an Internet champion in Congress and to portray Gore as a delusional braggart.

At times, the media jettisoned any pretext of objectivity. At a Democratic debate in New Hampshire between Gore and a Democratic rival, Senator Bill Bradley, reporters mocked Gore as they sat in a nearby press room and watched the debate on television. "Whenever Gore came on too strong, the room erupted in a collective jeer, like a gang of 15-year-old Heathers cutting down some hapless nerd," observed *Time*'s Eric Pooley.

The press corps' contempt for Gore carried over into the general election. Any verbal misstep by Gore became an example of his dishonesty, as happened when he misremembered visiting a disaster with the director of the Federal Emergency Management Agency when it was really a FEMA deputy director.

During the bitter Florida recount, the anti-Gore bias stayed strong with a widespread media acceptance that Bush was the rightful winner of the presidency even though Gore outpolled Bush by more than a half million votes nationwide.

The simple fact was that the Bush family had long been a pillar of the Washington Establishment, which had a fondness for many of the family's senior advisers, too. Some of the Bush entourage, such as James A. Baker III, were admired for their political savvy. Others, such as retired Gen. Colin Powell, were beloved as national security "wise men." Bush's Vice President Dick Cheney had a positive reputation as a tough-minded, no-nonsense leader.

While some Washington insiders doubted that George W. Bush possessed the skill set to make a great President, they were sure that his father's battle-tested team would step in whenever the son needed guidance. So, there wasn't much worry that the United States was under the control of a relative novice. The thinking was that the American people would get what many of them wanted, a leader they liked, and the government would get what it needed, the experienced hands of George H.W. Bush's old guard.

Both assumptions proved faulty, however. From the start, the headstrong George W. Bush was determined to craft his presidency as much as possible as a contrast to – and even a repudiation of – his father's political and foreign-affairs pragmatism. At key moments,

George H.W. Bush's "realists" found themselves not as counselors whispering from behind the throne, but on the outside looking in, helpless to shape policy or to rein in the son's rash instincts.

As far as the public was concerned, the first deception of the second Bush administration was the illusion that George W. Bush was the regular-guy Texan clearing brush in blue jeans and cowboy boots, when he was in reality a plutocrat in plebian clothes. Rather than an everyman who understood the normal challenges of day-to-day life on Main Street America, he was a pampered rich kid whose family estate in Kennebunkport, Maine, sat on a rocky point reaching out into the Atlantic Ocean and bearing Bush's middle name, Walker.

Those family connections, more than anything else, explained Bush's rise to the highest office in the land and offered important clues as to how he would handle the American presidency.

2

The Bush Family
Oil-igarchy

The two branches of the modern Bush family grew from the well-tended soil of 19th century respectability and privilege. The Bushes had deep Yankee roots in New England; the Walkers had the networking with Wall Street investment bankers. In the early 20th century, the merger of the respected Bush name and the Walkers' top-hat connections would start the family on its climb to the pinnacle of American power in the latter half of the 20th century.

George Herbert Walker, who was schooled in England during the late Victorian period, settled in St. Louis as an investment banker. In 1900, he founded an investment firm, G.H. Walker and Company, which he built into a financial power in the Mississippi Valley by 1914. Five years later, Walker made a jump to an even higher level in the financial world, teaming up with Averell Harriman of the Harriman railroad fortune.

With backing from the Rockefellers' National City Bank and the Morgan family's Guaranty Trust, Harriman founded a new investment banking firm, W.A. Harriman Company, with Walker at his side. Walker took the lead in developing overseas business investments, including Germany's Hamburg-Amerika steamship line and mineral interests in the Russian Caucasus.[3] Some of the Walker-Harriman foreign holdings were linked to industrialists who were instrumental in the rise of Adolf Hitler's Nazi regime.

The Walker family merged with the Bushes in 1921, when Walker's favorite daughter, Dorothy, married Prescott Bush. Handsome and athletic, Prescott Bush was a Yale graduate who became a legend in the school's exclusive Skull and Bones society. He was the leader of a group of Bonesmen who dug up the purported bones of legendary Apache chief Geronimo from his burial plot at Fort Sill, Oklahoma. Geronimo had died at the fort in 1909 and his grave site allegedly was ransacked by Bush and four other Yale men who had joined the Army during World War I and found themselves stationed at Fort Sill. Bush is credited with bringing back a skull, some other bones, a stirrup and a horse bit from Fort Sill to Skull and Bones at Yale in New Haven, Connecticut, where the relics were stored in the secret society's Tomb.

The authenticity of the bones – whether they are Geronimo's actual remains – has never been fully resolved.[4] But in May 2006, a Yale University historian lent new credibility to the Bush-Geronimo legend after uncovering a 1918 letter that identified Bush as one of the grave robbers. "The skull of the worthy Geronimo the Terrible, exhumed from its tomb at Fort Sill by your club … is now safe inside the [Tomb] together with his well worn femurs, bit & saddle horn," according to the letter written by Winter Mead.[5]

In his fondness for such elaborate pranks, Prescott Bush epitomized the popular upper-crust youth of his day. Bush also was admired by his peers for his easy grace as well as his golf and tennis skills. After graduating from Yale and marrying Dorothy Walker, Bush parlayed his father-in-law's contacts into a swift rise within the world of Wall Street finance. Further bonding the Walkers and the Bushes, Prescott Bush's first son, George Herbert Walker Bush, was born on June 12, 1924, in Milton, Massachusetts.

By 1926, George Herbert Walker had hired Prescott Bush as a vice president in the Harriman firm. There, the son-in-law climbed the ladder until he became a managing partner at the merged firm of Brown Brothers Harriman by the mid-1930s.[6] Bush's success, however, was soon tainted by scandal because of the firm's Nazi connections.

After Japan attacked Pearl Harbor on December 7, 1941, and Germany joined its fascist ally in declaring war on the United States, the U.S. government moved against the property of the Hamburg-Amerika line, seizing it under the Trading with the Enemy Act in August 1942. The government took action, too, against affiliates of the Union Banking Corporation where Nazi financial backer Fritz Thyssen had placed money. UBC was run by Brown Brothers Harriman and Prescott Bush was a UBC director. In November 1942, the U.S. government also seized the assets of the Silesian-American Corporation, another company connected to Harriman, Walker and Bush.[7]

For a citizen without blue-blood connections, the Nazi money scandal could have proved disastrous. But Bush, a Republican, and Harriman, a Democrat, brushed off the notoriety and continued on with their careers almost as if nothing had happened. In a pattern that would repeat itself through the Bush family's rise, Establishment friends would look the other way or treat any suggestion of impropriety by the Bushes as an impolite or outrageous thought. "Politically, the significance of these [Nazi] dealings – the great surprise – is that none of it seemed to matter much over the next decade or so," wrote Kevin Phillips in *American Dynasty*.[8]

Befitting the son of American aristocracy, George H.W. Bush received a first-rate education. He attended Phillips Andover Academy in Massachusetts, where he was a talented athlete excelling in baseball. He was accepted at Yale, but before starting he enlisted as a Navy pilot. At one point the nation's youngest naval aviator, he was shot down over the Pacific Ocean, earning the Distinguished Flying Cross and other medals.

Before the war ended, he married Barbara Pierce, the daughter of a publisher whose magazines included *Redbook* and *McCall's*. After the war, Bush enrolled at Yale and followed his father's footsteps into the Skull and Bones secret society. George H.W. Bush's first son, George Walker Bush, was born July 6, 1946, in New Haven.

After graduating in only three years, George H.W. Bush turned down a job from his father's Brown Harriman firm and struck out for West Texas to pursue his fortune as an oil man. He worked for Dresser Industries, where he sold drilling bits and learned the industry from the bottom up.

Though George H.W. Bush's oil-business career eventually would achieve middling success, his decision to relocate his family to Midland, Texas, would have profound consequences for American political history. Already possessing intimate contacts on Wall Street, the Bushes would add powerful alliances in the oil world of Texas – and through that to the oil-rich sheikhdoms of the Middle East. Eventually, the Bushes would come to lead what Sam Parry dubbed at *Consortiumnews.com* an "oil-igarchy."[9]

◆◆◆

In 1950, despite his brush with scandal over the Nazi financing, Prescott Bush ran for the U.S. Senate from Connecticut, mounting a strong but unsuccessful challenge to a popular Democratic incumbent. At about the same time, his son, George H.W. Bush, launched his first oil company in Midland. With financial backing from his uncle, Herbert Walker, and his Wall Street connections, the 26-year-old

George H.W. Bush joined an associate, John Overbey, to establish the Bush-Overbey Oil Development Company.

The new company received $350,000 in startup money from Herbert Walker's friends and family, including $50,000 from Prescott Bush, according to one of the few serious biographies about the 41st President, *George Bush: The Life of a Lone Star Yankee* by Herbert S. Parmet. To help the young George H.W. Bush launch his company, *Washington Post* publisher Eugene Meyer chipped in more than $50,000, some of which he put up in the name of his son-in-law, Phil Graham, whose wife Katharine Graham would later became chairman of the executive board at the Washington Post Company.

When Bush and Overbey were ready to expand their business in March 1953, they tapped their Midland network of oilmen friends to establish a new partnership, Zapata Petroleum Corporation, which specialized in offshore oil fields. Like Bush-Overbey, Zapata also received generous startup contributions from Herbert Walker's East Coast money connections.

In establishing Zapata, George H.W. Bush left behind the grinding work of buying and selling oil-rights leases and entered the more glamorous work of contract drilling for major suppliers. By the end of 1954, Zapata had 71 wells producing 1,250 barrels of oil per day.[10]

Back in Connecticut, Prescott Bush ran again for the U.S. Senate in a special election in 1952, this time winning. Once in Congress, Bush positioned himself as a moderate Republican, somewhere between the pragmatic conservatism of Dwight Eisenhower and the more liberal politics of Nelson Rockefeller. But his positions on issues related to the oil industry were more complicated.

In 1953, with his son heading up an offshore oil business, Senator Prescott Bush led the fight against legislation that would have federalized offshore resources, including oil, to raise revenue for the government. The bill's sponsor, Senator Lister Hill of Alabama, wanted to target that money for education. Senator Bush's leadership was instrumental in defeating Hill's legislation.[11]

George H.W. Bush also was expanding his West Texas business network. His early Zapata Petroleum partners included two brothers, J. Hugh Liedtke and William C. Liedtke, who ran a law firm across the street from Bush-Overbey's office in downtown Midland. The Liedtkes, whose father was the chief counsel for Gulf Oil, were already respected in the oil business. Hugh Liedtke had a special knack in the chancy field of energy exploration. He brought that skill to Zapata Petroleum which he soon guided to solid profitability.

While the Liedtkes brought the know-how, Bush supplied the family connections that attracted the needed capital.

By 1955, Zapata was involved in two distinct oil businesses, offshore drilling and land drilling. The operation seemed to be running smoothly. However, the Liedtkes grew impatient with the tight reins of control that Herbert Walker wanted over Zapata. Negotiations between Bush and the Liedtkes aimed for more flexibility. A series of stock swaps resulted in divided control over Zapata Offshore Oil Company and Zapata Petroleum. George H.W. Bush and Herbert Walker won control over the offshore business and the Liedtkes got to run the original Zapata Petroleum.[12]

The Liedtke brothers and Bush faced leaner years in the late 1950s but continued to grow Zapata's two businesses. In 1963, Hugh Liedtke expanded Zapata Petroleum by merging it with the Penn Oil Company. The combined company took the name Pennzoil, with Hugh Liedtke at the helm as president and chief executive officer. Liedtke's instincts, his business savvy and his aggressiveness would combine to help turn Pennzoil into one of the world's largest oil companies.

The Bush-Liedtke relationship also became a financial cornerstone for George H.W. Bush's political career. The relationship attracted the well-connected and wealthy by the dozens. Partly through these channels, Bush first came into contact with James A. Baker III, whose family had established itself as a preeminent force in the Texas legal profession going back almost to the Civil War. Beginning in 1870, Baker's grandfather helped build Baker & Botts, which had been founded four years earlier by two Confederate partisans, Judge Peter Gray and Walter Browne Botts.

After the 1963 merger of Zapata and Penn Oil, Baker & Botts became the chief legal firm to the growing oil conglomerate and enjoyed a remarkably close relationship with this client. "For 25 years, the internal legal department at Pennzoil had been almost indistinguishable from Baker & Botts," observed *Wall Street Journal* business journalist Thomas Petzinger.[13]

By this time, George H.W. Bush and Hugh Liedtke had moved their headquarters from Midland to Houston, a much larger and richer city. With the move to Houston, Bush's expanding Rolodex of Texas connections grew beyond the oil industry community and pulled in the Texas country club elites, foreshadowing the shift in Bush's ambitions from oil to politics.

In 1963, George H.W. Bush took a modest step onto the Texas political stage, running a successful campaign for chairman of the

Republican Party of Harris County. While tapping his oil friends to finance his own political ambitions, Bush also helped turn the spigot on a pipeline of cash that would flow from Texas oilmen to the national Republican Party.

In 1966, George H.W. Bush turned his eyes toward Washington, seeking and winning a congressional election from a district in Houston. As the son of an already prominent senator, Bush commanded immediate attention on Capitol Hill, evidenced by his selection to the powerful House Ways and Means Committee. No freshman had served on the committee for 63 years. From his seat on the tax-writing panel, Bush was perfectly positioned to defend the interests of the Texas oil industry.

Bush ran for the Senate in 1970, but lost to Democrat Lloyd Bentson. Bush had, however, attracted the favorable attention of President Richard Nixon, who enlisted Bush as Ambassador to the United Nations. In 1973, as the Watergate scandal began to eat away at the foundations of Nixon's political support, Bush stepped in as chairman of the Republican National Committee. After Nixon's forced resignation, President Gerald Ford appointed Bush to be the U.S. emissary to China and then director of the Central Intelligence Agency.[14]

◆◆◆

At times grudgingly, George W. Bush traced virtually every early step his father took. Like his father, George W. went to both Phillips Andover Academy and Yale and joined the secretive Yale fraternity Skull and Bones. Like his father – when starting out on his own career – George W. exploited both wealthy family connections and the nexus between oil and politics. Like his father, too, George W. joined the armed forces during war time.

But George W.'s early record had the look of a child shuffling around in his father's oversized shoes. In school, George W. was a C student, while his father graduated Phi Beta Kappa. In sports, George the father was captain of the Yale baseball team while George the son was captain of the cheerleading squad. George Sr. served under fire as a naval aviator in the Pacific theater of World War II, while George Jr. slipped past other better qualified candidates into the Texas Air National Guard where he would avoid service in Vietnam and leave behind long-term questions about his duty records and premature departure.

"My first impulse and first inclination was to support the country," Bush recalled in an interview about his backing for the Vietnam War.[15] Bush said no one to his knowledge helped him get into the National Guard. "I asked to become a pilot," Bush said. "I met the qualifications, and ended up becoming an F-102 pilot."[16]

The Bush family also denied pulling strings to land Bush a spot in the so-called "champagne unit" where he served with the offspring of other privileged Texas families, including the son of Senator Lloyd Bentsen. Still, George W. Bush jumped over other candidates to get into the unit despite having the lowest acceptable score for entry.

More than a quarter century later, in sworn testimony in a civil lawsuit, former Texas House Speaker Ben Barnes, a Democrat, added some details about Bush's route into the Guard. Barnes said he referred Bush's name to a senior Guard official, General James Rose, at the request of a Bush family friend, Houston businessman Sid Adger. Barnes testified about his Bush intervention in response to suspicions that Gtech, a company Barnes lobbied for, was allowed to keep a Texas state contract in exchange for Barnes's silence about Bush and the Guard. Barnes denied such a *quid pro quo*.[17]

Bush's service record in the Guard has been another source of mystery. After failing to take a mandatory physical in 1972 – a year after the Guard began testing for drug use – Bush was suspended from flying. He also arranged to transfer to an Alabama unit so he could work on Senator William Blount's reelection campaign, but Bush's appearance at Guard duty there was spotty at best.

"In his final 18 months of military service in 1972 and 1973, Bush did not fly at all," the *Boston Globe* reported. "And for much of that time, Bush was all but unaccounted for." Bush responded through a spokesman that he had "some recollection" of attending drills that year, "but maybe not consistently."[18]

The gaps in Bush's National Guard records continued to dog him through his 2004 campaign until a misstep by CBS News' "60 Minutes" enabled Bush's conservative backers on the Internet, Fox News and elsewhere to portray Bush as a victim of the old bugaboo, the "liberal news media." In a segment on Bush's National Guard duty, "60 Minutes" cited purported contemporaneous memos that described Bush as shirking his duty and disappointing his superiors in the Guard. But questions were raised about the authenticity of some memos and CBS admitted that it hadn't fully verified them.

As press critics ripped into CBS anchor Dan Rather and "60 Minutes," the larger point – that Bush had shirked his duty – was almost lost in the furor. For instance, Marian Carr Knox, a former

Texas Air National Guard secretary, told interviewers that she doubted the authenticity of the memos, but added that the information in them was "correct." Knox said her late boss, Lt. Col. Jerry Killian, indeed was "upset" that Bush had refused to obey his order to take a flight physical and that Bush's refusal to follow the rules had caused dissension among other National Guard pilots.

But instead of focusing on the actions of a man who in 2004 was President of the United States, the glare of attention remained on CBS and its failure to follow proper journalistic procedures. The dust-up left many American voters with the impression that Bush was innocent of the charges that he had skipped out on his National Guard duty. That impression held even when an important new piece of the puzzle was released by the U.S. government about a week after the CBS memo flap – Bush's hand-written resignation letter from the Texas Air National Guard.

After moving to Boston to attend Harvard Business School in 1974, Bush was supposed to finish up his National Guard service in Massachusetts. Instead, in November 1974, Bush scribbled a note saying he wanted out of the Guard. Bush explained that he had "inadequate time to fullfill [sic] possible future commitments." His request was granted. He was given an honorable discharge.[19]

◆◆◆

Bush's checkered history with the National Guard coincided with a period of his life when he drank heavily and apparently abused cocaine, although he never exactly admitted to that last fact.

During his presidential run in 2000, Bush acknowledged the drinking problem – in the context of saying he had licked the bottle with the help of his Christian faith – but he slid away from the cocaine question. When pressed, he didn't confirm or deny that he abused cocaine but asserted that he could have met his father's White House personnel requirement that set time limits on how far back an applicant would have to admit illegal drug use. Despite this implicit confirmation of drug abuse, many news outlets took Bush's side and reported that there was no evidence Bush had ever used illegal drugs.

What was known was that Bush drank heavily and could be surly when drunk. In one famous incident, a 26-year-old George W. Bush took his younger brother Marvin out drinking during a holiday visit to his parents' house in the Washington area. After getting intoxicated, George careened his car homeward through the residential neighborhood.

"Drunk and driving erratically, George W. barreled the car into a neighbor's garbage can, and the thing affixed itself to the car wheel," wrote his biographer Bill Minutaglio in *First Son*. "He drove down the street with the metal garbage can noisily banging and slapping on the pavement right up until he made the turn and finally started rolling up and onto the driveway of his parents' home in the pleasant, family-oriented neighborhood they had just moved into."

When George H.W. Bush demanded to talk with his son, George W. was neither contrite nor apologetic. Instead he threatened his father. "I hear you're looking for me," said George W. "You wanna go mano a mano right here?"[20]

Years later, explaining his fast living as a young man, George W. Bush would quip that "when I was young and irresponsible, I was young and irresponsible." But what he may have lacked in early accomplishments, he made up for in ambition and charm, two traits that served him well in both business and politics. In 1978, his ambition led George W. Bush to embrace his father's two career paths, oil and politics.

With almost no political experience, George W. launched an uphill campaign for the U.S. Congress in 1978. He lost badly to the Democratic incumbent, with George W. saying he learned a lesson about running in a race "he couldn't win."

That same year, he incorporated his own oil-drilling venture, Arbusto (Spanish for bush) Energy. Both his race for Congress and his oil business were based in Midland, his father's old stomping grounds. George W. even opened an office in Midland's Petroleum Building, the same office building where his father started out more than 25 years before.[21]

George W. Bush's oil business venture seemed promising at first. Just as his father had done nearly 30 years prior, George W. sought financial assistance from an uncle, this time, Jonathan Bush, a Wall Street financier. Jonathan Bush pulled together two dozen investors to raise $3 million to help launch Arbusto. Among the investors was Dorothy Bush, George W.'s grandmother and the daughter of the family's original Wall Street tycoon, George Herbert Walker. While lining up investors for Arbusto, Jonathan Bush also was raising money for a prospective presidential race by George H.W. Bush. Many of the funders gave to both causes.[22]

James Bath, one of George W.'s friends from the National Guard, also invested $50,000 for a five percent stake. At the time, Bath was the sole U.S. business representative for Salem bin Laden, scion of the wealthy Saudi bin Laden family and half-brother of

Osama bin Laden, who in the 1980s would be heading to Afghanistan to help Islamic fundamentalists resist the Soviet invasion. Though responsible for investments for Salem bin Laden, Bath insisted that the $50,000 for Arbusto came from his own personal funds. Salem bin Laden could not be questioned about the investment. He died in a 1988 plane crash in Texas.

Unfortunately for George W., 1978 was not the best time to start up an oil-drilling company in West Texas. After a brief price spike in the late 1970s, the price for a barrel of oil dropped through the 1980s to less than $10, which in turn sank many small businesses in the West Texas oil industry. Still, while other oil ventures failed, George W. kept his afloat thanks mostly to family connections and international financiers who sought to build or nurture relationships with his father, who became Vice President after Ronald Reagan defeated Jimmy Carter in November 1980.

George W. was the beneficiary of three major bailouts. The first occurred in 1982 when, despite the millions already pumped into Arbusto, the company faced a cash crunch. George W.'s balance sheet showed $48,000 in the bank and $400,000 owed to banks and other creditors. George W. realized that he had to raise additional cash and decided to take Arbusto public. With the company so deeply in debt, however, George W. would need a new infusion of money to clear the books.[23]

In stepped Philip Uzielli, a New York investor and friend of James Baker III from their days at Princeton University. Uzielli worked out a deal with George W. to purchase a 10 percent stake in Arbusto for $1 million, though the entire company was valued at less than $400,000. In a 1991 interview, Uzielli recalled the investment as a major money loser. "Things were terrible," he said.[24]

As bad as Uzielli's investment turned out to be, George W. now had enough money to seek public investors. But first he decided to make one other change. In April 1982, perhaps realizing the negative connotation of "bust" in Arbusto, George W. changed the name of his company to Bush Exploration. The change also made better use of Bush's primary asset, his family name.

In June 1982, George W. issued a prospectus, seeking $6 million in the initial public offering. But he managed to raise only $1.14 million. The shortfall was due in large part to the waning interest in the oil industry among investors. The price for a barrel of oil was falling and special tax breaks for losses incurred in oil investments had been slashed.[25]

Within two years, it was clear that Bush Exploration was in trouble. Michael Conaway, George W.'s chief financial officer, told *The Washington Post*, "We didn't find much oil and gas. We weren't raising any money." Something had to be done.

In walked bailout number two in the persons of Cincinnati investors, William DeWitt Jr. and Mercer Reynolds III. Heading up an oil exploration company called Spectrum 7, DeWitt and Mercer contacted George W. about a merger with Bush Exploration. For Bush and his struggling company, the decision wasn't hard to make.

In February 1984, George W. agreed to a merger with Spectrum 7 in which DeWitt and Reynolds would each control 20.1 percent and George W. would own 16.3 percent. George W. was named chairman and chief executive officer of Spectrum 7, which brought him an annual salary of $75,000.[26] Even though the merged companies still failed to make any money, the pieces were finally starting to fall into place for George W. Bush.

Spectrum 7 president Paul Rea remembers Bush's name as a definite "drawing card" for investors.[27] With oil prices collapsing in the mid-1980s, however, it became clear that George W.'s name alone would not save the company. In a six-month period in 1986, Spectrum 7 lost $400,000 and owed more than $3 million with no hope of paying those debts off. Once more, the situation was growing desperate.[28]

In September 1986, George W. was tossed his third lifeline, this time by Harken Energy Corporation, a medium-sized, diversified company that was purchased in 1983 by a New York lawyer, Alan Quasha. Quasha seemed interested in acquiring not just an oil company, but a relationship with the son of the Vice President. Harken agreed to acquire Spectrum 7 in a deal that handed over one share of publicly traded stock for five shares of Spectrum, which at the time were practically worthless.[29]

After the acquisition in 1986, George W. got a seat on the Harken board of directors, landed a $120,000-a-year job as a consultant and received $600,000 worth of Harken stock options. By any account, this wasn't a bad deal for an oilman who had never made any money in the oil business and, indeed, had lost lots of money for his investors.[30]

But Harken found that its investment at least in George W. appreciated. Though the company had acquired the son of the Vice President, it ended up in 1989 with the son of the President as George H.W. Bush became the 41st chief executive of the United States. Harken moved to exploit that upgrade by expanding its operations into the Middle East, where business and family connections are of legendary importance. In 1989, the government of Bahrain was in the middle of negotiations with Amoco for an agreement to drill for offshore oil. Negotiations were progressing until the Bahrainis suddenly changed direction.

Michael Ameen, who was serving as a State Department consultant assigned to brief Charles Hostler, the newly confirmed U.S. ambassador to Bahrain, put the Bahraini government in touch with Harken Energy. In January 1990, in a decision that shocked oil-industry analysts, Bahrain granted exclusive oil drilling rights to Harken, a company that had never before drilled outside Texas, Louisiana and Oklahoma – and that had never before drilled offshore.[31]

Nearly two years later, when *The Wall Street Journal* examined the curious Bahrain transaction, Bush declined to be interviewed but did agree to answer some questions in writing. Some of his responses were snippy, such as his answer to a question about whether his involvement in Dallas-based Harken lent it extra credibility in the Arab world. "Ask the Bahrainis," Bush shot back.[32]

Nevertheless, the January 1990 deal added to Harken's stock value, with its shares rising more than 22 percent to $5.50 from $4.50. The run-up in Harken's stock marked one of George W. Bush's first successes in the oil business.

But that year, Bush's father was focused on his own challenges in the Middle East. In August 1990, Iraqi dictator Saddam Hussein used force to settle a bitter border dispute with the sheikhdom of Kuwait over oil lands. Hussein sent his army across the border, overran the Kuwaiti army and quickly seized the Kuwaiti capital.

President Bush denounced Hussein for violating a fundamental principle of international law, the prohibition against aggressive war – even though Bush had ordered the invasion of Panama less than a year earlier. The U.S. military invaded Panama to arrest its military dictator, General Manuel Noriega, who was taken back to the United States to stand trial on drug charges.

But with the Middle East's vital oil reserves in play – and with the unsavory Hussein the culprit – consistency was afforded little respect. After Hussein invaded Kuwait, the inviolable principle against aggressive wars found itself back on Washington's pedestal. President Bush vowed that the Iraqi invasion "will not stand." He dispatched 500,000 U.S. troops as part of an international force to drive Iraqi soldiers from Kuwait. In the early months of 1991, the United States launched first an aerial offensive on Iraqi military and civilian targets, followed by a 100-hour land assault that routed the overmatched Iraqi army and restored the Kuwaiti royal family to power. Bush saw his popularity ratings soar above 90 percent among the American people.

Back in Texas, George W. Bush was winning acclaim himself as the popular new owner of the Texas Rangers. The beginning of that deal traced back to an idea of George W.'s Spectrum 7 partner, Bill DeWitt, whose father had owned the St. Louis Browns baseball team and later the Cincinnati Reds.

DeWitt wanted to pull together a group of investors to buy the Texas Rangers. To do so, DeWitt understood that he needed a native Texan in his group of investors. George W. fit the bill. The President's eldest son also brought with him family ties to the old owner of the Texas Rangers, Eddie Chiles. An aging Midland oilman, Chiles's links to the Bushes dated back to George H.W. Bush's days in the Midland oil business.[33]

George W. also had never given up his own political aspirations and recognized the public relations value that might come from being a part owner of a baseball team. The group of investors was missing only one thing – money. To address that need, George W. reached out to a Yale fraternity brother, Roland Betts, who brought with him a partner from a film-investment firm, Tom Bernstein, both from New York. The New York connection became a problem when Major League Baseball Commissioner Peter Ueberroth insisted on more financial backing from Texas-based investors.

But Ueberroth was eager to put together a deal for the son of the President, so the commissioner brought in a second investment group headed by Richard Rainwater, who had made much of his money working for the Bass family of Fort Worth. From 1970 to 1986, Rainwater had turned the family fortune of nearly $50 million into a $4 billion empire. He agreed to join Betts, Bernstein and George W. in the $86 million deal, but Rainwater imposed a strict limit on George W.'s active participation in the team. Bush got to be called a "managing partner." But – under Rainwater's conditions – George W. would only be the handsome front man for the team; he would have no actual say in how it was run.[34]

To finance his part of the purchase price, Bush decided to sell two-thirds of his holdings in Harken. He pressed ahead with this decision though he knew that Harken was struggling financially and was planning to sell shares in two subsidiaries to avert bankruptcy. Outside lawyers from the Haynes and Boone law firm advised Harken officers and directors on June 15, 1990, that if they possessed any negative information about the company's outlook, a stock sale might be viewed as illegal trading. Bush, who had attended a meeting four days earlier on the plan to sell off the two subsidiaries, went ahead anyway.

On June 22, 1990, Bush sold 212,140 shares to a still-unidentified buyer who spared Bush the trouble of selling on the open market, which likely would have tanked Harken's lightly traded stock and meant less money for Bush. The sale also preceded Harken's disclosure in August 1990 of more than $23 million in losses for the second quarter, which caused the stock to fall 20 percent before recovering for a time.[35]

To make matters worse, Bush missed deadlines by up to eight months for disclosing four stock sales to the Securities and Exchange Commission. After the missed deadlines were noted in published reports in 1991, the SEC opened an insider-trading investigation. At the time, Bush's father was President and thus the person responsible for appointing the SEC chairman.

George W. Bush denied any wrongdoing in the Harken stock sales. He insisted that he had sold into the "good news" of Harken landing offshore drilling rights in Bahrain. Bush's lawyers also argued that he had cleared the stock sale with the Haynes and Boone lawyers, a claim that proved to be important in the SEC's decision to close the investigation on August 21, 1991, without ever interviewing Bush.

But what the SEC didn't know at the time was that the Haynes and Boone lawyers had sent Bush and other Harken officials that letter warning against selling shares if they knew about the company's financial troubles. One day after the investigation was closed, Bush's lawyer Robert W. Jordan delivered a copy of the warning letter to the SEC.

Asked years later about the letter, SEC investigators said they had no memory of reading it. "The SEC investigation apparently never examined a key issue raised in the memo: whether Bush's insider knowledge of a plan to rescue the company from financial collapse by spinning off two troubled units was a factor in his decision to sell," the *Boston Globe* reported.[36]

Bush also was less than forthcoming about why he missed the deadlines for reporting the June 1990 stock sale and three others. For years, he claimed publicly that he had sent the reports in on time and the SEC had lost them, a sort of the bureaucrats-ate-my-stock-sale-reports argument.

The issue resurfaced again in 2002 when Bush positioned himself as a friend of embattled shareholders and demanded that corporate officers reveal their stock sales almost immediately. Asked why he had not lived up to his own admonition, Bush shifted the blame to Harken's lawyers for the late filings. He then changed his story again to say that he simply didn't know what had happened. He never apologized for claiming falsely for years that it had been the SEC's fault.[37]

On June 22, 1990, Bush made $848,560 on his Harken stock sale and used $606,000 of his profits to buy a 1.8 percent stake in the Texas Rangers baseball team. Then, after helping engineer public financing for a new baseball stadium in Arlington, Texas, he sold his interest in the Rangers for $14.9 million, more than 20 times his original investment.[38] The success of his Texas Rangers investment was even more dramatic when compared with what happened to the Harken stock that Bush sold for $4 a share. A dozen years later, each of those shares would have been worth two cents.

George W.'s time with Harken and his part ownership of the Rangers made him a millionaire and a well-known personality in Texas. That measure of success derived almost entirely from the family's triangle of oil-political-financial connections, from Texas to Washington to Wall Street. But he now had some achievements to list on a campaign pamphlet's résumé.

◆ ◆ ◆

In 1994, George W. Bush parlayed his family name and his All-American image as part owner of a Major League baseball team into a run for the Texas governorship. But Bush brought more to the table than just his reputation as the public face of the Texas Rangers and warm memories of his father, the former President. The younger George Bush had mastered the lessons of hardball politics at his father's knee in the 1988 and 1992 presidential campaigns.

In his father's presidential race in 1988, Bush had termed himself the campaign's "enforcer," demanding loyalty from the staff and likening his role to Robert Kennedy's in 1960. "Because of the access I had to George [H.W] Bush, I had the ability – and I think I used it judiciously – I had the ability to go and lay down some behavior modification," the younger George Bush said.[39]

Bush also picked up valuable techniques for drawing the Christian Right into his campaign tent. Doug Wead, a political adviser to the senior George Bush in 1987, had written a series of memos to the then-Vice President on how to communicate with evangelical Christians. Wead's motto was "signal early and signal often," meaning that sprinkling speeches with references to God and arranging public meetings with celebrity evangelicals sent a message to this influential political group – though the subtle signals mostly passed over the heads of non-evangelicals.

So, Wead argued, the signaling would make the evangelicals think the candidate was one of them – even if that relationship had to be hidden from the outside secular society. George H.W. Bush resisted these suggestions, apparently uncomfortable with exploiting religion for political gain. But Wead found George W. to be an avid fan of the memos. "George would read my memos, and he would be licking his lips saying, 'I can use this to win in Texas,'" Wead said.[40]

In the 1988 campaign, George W. Bush also grew close to political strategist Lee Atwater, a legendary master of ruthless politics.[*] Atwater's critics said his tactics included "baiting gays and blacks and scaring the holy hell out of nervous white voters," according to Bush biographer Bill Minutaglio in *First Son*. "George W. would grow to love Lee Atwater," Minutaglio wrote.[41]

When challenging popular Democratic Governor Ann Richards in 1994, George W. Bush reached into Atwater's bag of political dirty tricks, skewering Ann Richards as soft on crime, much as Atwater had savaged Democratic presidential nominee Michael Dukakis over the ill-fated Massachusetts furlough of prison inmate Willie Horton. George W. Bush's aggressive campaign – combined with the nationwide anti-Clinton backlash of 1994 – helped Bush defeat Richards with 54 percent of the Texas vote to her 45 percent. Four years later, Bush cruised to re-election with 69 percent of the vote.

The oil money ties that had served George W. Bush so well in his private life would continue to help him out in his political life, too. And, like his father before him, George W. would reward his oil benefactors while in office.

◆ ◆ ◆

During his six years in the governor's mansion, George W. presided over what was widely regarded as the most polluted state in the country. It ranked first in the amount of cancer-causing chemicals pumped annually into the air and water, first in the number of hazardous-waste incinerators, first in the total toxic releases to the

---

[*] Lee Atwater died in 1991 at the age of 40.

environment, and first in carbon dioxide and mercury emissions from industry.[42]

Amid this dismal record, Texas air quality was arguably the darkest blot on the state's environmental record. A majority of the 20 million Texans lived in areas that either flunked federal ozone standards or were close to flunking. Houston, the nation's oil- and petrochemical-industry headquarters, ranked as an ecological disaster zone. Chemical spills fouled its coastal waters and its air quality earned the dubious honor of eclipsing Los Angeles's famous smog as the most polluted in the country.

Water quality in Texas wasn't much better. More than 4,400 miles of Texas rivers, roughly one-third of the state's waterways, didn't meet basic federal standards set for recreational and other uses. Texans couldn't swim in them, fish in them or, without extensive treatment, drink them.

Despite this record, Bush's Texas administration continued a pattern of cutting water-testing programs. Between 1985 and 1997, the number of stations monitoring for pesticides in Texas waterways fell from 27 to two. The lack of attention given to these problems was further evidenced by the fact that the state of Texas ranked 49th in spending on environmental clean-up.[43]

While missing in action on environmental protection, Governor Bush jumped into the trenches when the oil industry felt threatened. In 1999, when international oil prices collapsed, Bush pushed for and won a $45 million tax break for the state's oil-and-natural-gas producers.[44]

Even when Bush announced what he claimed was a pro-environmental position on industrial pollution, there was a catch. In 1997, he vowed to "close the loophole" in the Texas Clean Air Act of 1971 that had granted 828 industrial plants a "grandfather clause" allowing them to operate without obtaining a permit. But Bush's plan turned out to be strictly voluntary and carried no penalties for industries that didn't seek a permit.

As it turned out, the plan was devised by the industries themselves. According to confidential memos obtained by the Sustainable Energy and Economic Development Coalition (SEED) under the state's Freedom of Information Act, it was shown that the Bush administration worked closely with the companies as they were crafting the proposal.[45]

Kinnan Goleman, who worked for an Austin-based law firm that represented a number of clients in the oil, petrochemical and electric industries, told the *Austin Chronicle* that he wrote "a good portion of certain aspects of the bill."[46]

Bush also recruited appointees who pleased the oil industry when he was filling seats on the Texas Natural Resource Conservation Commission (TNRCC), the Texas equivalent of the Environmental Protection Agency. His first choice, Barry McBee, was a former deputy commissioner at the Texas Department of Agriculture where he had led a drive to gut "right to know" laws that protected farm workers from unannounced aerial pesticide spraying.

Bush's second choice, Robert Huston, came from the oil industry consulting firm Espey, Huston & Associates, whose clients included Exxon, Chevron and Shell. Another of Bush's appointees to the TNRCC was Ralph Marquez, former vice chair of the Texas Chemical Council's environmental committee and a 30-year veteran of the chemical giant Monsanto.[47]

When Bush launched his presidential campaign, he turned to oil men around the country who shared his views on freeing up the industry from government interference. For Alaska state campaign co-chairman, he picked Bob Malone, who had served as president, chief executive and chief operating officer of the Alyeska Pipeline Services Co., a consortium owned by major oil companies active in the North Slope of Alaska.[48]

The other Bush co-chair in Alaska, Bill Allen, was the chairman of VECO Corp., which was formed to support offshore oil production in Alaska.[49]

George W.'s chairman of his campaign's finance committee was Donald Evans, CEO of Tom Brown Inc., an oil and gas company with the bulk of its production in Wyoming. According to *The Austin Chronicle*, Evans was "perhaps the governor's closest friend," having known George W. for three decades since their Midland days together. Evans helped pioneer the Pioneers, a group of Bush's biggest financial supporters who each raised at least $100,000.

In 1995, Bush rewarded Evans by appointing him to the University of Texas Board of Regents, one of the most "powerful patronage" jobs in Texas. With an annual budget of $5.4 billion and more than 76,000 employees, the Texas university system was one of the largest in the country. The Board of Regents also managed an investment portfolio of more than $14 billion. Evans rose to chairman of the board.[50]

Other Bush oil associates moved to Washington to help the Republican National Committee build up a war chest for Bush's expected presidential race. Ray Hunt, chairman and CEO of Dallas-based Hunt Oil Co., became finance chairman of the RNC's Victory 2000 Committee.[51]

Richard Kinder and Kenneth Lay, CEOs of Houston-based energy trader Enron Corp., also ranked as two of Bush's top contributors, both Pioneers. By the end of 1999 alone, funders connected to Enron had contributed $90,000 to the Bush presidential campaign, the fourth largest bundle at the time.[52]

As Texas governor, Bush had embraced energy deregulation, which was crucial to Enron's business as the No. 1 buyer and seller of natural gas and the top wholesale power marketer in the United States. Enron also had a spotty environmental record. In 1997, one Enron facility in Pasadena, Texas, released 274,361 pounds of toxic waste.[53]

Many of George W. Bush's senior foreign policy advisers also were close to the oil industry. His chief foreign policy aide, Condoleezza Rice, was a director of Chevron Corp., in charge of public policy for Chevron's board of directors. Chevron used Rice's expertise on Russian issues to help the energy company navigate its way to investments in the Caspian Sea oil fields. In 1993, Rice was granted a rare honor when Chevron named an oil tanker after her.

A grateful oil industry lubricated Bush's political machine with money. Of the $41 million Bush raised in two gubernatorial races, $5.6 million (14 percent) came from the energy and natural resources industries.[54] When Bush turned his gaze to the White House, the oil and gas industry donated 15 times more money to Bush than to his Democratic rival, Al Gore. Of the top-ten lifetime contributors to George W.'s political war chests, six either were in the oil business or had ties to it.[55]

From his family background to his personal business experience to his political career, George W. Bush was a man of the energy industry. It wasn't so much that industry executives owned him as that he was one of them.

3

Eyeing the White House

When he ran for President, George W. Bush had more going for him than just his father's old Rolodex of contacts, augmented by his own appeal to a younger generation of oil industry executives. As he ventured out into key primary states, even jaded political correspondents were impressed by his boyish charm and natural ease with the voters. His jovial big-man-on-campus confidence seemed contagious as he displayed a common touch and the look of a winner. He charmed some reporters by giving out nicknames which immediately bestowed on the reporter the treasured image of a campaign insider.

Bush's expertise in Lee-Atwater-style hardball politics also carried over to the fight for the Republican presidential nomination in 2000 as Bush's campaign targeted Senator John McCain of Arizona for personal attacks. By late October 1999, McCain, who spent five years in a North Vietnamese prisoner of war camp during the Vietnam War, had narrowed Bush's lead in the polls and the Bush assault began.

"Apparently the memo has gone out from the Bush campaign to start attacking John McCain, something that I'd hoped wouldn't happen," McCain said.[1]

Bush's negative attacks intensified after McCain won the New Hampshire primary. To undercut McCain, Bush's campaign ran a misleading ad lambasting the senator for not supporting breast cancer research. The ad cited an omnibus spending bill, which McCain voted against not because of the breast cancer research but because of the enormous spending included in the overall legislative package. There were also rumors about McCain undergoing Communist brainwashing while in a North Vietnamese prison camp, and mysterious "push-poll" calls to Southern voters asked if they would be less likely to vote for McCain if they knew he had a black child, without explaining that McCain had adopted the child from Bangladesh.

To burnish his own conservative credentials heading into the key South Carolina primary, Bush spoke at Bob Jones University and avoided criticizing the school's racist and anti-Catholic policies. After nailing down a victory in South Carolina, Bush shifted gears again, issuing a rare apology for not having criticized prejudice at Bob Jones University, a contrition that played well in the upcoming primaries in the North.

Despite his popular appeal and his tactical ruthlessness, Bush's biggest plus remained the public's generally fond memory of his father, which had grown warmer in light of the relentlessly negative media coverage that Bill Clinton was attracting as he slogged through the slime of endless scandals – some invented, some exaggerated and some self-inflicted. Early in Campaign 2000, a CBS News poll found 60 percent of Americans with a favorable view of former President Bush and only 17 percent with an unfavorable view.

As memories of Reagan-Bush-era scandals of illegal military aid to Iran, Iraq and the Nicaraguan contra rebels faded, Americans were left with the hazy impression of President George H.W. Bush as a "kinder and gentler" sort of fellow. He was perhaps remembered best from comedian Dana Carvey's imitation of him as an inarticulate preppie-president, with jerking hand gestures, saying, "Not gonna do it. Wouldn't be prudent." Bush's son was seen in the same benign light as he stressed his "compassionate conservatism." The fuzzy memories of the elder George Bush reassured voters who might otherwise have had doubts about his seemingly shallow and inexperienced son.

"People just automatically say, 'If this guy is George and Barbara Bush's son, we don't have any question about those personal qualities that we were fooled on by Clinton,'" explained Robert M. Teeter, George H.W. Bush's campaign manager in 1992.[2]

Indeed, without the glow of the Bush name, it was hard to imagine that the joshing-backslapping Texas governor would have been viewed as a favorite to win the White House or even be seen as serious presidential timber. He offered no comprehensive domestic policy and demonstrated only a rudimentary knowledge of world affairs.

Given Bush's lack of worldliness, the Daddy connection played out in another favorable way for George W. Bush. Many voters thought that if the younger Bush found himself over his head, he could reach out to some steady hands from his father's administration who would pull him – and the nation – to safety.

That concept played out when George W. Bush went looking for a running mate. He turned to Richard Cheney, who was five years older and had worked with George Sr. since their days together in the Ford administration. A hard-bitten conservative, Cheney had served as Gerald Ford's chief of staff in the mid-1970s after the Watergate scandal and the Vietnam War when the enhanced powers of the Cold War presidency were under siege. Along with then-CIA Director George H.W. Bush, Cheney developed strategies for watering down congressional initiatives aimed at constraining presidential authority.

Cheney later served as a Republican congressman from Wyoming. While in the House of Representatives, Cheney became known for his tough partisanship and his expertise on national security policy. During the Reagan-Bush years, Cheney rose up time and again to protect the presidency from investigations that threatened to reveal abuses of executive power.

In mid-1986, Cheney helped fend off early investigations into the secret channels of weapons and money overseen by White House aide Oliver North. In August 1986, after *Associated Press* reporters Robert Parry and Brian Barger exposed North's clandestine network for financing the contra rebels fighting in Nicaragua, Cheney took part in a House Intelligence Committee interview with North that concluded that the press stories were baseless and required no further investigation.

Only when one of North's supply planes was shot down over Nicaragua on October 5, 1986, did the superficiality of the initial House probe come into focus. The next month, after additional disclosures that North also was overseeing arms sales to Iran while funneling some profits back to the contras, the scandal exploded into the Iran-Contra Affair and led to the most publicized congressional investigation since Watergate.

Cheney returned to the front lines defending the White House and thwarting investigators who dug too deeply into the underlying secrets of the operation. Cheney and his aide David Addington were principal authors of the minority report on the Iran-Contra Affair issued by congressional Republicans. The report argued that "the bottom line ... is that the mistakes of the Iran-Contra Affair were just that – mistakes in judgment, and nothing more. There was no constitutional crisis, no systematic disrespect for 'the rule of law,' no grand conspiracy, and no Administration-wide dishonesty or cover-up."[3]

Cheney was laying down a marker on what had become the conservative Republican view on executive power – that the President could use his Commander-in-Chief authority to do almost anything he wanted in the name of national security. Though not fully understood at the time, the Iran-Contra operations represented the first significant resistance to the legal constraints that Congress had sought to place on the Executive in the 1970s.

Rather than publicly seek to repeal laws restricting presidential actions, Ronald Reagan and George H.W. Bush chose to brush aside many of the requirements, such as laws that mandated reporting U.S arms shipments, giving timely notification to the intelligence committees about covert operations and abiding by congressional limits on the President's war powers. In effect, the Oliver North operations – which had secret support from the CIA, the Vice President's office and the Pentagon – were devices to shield the broader evasion of law.

But, in Cheney's view, the Congress and the public had no business knowing about these national security activities in the first place; the President had the inherent right to make virtually all foreign policy decisions and then could parcel out information as he saw fit. So, while admitting that some mistakes were made, Cheney and the Republicans judged that the Iran-Contra operations represented "no systematic disrespect" for the law because the President's Commander-in-Chief powers superceded the law.

In March 1989, Cheney returned to the Executive Branch when former Texas Senator John Tower, George H.W. Bush's first choice for Defense Secretary, flamed out over accusations about his personal life. At the Pentagon, Cheney continued to be an advocate for the aggressive use of presidential power in foreign affairs. He was at Bush's side during the 1989 invasion of Panama, which was justified by an expansion of presidential war-making power to include invading other countries to enforce U.S. laws, such as the drug-trafficking indictment of Panamanian General Manuel Noriega. Cheney also was a hard-liner during the Persian Gulf War of 1990-1991.

Along with his belief in expansive executive power, Cheney was a stickler for secrecy, insistent on keeping embarrassing information away from political adversaries and the American public. In 1992, for instance, human rights advocates were demanding information about a long-time Pentagon training program known as "Project X," which had distilled lessons from decades of counterinsurgency operations into training manuals that were then distributed to U.S.-allied militaries around the world. Project X began in 1965 as a top-secret program at the U.S. Army Intelligence Center at Fort Holabird, Maryland, according to a brief history of the operation that was released in 1997.

Project X pulled together the field lessons from U.S. counterinsurgency operations around the world and put those lessons into training manuals. Translated into many languages, the booklets were to "provide intelligence training to friendly foreign countries," according to the Pentagon history.

Linda Matthews of the Pentagon's Counterintelligence Division recalled that in 1967-68, some of the Project X training material was prepared by officers connected to the Phoenix operation, a notorious assassination program in Vietnam. "She suggested the possibility that some offending material from the Phoenix program may have found its way into the Project X materials at that time," the Pentagon report said.

By the mid-1970s, Project X material was being shared with armies all over the world. In reviewing these training programs, the Pentagon acknowledged that Project X was the source for some of the "objectionable" lessons taught at the School of the Americas, where Latin American officers were trained in blackmail, kidnapping, murder and spying on non-violent political opponents.

But the full story of Project X – including the precise techniques taught to the Third World armies – was kept hidden. In the final days of the first Bush administration, Cheney's Defense Department ordered the collection of all Project X documents. The manuals and other materials were brought to a central location and systematically destroyed.

The ostensible rationale for the mass destruction of documents was to prevent Project X from being used as teaching material in the future. But the more immediate consequence was to conceal these unpleasant facts from the American people. Project X might have represented a smoking gun on long-standing allegations that U.S. authorities supported what amounted to anti-communist terrorism during the Cold War. Only the brief Project X history and some of the more innocuous records survived and were released in 1997.

After leaving office in January 1993, Cheney joined a conservative think tank, the American Enterprise Institute, before moving to Texas in 1995 as the chairman and chief executive of Halliburton, a Dallas-based oil-service giant that supported oil and gas exploration around the world. With Cheney at Halliburton's helm, the company grew into a global juggernaut, with two-thirds of its business overseas in nearly 130 countries. Halliburton counted about 700 wholly and partly owned subsidiaries, employed more than 100,000 workers worldwide, and boasted a 1999 income of $15 billion.[4]

Halliburton did much of its business in major oil-producing countries, some of which had poor records for human rights or democratic freedoms. Halliburton reported business operations in such countries as Nigeria, Indonesia, Saudi Arabia, Algeria, Kazakhstan, Azerbaijan, Iran, Libya, Angola and Russia. Halliburton's roster of subsidiaries also listed operations in countries known as offshore banking havens, such as the Cayman Islands, Barbados, Panama, Cyprus and Vanuatu.[5]

While Cheney the politician might have worried about these business ties to unsavory or suspect countries, Cheney the oilman apparently saw nothing wrong with lucrative investments in these places, even Iran and Libya which were on the State Department's list of terrorist states.

During Cheney's tenure, Halliburton built up operations in Nigeria despite the country's pattern of human rights abuses. Halliburton's subsidiaries signed contracts with Royal Dutch Shell and Chevron, two companies that have been at loggerheads with Nigerian indigenous groups in the Niger Delta.

In April 2000, Brown & Root Energy Services, a business unit of Halliburton, was selected by Shell Petroleum Development Co. of Nigeria to work on the development of an offshore oil and gas facility, the first of its kind for Shell. The deal, valued at $300 million, was questioned by those who worked to hold Shell accountable for its pollution and notorious human rights record in Ogoniland in the Niger Delta.

Shell had been involved in oil exploration and export in Nigeria for more than 40 years, much of it in the fertile lands belonging to the Ogoni people. During this period, Shell's activities led to repeated environmental calamities, caused by oil spills, noxious gas flares, cleared forests, despoiled farmland and pipeline blowouts.

Shell's operations poured money into the coffers of General Sani Abacha's military government, which used force to crush popular protests against the oil industry in the Niger Delta. In 1995 – the year Cheney joined Halliburton – renowned writer and environmental advocate Ken Saro-Wiwa and eight of his colleagues were hanged by the Abacha government for their efforts to prevent Shell from continuing to poison the environment of the Niger Delta. It was estimated that more than 2,000 people were murdered for their involvement in protests against Shell's activities in the Delta.

Back in the United States, Halliburton compensated Cheney handsomely for his work. As Halliburton's chairman and CEO, Cheney earned a $1.3 million salary, plus bonuses that went as high as $2 million.[6] When he quit in June 2000 – to be Bush's vice presidential running mate – Cheney sold 100,000 shares of Halliburton stock, bringing him an additional $5.1 million. During his five-year tenure, Cheney's accrued salary and stock options were worth an estimated $45 million.[7] The 59-year-old Cheney also got a $20 million parting gift from Halliburton when the board waived a requirement that Cheney would lose many of his stock options if he left before age 62.[8]

◆ ◆ ◆

At the Democratic convention in 2000, director/actor Rob Reiner joked that the Republican idea of diversity was "two guys at the head of the ticket that are from two different oil companies." Indeed, never before had both candidates on the same ticket come from the oil industry, yet that fact drew little serious discussion from the mainstream U.S. news media even though there were few more pressing issues facing the United States than problems related to energy.

The looming energy crisis threatened almost every aspect of American life from the economy to the environment to national security to leisure time. How Bush and Cheney approached these complex issues compared to how Al Gore and Joe Lieberman did represented one of the deeper divisions between the two parties.

There was also the potential catastrophe from global warming, which a growing consensus of scientists believed was driven primarily by the burning of fossil fuels. As Campaign 2000 was heating up, a team of scientists returned from the Arctic Ocean with additional alarming news, that much of the thick ice covering the North Pole was thinning and turning to water.[9]

Still, the U.S. media displayed only desultory interest in the Bush-Cheney oil ties, even as Bush counted himself among those traditional oil industry executives who mocked global warming as either a myth or an exaggeration. His official position was that global warming needed further study. But, to soften his image as a guy who didn't care about the environment, Bush made a campaign promise to set mandatory limits on carbon dioxide pollution from power plants.

Outside public view, however, Bush listened to think tanks that questioned either the science behind global warming or the widely accepted view that its consequences would be devastatingly harmful. Many of these think tanks were funded by oil or coal interests.

Bush and Gore also shied away from a full-scale battle over the environmental issue. Though the environment was a signature issue for Gore – whose commitment once prompted George H.W. Bush to dub him "Ozone Man" – Gore's political consultants knew the painful history of presidential candidates who had tried to get the American people to reduce their energy use. During the 1970s, Presidents Gerald Ford and Jimmy Carter tried to force energy efficiency down the throats of the American people and paid high prices at the polls.

Given the political fate of Ford and Carter – losing in consecutive elections in 1976 and 1980 – politicians have since avoided asking the American people to sacrifice their energy-loving lifestyles. The politically popular course was charted by Ronald Reagan and George H.W. Bush in the 1980s, essentially green-lighting America's switch to bigger and bigger gas-guzzling vehicles and promising to find additional supplies of oil somewhere. Instead of painful steps toward conservation, the smart political pitch to the American voter was Bobby McFerrin's reggae verse, "don't worry, be happy."

Gore, who wrote one of the hallmark pro-environmental books *Earth in the Balance* in 1992, perceived the growing energy crisis perhaps as fully as anyone in the U.S. government. He also tried to change the political rule book by erasing the old dichotomy that pitted jobs versus the environment. The Democratic nominee tried to sell the notion that protecting the environment could be good for the economy by creating new high-paying jobs as technology was applied to the energy problem.

Smart environmental policies could contribute to economic vibrancy, Gore said, by putting the United States in the world lead on building fuel-efficient cars and trucks and on developing alternative fuel sources. Gore's plan also aimed at encouraging energy savings through a detailed system of tax credits. But – like President Clinton – Gore wasn't willing to try the political gods too much by confronting the American people with tough demands for conservation. As the campaign progressed, Gore heeded the advice of his political consultants and soft-pedaled the environment.

Meanwhile, George W. Bush unveiled an energy policy built around the need for more oil drilling within the United States and in its coastal areas. He proposed opening a pristine section of Alaska's Arctic National Wildlife Refuge to the oil companies. As for foreign oil, Bush promised strengthened diplomacy toward oil-producing states to secure their petroleum at moderate prices. He also advocated construction of more nuclear reactors and research into cleaner burning coal.

Like his father, George W. Bush made Gore the butt of some environmental jokes. "The Vice President likes electric cars," Bush joshed during one speech, "he just doesn't like making electricity."

Bush's plan for drilling in the Arctic Refuge touched a sore point with environmentalists who grudgingly had accepted Alaskan oil exploration as part of a compromise in a 1980 bill signed by President Carter. Oil industry lobbyists opened 95 percent of Alaska's North Slope coastal plain for drilling, with the agreement that the remaining five percent – or about 19 million acres – be set aside as protected. Now, Bush was trying to pry loose about 1.5 million acres of that sanctuary.

Environmentalists see the refuge as a land of rare natural beauty, critical for maintaining the habitat of unique wildlife, including polar bears, musk oxen, grizzly bears, wolves, red and arctic foxes, lemmings, and a myriad of other bird species. The refuge also is vitally important to the 129,000-member Porcupine River caribou herd that calls Alaska's North Slope home. The Gwich'in Indians of northeast Alaska and northwest Canada depend on the land, too.

Beyond anger over what environmentalists saw as the bad faith of reneging on an earlier compromise, they warned that the drilling and the accompanying construction of almost 300 miles of new roads, hundreds of miles of pipelines and other facilities would permanently transform the natural landscape. Another objection was the limited quantity of oil that the Arctic Refuge would likely hold. By the most optimistic estimates, commercially recoverable oil from the refuge's coastal plain would provide about six months supply for the United States.[10]

While offending many environmentalists, Bush's energy policy was popular with the oil and coal industries. On September 27, 2000, Dick Cheney headlined a fundraiser in Washington, D.C., that tapped oil industry supporters to raise $8 million for Republican Senate candidates. Cheney found himself preaching to a very appreciative choir as he criticized the Clinton administration's unwillingness to exploit domestic oil reserves more aggressively. Among the oil executives were TXU Corp. chairman Erle Nye, El Paso Energy CEO William Wise and former ARCO chairman Lod Cook.[11]

By 2000, however, it was clear to many energy experts that there was no reasonable way for the United States to drill its way to energy security. The growing expectation was that the world would reach its peak oil production sometime in the next two to five decades after which supplies would decline. The Energy Information Agency of the U.S. Department of Energy estimated peak production to occur in 2037.[12]

Further, with large countries like China and India quickly modernizing their economies largely along Western lines, the oil markets were certain to tighten, driving up prices and forcing periodic oil shortages. The search for the remaining oil reserves was sure to present security challenges, including possible military conflicts with countries desperate to maintain their economies. Continued dependence on oil also threatened severe degradation of the environment, raising the specter of mass population dislocations, especially if global warming raises sea levels and worsens the intensity of hurricanes.

However, in Campaign 2000, Bush succeeded in spreading uncertainty about whether global warming was really something to fear and whether technological breakthroughs, such as the Internet, would hurt more than help. In a major address on energy policy on September 29, 2000, Bush offered a surprising assessment of the Internet as a heavy drain on the nation's electrical grid. He also cited it as a factor forcing the United States to build costly new power plants, including more coal-fired generators and nuclear reactors.

"Today, the equipment needed to power the Internet consumes 8 percent of all the electricity produced in the United States," Bush declared.

Bush's assertion astounded many energy experts who considered the Internet and similar technological advances, on balance, a way to improve American productivity and ease the U.S. economy's reliance on energy. Analysts for the Lawrence Berkeley National Labs and the Center for Energy and Climate Solutions calculated the Internet was drawing only about 1 percent of U.S. electricity, while helping to achieve a historic shift toward energy conservation for the country by reducing the need for researchers to visit the library or consumers to drive to the mall.

But Bush's curious remarks prompted virtually no attention from the national news media. Despite the significance of the Internet to the New Economy, the press corps put no questions to the Republican nominee about his unusual view about the Internet as an energy hog, nor did the press bother to find out who supplied Bush with his curious data.

If the news media had pursued the Internet-power-drain question, the journalists would have uncovered a peculiar relationship between Bush and a coal-industry-funded group that both produced dubious data and endorsed the view that more carbon dioxide in the atmosphere – and the global warming it would produce – was good for the earth, not the catastrophe that most mainstream scientists anticipate.

As Sam Parry wrote at *Consortiumnews.com* on October 9, 2000, Bush's Internet energy figure could be traced to a 1999 study entitled "The Internet Begins with Coal," written by Mark Mills, president of Mills McCarthy & Associates Inc. Based on Mills's calculations, the study stated, "The electricity appetite of the equipment on the Internet has grown from essentially nothing 10 years ago to 8 percent of the total U.S. electricity consumption today."

Though Bush cited Mills's 8 percent figure as fact, the estimate was vigorously challenged by many energy experts as a wild exaggeration of the Internet's energy requirements as well as a distortion of the fact that the high-tech New Economy had achieved significant net savings in energy use. The validity of Mills's findings also was put into question by his report's relationship to a coal-industry-funded think tank.

According to a summary of Mills's report, his Internet project grew "out of an inquiry by Greening Earth Society president Fred Palmer." Mills also was listed as a scientific adviser to the Greening Earth Society, a think tank dedicated to the proposition that the rising level of carbon dioxide in the atmosphere was beneficial to the earth because it would shift the climate and thus open up new lands for agriculture and other development.

The truth, according to the Greening Earth Society, is that increased levels of carbon dioxide help the environment by providing sustenance for plant growth. In a report entitled "The CO2 Issue," the Greening Earth

Society painted a rosy picture of greenhouse gases: "Evidence of very modest nighttime winter warming, robust plant growth, rejuvenating forests and ample harvests abounds."

The Greening Earth Society, however, was not a disinterested scientific body. It was established by the Western Fuels Association, a cooperative owned by seven coal-burning utilities mostly in the West and Midwest. According to its annual report, the Western Fuels Association delivered 22.7 million tons of coal to member utilities in 1999. Greening Earth Society president Palmer, who commissioned the Internet study, also was Western Fuels' chief executive.

In its 2000 annual report, Western Fuels condemned the "anti-coal activities" of the Clinton-Gore administration. The report also criticized efforts to address the problem of global warming through the international agreement, reached in Kyoto, Japan, aimed at reducing greenhouse gas emissions.

Although scientists couldn't forecast with precision the climate impact of global warming, there was widespread agreement in 2000 that sudden and drastic climate change would have a devastating impact on the earth's environment. From rising sea levels to sudden changes in habitats for wildlife to more extreme weather patterns, droughts in some places, floods in others, the warning signs were clear

The Intergovernmental Panel on Climate Change, which was established in 1988 jointly by the United Nations Environment Programme and the World Meteorological Organization for the purpose of assessing information related to global warming, warned that there was already a discernable impact on the earth's climate.

On November 2, 1999, Robert Watson, the panel's chairman, said: "It is not a question of whether the Earth's climate will change, but rather *when, where and by how much*. It is undisputed that the last decade has been the warmest this century, indeed the warmest for hundreds of years, and many parts of the world have suffered major heat waves, floods, droughts and extreme weather events leading to significant economic losses and loss of life. While individual events cannot be directly linked to human-induced climate change, the frequency and magnitude of these types of events are expected to increase in a warmer world."

Environmentalists also were alarmed because Bush seemed to be embracing the coal industry's propaganda about the desperate need for a rapid expansion of coal-fired generating plants. The dependence on coal-fired power plants is a major source of pollution on the air, land and water. And, coal is a principal source of greenhouse gas emissions, which contribute to global warming. The Energy Information Administration of the U.S. Energy Department estimated that burning coal releases 36 percent of the total greenhouse gas emissions in the United States.

Bush's energy policy speech was a troubling warning sign that the potential next President of the United States was hostile to both the environment and science.

4

Goring Gore

Some analysts likened the latter half of the 1990s to the period of economic boom and relative peace three-quarters of a century earlier. But even the comparison to the Roaring Twenties missed the unique quality of that pre-Millennium moment of excess and comfort just before the dawn of the 21st century. Not only was the long Cold War a quickly fading memory – with the old Soviet Union a shattered relic and the United States hailed as the last remaining superpower – but an Internet-driven New Economy was luring investors toward a high-technology gold rush with promises of overnight fortunes in companies with funny names like Yahoo! and Amazon.

A new technology-heavy stock market called Nasdaq was doubling and tripling in value, while more traditional economic measures – the S&P 500 and the Dow Jones Industrial Average – were also making historic gains. One all-time record would be shattered one day and then be surpassed again the next day and again the next. The Dow surged past 10,000 and some bullish stock watchers predicted the Dow hitting 36,000.

To the amazement of many in Washington, other seemingly intractable problems, like the gigantic federal budget deficit, suddenly became manageable. For decades, the federal debt had acted like a giant inland ocean draining the nation's economic vitality. Red ink "as far as the eye could see," said Ronald Reagan's budget director David Stockman.

Suddenly, it had become a large salt lake in the desert, rapidly drying up. The hot sun, primarily responsible for evaporating the deficit, turned out to be the capital gains taxes on sizzling stock values. Federal Reserve Board Chairman Alan Greenspan began to fret about the Fed's ability to regulate interest rates if the federal debt were eliminated *entirely*.

Even military engagements were different in this *fin-de-siecle* golden age. During the latter part of the Clinton administration, military operations, as in Kosovo, ended with virtually no loss of American lives in combat. U.S. military superiority versus opponents like Yugoslavia was so unprecedented that it was like the gods in ancient Greek mythology matched up against mere mortals.

Beyond the unparalleled military power, the United States also boasted the world's preeminent economy, the most dominant culture and the most appealing educational system attracting the planet's best and brightest. Never in history had one country possessed so much power of so many types. If anything, America's "hard" military clout may have been overshadowed by the pervasive influence of America's "soft" economic and cultural power. President Bill Clinton often seemed more popular abroad, where he was mobbed while on foreign trips, than he was at home.

But, as has happened throughout history, success and safety bred arrogance and complacency. As the clock counted down on the 20th century, with few foreign threats and with millions prospering from a historic economic boom, Americans let their political attention wander to more recreational interests.

Americans of the Clinton Era became fascinated with lifestyle issues and scandals of the rich-and-famous. Cable news networks, which were launched amid high-brow promises of in-depth examinations of a wide variety of neglected issues, found their ratings tied to round-the-clock coverage of sensational cases like the murder of child beauty queen JonBenet Ramsey.

As Bill Clinton's presidency ground on, another emerging factor in American life was the anger of Republicans who despised this "pretender" in the White House whom they saw as both a political *poseur* with Ivy League credentials and a randy hick from Arkansas. From Clinton's first days in office, right-wing operatives saw their eventual comeback tied to dragging down Clinton, denigrating his wife Hillary and cultivating public doubts about them both.

Professionally produced videos, such as "The Clinton Chronicles" promoted by right-wing Christian evangelist Jerry Falwell, attempted to link Clinton to mysterious deaths, drug trafficking and other nefarious activities. Over the eight years of Clinton's presidency, Republicans also pushed complicated – and ultimately flimsy – accusations about a failed real-estate deal called Whitewater. Leading conservative magazines, like *The American Spectator*, spread rumors about the Clintons' sex lives.

These two strands of political and cultural attitudes – America's fascination with personal scandal and the Right's determination to destroy Clinton's presidency – connected with disclosures in 1998 about Clinton's sexual liaison with former White House intern Monica Lewinsky. Whitewater special prosecutor Kenneth Starr, a right-wing legal activist and former Solicitor General under President George H.W.

Bush, recognized in the Lewinsky sex scandal the potential to revive his faltering Whitewater investigation and to restore his fading reputation. The Lewinsky liaison and Clinton's semantic attempts to conceal it allowed Starr to finally nail the elusive "Slick Willie."

In 1998, the Lewinsky case also perfectly suited the needs of the mainstream national news media, which had been tagging along behind the right-wing press in its coverage of the "Clinton scandals." Since the 1970s, mainstream journalists had carried around the albatross of the "liberal bias" accusation. Then, as the Right built up its own media apparatus in the 1980s and 1990s – from *The Washington Times* and *The Wall Street Journal*'s editorial page to Rush Limbaugh, Fox News and Matt Drudge – the pressure grew on mainstream journalists to tilt their reporting to the right and thus protect themselves from the increasingly dangerous accusation of "liberal."

Starr's decision to expand his Whitewater investigation into allegations that Clinton had tried to cover up his sexual contacts with Lewinsky was irresistible to the mainstream media. *The Washington Post* immediately headlined the disclosure of the Lewinsky probe; CNN switched to all-day coverage of developments; the major networks, the national newsmagazines and all the big newspapers followed, devoting time, space and resources to the Lewinsky affair as if it were a matter of national survival. Only a few Internet sites, like *Salon.com* and our own *Consortiumnews.com*, took note of the other side of the scandal, that it had the smell and feel of a political *coup d'etat*, albeit one relying on media clout, not tanks in the streets.

Ultimately, the Republican drive to unseat Clinton came up short. The Republican-controlled House voted for his impeachment, but opinion polls showed the American public opposing Clinton's ouster and the Senate trial failed to gain the two-thirds super-majority necessary to remove a President from office. A humiliated Clinton struggled on through his final two years in office, kept afloat by the rising economy and by the improbable federal budget *surplus*.

The seeming ease of the pre-millennium period led many Americans to feel that the nation had switched on to a kind of presidential auto-pilot. Most of the daunting challenges that had bedeviled presidents in previous decades – painful economic recessions and scary military challenges – looked like relics of the past. Politics became primarily about personality.

◆ ◆ ◆

In 1999, both the mainstream media and the right-wing press felt let down by the failure to bring down Clinton. As the impeachment battle ended with Clinton still standing, the Washington press corps turned almost as one against Clinton's favored successor, Vice President Al Gore. Among much of the mainstream press corps, the preferred Democrat was Senator Bill Bradley of New Jersey, a onetime Rhodes scholar and former New York Knicks basketball star.

While fawning over Bradley's ethical standards and other attributes, political reporters competed to attach negative characteristics to Gore. Gore was ruthless; he was a braggart; he was calculating; he was corrupt; he was a phony. To read the major newspapers and to watch the TV pundit shows in late 1999 and 2000, one couldn't avoid the impression that many in the national press corps had decided that Gore was unfit to be elected the President of the United States.

Across the board – from *The Washington Post* to *The Washington Times,* from *The New York Times* to the *New York Post,* from NBC's cable networks to the traveling campaign press corps – journalists didn't even bother to disguise their contempt for Gore. Every perceived Gore misstep, including his choice of clothing, was treated as a new excuse to put him on a psychiatrist's couch and find him wanting.

Some journalists and talking heads took to calling Gore "delusional" and "a liar." Yet, to back up these sweeping denunciations, the media relied on a series of distorted quotes and tendentious interpretations of Gore's words, at times following scripts written by the national Republican leadership.

In December 1999, for instance, the news media generated dozens of stories about Gore's supposed claim that he discovered the infamous Love Canal toxic waste dump. "I was the one that started it all," he was quoted as saying. This "gaffe" then was used to recycle other situations in which Gore allegedly exaggerated his role or, as some writers put it, told "bold-faced lies."

But behind this example of Gore's "lying" was some very sloppy journalism. The Love Canal flap started when *The Washington Post* and *The New York Times* misquoted Gore on a key point and cropped out the context of another sentence to give readers a false impression of what he meant. The error was then exploited by national Republicans and amplified endlessly by the rest of the news media, even after the *Post* and *Times* grudgingly filed corrections.

The Love Canal quote controversy began on November 30, 1999, when Gore was speaking to a group of high school students in Concord, New Hampshire. He was exhorting the students to reject cynicism and to recognize that individual citizens can contribute to important changes. As an example, he cited a high school girl from Toone, Tennessee, a town that had experienced problems with toxic waste. She brought the issue to the attention of Gore's congressional office in the late 1970s, he said.

"I called for a congressional investigation and a hearing," Gore told the Concord students. "I looked around the country for other sites like that. I found a little place in upstate New York called Love Canal. Had the first hearing on that issue, and Toone, Tennessee – that was the one that you didn't hear of. But that was the one that started it all."

After those congressional hearings, Gore said, "we passed a major national law to clean up hazardous dump sites. And we had new efforts to stop the practices that ended up poisoning water around the country. We've still got work to do. But we made a huge difference. And it all happened because one high school student got involved."

The context of Gore's comment was clear. What sparked his interest in the toxic-waste issue was the situation in Toone, Tennessee – "that was the one that you didn't hear of. But that was the one that started it all." After learning about the Toone situation, Gore looked for other examples and "found" a similar case at Love Canal. He was not claiming to have been the first one to discover Love Canal, which already had been evacuated. He simply needed other case studies for the hearings.

In the next day's *Washington Post,* a story by political writer Ceci Connolly stripped Gore's comments of their context and gave them a negative twist. "Gore boasted about his efforts in Congress 20 years ago to publicize the dangers of toxic waste," Connolly's story said. "'I found a little place in upstate New York called Love Canal,' [Gore] said, referring to the Niagara homes evacuated in August 1978 because of chemical contamination. 'I had the first hearing on this issue.' ... Gore said his efforts made a lasting impact. 'I was the one that started it all,' he said."[1]

The New York Times ran a slightly less contentious story with the same false quote: "I was the one that started it all."

The Republican National Committee spotted Gore's alleged boast and was quick to fax around its own take. "Al Gore is simply unbelievable – in the most literal sense of that term," declared Republican National Committee Chairman Jim Nicholson. "It's a pattern of phoniness – and it would be funny if it weren't also a little scary."

The GOP release then doctored Gore's quote a bit more. After all, it would be grammatically incorrect to have said, "I was the one *that* started it all." So, the Republican handout fixed Gore's grammar to say, "I was the one *who* started it all." In just one day, the key quote had transformed from a reference to the waste dump in Toone, Tennessee, as "*that* was the one *that* started it all" to "*I* was the one *that* started it all" to "*I* was the one *who* started it all."

Instead of taking the offensive against these misquotes – and thus face accusations of being overly defensive – Gore tried to head off the controversy by clarifying his meaning and apologizing if anyone got the wrong impression. But the fun was just beginning.

The national pundit shows quickly picked up the story of Gore's latest "exaggeration," mixing the Love Canal case with other hostile interpretations of Gore's words relating to the movie *Love Story* and his support for creating the modern Internet.

"Let's talk about the 'love' factor here," chortled Chris Matthews of CNBC's "Hardball." "Here's the guy who said he was the character Ryan O'Neal was based on in 'Love Story.' ... It seems to me ... he's now the guy who created the Love Canal [case]. I mean, isn't this getting ridiculous? ... Isn't it getting to be delusionary?"

Matthews turned to his baffled guest, Lois Gibbs, the Love Canal resident who is widely credited with bringing the issue to public attention. She sounded confused about why Gore would claim credit for discovering Love Canal, but defended Gore's hard work on the issue.

"I actually think he's done a great job," Gibbs said. "I mean, he really did work, when nobody else was working, on trying to define what the hazards were in this country and how to clean it up and helping with the Superfund and other legislation."[2]

The next morning, *Post* political writer Ceci Connolly highlighted Gore's supposed Love Canal boast, putting it into his alleged pattern of falsehoods. "Add Love Canal to the list of verbal missteps by Vice President Gore," she wrote. "The man who mistakenly claimed to have inspired the movie 'Love Story' and to have invented the Internet says he didn't quite mean to say he discovered a toxic waste site."[3]

That night, CNBC's "Hardball" returned to Gore's Love Canal quote by playing the actual clip but altering the context by starting Gore's comments with the words, "I found a little town..."

"It reminds me of Snoopy thinking he's the Red Baron," laughed Chris Matthews. "I mean how did he get this idea? Now you've seen Al Gore in action. I know you didn't know that he was the prototype for Ryan O'Neal's character in 'Love Story' or that he invented the Internet. He now is the guy who discovered Love Canal."

Matthews compared the Vice President to Zelig, Woody Allen's character whose face appeared at an unlikely procession of historic events. "What is it, the Zelig guy who keeps saying, 'I was the main character in 'Love Story.' I invented the Internet. I invented Love Canal."

Former Secretary of Labor Robert Reich, a Bradley supporter, added, "I don't know why he feels that he has to exaggerate and make some of this stuff up."

The following day, Rupert Murdoch's right-wing *New York Post* elaborated on Gore's supposed pathology of deception.

"Again, Al Gore has told a whopper," a *Post* editorial said. "Again, he's been caught red-handed and again, he has been left sputtering and apologizing. This time, he falsely took credit for breaking the Love Canal story. ... Yep, another Al Gore bold-faced lie. ... Al Gore appears to have as much difficulty telling the truth as his boss, Bill Clinton. But Gore's lies are not just false, they're outrageously, stupidly false. It's so easy to determine that he's lying, you have to wonder if he wants to be found out. Does he enjoy the embarrassment? Is he hell-bent on destroying his own campaign? ... Of course, if Al Gore is determined to turn himself into a national laughingstock, who are we to stand in his way?"

The Love Canal controversy soon moved beyond the Washington-New York power axis. On December 6, 1999, *The Buffalo News* ran an editorial entitled, "Al Gore in Fantasyland," that echoed the words of RNC chief Nicholson. It stated, "Never mind that he didn't invent the Internet, serve as the model for 'Love Story' or blow the whistle on Love Canal. All of this would be funny if it weren't so disturbing."

The next day, the right-wing *Washington Times* judged Gore simply crazy. "The real question is how to react to Mr. Gore's increasingly bizarre utterings," the *Times* said in an editorial. "Webster's New World Dictionary defines 'delusional' thusly: 'The apparent perception, in a nervous or mental disorder, of some thing external that is actually not present ... a belief in something that is contrary to fact or reality, resulting from deception, misconception, or a mental disorder.'"

The editorial denounced Gore as "a politician who not only manufactures gross, obvious lies about himself and his achievements but appears to actually believe these confabulations."

Yet, while the national media was excoriating Gore, the Concord students were learning more than they had expected about how media and politics worked in modern America. For days, the students pressed for a correction from *The Washington Post* and *The New York Times*. But the newspapers balked, insisting that the error was insignificant.

"The part that bugs me is the way they nit pick," said Tara Baker, a Concord High junior. "[But] they should at least get it right."[4]

When the David Letterman TV show made Love Canal the jumping off point for a joke list: "Top 10 Achievements Claimed by Al Gore," the students responded with a press release entitled "Top 10 Reasons Why Many Concord High Students Feel Betrayed by Some of the Media Coverage of Al Gore's Visit to Their School."[5] Bob Somerby, the editor of a media-criticism Web site, *The Daily Howler,* also was hectoring what he termed a "grumbling editor" at the *Post* to correct the error.

Finally, on December 7, 1999, a week after Gore's comment, the *Post* published a partial correction, tucked away as the last item in a corrections box. But the *Post* still misled readers about what Gore actually said. The *Post* correction read: "In fact, Gore said, 'That was the one that started it all,' referring to the congressional hearings on the subject that he called."

The revision fit with the *Post*'s insistence that the two quotes meant pretty much the same thing, but again, the newspaper was distorting Gore's clear intent by attaching "that" to the wrong antecedent. From the full quote, it's obvious the "that" refers to the Toone toxic waste case, not to Gore's hearings.

Three days later, *The New York Times* followed suit with a correction of its own, but again without fully explaining Gore's position. "They fixed how they misquoted him, but they didn't tell the whole story," said Lindsey Roy, another Concord High junior.

While the students voiced disillusionment, the two reporters involved showed no remorse for their mistake. "I really do think that the whole thing has been blown out of proportion," said Katharine Seelye of the *Times.* "It was one word."

The *Post*'s Ceci Connolly even defended her inaccurate rendition of Gore's quote as something of a journalistic duty. "We have an obligation to our readers to alert them [that] this [Gore's false boasting] continues to be something of a habit," she said.[6]

The half-hearted corrections also did not stop newspapers around the country from continuing to use the bogus quote. A December 9 editorial in the Lancaster, Pennsylvania, *New Era* even published the polished misquote that the Republican National Committee had stuck in its press release: "*I* was the one *who* started it all."

The *New Era* then went on to psychoanalyze Gore. "Maybe the lying is a symptom of a more deeply-rooted problem: Al Gore doesn't know who he is," the editorial stated. "The Vice President is a serial prevaricator."[7]

In the *Milwaukee Journal Sentinel,* writer Michael Ruby concluded that "the Gore of '99" was full of lies. He "suddenly discovers elastic properties in the truth," Ruby declared. "He invents the Internet, inspires the fictional hero of 'Love Story,' blows the whistle on Love Canal. Except he didn't really do any of those things."[8]

The National Journal's Stuart Taylor Jr. cited the Love Canal case as proof that President Clinton was something of a political toxic waste dump himself, contaminating those around him. The problem was "the Clintonization of Al Gore, who increasingly apes his boss in fictionalizing his life story and mangling the truth for political gain. Gore

– self-described inspiration for the novel *Love Story*, discoverer of Love Canal, co-creator of the Internet," Taylor wrote.[9]

On December 19, GOP chairman Nicholson was back on the offensive. Far from apologizing for the RNC's misquotes, Nicholson was reprising the allegations of Gore's falsehoods that had been repeated so often by then that they had taken on the color of truth: "Remember, too, that this is the same guy who says he invented the Internet, inspired *Love Story* and discovered Love Canal."

More than two weeks after the *Post* correction, the bogus quote was still spreading. *The Providence Journal* in Rhode Island lashed out at Gore in an editorial that reminded readers that Gore had said about Love Canal, "I was the one that started it all."

The editorial then turned to the bigger picture: "This is the third time in the last few months that Mr. Gore has made a categorical assertion that is – well, untrue. ... There is an audacity about Mr. Gore's howlers that is stunning. ... Perhaps it is time to wonder what it is that impels Vice President Gore to make such preposterous claims, time and again."[10]

The characterization of Gore as a clumsy liar continued into the New Year, election year 2000.

In *The Washington Times,* R. Emmett Tyrrell Jr. put Gore's falsehoods in the context of a sinister strategy: "Deposit so many deceits and falsehoods on the public record that the public and the press simply lose interest in the truth. This, the Democrats thought, was the method behind Mr. Gore's many brilliantly conceived little lies. Except that Mr. Gore's lies are not brilliantly conceived. In fact, they are stupid. He gets caught every time ... Just last month, Mr. Gore got caught claiming ... to have been the whistle-blower for 'discovering Love Canal.'"[11]

It was unclear where Tyrrell got the quote, "discovering Love Canal," since not even the earlier false quotes had put those words in Gore's mouth. But Tyrrell's description of what he perceived as Gore's strategy of flooding the public debate with "deceits and falsehoods" might have better fit what the U.S. news media and the Republicans were doing to Gore.

◆ ◆ ◆

Beyond the media's Love Canal tall tale, the other prime examples of Gore's "lies" – inspiring the male lead in *Love Story* and working to create the Internet – also stemmed from a quarrelsome reading of his words, followed by exaggeration and ridicule rather than a fair assessment of how his comments and the truth matched up.

The earliest of these Gore "lies" dated back to 1997 when Gore reportedly made a passing reference in a *Time* magazine interview to an article in the *Tennessean*, which quoted *Love Story* author Erich Segal as saying that the lead characters in his sentimental novel were based on Al and Tipper Gore, whom Segal knew during college days at Harvard.

That brief reference in *Time* magazine was then picked up as part of a Gore profile in *The New York Times*, which noted that Segal had clarified the point, saying that the hockey-playing male lead, Oliver Barrett IV, was partly based on Gore and partly on Gore's Harvard roommate, actor Tommy Lee Jones. But Segal said the female lead, Jenny, was not modeled after Tipper Gore.[12]

Rather than treating this distinction as a minor point of legitimate confusion that wasn't worthy of attention during a presidential campaign, the news media – virtually across the political spectrum – seized on the *Love Story* story to conclude that Gore had willfully lied. In doing so, however, the media repeatedly misstated the facts, insisting that Segal had denied that Gore was the model for the lead male character. In reality, Segal had confirmed that Gore was, at least partly, the inspiration for the character, Barrett, played by Ryan O'Neal.

Some journalists seemed to understand the nuance but still couldn't resist disparaging Gore's honesty. For instance, in its attack on Gore over the Love Canal case, the *Boston Herald* conceded that Gore "did provide material" for Segal's book, but the newspaper added that it was "for a minor character."[13] That, of course, was untrue, since the Barrett character was one of *Love Story*'s two principal characters.

The news media's treatment of apocryphal "inventing the Internet" comment followed a similar course. Gore's actual statement may have been poorly phrased, but its intent was clear: he was trying to say that he worked in Congress to help create the modern Internet. Gore wasn't claiming to have "invented" the Internet, with its connotation of a computer engineer tinkering with some hardware and achieving a technological breakthrough.

Gore's actual comment, in an interview with CNN's Wolf Blitzer that aired on March 9, 1999, was as follows: "During my service in the United States Congress, I took the initiative in creating the Internet." While the phrasing may have been inelegant, Gore's point was correct. He had led the way in Congress to fund the development of what the world now knows as the Internet, or what Gore earlier dubbed, "the information super-highway."

But Republicans quickly went to work on Gore's statement. In press releases, they noted that the precursor of the Internet, called ARPANET, existed in 1971, a half dozen years before Gore entered Congress. But

ARPANET was a tiny networking of about 30 universities, a far cry from today's Internet. Nevertheless, a media clamor soon arose over Gore's Internet statement.

Gore's spokesman Chris Lehane tried to clarify the point by noting that Gore "was the leader in Congress on the connections between data transmission and computing power, what we call information technology. And those efforts helped to create the Internet that we know today."[14]

There was no disputing Lehane's description of Gore's lead congressional role in developing today's Internet. But any plaintive appeals for fairness were hopeless. Reporters soon had lopped off the introductory clause "during my service in the United States Congress" or simply jumped to word substitutions, asserting that Gore claimed that he "invented" the Internet. Whatever imprecision may have existed in Gore's original comment, it paled beside the media's exaggerated efforts to attack Gore for exaggerating.

As Campaign 2000 swung into high gear, campaign reporters acted as if they had reached a collective decision that Gore should be disqualified. At times, they jettisoned even the pretext of objectivity. According to various accounts of the first Democratic debate in Hanover, New Hampshire, reporters openly mocked Gore as they sat in a nearby press room and watched the debate on television. Several journalists later recounted the incident, but without overt criticism of their colleagues.

As *The Daily Howler* observed, *Time*'s Eric Pooley cited the reporters' reaction only to underscore how Gore was failing in his "frenzied attempt to connect" with the voters. "The ache was unmistakable – and even touching – but the 300 media types watching in the press room at Dartmouth were, to use the appropriate technical term, totally grossed out by it," Pooley wrote. "Whenever Gore came on too strong, the room erupted in a collective jeer, like a gang of 15-year-old Heathers cutting down some hapless nerd."

Hotline's Howard Mortman described the same behavior as the reporters "groaned, laughed and howled" at Gore's comments. Later, during an appearance on C-SPAN's "Washington Journal," *Salon*'s Jake Tapper cited the Hanover incident, too. "I can tell you that the only media bias I have detected in terms of a group media bias was, at the first debate between Bill Bradley and Al Gore, there was hissing for Gore in the media room up at Dartmouth College. The reporters were hissing Gore, and that's the only time I've ever heard the press room boo or hiss any candidate of any party at any event."[15]

Traditionally, journalists pride themselves in maintaining deadpan expressions in such public settings, at most chuckling at a comment or raising an eyebrow, but never demonstrating derision for a public figure.

But, in Gore's case, the reporters must have felt there was no career downside to mocking Gore and there may have been an upside by demonstrating to the conservative journalists present that no one here was one of those Clinton-Gore-loving "liberals."

But – while the Gore bashing might have made sense in light of the career interests of the national press corps – how could the American voters be expected to make an informed judgment when the media intervened to transform one of the principal candidates – an individual who, by all accounts, was a well-qualified public official and a decent family man – into a national laughingstock?

What hope did American democracy have when the media could misrepresent a candidate's words so thoroughly that they became an argument for his mental instability? As *The Daily Howler*'s Somerby observed, the concern about deception and its corrosive effect on democracy dated back to the ancient Greeks. "Democracy won't work, the great Socrates cried, because sophists will create mass confusion," Somerby recalled at his Web site. "Here in our exciting, much-hyped new millennium, the Great Greek's vision remains crystal clear."[16]

5

A Misshapen Campaign

The national news media's disdain for Al Gore – and generally friendly treatment of George W. Bush – remained a key factor in shaping the presidential race through to the end. While bird-dogging every questionable remark by Gore, the national press corps acted more like playful pups around Bush. Gore was regarded as the inveterate liar; Bush was the well-meaning guy who spoke from the heart even if what he said wasn't always exactly true. Dick Cheney, too, got a mostly positive press, admired as a tough but reasonable operative who brought maturity and experience to the race.

So, when Gore made an innocuous mistake, such as remembering inaccurately being at a Texas disaster scene in 1998 with the director of the Federal Emergency Management Agency – when he actually was with the director's deputy – the news media went into a press riot over the Gore-as-serial-exaggerator "theme." It was a chance to show that the reporters were right all along. You see, here was more proof that Gore lies.

However, getting confused about whether you were on a trip with the FEMA director or his deputy wasn't the kind of detail that would stick in your head like whether you were hanging out with Nelson Mandela or Bono. Indeed, it made no sense to think that the Vice President of the United States would seek to polish his record by dropping the name of the FEMA director. Yet that was exactly the ugly conclusion that the Republicans and the press corps reached.

In contrast to the front-page coverage of Gore's FEMA mistake or the dispute over Gore's description of an overcrowded Florida high school, the press shrugged its shoulders at false statements by Bush and Cheney – on the grounds that, hey, everyone's human. In the second presidential debate, for instance, Bush said he opposed a hate-crimes law in Texas because three white men found guilty of dragging a black man, James Byrd, to his death behind a pickup truck were already facing the death penalty.

"It's going to be hard to punish them any worse after they're put to death," Bush said with a smirk. But Bush wasn't telling the truth. One of the three killers actually had received life imprisonment, not the death penalty. Bush had misstated or "exaggerated" the facts of a major criminal case that had occurred during his tenure as Texas governor. One could only imagine how the press would have played up a similar mistake by Gore. It would have been a huge topic of debate for a week.

Given the media's endless search for a personality flaw behind Gore's supposed exaggerations, a similar standard might have been expected to apply to Bush. With its penchant for cookie-cutter "themes" used to define candidates, the press might have seized on Bush's smirking comment about the condemned men and used it to remind the public about Bush's earlier insensitivity when he mimicked condemned murderer Carla Faye Tucker as she was pleading for her life.

In a 1999 interview with conservative writer Tucker Carlson for *Talk* magazine, Bush had ridiculed the woman's clemency appeal: "With pursed lips in mock desperation, [Bush said] 'Please don't kill me.'" In view of Bush's jocular comments about the killers in the Byrd case, the press might have asked: What is it about Bush's make-up that he likes to mock people he is about to have put to death?

But the major news media didn't see Bush's misstatement or his smirk as much of a story. The next day, *The Washington Post* stuck the governor's exaggeration about the three condemned killers in a story on A6. The media's rationale apparently was that Bush's error was the kind of mistake that a candidate can make in the course of a 90-minute debate and the press shouldn't be too picky. Yet, the opposite standard was applied to Gore.

The imbalance in press coverage was apparent, too, with Dick Cheney, a longtime favorite of official Washington. At the vice presidential debate, Cheney depicted himself as a self-made multi-millionaire from his years as chairman of Halliburton. As for his success in the private sector, Cheney told Democratic nominee Joe Lieberman that "the government had absolutely nothing to do with it."

If the Gore rules had applied, the major media would have jumped all over Cheney for puffing up his résumé. But the big newspapers and the major television networks offered no challenge to Cheney's comment. *Bloomberg News*, a business wire where Robert Parry was then an editor, was one of the few outlets that took note of the variance between Cheney's assessment and the facts. "Cheney's reply left out how closely … Halliburton's fortunes are linked to the U.S. government," *Bloomberg News* reported.

Bloomberg News noted that Halliburton was a leading defense contractor (with $1.8 billion in contracts from 1996-99) and a major beneficiary of federal loan guarantees (another $1.8 billion in loans and loan guarantees from the U.S.-funded Export-Import Bank during Cheney's years). The article also cited internal Ex-Im Bank e-mails showing that Cheney personally lobbied bank chairman James Harmon for a $500 million loan guarantee for Russia's OAO Tyumen Oil Co. The Ex-Im loan guarantee, approved in March 2000, helped finance Halliburton's contract with Tyumen.

In further contradiction of his self-made-man claim, Cheney gave a speech to the Ex-Im Bank in 1997 in which he said: "I see that we have in recent years been involved in projects in the following (countries) supported, in part, through Ex-Im activities: Algeria, Angola, Colombia, the Philippines, Russia, the Czech Republic, Thailand, China, Turkey, Turkmenistan, Kuwait, India, Kenya, the Congo, Brazil, Argentina, Trinidad and Tobago, Venezuela, Indonesia, Malaysia and Mexico. ... Export financing agencies are a key element in making this possible, helping U.S. businesses blend private sector resources with the full faith and credit of the U.S. government."[1]

So, in Cheney's own words in 1997, U.S. government loan guarantees had been "a key element in making" Halliburton's worldwide operations "possible." Three years later, however, Cheney insisted that "the government had absolutely nothing to do with" his business success.

Fresh from this false pronouncement about his self-reliance, Cheney took the offensive denouncing Gore for alleged exaggerations about his own history. "He [Gore] seems to have a compulsion to embellish his arguments or ... his résumé," Cheney said on October 6, 2000. "He seems to have this uncontrollable desire periodically to add to his reputation, to his record, things that aren't true. That's worrisome and I think it's appropriate for us to point that out."

As Sam Parry pointed out at *Consortiumnews.com*, "Normally, hypocrisy is considered a big story, especially when the accuser's behavior is more egregious than the actions of his target. Yet, Cheney's own résumé polishing was barely mentioned in the major media."[2]

The campaign press corps continued its disinterest even as Cheney went out of his way to defend his self-made-man statement in comments on National Public Radio. He insisted that the government contracts with Halliburton had predated his arrival at the company in 1995.

"We did do some" work for the government, Cheney told NPR interviewer Bob Edwards on October 11. "The fact is the company I worked for won a competitive bid before I ever got there. So it's not as though this were some kind of gift."[3] However, contrary to Cheney's suggestion that he was not responsible for bringing in any of Halliburton's government business, Halliburton actually moved up the list of Pentagon contractors during Cheney's tenure, reaching 17 in 1999, the latest available rankings in 2000.

The documents, which were cited in the *Bloomberg News* article, also made clear that Cheney personally lobbied for loan guarantees from the Ex-Im Bank, what some critics call "corporate welfare." Yet, the major news media's one-way microscope on Gore's credibility missed Cheney's exaggeration about his career while letting Cheney continue attacking Gore over alleged exaggerations about his career.

♦♦♦

Similarly, the press let Governor Bush escape any serious attention over false and misleading statements about the environment and global warming, issues that could affect the future of the planet.

In the presidential debate on October 11, Bush offered conflicting statements within the space of a few minutes. Bush's first swing at the issue of pollution-causing industrial plants went this way: "We need to make sure that if we decontrol our plants that there's mandatory – that the plants must conform to clean air standards, the grand-fathered plants. That's what we did in Texas. No excuses. I mean, you must conform."

Just minutes later, however, he had shifted toward what sounded like a call for a voluntary program. "Well, I – I – I don't believe in command-and-control out of Washington, D.C. I believe Washington ought to set standards, but I don't – again, I think we ought to be collaborative at the local levels. And I think we ought to work with people at the local levels."

Beyond the question of coherence, Bush's statements appeared contradictory. Either the national government sets standards and requires compliance or local governments can be allowed to set their own environmental rules, possibly in cooperation with business. Bush seemed to be having it both ways.

In Texas, Bush's record suggested that he opposed mandatory standards even at the local and state levels. Bush cited as his most significant environmental accomplishment the setting of new rules for grand-fathered industrial plants, previously exempt from Texas clean air laws – what he apparently was referring to in his debate remarks.

But those plants were asked only to comply voluntarily with the clean air rules. The 1997 law carried no penalties for industries that didn't seek a permit under the law. It was the kind of standard that polluting industries would salivate over at the national level.

On global warming, Bush's debate comments were perhaps even more misleading. "I just – I think there's been some – some of the scientists. I believe, Mr. Vice President, haven't they been changing their opinion a little bit on global warming?" Bush said.

In reality, the only change within the scientific community had been to revise global warming projections upward, recognizing that the rising temperatures were a greater threat than had been thought. By fall of 2000, no credible scientist denied that global warming was a real environmental development.

In the debate, Bush also protested the Kyoto Protocol, an amendment to the United Nations Framework Convention on Climate Change that assigned mandatory limitations on greenhouse gas emissions. Bush said, "I'll tell you one thing I'm not going to do is I'm not going to let the United States carry the burden for cleaning up the world's air, like the Kyoto Treaty would have done. China and India were exempted from that treaty."

In fact, China and India were not exempted from the treaty. It's true they weren't subjected to the same requirements as the developed world, but they committed themselves to reducing emissions. Plus, the Kyoto Protocol required steeper emissions reductions from European countries than it required from the United States.

At another point in the debate, Bush said the Clinton-Gore administration "took 40 million acres of land out of circulation without consulting local officials. ... I just cited an example of the administration just unilaterally acting without any input." Bush was referring to an administration proposal to protect 40 million acres of roadless areas in national forests from more road building and logging. But, as the Sierra Club noted in a press release, Bush's statement was false.

"In fact, the Forest Service conducted 600 public meetings about the proposal nationwide and more than one million Americans urged the administration to strengthen the proposal," the Sierra Club said. "There was ample opportunity for local officials and others to comment on the proposal."[4]

Defending his own record in Texas, Bush also asserted that "our water is cleaner now." False again, the Sierra Club said. "The discharge of industrial toxic pollution into surface waters in Texas increased from 23.2 million pounds in 1995 to 25.2 million pounds in 1998, the last year with data available," a Sierra Club press release said.[5]

In other dubious debate comments, Bush insisted he was not a man who needed a focus group or polls to tell him what to think. "I think you've got to look at how one has handled responsibility in office, whether or not ... you've got the capacity to convince people to follow;

whether or not one makes decisions based upon sound principles; or whether or not you rely upon polls and focus groups on how to decide what the course of action is," Bush said. "We've got too much polling and focus groups going on in Washington today. We need decisions made on sound principles."

Left out was that Bush's campaign had spent roughly $1 million on polls and focus groups during the campaign, about equal to the Gore campaign's spending, according to a report by NBC News.[6] Indeed, Bush changed his campaign slogan from "Compassionate Conservative" to "Real Plans for Real People" because of poll analysis done by his campaign.

In another debate, Bush tried to make an issue out of President Clinton's practice of allowing his friends and supporters to sleep over at the White House. "I believe they've moved that sign, 'The buck stops here,' from the Oval Office desk to 'The buck stops here' on the Lincoln bedroom, and that's not good for the country. It's not right. We need to have a new look about how we conduct ourselves in office," Bush said.

What Bush left out was that since he took office in 1995, he had 203 guests stay over at the Governor's Mansion in Austin, Texas. More than half of them had contributed to his campaign, amounting to $2.2 million.[7]

In perhaps Bush's most obvious whopper in the first presidential debate, the Republican claimed that the Gore campaign had out-spent his. "This man has out-spent me," Bush said.

In fact, Bush raised $193 million and spent $186 million in Election 2000, compared with Gore's $133 million raised and $120 million spent. There was no explanation from the Bush campaign about this remarkable claim and the national news media didn't press for one.

Rather than deal with Bush's numerous debate distortions, the press flew into a frenzy over Gore's audible sighs when Bush would misrepresent some fact and over Gore's mistake about the FEMA director. At times, the press seemed to be in a competition over who could find the next big Gore "exaggeration" or "character flaw."

A day after the first debate, Mickey Kaus of *Slate.com* wrote that the media had come to the conclusion that Gore's "stereotyped fatal flaw" was that he exaggerates and that reporters were on the hunt for examples of Gore "fiblets." This, according to Kaus, explained the press reaction to Gore's FEMA remark.

While this press fixation might seem trivial to some Americans, its cumulative effect was to transform the presidential election campaign from one that had been focused on issues to one dominated by the Republican/media's harsh assessment of Gore's character and credibility. What made this development a direct threat to the democratic process was that the media's treatment was extraordinarily one-sided and often erroneous.

Besides George W. Bush's lies and distortions, Bush's hypocrisies also received only spotty attention from the news media. For instance, after securing the Republican nomination by smearing John McCain, Bush renewed his pledge to run a positive general election campaign. But again, the promise lasted only until Bush found himself in a tight race. Bush then unleashed his campaign operatives to tear down Gore.

The news media observed the changed tactics but made little of how Bush was violating his own pledge. In fact, the Republican strategy to destroy Al Gore's reputation had been underway, often beneath the surface, for many months. *The New York Times* described what it called "a skillful and sustained 18-month campaign by Republicans to portray the Vice President as flawed and untrustworthy."[8]

In one example, the *Times* noted that the Republicans had successfully portrayed Gore as a liar for having talked about his work as a boy on the family's Tennessee farm. Republican National Chairman Jim Nicholson mocked Gore as a pampered city kid misrepresenting his past. But Gore, who split his time between life in a Washington hotel suite when his father was busy with Senate work and the family farm much of the rest of year, had not been lying.

"Friends later told reporters that Mr. Gore's father had kept him on a backbreaking work schedule during summers on the family farm," the *Times* noted.

But there was no sustained media effort to hold the Bush campaign accountable for its dishonest tactics against Gore and virtually no self-criticism about how the Washington press corps had consistently played into Republican hands.

♦♦♦

Conservative groups also were given wide leeway in smearing Gore without being called to account, even when the Vice President was falsely portrayed as a traitor.

For instance, in the weeks before Election 2000, a pro-Republican group from Texas, called Aretino Industries, ran an emotional ad modeled after Lyndon Johnson's infamous 1964 commercial that showed a girl picking a daisy before the screen dissolved into a nuclear explosion. The ad remake accused the Clinton-Gore administration of selling vital nuclear secrets to communist China, in exchange for campaign donations in 1996. The compromised nuclear secrets, the ad stated, gave China "the ability to threaten our homes with long-range nuclear warheads."[9]

But the ad – which aired in "swing" states including Ohio, Michigan, Missouri and Pennsylvania – was filled with disinformation. The actual evidence was that the key breach in national security, contributing to the modernization of China's nuclear arsenal, occurred in the 1980s, not the 1990s. The secrets were lost during the Reagan-Bush administration, not the Clinton-Gore administration.

The most important compromised U.S. secret that allegedly helped China's nuclear weapons program was the blueprint for the W-88 miniaturized nuclear warhead, which was smuggled to the Chinese in 1988, the last year of Ronald Reagan's presidency, according to documents later given to U.S. authorities by a Chinese defector. China tested their W-88-style warhead in 1992, the last year of the first Bush administration.

Therefore, the W-88 secret was lost – and acted upon – before Bill Clinton and Al Gore took office. Indeed, the only significant part of this nuclear-secrets case that happened during the Clinton-Gore administration was that a Chinese defector exposed the espionage breach in 1995. However, when the American public first learned of the compromised secrets a few years later, the Republicans applied fuzzy logic and a blurred chronology to transform the lost nuclear blueprints, apparently compromised on the Reagan-Bush watch, into an attack theme on Clinton and Gore.

This clever strategy could be traced back to a May 1999 report prepared by a Republican-controlled congressional investigation headed by Representative Christopher Cox of California. The so-called Cox report accused the Clinton-Gore administration of failing to protect the nation against China's theft of top-secret nuclear designs and other sensitive data.

When released on May 25, 1999 – shortly after the Clinton impeachment battle had ended – the Cox report was greeted by conservative groups and the national news media as another indictment of the Clinton administration. By then, the Washington press corps had long been addicted to "Clinton scandals" and viewed almost any allegation through that prism, regardless of the details.

Despite the media spotlight, little attention was paid to the shallowness of the Cox report. Though filling three glossy volumes and toting up 872 pages, the report had the look of a term paper written by a student trying to stretch the length by expanding the margins and triple-spacing. The Cox report certainly didn't resemble the typical green- or beige-bound congressional report. Inside a shiny black-red-white-and-gold cover, the Cox report used 14-point type, more fitting for a first-grade reading primer than a government document. (By comparison, most congressional reports use 10-point type or smaller.)

However, with its physical heft, the report gave weight in the public's mind to the suspicion that there was something far more sinister behind earlier allegations that a Chinese government front had funneled $30,000 in illegal "soft money" donations to the Democrats in 1996. Cox pulled off his sleight of hand with barely anyone spotting the trick card up his sleeve.[*]

The key ruse was to leave out dates of alleged Chinese spying in the 1980s and thus obscure the fact that the floodgates of U.S. nuclear secrets to China – including how to build the miniaturized W-88 nuclear warhead – had opened wide during the Reagan-Bush era. While leaving out those Republican time elements, Cox shoved references to the alleged lapses into the presidencies of Jimmy Carter and Bill Clinton.

So, the Cox report's "Overview" stated that "the PRC (People's Republic of China) thefts from our National Laboratories began at least as early as the late 1970s, and significant secrets are known to have been stolen as recently as the mid-1990s."

In this way, Cox started with the Carter presidency, jumped over the 12 years of Ronald Reagan and George H.W. Bush and landed in the Clinton years. In the "Overview" alone, there were three dozen references to dates from the Clinton years and only five mentions of dates from the Reagan-Bush years, with none of those citations related to alleged wrongdoing.

Cox's stacking of the deck carried over into the report's two-page chronology of the Chinese spy scandal. On pages 74-75, the Cox report put all the information boxes about Chinese espionage suspicions into the Carter and Clinton years. Nothing sinister is attributed specifically to the Reagan-Bush era, other than a 1988 test of a neutron bomb built from secrets that the report says were believed stolen in the "late 1970s," the Carter years. Only a careful reading of the text inside the chronology's boxes made clear that many of the worst national security breaches could be traced to the Reagan-Bush era.

When federal investigators translated more documents turned over by the Chinese defector, they learned that the exposure of nuclear secrets in the Reagan-Bush years was even worse than previously thought. According to an article in *The Washington Post*, "the documents provided by the defector show that during the 1980s, Beijing had gathered a large

---

[*] A key behind-the-scenes figure in the Cox investigation was an up-and-coming neoconservative lawyer named I. Lewis "Scooter" Libby, who later became Vice President Dick Cheney's chief of staff.

amount of classified information about U.S. ballistic missiles and reentry vehicles."[10] But the major news outlets rarely spelled out the significance of that timing.

Other evidence suggested that conscious decisions by senior Reagan-Bush officials may have put communist China in a position to glean these sensitive secrets. The rupture followed a secret decision by Ronald Reagan's White House in 1984 to collaborate with Beijing on a highly sensitive intelligence operation. The project was the clandestine shipment of weapons to the Nicaraguan contra rebels, in defiance of U.S. law and while the administration was denying to Congress that such shipments were occurring. The point man for enlisting China into the off-the-books contra operation was Marine Lt. Col. Oliver North, then assigned to Reagan's National Security Council staff.

Reagan's White House turned to the Chinese for surface-to-air missiles for the contras because Congress had banned military assistance to the rebel force and the contras were suffering heavy losses from Soviet-built attack helicopters deployed by Nicaragua's leftist Sandinista government. Some of the private U.S. operatives working with North believed China was the best source for SA-7 anti-aircraft missiles. In his 1989 Iran-Contra trial, North described this procurement as a "very sensitive delivery."

For the Chinese missile deal in 1984, North said he received help from the CIA in arranging false end-user certificates from the right-wing government of Guatemala. North testified that he "had made arrangements with the Guatemalan government, using the people [CIA] Director [William] Casey had given me." But China balked at selling missiles to the Guatemalan military, which was then engaged in a scorched-earth war against its own leftist guerrillas. To resolve this problem, North was dispatched to a clandestine meeting with a Chinese military official.

In fall 1984, North enlisted Gaston J. Sigur, the NSC's expert on East Asia, to make the arrangements for a meeting with a Chinese representative, according to Sigur's testimony at North's 1989 trial. "I arranged a luncheon and brought together Colonel North and this individual from the Chinese embassy" responsible for military affairs, Sigur testified.

"At lunch, they sat and they discussed the situation in Central America," Sigur said. "Colonel North raised the issue of the need for weaponry by the contras, and the possibility of a Chinese sale of weapons, either to the contras or, as I recall, I think it was more to countries in the region but clear for the use of the contras."

North described the same meeting in his autobiography, *Under Fire*. To avoid coming under suspicion of being a spy for China, North said he first told the FBI that the meeting had been sanctioned by National Security Adviser Robert C. McFarlane.

"Back in Washington, I met with a Chinese military officer assigned to their embassy to encourage their cooperation," North wrote. "We enjoyed a fine lunch at the exclusive Cosmos Club in downtown Washington."[11]

North said the Chinese saw the collaboration as a way to develop "better relations with the United States." Possession of this knowledge also put Beijing in position to leverage future U.S. policies. It was in this climate of cooperation that other secrets, including how to make miniaturized hydrogen bombs, allegedly reached communist China. While the details of a possible U.S.-China tradeoff are still unknown, the Reagan administration did authorize a broader exchange program between U.S. and Chinese nuclear physicists. The Chinese were given access to the Los Alamos nuclear facility.

◆◆◆

Los Alamos nuclear physicist Wen Ho Lee first came to the FBI's attention in 1982 when he called another scientist who was under investigation for espionage, but Lee's contacts with China – along with trips there by other U.S. nuclear scientists – increased in the mid-1980s as relations warmed between Washington and Beijing, according to a *New York Times* chronology that was not published until after George W. Bush had become President.[12]

In March 1985, Wen Ho Lee was seen talking with Chinese scientists during a scientific conference in Hilton Head, South Carolina, according to the *Times* chronology. The next year, with approval of the Los Alamos nuclear lab, Wen Ho Lee and another scientist attended a conference in Beijing. Wen Ho Lee traveled to Beijing again in 1988. The *Times* reported that limited exchanges between nuclear scientists from the United States and China began after President Carter officially recognized China in 1978, but those meetings grew far more expansive and less controlled during the 1980s.[13]

"With the Reagan administration eager to isolate the Soviet Union, hundreds of scientists traveled between the United States and China, and the cooperation expanded to the development of torpedoes, artillery shells and jet fighters," the *Times* wrote. "The exchanges were spying opportunities as well."[14]

"On September 25, 1992, a nuclear blast shook China's western desert," the *Times* wrote. "From spies and electronic surveillance, American intelligence officials determined that the test was a breakthrough in China's long quest to match American technology for smaller, more sophisticated hydrogen bombs."[15] In September 1992, George H.W. Bush was still President.

In the early years of the Clinton administration, U.S. intelligence experts began to suspect that the Chinese nuclear breakthrough most likely came from purloined U.S. secrets. "It's like they were driving a Model T and went around the corner and suddenly had a Corvette," said Robert M. Hanson, a Los Alamos intelligence analyst.[16]

Looking for possible espionage, investigators began examining the years of the mid-1980s when the Reagan-Bush administration had authorized U.S. nuclear scientists to hold a number of meetings with their Chinese counterparts. Though the American scientists were under restrictions about what information could be shared, it was never clear exactly why these meetings were held in the first place – given the risk that a U.S. scientist might willfully or accidentally divulge nuclear secrets.

But the Chinese-espionage story didn't gain national attention until March 1999 when *The New York Times* published several imprecise front-page stories fingering Wen Ho Lee as an espionage suspect. During those chaotic first weeks of "Chinagate," Republicans and political pundits mixed together the suspicions of Chinese spying and allegations about Chinese campaign donations to the Democrats in 1996.

Clinton's Justice Department officials then overcompensated by demonstrating how tough they could be on suspect Wen Ho Lee. Yet, virtually no one in official Washington noted the logical impossibility of Democrats selling secrets to China in 1996 that China apparently had obtained a decade or so earlier during a Republican administration.

Instead, conservative groups grasped the political and fund-raising potential. Larry Klayman's right-wing Judicial Watch sent out a solicitation letter seeking $5.2 million for a special "Chinagate Task Force" that would "hold Bill Clinton, Al Gore and the Democratic Party Leadership fully accountable for election fraud, bribery and possibly treason in connection with the 'Chinagate' scandal."

Despite the frenzy, cooler heads began to prevail in June 1999. A study was issued by the President's Foreign Intelligence Advisory Board – chaired by former Senator Warren Rudman, a New Hampshire Republican – concluding that Chinese spying was less than had been "widely publicized." In September 1999, *The New York Times* weighed in with an article stating that the evidence of Chinese spying was far more tenuous than the Cox report had represented. "The congressional report went beyond the evidence in asserting that stolen secrets were the main reason for China's breakthrough," the article said.[17]

Still, the fallout from the spy hysteria continued. The 60-year-old Wen Ho Lee was imprisoned on a 59-count indictment for mishandling classified material. The Taiwanese-born naturalized U.S. citizen was put in solitary confinement with his cell light on at all times. He was allowed out of his cell only one hour a day, when he shuffled around a prison courtyard in leg shackles. As the case against Wen Ho Lee began to collapse, the government accepted a plea bargain on September 13, 2000. The scientist pled guilty to a single count of mishandling classified material.

A furious U.S. District Judge James A. Parker complained that he had been "led astray" by government prosecutors and apologized to Lee for the "demeaning, unnecessarily punitive conditions" under which Lee had been held. Parker ordered Lee released with no further jail time.

Still, the Cox report's suspicions about Clinton-Gore treachery lingered and reemerged during the final days of Campaign 2000 with the "daisy ad" remake. The closing message was blunt: "Don't take a chance," the ad said. "Please vote Republican."[18]

In its appeal, the message was unintentionally ironic, since the worst compromises of nuclear secrets to China had occurred under Ronald Reagan and George H.W. Bush, the team that would be restored to power if the voters followed the ad's advice.

George W. Bush's campaign also exploited the "Chinagate" suspicions, albeit a touch more subtly, by running ads showing Gore meeting with saffron-robed monks at a Buddhist temple in California. So, millions of Americans went to the polls in November 2000 thinking that Gore's temple appearance and the Chinese nuclear spying were somehow linked.

The national news media – still bristling with hostility toward Clinton and Gore – contributed to the confusion by failing to explain to the American public in a timely fashion that the Chinese security breaches represented a Reagan-Bush scandal, not a Clinton-Gore scandal.

6

The Election

In the days before the November 7, 2000, election, Republicans were nervous. Despite their best efforts, they feared that Democrat Al Gore might sneak into the White House by winning a majority in the Electoral College – at least 270 electoral votes – while losing the national popular vote to Texas Governor George W. Bush. This Republican worry sprang from the possibility that Green Party candidate Ralph Nader might siphon off millions of votes from Gore nationwide, but not enough in key states to keep them out of Gore's column.

To stop Gore under those circumstances, advisers to the Bush campaign weighed the possibility of challenging the legitimacy of a popular-vote loser gaining the White House. "The one thing we don't do is roll over – we fight," a Bush aide told *New York Daily News* writer Michael Kramer a week before the election.

The article reported that "the core of the emerging Bush strategy assumes a popular uprising, stoked by the Bushies themselves, of course. In league with the campaign – which is preparing talking points about the Electoral College's essential unfairness – a massive talk-radio operation would be encouraged."[1]

"We'd have ads, too," said a Bush aide, "and I think you can count on the media to fuel the thing big-time. Even papers that supported Gore might turn against him because the will of the people will have been thwarted."[2]

The Bush strategy for overturning a hypothetical Gore majority in the Electoral College went even further, close to insurrection. "Local business leaders will be urged to lobby their customers, the clergy will be asked to speak up for the popular will and Team Bush will enlist as many Democrats as possible to scream as loud as they can," the article said.

"You think 'Democrats for Democracy' would be a catchy term for them?" asked one Bush adviser.[3]

The Bush strategy also would target the members of the Electoral College, the 538 electors who are picked by the campaigns and state party organizations to go to Washington for what is normally a ceremonial function, casting their ballots for the candidate who got the most votes in their state. Many of the electors are not legally bound to the specific candidate who carried their state, so theoretically some Gore electors could be peeled off to the Bush column if they came under enough pressure and persuasion.[4]

Another article describing Republican thinking on this contingency appeared in *The Boston Herald* two days later. It quoted Republican sources outlining plans to rally public sentiment against Gore's election if he won the Electoral College but lost the popular vote. "The Bush camp, sources said, would likely challenge the legitimacy of a Gore win, casting it as an affront to the people's will and branding the Electoral College as an antiquated relic," said the article by Andrew Miga.[5]

"One informal Bush adviser, who declined to be named, predicted Republicans would likely benefit from a storm of public outrage if Bush won the popular vote but was denied the presidency," the article said. The article quoted the Bush adviser as saying: "That's what America is all about, isn't it? I'm sure we would make a strong case."[6]

This contingency planning showed how determined the Bush campaign was to prevail in Election 2000, almost at whatever cost. After eight years of a Clinton-Gore administration, Republicans saw a danger in the Democrats demonstrating over another four or eight years that they could govern effectively and responsibly, that the Democrats could bring the country both peace and prosperity. Even worse, they were making progress in addressing longer-range problems like the federal debt, Social Security, national health insurance and environmental threats. Another Democratic presidency also might doom conservative dreams about securing control of the U.S. Supreme Court.

Though there had not been a case of a popular-vote loser winning the Electoral College for over a century, the Republicans weren't about to lie down and give up if Bush won the popular vote and Gore won the electoral vote. Electoral votes, apportioned to states in line with their seats in Congress plus three for the District of Columbia, were the ones that counted in the official selection of a President.

But, citing the democratic principle of majority rule, the Republicans were gearing up to risk a constitutional crisis if necessary to stop Al Gore from claiming the White House without a popular mandate. However, the November 7 election didn't exactly turn out that way.

◆◆◆

Election Night was a back-and-forth affair. It looked at first like Al Gore was doing well in the East, but George W. Bush came on strong across the South, Midwest and Rocky Mountain States. When many Americans on the East Coast went to bed, it looked as if Bush would prevail, but Gore rallied in the Pacific states and crept close to the 270 electoral votes needed for victory.

In the early-morning hours, Florida and its 25 electoral votes took center stage. Most political observers had expected the state, with Bush's brother Jeb as governor, to land in Bush's column, but Gore had mounted a surprisingly determined and effective campaign. His running mate, Connecticut Senator Joe Lieberman, the first person of the Jewish faith on a major national party ticket, had devoted large chunks of time to Florida and especially to the state's large communities of Jewish retirees.

To the shock of many pundits, the exit polling and available state returns suggested Gore's gamble may have paid off. On Election Night, the TV networks, including pro-Republican Fox News, put Florida's crucial 25 electoral votes in Gore's column. John Ellis, the head of the Fox election team and a cousin to George W. and Jeb Bush, later recalled that Jeb was soon on the phone complaining about the networks' judgment that Florida would go for Gore. Ellis said it was one of a half dozen or more calls he got on Election Night from his Bush cousins.[7]

Ellis said he was looking at a computer "screenful for Gore." But the two Bush brothers still voiced confidence that Florida would end up in George W.'s column before the election was finished.

By 2:16 a.m. on November 8, their confidence appeared vindicated when Ellis and his Fox team became the first of the networks to flip Florida from the Gore column to the Bush column. The other members of the Voter News Service, a consortium of major TV networks and *The Associated Press*, followed suit, except for the AP, which treated Florida as still a toss-up.[8]

"Anchors and show producers and analysts and commentators all hate reversals with a white-hot passion because it makes them look stupid instead of omniscient," Ellis later observed.[9]

But the reversals in the early hours of Wednesday would have weighty consequences for the future. Suddenly, the TV network anchors were hailing George W. Bush as the President-elect of the United States, a stamp of legitimacy that would influence the course of events over the next month.

Persuaded by the network projections of Bush's victory, an exhausted Al Gore called to congratulate Bush and headed off to a somber rally to concede defeat. Only last-minute protests from Democrats on the ground in Florida, who began questioning the news media's certainty, stopped Gore from going through with his public concession.

Ellis said that in the final call that night from his cousin George W. Bush, the presumptive President-elect said Gore had just taken back his private concession to Bush. "I hope you're taking all this down, Ellis," Bush told his cousin at Fox News. "This is good stuff for a book."[10]

By the morning of November 8, as Americans on the East Coast were awakening and turning on their televisions, many were stunned to find that the election remained unsettled. Bush was clinging to a narrow lead in Florida but Gore was winning decisively in the most populous state, California, and thus was building a significant lead in the national popular vote.

It looked as if Bush might eke out a win in Florida and claim the presidency via the Electoral College, while simultaneously losing the popular vote. Those Republican contingency plans for mounting a principled battle against letting a popular-vote loser into the White House were quickly shelved.

But it seemed possible, too, that Gore might chip away at Bush's narrow lead of a few thousand votes in Florida and emerge as both the popular-vote and electoral-vote winner. If Gore did so, it would vindicate the exit polls that had convinced the TV networks that Gore was headed to a close but clear victory in the Sunshine State.

In those first hours of the Florida election battle, it became obvious, too, that there had been major irregularities in the state's voting. Reform Party candidate Patrick Buchanan showed surprising strength in West Palm Beach precincts where Jewish retirees apparently were confused by a butterfly-shaped ballot and poked holes for Buchanan while meaning to vote for Gore.

There were also reports that a number of African-American voters, among the most loyal Democratic constituency, had been turned away from the polls or had been intimidated by police roadblocks. Thousands of other ballots were being spit out by vote-counting machines because old voting devices, especially in poorer precincts, had failed to punch holes completely through the ballots.

It appeared that the exit polls showing Gore as the choice of most Florida voters were correct – because voters thought they had voted for Gore and so informed the pollsters – but for a variety of reasons, their ballots were counted for someone else or were thrown out for not recording a clear choice for President.

A simple recalculation of the Florida ballots was not likely to correct these inaccuracies. Plus, nothing could be done about the mistaken votes for Buchanan. But a statewide manual recount, in which canvassers

would decide whether a ballot reflected the clear intent of the voters, still
could recover enough Gore votes to overcome Bush's tiny lead.

The recount battle, which would hold the nation transfixed for 36
days, would represent an effort by the Gore forces to compel a statewide
recount – or at least, recounts in some of Florida's largest cities – versus a
fierce determination by the Bush campaign to prevent anything
approaching a careful examination of the disputed ballots.

◆◆◆

Within the first hours and days of the Florida recount battle, the
Republicans demonstrated their dexterity in getting out their desired
message, both through their own media mouthpieces like Rush Limbaugh
and Fox News and through leading mainstream media outlets that still
nursed resentment toward Gore and Clinton.

The Republicans, who only days earlier were preparing to man the
barricades if Gore had won the electoral vote but lost the popular vote,
smoothly shifted to a new rationale to justify Bush's claim to the
presidency, even as a popular-vote loser. The new GOP theme was that
Republicans had politely stepped aside during other close elections to
maintain national unity and now the Democrats should return the favor.

On November 10, *The New York Times* highlighted on its op-ed page
the supposed example of Richard Nixon's gracious acceptance of defeat
in 1960, despite questions of voting irregularities by John F. Kennedy's
campaign in Illinois and Texas. "Whatever else he was, Nixon was a
patriot," wrote author Richard Reeves. "He understood what recounts and
lawsuits and depositions carried out over months – even years – would do
to the nation."

On November 11, *The Washington Post* gave prominent play to a
similar op-ed column by former Senator Bob Dole with the title, "Do the
Right Thing, Mr. Gore." The point of the article was that Gore was acting
in a selfish manner when he demanded that the Florida votes be
recounted. "It was a close election, but it's over," wrote Dole, the
Republican presidential nominee in 1996. "I urge Al Gore to put his
country's agenda ahead of his agenda; to put the people's interests before
his personal interests."

Dole then cited the examples of Nixon conceding defeat in 1960 and
Gerald Ford conceding in 1976. Dole, who was Ford's vice presidential
running-mate, described Ford as rebuffing calls from aides who felt "a
few changed votes in a couple of key states" would have elected him.

But neither the Ford example nor the Nixon case was parallel to
Election 2000. What was left out of those op-eds was that Jimmy Carter

defeated Ford by 1.7 million votes nationwide in 1976. Even if Ford could have reversed enough votes in a few states to claim the Electoral College, he would have won by defying the popular will. The same was true of Nixon in 1960, although the popular vote was much closer. John F. Kennedy won by about 119,450 ballots.[11]

Though the stories of Nixon's graceful exit have taken on the color of history from constant retelling, they also don't match the historical record. Contrary to the image of Republicans meekly accepting the 1960 results, the GOP sought recounts in 11 states and mounted aggressive legal challenges in some. The outgoing Eisenhower administration, in which Nixon was Vice President, even launched criminal investigations of voting irregularities, though without much result.

While the cherished myths of political statesmanship may seem innocent enough, they fed a growing resentment by Republicans who – with increasing bitterness – demanded that Gore step aside and accept Bush as the rightful winner. The thinking went that it was the Democrats' turn to do "what's right for the country."

◆◆◆

In the weeks after the November 7 election, a lot was written about the Florida recount battle, but very little of it explained to the American people how extraordinary the struggle was. In a representative democracy, nothing is perhaps more important than an accurate counting of the votes. It is not just the way in which the governed bestow their consent upon their elected representatives; it's how a free society settles its differences in a peaceful fashion.

But the Florida recount battle – which would decide who would sit in the most powerful office on earth – was treated by most of the U.S. news media as a spectacle, grist for talk-show mills, another chance to elevate personality over substance. While there was smirking commentary on the sexual implications of the various types of chads – "pregnant, hanging and dimpled" – there was little in the way of serious or timely examination of Florida's racially tinged election abuses, such as use of faulty computerized data to disqualify thousands of black voters who were improperly knocked off the rolls after being misidentified as felons.

From the first days of the recount struggle, the focus was not on how historically remarkable the story was. Instead, the news media seemed perpetually annoyed that the election hadn't been quickly settled. In part, that was because some of the tired political reporters had no choice but to postpone previously scheduled vacations.

◆◆◆

For decades, political scientists had fretted over the prospect of a popular-vote loser slipping into the White House through the creaky back door of the Electoral College. That anti-democratic result had not occurred in the United States since 1888 – 112 years earlier – when Grover Cleveland beat Benjamin Harrison in the popular vote but lost in the Electoral College. Yet, when this eventuality finally presented itself again in 2000, it prompted little commentary from either political scientists or advocates of democracy. Presumably that was because the outcome – a Bush victory – was what most of the political insiders wanted to see happen.

Still, the facts were these: Al Gore was the clear choice of the American people, albeit by a narrow margin of slightly over a half million votes out of 105 million cast.[12] Also, without any real doubt, he was the favorite of the voters of Florida, except that a variety of irregularities had conspired to cost him tens of thousands of votes and leave Bush with a lead of 930 votes after the initial tallies.

Helping Bush even more, the Florida electoral process was overseen by Bush partisans, including Secretary of State Katherine Harris, a co-chairman of Bush's Florida campaign and a close political ally of Bush's younger brother, Governor Jeb Bush. Under international standards for judging elections, voting is supposed to be overseen by non-partisan experts, but this serious flaw in America's electoral system had never been addressed. In Florida, the pro-Bush institutional bias would prove crucial as Harris ruled in Bush's favor on every key issue.

Some of Gore's lost votes could never be reclaimed no matter who was in charge of the vote counting. The most famous of those lost votes were the mis-punched "butterfly ballots" in Palm Beach County, which may have slashed about 13,000 votes from Gore's tally. Many elderly Palm Beach voters had trouble reading the complex ballot, which listed presidential choices in two side-by-side columns rather than in one vertical column as required by Florida law.

Many of these voters said they feared they accidentally cast their votes for Reform Party nominee Patrick Buchanan. After the election, Buchanan acknowledged that his surprising blip of 3,704 votes in the staunchly Democratic county, with a large Jewish population, almost certainly resulted from confusion. Buchanan, who has found himself in controversies over alleged anti-Semitic comments, said he believed those votes were meant for Gore.

But it appeared that Gore lost even more votes when voters tried to correct their error. After mistakenly punching a hole for Buchanan, these Palm Beach voters punched a second hole for Gore. In Palm Beach

County, there were 19,120 ballots disqualified because of double-voting. The Palm Beach County canvassing board analyzed a sample of these disqualified ballots. From that sample of 144 ballots, 80 ballots – or 56 percent – showed punches for both Buchanan and Gore. If that sample percentage were applied to the entire batch, Gore potentially lost 10,622 votes. If one counts 2,700 of the Buchanan votes as likely confused voters for Gore, that would put Gore's lost vote in Palm Beach County alone at more than 13,000.[13]

In other counties, allegations of outright misconduct had been raised. The NAACP complained that Florida authorities intimidated African-Americans who were trying to vote. Across the state, hundreds of likely Gore voters were told their names had been purged from the voting lists, though they were fully qualified to vote. This phenomenon apparently resulted from Jeb Bush's administration falsely identifying them as felons who are barred from voting under Florida law even after completing prison terms.

In Seminole County, election officials gave Republicans special access to absentee-ballot applications so corrections could be made and the votes counted for Bush. Democrats and individual voters with similar deficiencies in their applications were not given an opportunity to make corrections. Their votes were tossed out.[14] Bush outpolled Gore among Seminole County's absentee ballots by nearly 5,000 votes, far more than Bush's statewide lead.

Yet, while these irregularities boosted Bush's totals or held Gore's down, there was little or nothing that could be done to fix most of those problems. So, the question became whether the state at least should examine the ballots that had been rejected by counting machine to see if the clear intent of the voter could be discerned. Gore first sought an agreement with Bush for a statewide review of the uncounted ballots, a proposal that Bush rebuffed. Gore and his advisers then tried to make a case for a review of ballots in three of Florida's major metropolitan areas.

As the recount battle took shape, the two sides also adopted different tactics. Gore tamped down the anger of his supporters, called on them to trust in the rule of law and sought relief in the state courts. By contrast, Bush revved up his backers, played hardball politics at every turn and deployed smart lawyers to stop a recount.

Bush flew into a rage when the Florida Supreme Court ruled that Florida law permitted hand recounts, which would seem to have been a rather obvious point and well within the normal authority of a state court. But Bush accused the Democratic-majority court of overstepping its bounds. Bush said the ruling sought "to change Florida's election laws and usurp the authority of Florida's election officials." Bush added that "writing laws is the duty of the legislature; administering laws is the duty of the executive branch."

Bush left out the third component of the U.S. system of checks and balances, a fact taught to every American child in grade-school civics class – that it is the duty of the judiciary to interpret the laws. It's also the responsibility of the courts to resolve differences between parties under the law. Besides suggesting an ignorance of the U.S. political system, Bush's harsh language sent a strong message to Republican demonstrators who were already assembling to contest the examination of disputed ballots.

◆◆◆

While some of the pro-Bush demonstrators were local, including the notoriously aggressive right-wing Cuban exiles, scores of others were being recruited from Republican congressional offices in Washington and flown down to Florida. These two groups merged together on November 22, the day before Thanksgiving to present a shocking scene on U.S. television.

After learning that the Dade County canvassing board was starting an examination of 10,750 disputed ballots that had not been previously counted, a mob – egged on by Republican phone banks and heated rhetoric over Cuban-American radio – descended on the board's Miami offices. They shouted slogans and carried anti-Gore signs, such as one that read "Rotten to the Gore."

As the count was about to begin, Representative John Sweeney, a New York Republican, called on the protesters to "shut it down." Other Republicans used megaphones to shout inflammatory rhetoric to incite the already angry crowd. "A lawyer for the Republican Party helped stir ethnic passions by contending that the recount was biased against Hispanic voters," The New York Times reported.[15]

"Emotional and angry, they immediately make their way outside the larger room in which the tabulating room is contained," wrote Jake Tapper in his Election 2000 book, Down and Dirty. "The mass of 'angry voters' on the 19th floor swells to maybe 80 people."

News cameras captured the chaotic scene. The mob charged the offices of the supervisor of elections, shouting slogans and pounding on the doors and walls. Security officials feared the confrontation was spinning out of control.

The unruly protest prevented official observers and members of the press from reaching the room. Miami-Dade county spokesman Mayco Villafana was pushed and shoved. The canvassing board suddenly reversed its decision and canceled the recount. "Until the demonstration stops, nobody can do anything," said David Leahy, Miami's supervisor of elections, although the canvassing board members would later insist that they were not intimidated into stopping the recount.[16]

While the siege of the canvassing board office was underway, county Democratic chairman Joe Geller stopped at another office seeking a sample ballot. He wanted to demonstrate his theory that some voters had intended to vote for Gore but instead marked an adjoining number that represented no candidate. As Geller took the ballot marked "sample," one of the Republican activists began shouting, "This guy's got a ballot!"[17]

In *Down and Dirty*, Tapper wrote: "The masses swarm around him, yelling, getting in his face, pushing him, grabbing him. 'Arrest him!' they cry. 'Arrest him!' With the help of a diminutive DNC aide, Luis Rosero, and the political director of the Miami Gore campaign, Joe Fraga, Geller manages to wrench himself into the elevator. Rosero, who stays back to talk to the press, gets kicked, punched. A woman pushes him into a much larger guy, seemingly trying to instigate a fight. In the lobby of the building, a group of 50 or so Republicans are crushed around Geller, surrounding him. ...

"The cops escort Geller back to the 19th floor, so the elections officials can see what's going on, investigate the charges. Of course, it turns out that all Geller had was a sample ballot. The crowd is pulling at the cops, pulling at Geller. It's insanity! Some even get in the face of 73-year-old Representative Carrie Meek. Democratic operatives decide to pull out of the area altogether."[18]

When the canvassing board halted the recount, the Bush supporters cheered. Only later would examination of photos of the protest reveal that many of the well-dressed demonstrators actually were Republican staffers from Capitol Hill. Because of their preppie clothing, the noisy demonstration became known as the "Brooks Brothers Riot."

Bush and his top aides refused to criticize these disruptive tactics, which they called spontaneous expressions by "angry voters." But GOP operatives spotted among the demonstrators included Tom Pyle, an aide to House Majority Whip Tom DeLay of Texas, and Doug Heye, a spokesman for Representative Richard W. Pombo of California.[19]

The Wall Street Journal reported that the assault on the canvassing board was led by national Republican operatives "on all expense-paid trips, courtesy of the Bush campaign." After their success in Dade, the rioters moved on to Broward County, where the protests remained unruly but failed to stop that count. The *Journal* noted that "behind the rowdy rallies in South Florida this past weekend was a well-organized effort by

Republican operatives to entice supporters to South Florida," with DeLay's Capitol Hill office taking charge of the recruitment.[20]

About 200 Republican congressional staffers signed on and were put up at hotels, given $30 a day for food and invited to an exclusive Thanksgiving Day party in Fort Lauderdale. The *Journal* reported that there was no evidence of a similar Democratic strategy to fly in national party operatives. "This has allowed the Republicans to quickly gain the upper hand, protest-wise," the *Journal* said.[21]

The Bush campaign also worked to conceal its hand. "Staffers who joined the effort say there has been an air of mystery to the operation. 'To tell you the truth, nobody knows who is calling the shots,' says one aide. Many nights, often very late, a memo is slipped underneath the hotel-room doors outlining coming events," the *Journal* reported.[22]

The reinforcements from Capitol Hill added an angrier tone to the dueling street protests already underway between supporters of Bush and Gore. The new wave of Republican activists injected "venom and volatility into an already edgy situation," wrote reporter Jake Tapper in *Down and Dirty*.

"This is the new Republican Party, sir!" Brad Blakeman, Bush's campaign director of advance travel logistics, bellowed into a bullhorn to disrupt a CNN correspondent interviewing a Democratic congressman. "We're not going to take it anymore!"[23]

Around the country, the conservative media apparatus, led by talk show host Rush Limbaugh and other pro-Bush pundits, rallied the faithful with charges that a hand recount was fraudulent and amounted to "inventing" votes for Gore.

◆ ◆ ◆

At a Bush campaign-sponsored celebration on the night of Thanksgiving Day, one day after the Miami melee, George W. Bush offered personal words of gratitude. "The night's highlight was a conference call from Mr. Bush and running mate Dick Cheney, which included joking reference by both running mates to the incident in Miami, two [Republican] staffers in attendance say," according to the *Wall Street Journal*.

Another high point of the celebration at the Hyatt on Pier 66 in Fort Lauderdale was a performance by crooner Wayne Newton who sang "Danke Schoen," the German words for thank you very much.[24] On November 25, two days after the celebration, the Bush campaign issued "talking points" to justify the Miami protest, calling it "fitting, proper" and blaming the canvassing board for the disruptions.

Nineteen months later, the Bush campaign grudgingly spelled out how it had spent $13.8 million to frustrate the Florida recount. In a filing with the Internal Revenue Service, the Bush campaign reported it had put about 250 staffers on the payroll, spent about $1.2 million to fly operatives to Florida and elsewhere, and paid for hotel bills adding up to about $1 million. Bush's total of $13.8 million was about four times the $3.2 million spent by the Gore recount committee. Bush, who on the stump was a fierce critic of lawyers, spent more just on lawyers – $4.4 million – than Gore did on his entire effort.

To add flexibility to the travel arrangements, a fleet of corporate jets also was assembled, including planes owned by Enron Corp., then run by Bush backer Kenneth Lay, and Halliburton Co., where Dick Cheney had served as chairman and chief executive.

Only a handful of the Brooks Brothers rioters were publicly identified, some through photographs published in *The Washington Post*. Jake Tapper's book, *Down and Dirty*, listed 12 Republican operatives who took part in the Miami riot. Half of those individuals received payments from the Bush recount committee, according to the IRS records.

The publicly identified Miami protesters who were paid by Bush recount committee were: Matt Schlapp, a Bush staffer who was based in Austin and received $4,276.09; Thomas Pyle, a staff aide to House Majority Whip Tom DeLay, $456; Michael Murphy, a DeLay fund-raiser, $935.12; Garry Malphrus, House majority chief counsel to the House Judiciary subcommittee on criminal justice, $330; Charles Royal, a legislative aide to Representative Jim DeMint of South Carolina, $391.80; and Kevin Smith, a former GOP House staffer, $373.23.

At least three of the Miami protesters became members of Bush's White House staff, the *Miami Herald* reported in 2002. They included Schlapp, a special assistant to the President; Malphrus, deputy director of the President's Domestic Policy Council; and Joel Kaplan, another special assistant to the President.[25]

Bush's recount committee also paid $35,501.52 to the Hyatt Regency Pier 66 in Fort Lauderdale, where the Republican protesters celebrated on Thanksgiving Day. A number of miscellaneous expenses also appear to have gone for party items, such as lighting, sound systems and even costumes. Garrett Sound and Lighting in Fort Lauderdale was paid $5,902; Beach Sound Inc. in North Miami was paid $3,500; and the House of Masquerades, a costume shop in Miami, had three payments totaling $640.92, according to the Bush records.

Though the Bush records received little attention when they were released in July 2002, they represented hard evidence that the Bush campaign had financed an operation to bring rioters across state lines to rough up political adversaries and interfere with the counting of votes. Thirty-two years earlier, when anti-Vietnam War protests disrupted the Democratic National Convention in Chicago, federal prosecutors brought criminal charges against alleged ringleaders, known as the Chicago Seven, for "conspiring to cross state lines with the intent to incite a riot."

In the Chicago Seven case, the jury eventually acquitted all defendants of conspiracy charges, though finding five defendants – David Dellinger, Tom Hayden, Rennie Davis, Abbie Hoffman and Jerry Rubin – individually guilty of inciting a riot, charges that later were reversed on appeal. Ironically, the kind of documentary evidence that might have proved valuable in tying up the loose ends of the Chicago Seven conspiracy was present in the filings that the Bush recount committee made to the IRS.

Obviously, no case was ever brought against George W. Bush or other Republican leaders who helped finance and organize the Brooks Brothers Riot. But the disruption of the Dade County vote count on November 22, 2000, made clear how far Bush's supporters were prepared to go to put their man in the White House.

◆◆◆

By stopping the Dade County recount, the Republicans effectively guaranteed that Bush's 930-vote lead would survive any Gore gains in Broward and Palm Beach counties. That, in turn, meant that four days later, on November 26, Republican Secretary of State Katherine Harris would declare Bush the winner of Florida's 25 electoral votes and thus the presidency.

That prospect was welcomed by many Washington insiders, whose views were expressed by *Washington Post* columnist Richard Cohen on November 24. "Given the present bitterness, given the angry irresponsible charges being hurled by both camps, the nation will be in dire need of a conciliator, a likable guy who will make things better and not worse," Cohen wrote. "That man is not Al Gore. That man is George W. Bush."[26]

But the recount drama pressed on. By the evening of the November 26 deadline, the Broward County vote had whittled down Bush's lead. Gore was gaining slowly in Palm Beach's recount, too, despite constant challenges from Republican observers. To boost Bush's margin back up by 52 votes, Secretary of State Harris allowed Nassau County to throw out its recounted figures that had helped Gore. The county reverted back to the original Election Night count that had been more favorable to Bush.

As a 5 p.m. deadline approached, the Palm Beach canvassing board asked for a short extension to finish the contentious recount. Harris refused, rejecting even the partial recount figures that Palm Beach sent in the interim. With Palm Beach excluded and Dade County shut down, Harris certified Bush the winner by 537 votes, a victory margin of 0.009 percent of the 5.9 million ballots cast.

The certification ceremony was conducted with all the fanfare of an international treaty being signed. Bush partisans cheered their victory and began demanding that Bush be called the president-elect. Soon afterwards, Bush appeared on national television to pronounce himself the winner and to call on Gore to concede defeat.

"Now," Bush said, "we must live up to our principles. We must show our commitment to the common good, which is bigger than any person or any party. ... The end of an election is the beginning of a new day. Together we can make this a positive day of hope and opportunity for all of us who are blessed to be Americans."

But the Gore campaign still announced it would fight on in the courts to try to make sure that every legal vote was counted. Yet, Republicans were leaving little doubt that whatever the actual vote tally was, they would block Gore from ever getting Florida's 25 electoral votes, either by having the Republican-controlled state legislature intervene or by turning to the U.S. House of Representatives, which also had a GOP majority.

The voters' will on Election Day – both nationally and in Florida – may have been to elect Al Gore and Joe Lieberman. But Bush and the Republicans had demonstrated through their hardball political strategies – and their readiness to use mob tactics – that they had the will to win.

Indeed, it was remarkable, though little noted, that the Republicans had dropped any pretense of suggesting that Bush's election actually reflected the desires of the American voters. Nationally, Republicans termed Gore's popular-vote victory irrelevant. In Florida, they called the confusion and irregularities simply the way the system works, tough luck. To the Bush camp, winning became everything, while Gore was excoriated as a "sore loser man," a play on words of Gore-Lieberman.

Before the world, "President-Elect" George W. Bush had demonstrated his triumph of the will.

7

Judicial Coup

During the Iran-Contra investigation in the 1980s, special prosecutor Lawrence Walsh likened the Reagan-appointed federal judges in Washington to "the strategic reserve of an embattled army." When President Ronald Reagan's political troops were under the gun of legal accountability, the judges could be counted on to jump into the trenches and find some legal excuse to pull the endangered operatives to safety.

At a crucial moment of the Iran-Contra scandal, tough law-and-order appeals court judges Laurence H. Silberman and David Sentelle – both Reagan appointees – suddenly went soft on criminals and carved out a broad new legal right for defendants relating to grants of limited immunity. The defendant who benefited from this new liberal legal construction was named Oliver North. Silberman and Sentelle overturned North's conviction on three Iran-Contra felonies.

Similarly, George W. Bush turned to Republicans on the U.S. Supreme Court when it looked like the Florida Supreme Court might actually require disputed votes to be examined and counted. The Florida court was one place where Bush didn't have enough allies. In its various rulings on the recount issue, the court hewed to the principle that the right of voters to have their votes counted – when their intent could be clearly discerned – trumped technical legal provisions. The state court took that position both when it helped Gore and when it helped Bush.

Yet, even before the Florida Supreme Court considered a statewide recount of disputed ballots, Bush went to the U.S. Supreme Court to head off that possibility. He requested and got the U.S. Supreme Court to consider his appeal seeking to throw out hundreds of votes for Gore that had been discovered in a recount in Broward County. Oral arguments made clear that the U.S. Supreme Court's Republican majority sympathized with Bush's position that the Florida Supreme Court had erred in citing the state constitution and the broader principle that the right to vote was more important than legal technicalities.

But – rather than prevail in a narrow partisan decision – Chief Justice William Rehnquist opted for a compromise that won over all nine justices. The court chose to vacate the Florida Supreme Court's ruling with a request for clarification of the state court's justification for extending a certification deadline that had allowed recounts to continue. Effectively, the U.S. Supreme Court was signaling that the state court could not cite constitutional provisions regarding a citizen's right to vote and must confine its reasoning to narrow statutory interpretations.

In another court ruling adverse to Gore, Florida Circuit Judge N. Sanders Sauls denied Gore's lawsuit seeking to require completion of Dade County's aborted recount – that had ended on November 22 as paid Republican demonstrators were pounding on the walls. Sauls refused even to look at the ballots in question, a judgment that became the basis for Gore's appeal back to the Florida Supreme Court.

These legal setbacks for Gore were welcomed by both conservative and mainstream commentators. The new watchword among the pundits was "legitimacy" – meaning the acceptance of Bush's "victory," rather than what the voters of the United States and Florida wanted.

Speaking for many of his mainstream compatriots, *New York Times* columnist Thomas L. Friedman hailed the two pro-Bush judicial rulings. "Slowly but surely, in their own ways, the different courts seem to be building a foundation of legitimacy for Governor George W. Bush's narrow victory," Friedman wrote. "That is hugely important. Our democracy has taken a hit here, and both Democrats and Republicans must think about how they can start shoring it up."[1]

Searching for a silver lining in this cloudy predicament, Friedman expressed hope that Bush – after having taken office in defiance of the people's will – could become the "democracy President" who would push for democratic principles at home and abroad. It apparently didn't cross Friedman's mind that if George W. Bush wished to be the "democracy President," he might want to start by ensuring that all legal votes in Florida be counted, even if they might help elect Bush's opponent.

◆ ◆ ◆

Late on the afternoon of December 8, by a single vote, the Florida Supreme Court dealt a dramatic blow to Bush's desire to discard thousands of uncounted Florida ballots. Four justices – Peggy Quince, Barbara Pariente, Fred Lewis and Harry Lee Anstead – ruled that not only must the disrupted Miami-Dade recount be completed but ballots kicked out by counting machines across the state must be examined and added to the tally if the intent of the voter could be discerned.

The 4-3 decision sought to include hundreds of votes not counted because antiquated voting machines did not discern a choice for President. This fuller tally would address some of the injustice of disenfranchising many voters from poorer communities and held out the hope of bestowing greater legitimacy on whoever turned out to be the winner.

But the ruling of the Florida Supreme Court – where a majority of justices were Democratic appointees – infuriated Bush and his supporters. Bush's team of lawyers quickly devised a strategy that turned the concept of a court injunction inside out. They rushed into federal court seeking to stall the state-court-ordered recount until after December 12 when Bush's certified victory was scheduled to become official and thus render any recount meaningless.

In demanding the stay, Bush's lawyers argued that the vote counting was a threat to "the integrity of the electoral process" and could cause Bush "irreparable injury." But there would be nothing irreparable about conducting the recount and then, if the U.S. Supreme Court agreed with Bush, to throw out the newly discovered votes. On the other hand, there would be irreparable harm to Gore's campaign if an injunction blocked the counting of the votes and the December 12 deadline preserved Bush's margin which by then had shrunk to 154 votes.

When Bush's legal arguments were presented to the conservative-dominated U.S. Court of Appeals in Atlanta, the case was promptly rejected. But Bush's lawyers then hastened to a friendlier venue, the U.S. Supreme Court.

Meanwhile, in Florida, the state-court-ordered recount was underway. County by county, election canvassing boards were moving smoothly through the machine-rejected ballots, discovering hundreds that clearly had registered choices for presidential candidates. Gore gained some and Bush gained some. When there was a dispute, the ballots were set aside for later presentation to Leon County Circuit Judge Terry Lewis, who had been named by the Florida Supreme Court to oversee the process and was given wide leeway to make judgments about which ballots should be counted.

"The Circuit Court is directed to enter such orders as are necessary to add any legal votes to the total statewide certifications and to enter any orders necessary," the Florida Supreme Court ruling stated. "In tabulating the ballots and in making a determination of what is a 'legal' vote, the standard to be employed is that established by the Legislature in our election code which is that the vote shall be counted as a 'legal' vote if there is 'clear indication of the intent of the voter.'"

As the recount proceeded, the chairman of the Charlotte County canvassing board posed a question to Judge Lewis: what should be done with ballots in which a voter both punched the name of a presidential candidate and wrote the name in? These so-called "over-votes" – containing two entries for President although for the same candidate – had been kicked out of the counting machines, too, along with the "under-votes," those where the machine couldn't discern a vote for President.

The Florida Supreme Court ruling had only specified tallying the under-votes, but the ruling also had instructed Judge Lewis to count every vote where there was a "clear indication of the intent of the voter." The over-votes demonstrated even more clearly than the under-votes who the voter wanted. So Lewis sent a memo to the state canvassing boards, instructing them to collect these over-votes and send them along with under-votes still in dispute.

"If you would segregate 'over-votes' as you describe and indicate in your final report how many where you determined the clear intent of the voter," Judge Lewis wrote, "I will rule on the issue for all counties."

Lewis's memo – a copy of which was later obtained by *Newsweek* magazine – might not have seemed very significant at the time, but it would grow in importance because the over-votes were discovered to heavily favor Gore. If they were counted – as they almost surely would have been under Lewis's instructions – Gore would have carried Florida regardless of what standard was applied to the "chads," the tiny pieces of paper that were not completely dislodged from the punch-through ballots that were then kicked out by the counting machines.

After the Lewis memo surfaced almost a year later, the *Orlando Sentinel* of Florida was virtually alone in asking the judge what he would have done with the over-votes if the Florida recount had been permitted to go forward. Lewis said that while he had not fully made up his mind about counting the over-votes in December 2000, he added: "I'd be open to that."[2]

In effect, Lewis's instructions had signaled an obvious decision to count the over-votes because once the votes – that were legal under Florida law – had been identified and collected there would be no legal or logical reason to throw them out, especially since some counties had already included over-votes in their counts

◆ ◆ ◆

But only hours after Lewis issued his instructions, five Republicans on the U.S. Supreme Court did something unprecedented. The narrow court majority ordered a halt in the counting of ballots cast by citizens for the election of the President of the United States. It was a heart-stopping moment in the history of a democratic Republic. It carried the unmistakable odor of a new order imposing itself in defiance of the popular will. There were no tanks in the streets, but the court's ruling was as raw an imposition of political power as the United States had seen in modern times.

In the 5-4 decision, the highest court in the land told vote-counters across Florida to stop the recount out of fear that it would show that Gore got more votes in Florida than Bush did. Such an outcome would "cast a cloud" over the "legitimacy" of an eventual Bush presidency if the U.S. Supreme Court later decided to throw out the Gore gains as illegal, explained Justice Antonin Scalia in an opinion speaking for the majority, which included Chief Justice Rehnquist and Justices Anthony Kennedy, Sandra Day O'Connor and Clarence Thomas.

"Count first, and rule upon the legality afterwards, is not a recipe for producing election results that have the public acceptance democratic stability requires," wrote Scalia, an appointee of President Ronald Reagan.

In other words, it was better for the U.S. public not to know for sure that Gore got the most votes if – as expected – the Supreme Court later decided simply to award the presidency to Bush. For the American people to realize that Gore got more votes nationally – as well as in Florida – while Bush was moving into the White House might cause public dissatisfaction – or as Scalia put it, might not generate "the public acceptance [that] democratic stability requires."

In a sharply worded dissent, Justice John Paul Stevens took Scalia's reasoning to task. Stevens, a moderate who was appointed by Republican President Gerald Ford, said the injunction against the vote tally violated the traditions of "judicial restraint that have guided the Court throughout its history." Stevens complained that the high court's action overrode the judgment of a state supreme court, took sides on a constitutional question before that issue was argued to the justices, and misinterpreted the principles of "irreparable harm."

"Counting every legally cast vote cannot constitute irreparable harm," Stevens argued. "On the other hand, there is a danger that a stay may cause irreparable harm to the respondents [the Gore side] and, more importantly, the public at large" because the stay could prevent a full tally of the votes before the impending deadline of December 12 for selecting Florida's electors.

As for the "legitimacy" issue, Stevens answered Scalia's rhetoric directly. "Preventing the recount from being completed will inevitably cast a cloud on the legitimacy of the election," Stevens wrote.

Immediately after the U.S. Supreme Court's unprecedented injunction, we wrote at *Consortiumnews.com* that if the high court insisted "on stopping the vote count and handing the presidency to George W. Bush, the United States will have embarked upon a dangerous political journey whose end could affect the future of all mankind. For American political institutions to ignore the will of the voters – and to wrap partisanship in the judicial robes of the nation's highest court – will almost certainly be followed by greater erosion of political freedom in the United States and eventually elsewhere.

"Illegitimacy and repression are two of history's most common bedfellows. Perhaps most chilling, at least for the moment, is the now-unavoidable recognition that the U.S. Supreme Court, the country's final arbiter of justice, has transformed itself into the right wing's ultimate political weapon. A dark cloud is descending over the nation."[3]

◆ ◆ ◆

Three days later, the other shoe from the U.S. Supreme Court was expected to drop. The days leading up to the decision were marked by impassioned protests in front of the court, which sometimes degenerated into shouting matches between Bush supporters and those who supported a full counting of votes in Florida. The Bush partisans would begin a chant of "President Bush!" only to be shouted down by chants of "Fascists!"

Jesse Jackson led one of the rallies, and despite his fiery rhetoric, it was clear that many of his followers were growing increasingly impatient with the lack of real leadership challenging the electoral shenanigans in Florida. As Jackson spoke about the importance of counting every vote, one young African-American called out, "Tell them about the roadblocks, Jesse! Tell them about the roadblocks!"

Despite the protests, there should have been no real doubt how Scalia and the other four would rule – they clearly had decided that George W. Bush should be President – but it was less certain what legal reasoning they would employ.

As Stevens wryly noted, the court's right-wing justices had long derided "judicial activism" by federal judges and preached respect for states' rights. Now those same justices were moving to overturn not only the judgment of the Florida Supreme Court but of the U.S. Court of Appeals in Atlanta that had found no merit to Bush's position. This appeared to be a case of the U.S. Supreme Court's majority starting with a conclusion that went against its own principles and then drafting some legal language to create at least the appearance of jurisprudence.

Consortiumnews.com political reporter Mollie Dickenson reported that "one of the court's supposed 'swing votes,' Justice Sandra Day O'Connor, is firmly on board for George W. Bush's victory. According to a knowledgeable source, O'Connor was visibly upset – indeed furious – when the networks called Florida for Vice President Al Gore on Election Night. 'This is terrible,' she said, giving the impression that she desperately wanted Bush to win."[4]

But one optimist who thought that O'Connor would transcend partisanship and demand a ruling respectful of democratic principles was Al Gore. Dickenson reported that as late as 4 p.m. on December 12, Gore was making campaign thank-you calls, including one to Sarah Brady, the gun-control advocate whose husband James Brady had been wounded in the 1981 assassination attempt against President Ronald Reagan.

"We're going to win this thing, Sarah," Gore said. "I just have all the faith in the world that Sandra Day O'Connor is going to be with us on this one."[5]

As it turned out, Gore's confidence in O'Connor had been misplaced. She was more of a Republican partisan than he had understood. As the clock ticked toward a midnight deadline for Florida to complete any recount, O'Connor was working with Justice Anthony Kennedy to fashion a ruling that would sound principled but still would prevent a full recount and thus guarantee both George W. Bush's inauguration and Republican control over the appointment of future federal judges.[*]

Yet, behind the closed doors of the court chambers, O'Connor and the other four pro-Bush justices were having a harder time than expected coming up with even a marginally plausible legal case. Indeed, outside public view, the five justices tentatively decided on one set of arguments on December 11 but then reversed their thinking nearly 180 degrees heading into the evening of December 12.

USA Today disclosed the inside story in a later article that focused on the stress that the *Bush v. Gore* ruling had caused within the court. While sympathetic to the pro-Bush majority, the article by reporter Joan Biskupic explained the court's flip-flop in legal reasoning. The five justices had been planning to rule for Bush after oral arguments on

---

[*] Five years later, O'Connor seemed to regret the role she played in getting Bush elected and the impact that this may have had on judicial independence. After retiring from the court in early 2006, she lamented what she saw as an ongoing Republican assault on the judiciary, warning that interference with judicial independence could lead to dictatorship in America. "It takes a lot of degeneration before a country falls into dictatorship," she said, "but we should avoid these ends by avoiding these beginnings."

December 11. The court even sent out for Chinese food for the clerks, so the work could be completed that night, but events took a different turn.[6]

The December 11 legal rationale for stopping the recount was to have been that the Florida Supreme Court had made "new law" when it referenced the state constitution in an initial recount decision – rather than simply interpreting state statutes. Even though this pro-Bush argument was highly technical, the rationale at least conformed with conservative principles, supposedly hostile to "judicial activism."

But the Florida Supreme Court threw a wrench into the plan. On the evening of December 11, the state court submitted a revised ruling that deleted the passing reference to the state constitution. The revised state ruling based its reasoning entirely on state statutes that permitted recounts in close elections.[7]

The revision drew little attention from the national press, but it created a crisis within the U.S. Supreme Court's majority. Justices O'Connor and Kennedy no longer felt they could agree with the "new law" rationale for striking down the recount, though Rehnquist, Scalia and Thomas still were prepared to use that argument despite the altered reasoning from the state court.[8]

Searching for a new rationale, O'Connor and Kennedy veered off in a different direction. Through the day of December 12, the pair worked on an opinion arguing that the Florida Supreme Court had failed to set consistent standards for the recount and that the disparate county-by-county standards constituted a violation of the "equal protection" rules of the 14th Amendment.[9] But this argument was so thin and so tendentious that Kennedy reportedly had trouble committing it to writing – with good reason.

To anyone who had followed the Florida election, it was clear that varied standards already had been applied throughout the state. Wealthier precincts had benefited from optical voting machines that were simple to use and eliminated nearly all errors, while poorer precincts – where many African-Americans and retired Jews lived – were stuck with outmoded punch-card systems with far higher error rates. Some Republican counties also had conducted manual recounts on their own and those totals were part of the tallies giving Bush a tiny lead.

The suspended statewide recount, even if there were slight variations of standards regarding "intent of the voters," was designed to reduce these disparities and thus bring the results closer to equality. Applying the "equal protection" provision, as planned by O'Connor and Kennedy, turned the 14th Amendment on its head, guaranteeing less equality than would occur if the recount went forward. Plus, the losers in this perverse application of the 14th Amendment would include African-Americans whose legal rights the amendment had been created to protect.

Further, if one were to follow the O'Connor-Kennedy position to its logical conclusion, the only fair outcome would have been to throw out Florida's presidential election in total. After all, Florida's disparate standards were being judged unconstitutional, and without some form of recount to eliminate those disparities, the entire statewide results would violate the 14th Amendment. That, however, would have left Al Gore with a majority of the remaining electoral votes nationwide. Clearly, the five pro-Bush justices had no intention of letting their "logic" lead to that result.

Yet possibly even more startling than the stretched logic of O'Connor-Kennedy was the readiness of Rehnquist, Scalia and Thomas to sign on to the revamped opinion that was almost completely at odds with their own legal rationale for blocking the recount in the first place. On the night of December 11, that trio was ready to bar the recount because the Florida Supreme Court had created "new law." A day later, they agreed to bar the recount because the Florida Supreme Court had *not* created "new law," the establishment of precise statewide recount standards.

The pro-Bush justices had devised a Catch-22. If the Florida Supreme Court set clearer standards, they would be struck down as creating "new law." Yet, if the state court didn't set clearer standards, that would be struck down as violating the "equal protection" principle. Heads Bush wins; tails Gore loses.

Never before in American history had U.S. Supreme Court justices exploited their extraordinary powers as brazenly to advance such clearly partisan interests as did these five justices. There was also the troubling fact that Chief Justice Rehnquist had a track record when it came to diminishing the electoral influence of African-Americans. In the 1960s, Rehnquist had opposed desegregation in Phoenix and had worked on Republican "ballot security" in Arizona, a program criticized as intimidation of African-American and other minority voters.

◆ ◆ ◆

The *Bush v. Gore* decision was finally released at 10 p.m., December 12, just two hours before the deadline for completing the recount. After having delayed any remedy up to the deadline, the five pro-Bush justices then demanded that any revised plan and recount be finished in 120 minutes, a patently impossible task.

In a dissenting opinion, Justice Stevens said the majority's action in blocking the Florida recount "can only lend credence to the most cynical appraisal of the work of judges throughout the land." Justices Stephen Breyer and Ruth Bader Ginsburg, appointees of President Bill Clinton, said in another dissent, "Although we may never know with complete certainty the identity of the winner of this year's presidential election, the identity of the loser is perfectly clear. It is the nation's confidence in the judge as an impartial guardian of the rule of law."

Tacitly recognizing the nonsensical nature of its own ruling, the majority justices barred the *Bush v. Gore* decision from ever being cited as a precedent in any other case. It was a one-time deal to put Bush in the White House.

The next day, Al Gore – whose final national plurality by then had grown to about 540,000 votes, more than the winning margins for Kennedy in 1960 or Nixon in 1968 – conceded Election 2000 to George W. Bush.

After Gore's concession, Justice Thomas told a group of high school students that partisan considerations played a "zero" part in the court's decisions. Later, asked whether Thomas's assessment was accurate, Rehnquist answered, "Absolutely."

On January 6, 2001, in his ceremonial role as President of the Senate, Vice President Gore presided over a joint session of Congress that officially received and tabulated the final electoral vote count making Bush the 43rd President of the United States. Members of the Congressional Black Caucus, rose – again and again – to object to the travesty of the Florida vote count. However, when no senator joined the House objectors as required by the rules of the joint session, Gore gaveled the protests down.

Near the end, Representative Alcee L. Hastings of Florida turned to Gore and said, "We did all we could." Gore smiled and replied, "The chair thanks the gentleman."

◆◆◆

The next day in a speech to a Catholic service organization, Rehnquist seemed unfazed by the inconsistency of the logic behind *Bush v. Gore*. His overriding rationale for the ruling seemed to be that he viewed Bush's election as good for the country – whether most voters thought so or not – and that it was the Supreme Court's duty to intervene to extricate the nation from a political crisis.

Rehnquist's remarks were made in the context of the Hayes-Tilden race in 1876, when another popular vote loser, Rutherford B. Hayes, was awarded the presidency after justices participated in a special election commission.

"The political processes of the country had worked, admittedly in a rather unusual way, to avoid a serious crisis," Rehnquist said.

Scholars interpreted Rehnquist's remarks as shedding light on his thinking during the *Bush v. Gore* case. "He's making a rather clear statement of what he thought the primary job of our governmental process was," said Michael Les Benedict, a history professor at Ohio State University. "That was to make sure the conflict is resolved peacefully, with no violence."[10]

But where were the threats of violence in Election 2000? Although some demonstrations had taken place in Florida and Washington, DC, Gore had largely reined in his supporters, urging them to avoid confrontations and to trust in the "rule of law." The only serious violence had come from the Bush side, when protesters were flown from Washington to Miami to put pressure on local election boards.

If one were to take Rehnquist's "good-for-the-country" rationale seriously, it would mean that the U.S. Supreme Court was ready to award the presidency to the side most willing to use violence or other anti-democratic means to overturn the will of the voters.

8

The Legend

One explanation for the national press corps' tilt toward George W. Bush in Election 2000 was the media's consensus that the inexperienced Texas governor would bring back a cast of well-respected figures from George H.W. Bush's presidency. Perhaps the most admired of these so-called "adults" was Colin Powell, who was regarded as a war hero for his service in conflicts from Vietnam to Panama to the Persian Gulf. In 1989, Powell became the first African-American chairman of the Joint Chiefs of Staff. In 1995, he flirted with a run for the presidency while he was on the book-tour circuit touting his best-selling memoirs, *My American Journey*.

Powell was a political rock star, beloved by the Inside-the-Beltway crowd for his savvy, his intelligence and his reputation as a man of honor and decency. His fans included center-right Republicans who appreciated his loyalty to Ronald Reagan and George H.W. Bush. But Powell's attraction crossed the aisle to attract liberal Democrats who admired him as a black man who rose through the challenging ranks of the U.S. military and then maneuvered through the even more treacherous corridors of Washington power.

Powell had a huge following among average Americans, too. He always ranked at or near the top of those "most-admired." When he appeared one day to testify behind closed doors in the Iran-Contra scandal, special prosecutor Lawrence Walsh marveled at how his own office staff, especially the African-Americans, scrambled to get a glimpse of the handsome general arriving in his Army uniform.

Without doubt, Powell was a man with a legend, a charismatic figure who radiated seriousness of purpose and moved with an aura of confidence. By Election 2000, there was possibly no person in America who was more universally praised than Colin Powell. So, as the bitter Florida recount battle raged – and Bush stood accused of disenfranchising thousands of black voters – Powell was someone who could blunt the ugly suspicions that the Republicans had again played games with race to put themselves in position to win an election.

To bolster Bush at this time of need, Powell made a well-publicized trip to Bush's ranch in Crawford, Texas, bringing with him his *gravitas* as a national leader and his immense credibility with the African-American community. The import of the tableau of George W. Bush and Dick Cheney standing with Colin Powell was not lost on the national press corps, either. First, it showed that Bush could reach across the racial divide. Second, it reminded the journalists that if Bush prevailed, one of their favorites, Colin Powell, would be reinstalled in a position of power in Washington. Indeed, on December 16, just four days after the U.S. Supreme Court ruling, Bush appointed Powell to be Secretary of State, the first African-American who would hold that post.

But did Colin Powell really deserve his hero worship? How did he really navigate his American journey? Was he more a profile in courage or a case study in brilliant careerism? What did it say about Powell, a black man who supposedly never forgot who he was, that he wouldn't challenge Bush to make sure that the votes of African-Americans were counted in Florida? Why did he let himself be used as a prop at a time Bush's lawyers were exploiting the "equal protection" standard of the 14th Amendment? In short, what was the truth behind Colin Powell's legend?

Five years earlier, as Powell was promoting his memoirs and testing the presidential waters, Robert Parry and Norman Solomon examined this question and published a series of articles at *Consortiumnews.com*, tracing Powell's rise from obscurity to national acclaim. They found a very different character than the one Americans thought they knew. The story began with Powell's first tour in Vietnam.

◆ ◆ ◆

On January 17, 1963, in South Vietnam's monsoon season, U.S. Army Capt. Colin Powell jumped from a military helicopter into a densely forested combat zone of the A Shau Valley, not far from the Laotian border. Carrying an M-2 carbine, Capt. Powell was starting his first – and only – combat assignment. He was the new adviser to a 400-man unit of the Army of the Republic of Vietnam (ARVN). Across jungle terrain, these South Vietnamese government troops were arrayed against a combined force of North Vietnamese regulars and local anti-government guerrillas known as the Viet Cong.

The 25-year-old Powell was arriving at a pivotal moment in the Vietnam War. To forestall a communist victory, President John F. Kennedy had dispatched teams of Green Beret advisers to assist the ARVN, a force suffering from poor discipline, ineffective tactics and bad morale. Already, many U.S. advisers, most notably the legendary Col.

John Paul Vann, were voicing concerns about the ARVN's brutality toward civilians. Vann feared that the dominant counterinsurgency strategy of destroying rural villages and forcibly relocating inhabitants while hunting down enemy forces was driving the people into the arms of the Viet Cong.

But as Colin Powell arrived, he was untainted by these worries. He was a gung-ho young Army officer with visions of glory. He brimmed with trust in the wisdom of his superiors. Capt. Powell also felt deep sympathy for the ARVN troops under his command, but only a cold contempt for the enemy. Soon after his arrival, Powell and his ARVN unit left for a protracted patrol that fought leeches as well as Viet Cong ambushes. From the soggy jungle brush, the Viet Cong would strike suddenly against the advancing government soldiers. Often invisible to Powell and his men, the VC would inflict a few casualties and slip back into the jungles.

In *My American Journey*, Powell recounted his reaction when he spotted his first dead Viet Cong. "He lay on his back, gazing up at us with sightless eyes," Powell wrote. "I felt nothing, certainly not sympathy. I had seen too much death and suffering on our side to care anything about what happened on theirs."

While success against the armed enemy was rare, Powell's ARVN unit punished the civilian population systematically. As the soldiers marched through mountainous jungle, they destroyed the food and the homes of the region's Montagnards, who were suspected of sympathizing with the Viet Cong. Old women would cry hysterically as their ancestral homes and worldly possessions were consumed by fire.

"We burned down the thatched huts, starting the blaze with Ronson and Zippo lighters," Powell recalled. "Why were we torching houses and destroying crops? Ho Chi Minh had said the people were like the sea in which his guerrillas swam. ... We tried to solve the problem by making the whole sea uninhabitable. In the hard logic of war, what difference did it make if you shot your enemy or starved him to death?"

For nearly six months, Powell and his ARVN unit slogged through the jungles, searching for Viet Cong and destroying villages. Then, while on one patrol, Powell fell victim to a Viet Cong booby trap. He stepped on a punji stake, a dung-poisoned bamboo spear that had been buried in the ground. The stake pierced Powell's boot and quickly infected the young officer's right foot. The foot swelled, turned purple and forced his evacuation by helicopter to Hue for treatment.

Although Powell's recovery from the foot infection was swift, his combat days were over. He stayed in Hue, reassigned to the operations staff of ARVN division headquarters. As part of his work, he handled intelligence data and oversaw a local airfield. By late autumn 1963, Powell's first Vietnam tour ended.

On his return to the United States, Powell did not join Vann and other early American advisers in warning the nation about the self-defeating counterinsurgency strategies. In 1963, Vann carried his prescient concerns back to a Pentagon that was not ready to listen to doubters. When his objections fell on deaf ears, Vann resigned his commission and sacrificed a promising military career.

In contrast, Powell recognized that his early service in Vietnam put him on a fast track for military success. He signed up for a nine-month Infantry Officer Advanced Course that trained company commanders. In May 1965, Powell finished third in a class of 200 and was the top-ranked infantryman. A year later, he became an instructor.

In 1966, as the numbers of U.S. servicemen in Vietnam swelled, Powell received a promotion to major, making him a field-grade officer before his 30th birthday. In 1968, Powell continued to impress his superiors by graduating second in his class at Fort Leavenworth's Command and General Staff College, a prestigious school regarded as an essential way station for future Army generals.

Recognizing Powell as an emerging "water-walker" who needed more seasoning in the field, the Army dispatched Powell to a command position back in Vietnam. But on his second tour, Powell would not be slogging through remote jungles. On July 27, 1968, he arrived at an outpost at Duc Pho to serve as an executive officer.

Then, to the north, at the American Division headquarters in Chu Lai, the commander, Maj. Gen. Charles Gettys, saw a favorable mention of Powell in the *Army Times*. Gettys plucked Powell from Duc Pho and installed him on the general's own staff at Chu Lai. Gettys jumped the young major ahead of more senior officers and made him the G-3 officer in charge of operations and planning. The appointment made "me the only major filling that role in Vietnam," Powell wrote in his memoirs.

But history again was awaiting Colin Powell. The American Division was already deep into some of the cruelest fighting of the Vietnam War. The "drain-the-sea" strategy that Powell had witnessed near the Laotian border continued to lead American forces into harsh treatment of Vietnamese civilians. Though it was still a secret when Powell arrived at Chu Lai, American troops had committed an act that would stain forever the reputation of the U.S. Army. As Major Powell settled into his new assignment, a scandal was waiting to unfold.

◆ ◆ ◆

On March 16, 1968, a bloodied unit of the Americal division stormed into a hamlet known as My Lai 4. With military helicopters circling overhead, revenge-seeking American soldiers rousted Vietnamese civilians – mostly old men, women and children – from their thatched huts and herded them into the village's irrigation ditches. As the round-up continued, some Americans raped the girls. Then, under orders from junior officers on the ground, soldiers began emptying their M-16s into the terrified peasants. Some parents used their bodies futilely to shield their children from the bullets. Soldiers stepped among the corpses to finish off the wounded.

The slaughter raged for four hours. A total of 347 Vietnamese, including babies, died in the carnage. But there also were American heroes that day in My Lai. Some soldiers refused to obey the direct orders to kill and some risked their lives to save civilians from the murderous fire. A pilot named Hugh Clowers Thompson Jr. from Stone Mountain, Georgia, was furious at the killings he saw happening on the ground. He landed his helicopter between one group of fleeing civilians and American soldiers in pursuit.

Thompson ordered his helicopter door gunner to shoot the Americans if they tried to harm the Vietnamese. After a tense confrontation, the soldiers backed off. Later, two of Thompson's men climbed into one ditch filled with corpses and pulled out a three-year-old boy whom they flew to safety.

Several months later, the Americal's brutality would become a moral test for Major Powell, too. A letter had been written by a young specialist fourth class named Tom Glen, who had served in an Americal mortar platoon and was nearing the end of his Army tour. In the letter to Gen. Creighton Abrams, the commander of all U.S. forces in Vietnam, Glen accused the Americal Division of routine brutality against civilians. Glen's letter was forwarded to the Americal headquarters at Chu Lai where it landed on Major Powell's desk.

"The average GI's attitude toward and treatment of the Vietnamese people all too often is a complete denial of all our country is attempting to accomplish in the realm of human relations," Glen wrote. He added that many Vietnamese were fleeing from Americans who "for mere pleasure, fire indiscriminately into Vietnamese homes and without provocation or justification shoot at the people themselves. ...

"What has been outlined here I have seen not only in my own unit, but also in others we have worked with, and I fear it is universal. If this is indeed the case, it is a problem which cannot be overlooked, but can through a more firm implementation of the codes of MACV (Military Assistance Command Vietnam) and the Geneva Conventions, perhaps be eradicated."

When interviewed in 1995, Glen said he had heard second-hand about the My Lai massacre, though he did not mention it specifically. The massacre was just one part of the abusive pattern that had become routine in the division, he said.

The letter's troubling allegations were not well received at American headquarters. Major Powell undertook the assignment to review Glen's letter, but did so without questioning Glen or assigning anyone else to talk with him. Powell simply accepted a claim from Glen's superior officer that Glen was not close enough to the front lines to know what he was writing about, an assertion Glen denied.

After that cursory investigation, Powell drafted a response on December 13, 1968. He admitted to no pattern of wrongdoing. Powell claimed that U.S. soldiers in Vietnam were taught to treat Vietnamese courteously and respectfully. The American troops also had gone through an hour-long course on how to treat prisoners of war under the Geneva Conventions, Powell noted.

"There may be isolated cases of mistreatment of civilians and POWs," Powell wrote. But "this by no means reflects the general attitude throughout the Division. ... In direct refutation of this [Glen's] portrayal ... is the fact that relations between American soldiers and the Vietnamese people are excellent."

It would take another American veteran, an infantryman named Ron Ridenhour, to piece together the truth about the atrocity at My Lai. After returning to the United States, Ridenhour interviewed American comrades who had participated in the massacre. On his own, Ridenhour compiled this shocking information into a report and forwarded it to the Army inspector general. The IG's office conducted an aggressive official investigation, in contrast to Powell's review.

Courts martial were held against officers and enlisted men who were implicated in the murder of the My Lai civilians. But Powell's peripheral role in the My Lai cover-up did not slow his climb up the Army's ladder. Luckily for Powell, Glen's letter also disappeared into the National Archives – to be unearthed only years later by British journalists Michael Bilton and Kevin Sims for their book, *Four Hours in My Lai*.

In his memoirs, Powell did not mention his brush-off of Tom Glen's complaint. Powell did include, however, another troubling recollection that belied his 1968 official denial of Glen's allegation that American soldiers "without provocation or justification shoot at the people themselves." After a brief mention of the My Lai massacre, Powell penned a partial justification of the American's brutality. Powell explained the routine practice of murdering unarmed male Vietnamese.

"I recall a phrase we used in the field, MAM, for military-age male," Powell wrote. "If a helo spotted a peasant in black pajamas who looked remotely suspicious, a possible MAM, the pilot would circle and fire in front of him. If he moved, his movement was judged evidence of hostile intent, and the next burst was not in front, but at him. Brutal? Maybe so. But an able battalion commander with whom I had served at Gelnhausen [West Germany], Lt. Col. Walter Pritchard, was killed by enemy sniper fire while observing MAMs from a helicopter. And Pritchard was only one of many. The kill-or-be-killed nature of combat tends to dull fine perceptions of right and wrong."

While it's certainly true that combat is brutal and judgments can be clouded by fear, the mowing down of unarmed civilians in cold blood does not constitute combat. It is murder and, indeed, a war crime. Neither can the combat death of a fellow soldier be cited as an excuse to murder civilians. That was precisely the rationalization that the My Lai killers cited in their own defense.

After returning home from Vietnam in 1969, Powell was drawn into another Vietnam controversy involving the killing of civilians. In a court martial proceeding, Powell sided with an American Division general who was accused by the Army of murdering unarmed civilians while flying over Quang Ngai province. Helicopter pilots who flew Brig. Gen. John W. Donaldson had alleged that the general gunned down civilian Vietnamese almost for sport.

In an interview in 1995, a senior investigator from the Donaldson case told Robert Parry that two of the Vietnamese victims were an old man and an old woman who were shot to death while bathing. Though long retired – and quite elderly himself – the Army investigator still spoke with a raw disgust about the events of a quarter century earlier. He requested anonymity before talking about the behavior of senior Americal officers.

"They used to bet in the morning how many people they could kill – old people, civilians, it didn't matter," the investigator said. "Some of the stuff would curl your hair."

For eight months in Chu Lai during 1968-69, Powell had worked with Donaldson and apparently developed a great respect for this superior officer. When the Army charged Donaldson with murder on June 2, 1971, Powell rose in the general's defense.

Powell submitted an affidavit dated August 10, 1971, which lauded Donaldson as "an aggressive and courageous brigade commander." Powell did not specifically refer to the murder allegations, but added that helicopter forays in Vietnam had been an "effective means of separating hostiles from the general population."

The old Army investigator claimed that "we had him [Donaldson] dead to rights," with the testimony of two helicopter pilots who had flown Donaldson on his shooting expeditions. Still, the investigation collapsed after the two pilot-witnesses were transferred to another Army base and apparently came under pressure from military superiors. The two pilots withdrew their testimony, and the Army dropped all charges against Donaldson.

While thousands of other Vietnam veterans joined the anti-war movement upon returning home and denounced the brutality of the war, Powell held his tongue. To this day, Powell has avoided criticizing the Vietnam War other than to complain that the politicians should not have restrained the military high command.

◆ ◆ ◆

The middle years of Colin Powell's military career – bordered roughly by the twin scandals of My Lai and Iran-Contra – were a time for networking and advancement. The Army footed the bill for Powell's masters degree in business at George Washington University. He won a promotion to lieutenant colonel and a prized White House fellowship that put him inside Richard Nixon's White House.

Powell's work with Nixon's Office of Management and Budget brought Powell to the attention of senior Nixon aides, Frank Carlucci and Caspar Weinberger, who soon became Powell's mentors. The high-powered contacts would prove invaluable to Powell as the personable young officer rose swiftly through the ranks.

When Ronald Reagan swept to victory in 1980, Powell's allies – Weinberger and Carlucci – took over the Defense Department as secretary of defense and deputy secretary of defense, respectively. When they arrived at the Pentagon, Powell, then a full colonel, was there to greet them. But before Powell could move to the top echelons of the U.S. military, he needed to earn his first general's star. That required a few command assignments in the field. So, under Carlucci's sponsorship, Powell received brief assignments at Army bases in Kansas and Colorado.

By the time Powell returned to the Pentagon in 1983, at the age of 46, he had a general's star on his shoulder. But Powell had returned to an administration caught up in an anti-communist crusade that courted danger by sending money and shipping arms to brush-fire wars against alleged Soviet surrogates. Reagan's operatives also were battling Democrats in Congress whom the White House sometimes viewed as little more than Moscow's fellow-travelers.

At the Central Intelligence Agency, the aging director William J. Casey was pressuring the Soviet Union on all fronts, through wars that often pitted desperately poor peasants and rival tribes against one another. Whether in Angola or Mozambique, in Nicaragua or Guatemala, in Lebanon or Afghanistan, Casey was spoiling for fights: to finish off the Cold War in his lifetime.

Though often disengaged on other matters, Ronald Reagan snapped to attention when Central American battlefield maps were put before him, with pins representing Nicaraguan contras outmaneuvering other pins for forces loyal to Nicaragua's leftist Sandinista government. Reagan, the onetime war-movie actor, and Casey, the onetime World War II spymaster, loved the game of international conflict and intrigue.

But many of their fiercest battles were fought in Washington. Liberal Democrats, led by old political war-horse, House Speaker Thomas P. "Tip" O'Neill, thought that Reagan and Casey were overzealous and maybe a bit crazy. Democrats, as well as some Republicans, suspected, too, that Casey, the mumbling dissembler, was treating Congress like a fifth column, agents of influence slipped behind his lines to disrupt his operations.

Still, the hub of any American military activity – whether overt or covert – remained the Pentagon. It was from the Defense Department that the special operations units were dispatched, that the military supplies were apportioned, that the most sensitive electronic intelligence was collected. All these military responsibilities were vital to Casey and Reagan, but came under the jurisdiction of Defense Secretary Weinberger.

To Casey's and Reagan's dismay, the Pentagon brass favored greater caution when it came to offending Congress. After all, Congress held the strings to the Pentagon's bulging purse. Maybe Casey could blow off a senator or offend a congressman, but the Pentagon could not detonate too many bridges to its rear.

Onto that political battlefield stepped Brig. Gen. Colin Powell, who was named military assistant to Weinberger. It was a position that made Powell the gatekeeper for the Defense Secretary, one of Reagan's closest advisers. Top Pentagon players quickly learned that Powell was more than Weinberger's coat holder or calendar handler. Powell was the "filter," the guy who saw everything when it passed into the secretary for action and who oversaw everything that needed follow-up when it came out.

Powell's access to Weinberger's most sensitive information would be a mixed blessing, however. Some of the aggressive covert operations ordered by Reagan and managed by Casey were spinning out of control.

Like a mysterious gravitational force, the operations were pulling in the Pentagon, whatever the reservations of the senior generals.

This expanding super nova of covert operations began to swallow the Pentagon a few months after Powell's return. On September 1, 1983, an Army civilian, William T. Golden, stumbled onto billing irregularities at a U.S. intelligence front company in suburban Annandale, Virginia, which was handling secret supplies for Central America.

The supply operation fell under the code name "Yellow Fruit," an ironic reference to the region's banana republics. The billing irregularities seemed modest at first, the doctoring of records to conceal vacation flights to Europe. But Golden began to suspect that the corruption went deeper. By October 1983, Yellow Fruit had turned thoroughly rotten, and the Army began a criminal inquiry.

"The more we dig into that," Gen. Maxwell R. Thurman, vice chief of the U.S. Army, later told congressional Iran-Contra investigators, "the more we find out that it goes into agencies using money, procuring all sorts of materiel." Reacting to the scandal, Thurman implemented new secret accounting procedures for supporting CIA activities. "We have tried to do our best to tighten up our procedures," Thurman said. [1]

But the muck of the Central American operations was oozing out elsewhere, too, as Casey recruited unsavory characters from the region to carry out his bidding. One was Panama's Gen. Manuel Noriega, whom Casey found useful funneling money and supplies to the Nicaraguan contras. In *My American Journey*, Powell recalled when meeting Noriega, "the crawling sense that I was in the presence of evil."

Powell's retrospective disdain for Noriega, however, didn't square with the enthusiasm some of Powell's Pentagon friends expressed for the Panamanian at the time. Powell's pal, Richard Armitage, the assistant defense secretary for inter-American affairs, hosted a Washington lunch in November 1983, honoring Noriega. "Pentagon officials greeted Noriega's rise to power with great satisfaction," noted author John Dinges. [2]

Noriega's visit coincided with another growing political problem for the Reagan administration: the refusal of an angry Congress to continue funding the contra war in Nicaragua. The rebel force was gaining a reputation for brutality, as stories of rapes, summary executions and massacres flowed back to Washington. Led by Speaker O'Neill, the Democratic-controlled House capped the CIA's contra funding at $24 million in 1983 and then moved to ban contra aid altogether.

Meanwhile, in the Middle East, Reagan's policies were encountering more trouble. Reagan had deployed Marines as peacekeepers in Beirut, but he also authorized the USS New Jersey to shell Shiite Muslim villages. On October 23, 1983, Islamic militants struck back, sending a suicide truck bomber through U.S. security positions and demolishing a high-rise Marine barracks. A total of 241 U.S. servicemen died.

"When the shells started falling on the Shiites, they assumed the American 'referee' had taken sides," Powell wrote in his memoir.

After the bombing, U.S. Marines were withdrawn to the USS Guam off Lebanon's coast. But Casey ordered secret counterterrorism operations against Islamic radicals. As retaliation, the Shiites targeted more Americans. Another bomb destroyed the U.S. Embassy and killed most of the CIA station.

Casey dispatched veteran CIA officer William Buckley to fill the void. But on March 14, 1984, Buckley was spirited off the streets of Beirut to face torture and eventually death. The grisly scenes – in the Middle East and in Central America – had set the stage for the Iran-Contra scandal.

◆◆◆

Defense Secretary Weinberger was one of the first officials outside the White House to learn that Reagan had put the arm on Saudi Arabia to give the contras $1 million a month in 1984, as Congress was cutting off the CIA's covert assistance through what was known as the Boland Amendment. Handling the contra-funding arrangements was Saudi ambassador Prince Bandar, a close friend of both Weinberger and Powell. Bandar and Powell had met in the 1970s and were frequent tennis partners in the 1980s.

So it was plausible – perhaps even likely – that Bandar would have discussed the contra funding with Powell, Weinberger or both. But exactly when Weinberger learned of the Saudi contributions and what Powell knew remain unclear to this day. The Iran-Contra trial of Weinberger for alleged obstruction of justice – scheduled for early 1993 and expected to include Powell's testimony – was derailed by President George H.W. Bush on Christmas Eve 1992 when he pardoned Weinberger and five other Iran-Contra defendants.

What is known from the public record, however, is that on June 20, 1984, Weinberger attended a State Department meeting about the contra operation. His scribbled notes cited the need to "plan for other sources for $." But secrecy would be vital, the Defense Secretary understood. "Keep US fingerprints off," he wrote.

In 1985, the White House also maneuvered into dangerous geopolitical straits in its policy toward Iran. The Israelis were interested in trading U.S. weapons to Iran's radical Islamic government to expand

Israel's influence in that important Middle Eastern country. It was also believed that Iran might help free American hostages held by Islamic extremists in Lebanon.

Carrying the water for this strategy within the Reagan administration was National Security Adviser Robert McFarlane. He circulated a draft presidential order in June 1985, proposing an overture to supposed Iranian moderates. The paper passed through Weinberger's "filter," Colin Powell. In his memoir, Powell called the proposal "a stunner" and a grab by McFarlane for "Kissingerian immortality." After reading the draft, Weinberger scribbled in the margins, "this is almost too absurd to comment on."

On June 30, 1985, as the paper was circulating inside the administration, Reagan declared that the United States would give no quarter to terrorism. "Let me further make it plain to the assassins in Beirut and their accomplices, wherever they may be, that America will never make concessions to terrorists," the President said.

But in July 1985, Weinberger, Powell and McFarlane met to discuss details for doing just that. Iran wanted 100 anti-tank TOW missiles that would be delivered through Israel, according to Weinberger's notes. Reagan gave his approval, but the White House wanted to keep the operation a closely held secret. The shipments were to be handled with "maximum compartmentalization," the notes said.

On August 20, 1985, the Israelis delivered the first 96 missiles to Iran. It was a pivotal moment for the Reagan administration. With that missile shipment, the Reagan administration stepped over an important legal line. The transfer violated laws requiring congressional notification for shipment of U.S. weapons and prohibiting arms to Iran or any other nation designated a terrorist state. Violation of either statute could be a felony.

The available evidence from that period suggested that Weinberger and Powell were very much in the loop, even though they may have opposed the arms-to-Iran policy. On August 22, two days after the first delivery, Israel notified McFarlane of the completed shipment. From aboard Air Force One, McFarlane called Weinberger. When Air Force One landed at Andrews Air Force Base outside Washington, McFarlane rushed to the Pentagon to meet Weinberger and Powell. The 40-minute meeting started at 7:30 p.m.

That much is known from the Iran-Contra public record. But the substance of the conversation remains in dispute. McFarlane said he discussed Reagan's approval of the missile transfer with Weinberger and Powell, and the need to replenish Israeli stockpiles. That would have put Weinberger and Powell in the middle of a criminal conspiracy. But

Weinberger denied McFarlane's account, and Powell insisted that he had only a fuzzy memory of the meeting without a clear recollection of any completed arms shipment.

"My recollection is that Mr. McFarlane described to the Secretary the so-called Iran Initiative and he gave to the Secretary a sort of a history of how we got where we were that particular day and some of the thinking that gave rise to the possibility of going forward ... and what the purposes of such an initiative would be," Powell said in an Iran-Contra deposition two years later.[3]

Congressional attorney Joseph Saba asked Powell if McFarlane had mentioned that Israel already had supplied weapons to Iran. "I don't recall specifically," Powell answered. "I just don't recall."[4]

In a later interview with the FBI, Powell said he learned at that meeting with McFarlane that there "was to be a transfer of some limited amount of materiel" to Iran. But he did not budge on his claim of ignorance about the crucial fact that the first shipment had already gone and that the Reagan administration had promised the Israelis replenishment for the shipped missiles.

This claim of only prospective knowledge of future arms shipments, not past knowledge of completed transfers, would be key to Powell's Iran-Contra defense. But it made little sense for McFarlane to learn of Israel's August 1985 missile delivery to Iran and the need for replenishment of the Israeli stockpiles, then hurry to the Pentagon, only to debate a future policy that, in reality, was already being implemented.

The behavior of Powell and Weinberger in the following days also suggested that they knew an arms-for-hostage swap was under way.

According to Weinberger's diary, he and Powell eagerly awaited a release of an American hostage in Lebanon, the payoff for the clandestine weapons shipment to Iran. In early September 1985, Weinberger dispatched a Pentagon emissary to meet with Iranians in Europe, another step that would seem to make little sense if Weinberger and Powell were indeed in the dark about the details of the arms-for-hostage operation. At the same time, McFarlane told Israel that the United States was prepared to replace 500 Israeli missiles, an assurance that would have required Weinberger's clearance since the missiles would be coming from Defense Department stockpiles.

On September 14, 1985, Israel delivered the second shipment, 408 more missiles to Iran. The next day, one hostage, the Rev. Benjamin Weir, was released in Beirut. Back at the Pentagon, Weinberger penned in his diary a cryptic reference to "a delivery I have for our prisoners."

But when the Iran-Contra scandal broke more than a year later, Weinberger and Powell would plead faulty memories about the Weir case, too. Saba asked Powell if he knew of a linkage between an arms delivery and Weir's release. "No, I have no recollection of that," Powell answered.

After Weir's freedom, the job of replenishing the Israel missiles fell to White House aide Oliver North, who turned to Powell for logistical assistance. "My original point of contact was General Colin Powell, who was going directly to his immediate superior, Secretary Weinberger," North testified in 1987.

But in their later sworn testimony, Powell and Weinberger continued to insist that they had no idea that 508 missiles had already been shipped via Israel to Iran and that Israel was expecting replenishment of its stockpiles.

Powell stuck to that story even as evidence emerged that he and Weinberger read top-secret intelligence intercepts in September and October 1985 in which Iranians described the U.S. arms delivery. One of those reports, dated October 2, 1985, and marked with the high-level classification, "SECRET SPOKE ORCON," was signed by Lt. Gen. William Odom, the director of the National Security Agency. According to Odom's report, a sensitive electronic intercept had picked up a phone conversation a day earlier between two Iranian officials, identified as "Mr. Asghari" who was in Europe and "Mohsen Kangarlu" who was in Teheran.

"A large part of the conversation had to do with details on the delivery of several more shipments of weapons into Iran," wrote Odom. "Asghari then pressed Kangarlu to provide a list of what he wanted the 'other four planes' to bring. ... Kangarlu said that he already had provided a list. Asghari said that those items were for the first two planes. Asghari reminded Kangarlu that there were Phoenix missiles on the second plane which were not on the first. ... [Asghari] said that a flight would be made this week."

In 1987, when congressional Iran-Contra investigators asked about the intercepts and other evidence of Pentagon knowledge, Powell again pleaded a weak memory. He repeatedly used phrases such as "I cannot specifically recall." At one point, Powell said, "To my recollection, I don't have a recollection."[5]

◆◆◆

In the next phase of the evolving Iran operation – the direct delivery of U.S. missiles to the Islamic fundamentalist government – Powell would play an even bigger role. Indeed, without the prodigious work of Colin

Powell, the unfolding disaster might never have happened, or might have stopped much sooner.

In early 1986, Powell exploited his bureaucratic skills to begin short-circuiting the Pentagon's covert procurement system that had been put in place after the Yellow Fruit scandal. Defense procurement officials said that without Powell's manipulation of the process, the Pentagon's internal auditing systems would have alerted the military brass that thousands of TOW anti-tank missiles and other sophisticated weaponry were headed to Iran, designated a terrorist state. But Powell managed to slip the missiles and the other hardware out of U.S. Army inventories without key Pentagon officials knowing where the equipment was going.

The story of Powell's maneuvers can be found in a close reading of thousands of pages from Iran-Contra depositions of Pentagon officials, who pointed to Weinberger's assistant as the key Iran-Contra action officer within the Defense Department. For his part, Powell insisted that he and Weinberger minimized the Pentagon's role. Powell said they delivered the missiles to the CIA under the Economy Act, which regulates transfers between government agencies.

"We treated the TOW transfer like garbage to be gotten out of the house quickly," Powell wrote in *My American Journey*.

But the Economy Act argument was disingenuous, because the Pentagon always uses the Economy Act when it moves weapons to the CIA. Powell's account also obscured his unusual actions in arranging the shipments without giving senior officers the information that Pentagon procedures required, even for sensitive covert activities.

Weinberger officially handed Powell the job of shipping the missiles to Iran on January 17, 1986. That was the day Reagan signed an intelligence finding, a formal authorization that is required by law for the conduct of covert operations, in this case, the transfer of arms from U.S. stockpiles and their shipment to Iran. In testimony, Powell dated his first knowledge of the missile transfers to this moment.[6]

A day after Reagan's finding, Powell instructed Gen. Max Thurman, then acting Army chief of staff, to prepare for a transfer of 4,000 TOW anti-tank missiles, but Powell made no mention that they were headed to Iran. "I gave him absolutely no indication of the destination of the missiles," Powell testified.

Though kept in the dark, Thurman began the process of transferring the TOWs to the CIA, the first step of the journey. Powell's orders "bypassed the formal [covert procedures] on the ingress line," Thurman acknowledged in later Iran-Contra testimony. "The first shipment is made without a complete wring-out through all of the procedural steps."[7]

As Powell's strange orders rippled through the top echelon of the Pentagon, Lt. Gen. Vincent M. Russo, the assistant deputy chief of staff for logistics, called Powell to ask about the operation. Powell immediately circumvented Russo's inquiry. In effect, Powell pulled rank by arranging for "executive instructions" commanding Russo to deliver the first 1,000 TOWs, no questions asked.

"It was a little unusual," commented then Army chief of staff, Gen. John A. Wickham Jr. "All personal visit or secure phone call, nothing in writing – because normally through the [covert logistics office] a procedure is established so that records are kept in a much more formal process. ... I felt very uneasy about this process. And I also felt uneasy about the notification dimension to the Congress."[8] Under federal law, the Executive was required to notify Congress both of covert action "findings" and the transfer of military equipment to third countries.

However, on January 29, 1986, thanks to Powell's intervention, 1,000 U.S. TOWs were loaded onto pallets at Redstone Arsenal and transferred to the airfield at Anniston, Alabama. As the shipment progressed, senior Pentagon officers grew edgier about Powell withholding the destination and other details. The logistics personnel also wanted proof that somebody was paying for the missiles.

Major Christopher Simpson, who was making the flight arrangements, later told Iran-Contra investigators that Gen. Russo "was very uncomfortable with no paperwork to support the mission request. He wasn't going to do nothin', as he said, without seeing some money. ... 'no tickey, no laundry.'"

The money for the first shipment was finally deposited into a CIA account in Geneva, Switzerland, on February 11, 1986. Three days later, Russo released the 1,000 TOWs. Inside the Pentagon, however, concern grew about Powell's unorthodox arrangements and the identity of the missile recipients. Major Simpson told congressional investigators that he would have rung alarm bells if he had known the TOWs were headed to Iran.

"In the three years that I had worked there, I had been instructed ... by the leadership ... never to do anything illegal, and I would have felt that we were doing something illegal," Simpson said.[9]

Even without knowing that the missiles were going to Iran, Simpson expressed concern about whether the requirement to notify Congress had been met. He got advice from a Pentagon lawyer that the 1986 intelligence authorization act, which mandated a "timely" notice to Congress on foreign arms transfers, had an "impact on this particular mission."

Major Simpson asked Gen. Russo, who got another legal opinion from the Army general counsel who concurred that Congress must be notified. The issue was bumped up to Secretary of the Army John Marsh. Though still blind about the shipment's destination, the Army high command was inclined to stop the peculiar operation in its tracks.

At this key moment, Colin Powell intervened again. Simpson said, "General Powell was asking General Russo to reassure the Secretary of the Army that notification was being handled, ... that it had been addressed and it was taken care of." Despite Powell's assurance, however, Congress had not been notified.[10]

Army Secretary Marsh shared the skepticism about Powell's operation. On February 25, 1986, Marsh called a meeting of senior Army officers and ordered Russo to "tell General Powell of my concern with regard to adequate notification being given to Congress," Russo testified. Marsh also instructed Russo to keep a careful chronology of events.[11]

Army chief of staff Wickham went further. He demanded that a memo on congressional notification be sent to Powell. "The chief wanted it in writing," stated Army Lt. Gen. Arthur E. Brown, who delivered the memo to Powell on March 7, 1986.[12]

Five days later, Powell handed the memo to President Reagan's national security adviser John Poindexter with the advice: "Handle it ... however you plan to do it," Powell later testified. Poindexter's plan for "timely notification" was to tell Congress on the last day of the Reagan presidency, January 20, 1989. Poindexter stuck the Pentagon memo into a White House safe, along with the secret "finding" on the Iran missile shipments.

Col. John William McDonald, who oversaw covert supply, added his voice to the Pentagon objections when he learned that key Army officials had no idea where the weapons were headed.

"One [concern] was inadvertent provision of supplies to the [Nicaraguan] contras in violation of the Boland Amendment," which prohibited military shipments to the contras, McDonald testified. "The second issue was inadvertent supply to countries that were on the terrorist list. ... There is a responsibility to judge the legality of the request."[13]

When McDonald was asked by congressional investigators how he would have reacted if told the weapons were going to Iran, he responded, "I would have told General Thurman ... that I would believe that the action was illegal and that Iran was clearly identified as one of the nations on the terrorist list for whom we could not transfer weapons."[14]

But when McDonald joined other Pentagon officers in appealing to Powell about the missile shipment's destination, they again were told not to worry. Powell "reiterated [that it was] the responsibility of the recipient" agency, the CIA, to notify Congress, "and that the Army did not have the responsibility to do that."[15]

Then, in March 1986, Powell conveyed a second order, this time for 284 HAWK antiaircraft missile parts and 500 HAWK missiles. This time, Powell's order set off alarms not only over legal questions, but whether the safety of U.S forces might be jeopardized. The HAWK order would force a drawdown of U.S. supplies to a dangerous level. Henry Gaffney, a senior supply official, warned Powell that "you're going to have to start tearing it out of the Army's hide."[16]

But the Pentagon again followed Powell's orders. It stripped its shelves of 15 spare parts for HAWK missiles that were protecting U.S. forces in Europe and elsewhere in the world.

"I can only trust that somebody who is a patriot ... and interested in the survival of this nation ... made the decision that the national policy objectives were worth the risk of a temporary drawdown of readiness," said Lt. Gen. Peter G. Barbules.[17]

If there had been an air attack on U.S. forces in Europe during the drawdown, the HAWK missile defense batteries might not have had the necessary spare parts to counter an enemy attack. As implemented by Powell, the Iran initiative had taken priority over both legal safeguards and the safety of U.S. soldiers around the world.

Ironically, after helping set in motion the Iranian arms shipments that left U.S. forces in Europe potentially vulnerable, Powell was dispatched to West Germany, where he was made commander of the V Corps in pursuit of another general's star.

◆ ◆ ◆

"We need you, Colin," pleaded Colin Powell's old mentor, Frank Carlucci, who in December 1986 was President Reagan's new national security adviser. "Believe me, the presidency is at stake."

With those words, Colin Powell re-entered the Iran-Contra scandal which had broken into public view in November with exposure of the secret shimpments of U.S. military hardware to Iran and revelations that some profits were diverted to the Nicaraguan contras.

Powell was reluctant to heed Carlucci's request. "You know I had a role in this business," Powell said. But Carlucci moved adroitly to wall Powell off from the spreading scandal. On December 9, 1986, the White House obtained from the FBI a statement that Powell was not a criminal suspect in the secret arms deals.

On December 12, Reagan formally asked Powell to become deputy national security adviser. "Yes, sir," Powell answered. "I'll do it." But

Powell was not enthusiastic. According to his memoir, Powell felt he "had no choice."

As usual, Powell took to his new task with skill and energy. His personal credibility was instrumental in persuading key journalists to accept White House explanations that Oliver North had undertaken a rogue operation and that matters were now back under control.

◆ ◆ ◆

On June 21, 1989, in secret, the Justice Department promulgated an extraordinary legal opinion, asserting the President's right to order the capture of fugitives from U.S. laws even if they were living in foreign countries, even if the arrest meant ignoring extradition treaties and international law. In 1989, the opinion had specific relevance to U.S.-Panamanian relations because a federal grand jury in Florida had indicted Gen. Manuel Noriega on drug-trafficking charges.

The legal opinion also would influence the course of Colin Powell's career. The four-star general had left Washington at the start of Bush's presidency to take charge of Forces Command at Fort McPherson. By August 1989, however, President George H.W. Bush and Defense Secretary Dick Cheney were urging Powell to return to Washington where he would become the first black chairman of the Joint Chiefs of Staff. Powell accepted the new assignment.

His first day on the new job was October 2, 1989 – and Powell immediately joined debates about whether to intervene in support of a home-grown Panamanian coup attempt led by Major Moises Giroldi against Noriega. "The whole affair sounded like amateur night," Powell wrote in *My American Journey*. "Cheney, [Gen. Max] Thurman and I ... agreed that the United States should not get involved."

Bush accepted the opinions of his military advisers. Receiving only minimal U.S. help, the coup failed. Noriega promptly executed Giroldi.

In the wake of the coup attempt, President Bush came under fierce criticism in the news media and in Congress. TV's armchair-warrior pundits had a field day mocking Bush's supposed timidity. On "The McLaughlin Group," conservative Ben Wattenberg charged that Bush's only policy was "prudence, prudence, prudence. Prudence is not a policy."

The New Republic's Fred Barnes chimed in that Bush's policy "is 'when in doubt, do nothing.' It was a massive failure of nerve. And then they come up with these whiny excuses. ... If this were a baseball game, the fans would be going – the choke sign."

Another pundit, Morton Kondracke, offered a joke line about the President. "Most of what comes from George Bush's bully pulpit is bull."

According to Bob Woodward's book, *The Commanders*, Powell was stunned. He had never seen "piling on of this intensity, and across the whole political spectrum. It was as if there was a lynch mob out there."[18]

Even more unsettling, Powell saw his own leadership at the JCS jeopardized by Washington's super-macho political environment of the late 1980s. Neither Bush nor Powell would make the same mistake again. They quickly built up U.S. forces in Panama, and the administration began spoiling for a fight.

"We have to put a shingle outside our door saying, 'Superpower Lives Here,'" declared Powell.

In mid-December 1989, the tensions between the United States and Panama exploded when four American officers in a car ran a roadblock near the headquarters of the Panamanian Defense Forces. PDF troops opened fire, killing one American. Another American officer and his wife were held for questioning. After their release, the officer alleged that he had been kicked in the groin and that his wife had been threatened with rape. When word of this humiliation reached Washington, President Bush saw American honor and his own manhood challenged.

This time, Powell also saw the need for decisive action. On December 17, he recommended to Bush that a large-scale U.S. military operation capture Noriega and destroy the PDF, even though the assault might result in many civilian casualties and violate international law. The authorization for the attack was found in the secret Justice Department legal opinion from almost six months earlier.

On Bush's orders, the invasion began on December 20, with Powell and Cheney monitoring developments at the Pentagon. The high-tech American assault force, using the F-117 Stealth aircraft for the first time, incinerated the PDF headquarters and the surrounding civilian neighborhoods. Hundreds of civilians – possibly thousands, according to some human rights observers – perished in the first few hours of the attack. An estimated 315 Panamanian soldiers also died, as did 23 Americans.

In the following days, as U.S. forces hunted for the little dictator, an edgy Powell demonized Noriega over the supposed discovery of drugs and voodoo artifacts in his safehouse. Powell started calling Noriega "a dope-sniffing, voodoo-loving thug."[19] (The white powder would turn out to be tamale flour, however.) When asked once too often about the failure to capture Noriega, Powell told a reporter to "stick it."[20]

On December 24, 1989, Manuel Noriega finally re-emerged. He entered the Papal Nuncio's residence and sought asylum. The United

States demanded his surrender and bombarded the house with loud rock music. On January 3, 1990, in full military uniform, Noriega surrendered to U.S. Delta Forces and was flown in shackles to Miami for prosecution on the drug charges. Two days later, the victorious Powell flew to Panama to announce that "we gave the country back to its people."[21]

However, the Panama invasion would soon be overshadowed by another military crisis, this time in the Middle East.

◆ ◆ ◆

An enduring image from the Persian Gulf War is the picture of the two generals – Colin Powell and Norman Schwarzkopf – celebrating the 1991 military victory in ticker-tape parades. They seemed the perfect teammates, a politically smooth chairman of the Joint Chiefs of Staff (Powell) and the gruff field commander (Schwarzkopf).

But the behind-the-scenes reality often was different. Time and again in the march toward a ground war in Kuwait and Iraq, Powell wavered between siding with Schwarzkopf, who was willing to accept a peaceful Iraqi withdrawal, and lining up with President George H.W. Bush, who hungered for a clear military victory.

According to insiders, Bush saw the war as advancing two goals: to inflict severe damage on Saddam Hussein's army and to erase the painful memories of America's defeat in Vietnam. Though secret from the American people at that time, Bush had long determined that a peaceful Iraqi withdrawal from Kuwait would not be tolerated. Bush, Defense Secretary Cheney and the White House political leadership desperately wanted a ground war to crown the American victory.

To Bush, exorcising the "Vietnam Syndrome" demons had become an important priority of the Persian Gulf War, almost as central to his thinking as ousting Saddam's army from Kuwait. On January 9, 1991, when Iraqi foreign minister Tariq Aziz rebuffed an ultimatum from Secretary of State James Baker III in Geneva, "Bush was jubilant because it was the best news possible, although he would have to conceal it publicly," Bob Woodward wrote in his book, *Shadow*.[22]

On January 15, 1991, U.S. and allied forces launched a punishing air war, hitting targets in Baghdad and other Iraqi cities as well as Iraqi forces in Kuwait. Weeks of devastating bombing left tens of thousands of Iraqis dead, according to estimates. The Iraqi forces soon seemed ready to crack. Soviet diplomats were meeting with Iraqi leaders who let it be known that they were prepared to withdraw their troops from Kuwait.

Still, Bush recognized the military and psychological value of a smashing ground offensive. But Schwarzkopf saw little reason for U.S.

soldiers to die if the Iraqis were prepared to withdraw and leave their heavy weapons behind. There was also the prospect of chemical warfare that might be used by the Iraqis against advancing American troops. Schwarzkopf saw the possibility of heavy U.S. casualties as an unnecessary risk.

As chairman of the Joint Chiefs, Powell found himself in the middle. He wanted to please Bush while still representing the concerns of the field commanders. Stationed at the front in Saudi Arabia, Schwarzkopf thought Powell was an ally. "Neither Powell nor I wanted a ground war," Schwarzkopf wrote in his memoirs, *It Doesn't Take a Hero*.

At key moments in White House meetings, however, Powell sided with Bush. "I cannot believe the lift that this crisis and our response to it have given to our country," Powell told Schwarzkopf as American air sorties pummeled Iraq.

In mid-February 1991, Powell also bristled when Schwarzkopf acceded to a Marine commander's request for a three-day delay to reposition his troops. "I hate to wait that long," Powell fumed. "The President wants to get on with this." Powell explained that Bush was worried about the pending Soviet peace plan which sought to engineer an Iraqi withdrawal with no more killing.

"President Bush was in a bind," Powell wrote in *My American Journey*. "After the expenditure of $60 billion and transporting half a million troops 8,000 miles, Bush wanted to deliver a knock-out punch to the Iraqi invaders in Kuwait. He did not want to win by a TKO that would allow Saddam to withdraw with his army unpunished and intact."

On February 18, Powell relayed a demand to Schwarzkopf from Bush's NSC for an immediate attack date. Powell "spoke in the terse tone that signaled he was under pressure from the hawks," Schwarzkopf wrote. But field commanders still protested that a rushed attack could mean "a whole lot more casualties," a risk that Schwarzkopf considered unacceptable.

"The increasing pressure to launch the ground war early was making me crazy," Schwarzkopf wrote. "There had to be a contingent of hawks in Washington who did not want to stop until we'd punished Saddam. We'd been bombing Iraq for more than a month, but that wasn't good enough. There were guys who had seen John Wayne in 'The Green Berets,' they'd seen 'Rambo,' they'd seen 'Patton,' and it was very easy for them to pound their desks and say, 'By God, we've got to go in there and kick ass! Got to punish that son of a bitch!' Of course, none of them was going to get shot at. None of them would have to answer to the mothers and fathers of dead soldiers and Marines."[23]

On February 20, Schwarzkopf sought a two-day delay because of bad weather. Powell exploded. "I've got a President and a Secretary of Defense on my back," Powell shouted. "They've got a bad Russian peace proposal they're trying to dodge. ... I don't think you understand the pressure I'm under."

Schwarzkopf yelled back that Powell appeared to have "political reasons" for favoring a timetable that was "militarily unsound." Powell snapped back, "Don't patronize me with talk about human lives."

By the evening of February 21, however, Schwarzkopf thought he and Powell were again reading from the same page, looking for ways to avert the ground war. Powell had faxed Schwarzkopf a copy of the Russian cease-fire plan in which Soviet president Mikhail Gorbachev proposed a six-week period for Iraqi withdrawal. Recognizing that six weeks would give Saddam time to salvage his military hardware, Schwarzkopf and Powell devised a counter-proposal.[24]

"The National Security Council was about to meet," Schwarzkopf wrote, "and Powell and I hammered out a recommendation. We suggested the United States offer a cease-fire of one week: enough time for Saddam to withdraw his soldiers but not his supplies or the bulk of his equipment. ... As the Iraqis withdrew, we proposed, our forces would pull right into Kuwait behind them. ... At bottom, neither Powell nor I wanted a ground war. We agreed that if the United States could get a rapid withdrawal we would urge our leaders to take it."

But when Powell arrived at the White House late that evening, he found Bush angry about the Soviet peace initiative. Still, according to Woodward's *Shadow*, Powell reiterated that he and Schwarzkopf "would rather see the Iraqis walk out than be driven out." Powell said the ground war carried serious risks of significant U.S. casualties and "a high probability of a chemical attack." But Bush was set: "If they crack under force, it is better than withdrawal," the President said.[25]

In *My American Journey*, Powell expressed sympathy for Bush's predicament. "The President's problem was how to say no to Gorbachev without appearing to throw away a chance for peace," Powell wrote. "I could hear the President's growing distress in his voice. 'I don't want to take this deal,' he said. 'But I don't want to stiff Gorbachev, not after he's come this far with us. We've got to find a way out.'"

Powell sought Bush's attention. "I raised a finger," Powell wrote. "The President turned to me. 'Got something, Colin?'" Bush asked. But Powell did not outline Schwarzkopf's one-week cease-fire plan. Instead, Powell offered a different idea intended to make the ground offensive inevitable.

"We don't stiff Gorbachev," Powell explained. "Let's put a deadline on Gorby's proposal. We say, great idea, as long as they're completely on their way out by, say, noon Saturday," February 23, less than two days away.

Powell understood that the two-day deadline would not give the Iraqis enough time to act, especially with their command-and-control systems damaged by the air war. The plan was a public-relations strategy to guarantee that the White House got its ground war.

"If, as I suspect, they don't move, then the flogging begins," Powell told a gratified President.

The next day, at 10:30 a.m., a Friday, Bush announced his ultimatum. There would be a Saturday noon deadline for the Iraqi withdrawal, as Powell had recommended. Schwarzkopf and his field commanders in Saudi Arabia watched Bush on television and immediately grasped its meaning. "We all knew by then which it would be," Schwarzkopf wrote. "We were marching toward a Sunday morning attack."

Conservative columnists Rowland Evans and Robert Novak were almost alone in describing Bush's obsession with a ground war in real time. They wrote that the Gorbachev initiative brokering Iraq's surrender of Kuwait "stirred fears" among Bush's advisers that the Vietnam Syndrome might survive the Gulf War.

"There was considerable relief, therefore, when the President ... made clear he was having nothing to do with the deal that would enable Saddam Hussein to bring his troops out of Kuwait with flags flying," Evans and Novak wrote. "Fear of a peace deal at the Bush White House had less to do with oil, Israel or Iraqi expansionism than with the bitter legacy of a lost war," the columnists wrote, quoting one senior aide as saying: "This is the chance to get rid of the Vietnam Syndrome."[26]

On February 28, the day the war ended with a decisive rout of Iraqi forces, Bush celebrated the victory. "By God, we've kicked the Vietnam Syndrome once and for all," the President exulted.

However, to the consternation of some neoconservative advisers and pundits, Bush decided against pursuing the Iraqi army back to Baghdad. In a 1998 book, which he coauthored with his national security adviser Brent Scowcroft, Bush explained that conquering Iraq would have led to a bloody occupation of the country and jeopardized the support of other Arab nations.

"We would have been forced to occupy Baghdad and, in effect, rule Iraq. The coalition would instantly have collapsed, the Arabs deserting it in anger and other allies pulling out as well," Bush and Scowcroft wrote. "Had we gone the invasion route, the U.S. could conceivably still be an occupying power in a bitterly hostile land. It would have been a dramatically different – and perhaps barren – outcome."[27]

◆ ◆ ◆

The Persian Gulf victory capped Colin Powell's rise to national hero. But, in the year that followed, some of his political compromises from the Reagan years returned to tarnish, at least slightly, the shining image.

To his dismay, Powell was not quite through with the Iran-Contra Affair. In testimony to special prosecutor Lawrence Walsh, Powell had denied knowing about illegal missile shipments to Iran through Israel in 1985, though acknowledging arranging legal shipments from Defense Department stockpiles in 1986. Then, in 1991, Iran-Contra investigators stumbled upon former Defense Secretary Caspar Weinberger's long-lost notes filed away in a corner of the Library of Congress.

Among those papers was a note dated October 3, 1985, indicating that Weinberger had received information from a National Security Agency intercept that Iran was receiving "arms transfers," a notice that would have gone through Powell. The belated discovery of the diaries led to Weinberger's indictment for obstruction of justice. Weinberger's trial, scheduled to start in January 1993, listed Powell as a prospective witness.

So, in late 1992, Powell joined an intense lobbying campaign to convince President Bush to pardon Weinberger. Bush had his own reasons to go along. Bush's role in the scandal also might have been exposed to the public if the trial went forward. Bush's insistence that he was "not in the loop" on the Iran-Contra business had been undermined by the Weinberger documents, too, when a batch was released on the Friday before Election 1992. Bush blamed the disclosure of the Weinberger documents for sinking his last hope of winning reelection

On Christmas Eve 1992, still stinging from his loss to Democrat Bill Clinton, Bush dealt a retaliatory blow to Walsh and the Iran-Contra investigation, granting pardons to Weinberger, neoconservative State Department official Elliott Abrams and four other Iran-Contra defendants. The pardons effectively killed the Iran-Contra probe. Weinberger was spared a trial – and Powell was saved from embarrassing attention over his dubious role in the scandal.

◆ ◆ ◆

In 1995, back in private life, Colin Powell was still remembered as the confetti-covered hero of Desert Storm. A star-struck national press corps seemed eager to hoist the four-star general onto its shoulders and into the

Oval Office. Any hint of a Powell interest in the White House made headlines.

Newsweek was one of the first publications to catch the Powell presidential wave. In its October 10, 1994, issue, the magazine posed the hyperbolic query: "Can Colin Powell Save America?" Powell was portrayed as a man of consummate judgment, intelligence and grace.

Not to be outdone, *Time* endorsed Powell as the "ideal candidate" for President. In *Time*'s view, Powell was "the perfect anti-victim, validating America's fondest Horacio Alger myth that a black man with few advantages can rise to the top without bitterness and without forgetting who he is."[28]

Soon, *Time* was detecting near-super-human powers: Powell could defy aging and even the middle-age paunch. While African-American leader Jesse Jackson had grown "older, paunchier and less energetic," Powell was "the Persian Gulf War hero who exudes strength, common sense and human values like no one else on the scene."[29]

But the newsmagazines were not alone in the accolades. Surveying the media scene, press critic Howard Kurtz marveled at how many supposedly hard-edged journalists were swooning at Powell's feet. "Even by the standards of modern media excess, there has never been anything quite like the way the press is embracing, extolling and flat-out promoting this retired general who has never sought public office," Kurtz wrote.[30]

Even normally clear-eyed journalists had their vision clouded by Powell fever. *Rolling Stone*'s analyst William Greider reprised the theme of Powell as the nation's savior. "Luck walks in the door, and its name is Colin Powell," Greider proclaimed.[31]

In one rare dissent, *The New Republic*'s Charles Lane reviewed Powell's second stint in Vietnam in 1968-69. The article focused on the letter from Americal soldier Tom Glen who complained to the U.S. high command about a pattern of atrocities against civilians, encompassing the My Lai massacre.

When Glen's letter reached Powell, the fast-rising Army major at Americal headquarters conducted a cursory investigation and dismissed the young soldier's concerns. "There is something missing," Lane observed, "from the legend of Colin Powell, something epitomized, perhaps, by that long-ago brush-off of Tom Glen."[32]

After Lane's article, a prominent *Washington Post* columnist rallied to Powell's defense. Richard Harwood, a former *Post* ombudsman, scolded Lane for his heresy, for trying "to deconstruct the image of Colin Powell." Harwood attacked this "revisionist view" which faulted Powell for "what he didn't do" and for reducing Powell's "life to expedient bureaucratic striving."

Harwood fretted that other reporters might join the criticism. "What will other media do with this tale?" Harwood worried. "Does it become part of a new media technique by which indictments are made on the basis of might-have-beens and should-have-dones?"[33]

But Harwood's fears were unfounded. The national media closed ranks behind Powell. Not only did the media ignore Powell's troubling actions in Vietnam, but the press turned a blind eye to Powell's dubious role in the Iran-Contra scandal. For the media, it was time for Powell-mania, a phenomenon that reached a frenzied climax in fall 1995 with the general's book tour and the drama about Powell running for President.

Then, in early November 1995, Powell said no to entering the presidential race and the media's balloon deflated with an almost audible whoosh. The disappointment was palpable as journalists filled a Northern Virginia banquet hall to hear Powell make the announcement.

The rest of that week, *The New York Times* op-ed page could have been draped in black crepe. Columnist Maureen Dowd compared her disappointment to Francesca's pining over her abortive love affair with Robert Kincaid in *The Bridges of Madison County.*

"The graceful, hard male animal who did nothing overtly to dominate us yet dominated us completely, in the exact way we wanted that to happen at this moment, like a fine leopard on the veld, was gone," Dowd wrote, mimicking the novel's overwrought style. "'Don't leave, Colin Powell,' I could hear myself crying from somewhere inside."[34]

Liberal and middle-of-the-road commentators were especially crushed. Columnists Anthony Lewis, A.M. Rosenthal and Bob Herbert proved that Dowd's column was not just satire. Lewis informed readers that Americans "across the political spectrum ... had just seen the dignity, the presence, the directness they long for in a President." Rosenthal proclaimed Powell to be "graceful, decisive, courteous, warm, also candid." Herbert hailed Powell as "honest, graceful, strong, intelligent, modest and resolute."[35]

Though also smitten by the Powell charisma, Frank Rich recognized that political reporters were acting a lot like love-sick adolescents. "The press coverage will surely, with hindsight, make for hilarious reading," Rich observed.[36]

In the years that followed – as Powell remained a figure of great national respect, earning millions of dollars on the lecture circuit – there was little of that critical hindsight. His selection as Secretary of State by President-elect George W. Bush was hailed by the news media with near universal praise.

9

Oil Futures

When George W. Bush was sworn in as the America's 43rd Chief
Executive, the widespread expectation was that he would recognize his
unusual position as the President Who Came in Second and would govern
with an eye toward compromise and consensus. In his Inaugural Address,
Bush declared, "Our unity, our union, is the serious work of leaders and
citizens in every generation. And this is my solemn pledge: I will work to
build a single nation of justice and opportunity."

But Bush's view of "unity" was not what many Americans might
have expected. Instead of going the extra mile to address the concerns
held by the plurality of voters who had favored Al Gore, Bush treated
"unity" as the opportunity for them to line up behind their new President.
The pugnacious tone of Bush's campaign and the bare-knuckled approach
toward the Florida recount carried over to the early months of Bush's
presidency.

The Republican national leadership quickly grasped that their first
objective must be to establish Bush's "legitimacy" and shove the ugly
facts of Election 2000 into a closet behind a locked door.

Toward that goal, the new Bush administration had the help of many
national journalists who treated the rookie President almost as if he were
a toddler who needed encouragement as he wobbled off on a new bike
with training wheels. While Bill Clinton had received a hazing during his
presidential transition and got virtually no honeymoon upon taking office,
the U.S. news media acted as if its patriotic duty in early 2001 were to
assist Bush in finding his balance and helping the nation get past the bitter
Florida recount battle.

Most leading Democrats adopted a similar approach, going silent
about the controversial election in the hope that predictions of Bush's
bipartisanship and "compassionate conservatism" would prove true.
Congressional Democrats didn't even press for full hearings on how Bush
engineered his victory – one of the most controversial political events in

the history of American democracy. Democratic pollsters warned activists, "don't be shrill" and "attack the positions, not the person."

Sensing this Democratic softness, Republican leaders took the offensive. In reference to the election, they sought to stigmatize anyone who "couldn't get over it." Criticism of how Bush gained power was quickly labeled spoiled-sport partisan rhetoric.

Without a more vocal demand from Democratic lawmakers to examine the Florida recount, Democratic National Chairman Terence McAuliffe and a few other party operatives raised their voices. The National Republican Senatorial Committee promptly accused McAuliffe of engaging in an unpatriotic smear campaign against America's President. An NRSC e-mail said McAuliffe was "openly undermining the legitimacy of George W. Bush's presidency."[1]

Meanwhile, Bush acted as if he had won in a landslide, brushing aside suggestions for a unity government and instead appointing conservatives to most key administration posts. (The only Democrat named to Bush's Cabinet was Norman Mineta who was given a relatively minor job as Transportation Secretary.) Bush also pressed a right-wing agenda that surprised many pundits and distressed the few moderate Republicans in his administration. The Colin Powells, the Christie Todd Whitmans and the Paul O'Neills began to look more and more like window-dressing.

Bush took a particularly hard line on environmental issues. His early decisions included repudiating the Kyoto Protocol on greenhouse gases; reneging on a campaign pledge to seek restrictions on carbon dioxide emissions; cutting funding for renewable energy and energy-efficiency programs; rolling back limits on arsenic in drinking water; promoting new oil and mineral extraction from public lands; and weakening a rule on roads in national forests.

The cuts in the energy conservation and renewal were especially puzzling because the moves contradicted the administration's stated desire to promote energy independence and to confront a "national energy crisis." Instead, the emphasis was all on finding new places to drill, both in and outside the United States.

Bush took direct aim at Alaska's Arctic National Wildlife Refuge. Via his first budget, Bush sent environmentalists a message that might have been composed like a ransom note with letters clipped from magazine headlines: "If you want money for renewable energy research, you'll have to let me drill the refuge."

Bush's proposed deal went like this: if oil companies were allowed to drill in the protected Alaska wilderness, Bush would earmark $1.2 billion raised from selling the drilling rights for research into renewable energy sources, such as solar, wind and other non-polluting alternatives to fossil fuels. To show the environmentalists that he meant business, Bush added a coercive element by slashing existing money for renewable energy sources by more than 50 percent, to $186 million from $376 million.[2]

In another move that had a touch of revenge, Bush gutted a program promoted by former Vice President Al Gore for developing a new generation of fuel-efficient automobiles. Gore's "Partnership for a New Generation of Vehicles," which aimed to boost gasoline mileage to as much as 85 miles a gallon, saw its funding cut by 35 percent to about $92 million, with that remainder shifted to research on bigger cars.

Environmental Protection Agency administrator Christie Todd Whitman, the former New Jersey governor who joined the Bush administration as a respected political moderate, found herself caught between serving as the nation's top environmental advocate and acting as a loyal administration defender. In a speech before the National Wildlife Federation on April 6, 2001, Whitman urged patience from the environmental community and blamed Bush's critics for exaggerating the impact of "one or two decisions that people might disagree with."

But even moderate Republicans in Congress weren't buying that. Senator Lincoln Chafee of Rhode Island, son of the late Republican environmental champion John Chafee, described the Bush administration's early environmental decisions as a reward to his conservative base. "There's a realization that some of the Western senators and more conservative elements of the party are calling some important shots," Chafee said.[3]

Republican President Theodore Roosevelt's granddaughter, Edith Williams, described herself as "fighting mad ... about what Bush is doing to the environment and to the environmental legacy of the Republican Party." Williams told *Seattle Post-Intelligencer* columnist Joel Connelly that "I'm desperately disappointed. ... I am deeply distressed at this administration."[4]

◆◆◆

Even before his first 100 days had ended, Bush had dropped all pretense of governing from the center. So much so that *The Wall Street Journal*'s ultra-conservative editorial page praised Bush for an administration that was to the right of Ronald Reagan's.

Bush's early policies and appointments made his right-wing base giddy. Two years earlier, prominent right-wing leader Paul Weyrich had written a despondent public letter in which he lamented "that politics itself has failed" and that conservatives had "lost the culture war." But after watching the Bush administration, Weyrich gushed that the new President's attention to the Republican right wing had eclipsed Reagan's and was "something that I've never experienced before."[5]

While Bush's right-wing supporters experienced a revival of their political spirits, White House spokesmen spun the press away from the idea that Bush had snookered the public with his talk of bipartisan moderation. The administration's new line was that conservative appointments and policies should come as no surprise given the fact that Bush himself was a conservative.

Some pundits publicly rued their earlier dismissive tone toward Al Gore. *New York Times* columnist Maureen Dowd – who made endless fun of Gore for his earth-tone sweaters, his Palm Pilot and his connection to the book/movie *Love Story* – coughed up a rare apology for her failing to recognize how far Bush would turn back the clock on the environment and in areas of foreign policy.

"Forgive me, Al Gore," Dowd wrote. "I'm going hungry for a shred of modernity."[6]

Instead of having Al Gore promoting a New Economy that would push the frontiers on fuel-efficient cars and pioneer advanced technologies for renewable energy resources, the American people found themselves with a government headed by George W. Bush, who seemed nostalgic for the Old Economy and its dependence on fossil fuels.

Bush's decision to withdraw the United States from the Kyoto Protocol earned condemnation even from close U.S. allies. Bush's unilateral move to drop out of Kyoto was seen as an early signal to the world that the new administration planned to embrace national-interest-unilateralism rather than the more traditional global-multilateral approach that had been favored not only by President Clinton, but presidents of both parties dating back to World War II.

Bush's environmental retrenchment prompted alarm from moderates angry that Bush's supposed centrist tendencies hadn't emerged on an issue dear to their hearts. The Bush administration felt "stung by the furious reaction to its early decisions on the environment," *The Washington Post* reported.[7]

Bush's approval ratings, which had risen to the mid-60s buoyed by America's hopes for its new President, slipped as many as 10 points by the week before Earth Day – April 22, 2001. Much of this drop came in the suburbs, where the critical swing-voting block of "soccer moms" frowned on Bush's early moves to rescind Clinton-era environmental protections. By a 2-to-1 margin, Americans agreed that Bush "cares more about protecting the interests of large corporations than of ordinary people," according to an ABC/*Washington Post* survey.[8]

Bush suddenly began polishing his green credentials. He decided not to block Bill Clinton's rules to protect wetlands; supported Clinton's proposal to tighten standards on lead pollution; and announced his intention to sign a global treaty negotiated by Clinton's State Department on toxic chemicals known as Persistent Organic Pollutants (POPs). When the dust settled, Bush had a string of pro-environment newspaper headlines, just in time for an Earth Day ceremony in the Rose Garden.

Bush kept up his pro-environmental rhetoric in interviews surrounding his first 100 days, though sometimes showing little comprehension of what he was talking about. In a CBS interview on April 25, 2001, Bush ticked off some of his pro-environmental stands. "I have made it clear we're going to do something on sulfur – sulfur oxide, nitrous – nitrous oxide, sulfur dioxide, and mercury, and we've got work to do with this greenhouse gas, this CO_2."

Though it's true that sulfur dioxide and mercury present pollution problems, it's unclear what "sulfur oxide" is. Nor did Bush seem to know what he was talking about when he mentioned "nitrous oxide," which is a mild anesthetic used by dentists, known popularly as "laughing gas." Bush's lack of precision aside, his pro-environmental rhetoric helped restore some luster to Bush's poll numbers.

◆◆◆

While part of Bush's energy agenda played out in public, the bulk of the new administration's thinking was taking shape behind closed doors, in Dick Cheney's secret Energy Task Force. In those first few months – and for years after – Cheney zealously defended the privacy of those deliberations, which involved discussions with energy-industry executives, geopolitical specialists and think-tank ideologues. Only much later would some of the details spill out.

In secret, the new Bush administration was already planning a radical new strategy toward the oil-rich Middle East. The Bush-Cheney strategy foresaw a much more muscular approach to countries in the region that got in the way of U.S. interests. "Regime change" in Iraq would no longer be just an idle wish. Not only would dictator Saddam Hussein have to go, but Iraq's oil riches would be parcelled off to international conglomerates that could exploit them and share the bounty with U.S. friends and allies.

Bush also made clear that the days of frustrating shuttle-diplomacy between the Israelis and the Palestinians were over. The United States, which for years had sought to mediate disputes between Israel and its Arab neighbors, would jettison any pretence of neutrality. Bush, who had once been the guest of Israel's Ariel Sharon on a helicopter tour over the cramped Palestinian city of Gaza, was ready to remove any restraints on what Israel would be allowed to do to finally break the will of the Palestinians.

Ten days after the Inauguration, at the first meeting of the National Security Council, Bush signalled a new "hands-off" policy toward the Israeli-Palestinian conflict, according to Treasury Secretary Paul O'Neill who later gave an insider account to author Ron Suskind for the book, *The Price of Loyalty.*

"We're going to correct the imbalances of the previous administration on the Mideast conflict," Bush was quoted as saying. "We're going to tilt it back toward Israel. And we're going to be consistent." Bush's analysis of the situation was that President Clinton had "overreached," causing negotiations to fall apart. "That's why we're in trouble," Bush said.[9]

Recalling the helicopter trip he took with Sharon over Palestinian refugee camps, Bush remarked, "Looked real bad down there. I don't see much we can do over there at this point. I think it's time to pull out of that situation."

Secretary of State Colin Powell expressed strong misgivings, predicting that U.S. disengagement would unleash Sharon and lead to "dire consequences," especially for the Palestinians. But Bush shrugged off the concerns, saying "Maybe that's the best way to get things back in balance."

Elaborating on this theory, Bush said, "Sometimes a show of strength by one side can really clarify things."[10]

So, years of U.S. diplomatic efforts to resolve the Middle East conflict abruptly ended. Sharon soon launched some of the deadliest attacks ever seen in the Israeli-Palestinian conflict, and Palestinians countered with suicide bombings that killed Israeli civilians. The cycle of violence spiralled out of control.

O'Neill, a member of Bush's National Security Council, said invading Iraq also was on the new administration's agenda starting with that first meeting. The message from Bush was "find a way to do this," O'Neill said. The linkage between overthrowing Saddam Hussein and securing oil supplies was also apparent. O'Neill described a map for a post-war occupation, marking out how Iraq's oil fields would be carved up.[11]

O'Neill's account, given after he was forced out of his job in December 2002, dovetailed with another account from *New Yorker* magazine writer Jane Mayer who discovered an NSC document dated Feb. 3, 2001 – only two weeks after Bush took office – that connected "regime change" in Iraq with exploitation of its oil fields. The NSC document instructed NSC officials to cooperate with Vice President Cheney's Energy Task Force, explaining that the task force was "melding" two previously unrelated areas of policy: "the review of operational policies towards rogue states" and "actions regarding the capture of new and existing oil and gas fields."[12]

While Cheney never discussed this hidden agenda publicly, he did make clear that his priority was to increase oil, natural gas, coal and nuclear energy as a way to meet American energy needs into the future. "Conservation may be a sign of personal virtue, but it is not a sufficient basis for a sound, comprehensive energy policy," said the former chief executive of Halliburton.

Some analysts interpreted Cheney's reference to "personal virtue" as a knock on Jimmy Carter and his cardigan-sweater-wearing speeches of the 1970s, a recollection that was sure to get a chuckle from Republicans of Cheney's age group. But the dismissal of conservation as a meaningful factor in meeting U.S. energy needs came across as a bit over the top to others. So, uncharacteristically, it fell to Bush – normally the one who needs bailing out on his own words – to do some damage control.

"I think conservation has got to be part of making sure we have got a reasonable energy policy, but what the Vice President was saying was we can't conserve our way to energy independence," Bush said. "We have got to do both. We've got to conserve, but we also have to find new sources of energy."[13]

Bush's more nuanced language, however, couldn't conceal the reality that his administration – dominated by oil men – was about to embark on an energy policy that would try to ensure that Americans could buy and use the energy they wanted, without asking much in lifestyle sacrifices or worrying about environmental consequences.

◆◆◆

Behind the Bush administration's grander energy plans were the more mundane politics of doing favors for friends in the oil industry – and no political supporter had earned a presidential back scratch from Bush more than Enron Corp. chairman Kenneth Lay.

Lay, who saw himself and his energy trading company as trailblazers in the exciting land of the New Economy, had served as a reliable Bush backer since Bush's days as Texas governor. By the early days of Campaign 2000, Lay – whom Bush called "Kenny Boy" – was another kind of Pioneer, the type that raised at least $100,000 for Bush. Enron also gave the Republicans $250,000 for the convention in Philadelphia and contributed $1.1 million in soft money to the Republican Party.

Not only was Lay a top fund-raiser for the campaign, but he helped out during the recount battle in Florida in November 2000. Lay and his wife donated $10,000 to Bush's Florida recount fund that helped pay for Republican lawyers and other expenses. Lay even let Bush operatives use Enron's corporate jet to fly in reinforcements. After Bush secured his victory, another $300,000 poured in from Enron circles – including $100,000 from Lay – for the Bush-Cheney Inaugural Fund.

The first several months of Bush's presidency presented Enron with a promising set of opportunities. Lay was thrilled to have an ally in the White House who agreed with the goal of deregulating the U.S. energy industry. Lay also had a strong say-so in the appointment of federal energy regulators. Plus, Enron had a friendly ear at the highest levels of government when the company found itself at odds with India over a white-elephant power plant that Enron had built in Dabhol, India.

But Enron faced growing challenges, too. With a steady decline in its stock, Enron was desperately seeking cash to cover mounting losses from its off-the-books partnerships, a bookkeeping black hole that was sucking Enron toward bankruptcy and scandal. As Enron's crisis worsened, Lay secured Bush's help in three key ways:

- Bush personally joined the fight against imposing caps on the soaring price of electricity in California at a time when Enron was artificially driving up the price of electricity by manipulating supply. Bush's resistance to price caps bought Enron extra time to gouge hundreds of millions of dollars from California's consumers.
- Bush granted Lay broad influence over the development of the administration's energy policies, including the choice of key regulators to oversee Enron's businesses. The chairman of the Federal Energy Regulatory Commission was replaced in 2001 after he began to delve into Enron's complex derivative-financing schemes.
- Bush had his National Security Council staff organize an administration-wide task force to pressure India to accommodate Enron's interests in selling the Dabhol generating plant for as much as $2.3 billion. The pressure on India went up the chain of command to Vice President Cheney, who personally pushed Enron's case.

Enron's financial crisis could be traced back to 2000 when the long-running stock market boom ended. During the boom, Enron had risen through the ranks of Fortune 500 companies to a perch at No. 7. In its rapid growth, Enron expanded beyond its core business in natural gas pipelines, branching out into complex commodity trading, which included electricity, broadband capacity and other ethereal items, such as weather futures.

The bursting of the dot-com bubble in March 2000 put pressure on Enron as it did many other companies. Even though Enron's stock held strong, hitting an all-time high of $90 a share on August 17, 2000, the tumbling market and some risky overseas energy projects left Enron with many poor-performing assets. To protect its image as a Wall Street darling – and to prop up its stock value – Enron began shifting more of its losing operations into off-the-books partnerships given names like Raptor and Chewco. Hedges were set up to limit Enron's potential losses from equity investments, but some hedges were backed by Enron stock, creating the possibility of a spiraling decline if investors lost faith in Enron.

Still, Enron saw a silver lining in the darkening economic clouds of 2000. A prospective George W. Bush victory could speed up Enron's deregulatory plans for the energy markets. Through energy trading in California alone, Enron stood to earn tens of billions of dollars. Meanwhile, in summer 2000, the first signs of suspicions arose that Enron was trying to manipulate the California energy market.

An employee with Southern California Edison sent the Federal Energy Regulatory Commission (FERC) a memo expressing concerns that Enron and other electricity providers to California's deregulated energy market were gaming the system by cutting off supply and creating phony congestion in the electricity grid to run up energy prices.[14]

By December 2000, Enron was implementing plans dubbed "Fat Boy," "Death Star" and "Get Shorty" to siphon electricity away from areas that needed it most and getting paid for phantom transfers of energy supposedly to relieve transmission-line congestion.[15] That same month, after a 36-day battle over Florida's vote count, Bush nailed down his presidential victory.

Once in the White House, a grateful Bush gave Ken Lay a major voice in shaping energy policy and picking personnel. Starting in late February 2001, Lay and other Enron officials took part in at least a half dozen secret meetings to develop Bush's energy plan. After one of the Enron meetings, Cheney's energy task force changed a draft energy proposal to include a provision to boost oil and natural gas production in India. The amendment was so narrow that it apparently was targeted only to help Enron's troubled Dabhol power plant.[16]

Key parts of Bush's energy plan echoed Enron's views. Seventeen of the proposals were sought by and benefited Enron. One proposal called for repeal of the Public Utility Holding Company Act of 1935, which hindered Enron's potential for acquisitions.

Bush also put Enron's allies inside the federal government. Two top administration officials, Lawrence Lindsey, the White House's chief economic adviser, and Robert Zoellick, the U.S. Trade Representative, both worked for Enron, Lindsey as a consultant and Zoellick as a paid member of Enron's advisory board. At least 14 administration officials owned stock in Enron, with Undersecretary of State Charlotte Beers and chief political adviser Karl Rove each reporting up to $250,000 worth of Enron stock when they joined the administration.

Lay exerted influence, too, over government regulators already in place. Curtis Hebert Jr., a conservative Republican and ally of Senator Trent Lott, a Mississippi Republican, had been appointed to the FERC during the Clinton administration. Like Bush and Lay, Hebert was a promoter of "free markets," and Bush elevated him to FERC chairman in January 2001. But Hebert ran into trouble when he broke ranks with Lay on Enron's plan to force consolidation of state utilities into four giant regional transmission organizations, or RTOs. By quickly pushing the states into RTOs, Enron and other big energy traders would have much larger markets for their energy sales.

Hebert, who advocated states' rights, told *The New York Times* that he got a call from Lay with a proposed deal. Lay wanted Hebert to support a faster transition to a national retailing structure for electricity. If he did, Enron would back him to keep his job. The FERC chairman said he was "offended" by the veiled threat. Lay already had demonstrated sway over selection of administration appointees by supplying Bush aides with a list of preferred candidates and personally interviewing a possible FERC nominee.

Lay offered a different account of the phone call. He said Hebert was the one "requesting" Enron's support, though Lay acknowledged that in the context of their discussion, the pair "very possibly" discussed issues involving FERC's authority over the nation's electricity grids.

Hebert raised Enron's ire when he started an investigation in early 2001 into how Enron's complex derivative financing instruments worked. "One of our problems is that we do not have the expertise to truly unravel the complex arbitrage activities of a company like Enron," Hebert said.[17] At the time, those complex – and deceptive – derivative schemes were concealing Enron's worsening losses.

The California energy crisis also was spinning out of control. Rolling blackouts crisscrossed the state, where the partially deregulated energy market, served by Enron and other traders, had seen electricity prices soar 800 percent in one year. After taking power, Bush turned a deaf ear to appeals from public officials in California to give the state relief from the skyrocketing costs of energy. Bush also reined in federal efforts to monitor market manipulations.

As California's electricity prices continued to soar, Democratic Governor Gray Davis and Democratic Senator Dianne Feinstein voiced suspicions that the "free market" was not at work. Rather they saw corporate price-fixing, gouging consumers and endangering California's economy. But California's suspicions mostly were mocked in official Washington as examples of finger-pointing and conspiracy theories. The administration blamed the problem on excessive environmental regulation that discouraged the building of new power plants.

Again, Lay was influencing policy behind the scenes. An April 2001 memo from Lay to Cheney advised the administration to resist price caps. "The administration should reject any attempt to re-regulate wholesale power markets by adopting price caps or returning to archaic methods of determining the cost-base of wholesale power," Lay said.[18]

Cheney and Bush echoed Lay's position in their political exchanges with Davis and other Democrats. On April 18, 2001, Cheney told the *Los Angeles Times* that the Bush administration opposed price caps because they would discourage investment.[19]

In May 2001, Bush traveled to California on a trip choreographed like a President visiting a disaster area. Only this time, Bush wasn't promising federal help to a state in need. He was carrying the same message that Lay had sent to Cheney. In effect, Bush was saying: Read my lips. No price caps. "Price caps do nothing to reduce demand, and they do nothing to increase supply," Bush said.[20]

After weeks of standoff, as electricity prices stayed high and began spreading to other Western states, the political showdown ended on June 18, 2001. FERC approved limited price caps, a reversal prompted by Republican fears of a political backlash that could cost them seats in Congress.[21]

Still, the administration's rear-guard defense of deregulation had bought Enron and other energy traders precious months to reap hundreds of millions of dollars in trading profits in California. The imposition of FERC's limited price caps – and the state's aggressive conservation efforts – brought the energy crisis under control. That may have been good news for California, but not for Enron. By losing control over its ability to keep electricity prices artificially high, Enron faced new economic pressures.

"There are some hints of a connection [between the price caps and Enron's collapse], including the billions of dollars in cash that flowed in and out of Enron as the crisis waxed and waned," *The New York Times* reported later.[22]

With the easing of the California energy crisis, Enron's stock price began to decline, slipping from around $80 early in the year to the high-$40's. That began to put pressure on the stock hedges tucked inside the off-the-books partnerships.

In June 2001, the White House went to bat for Enron on another touchy issue, the natural gas power plant that Enron had built in Dabhol, India. The plant had become a financial disaster because its cost of electricity was several times higher than what India was paying other providers. That, in turn, led to an impasse over unpaid bills. Enron wanted India to pay $250 million for the electricity or buy out Enron's stake in the plant for about $2.3 billion.

These sorts of contract disputes between U.S. companies and foreign governments are normally handled by the Commerce Department or possibly the State Department. But Enron's Dabhol problem became a priority for Bush's National Security Council staff, a level of interest over a contract dispute that was almost unprecedented, according to former NSC officials from both Republican and Democratic administrations.

On June 27, 2001, Vice President Cheney personally discussed Enron's problem with Sonia Gandhi, the leader of India's opposition Congress Party. "Good news is that the Veep mentioned Enron in his meeting with Sonia Gandhi yesterday," said one NSC e-mail dated June 28, 2001 and obtained under a Freedom of Information Act request.

Throughout summer 2001, the NSC staff met frequently to coordinate U.S. pressure on India over Enron's plant, drawing in the State Department, the Treasury Department, the Office of U.S. Trade Representative and the Overseas Private Investment Corp., which had committed $360 million in risk insurance to the Dabhol project. National Security Adviser Condoleezza Rice organized and led this "Dabhol Working Group."

The working group sought to broker meetings between Lay and senior Indian officials, including Brajesh Mishra, the national security adviser to Indian Prime Minister Atal Bihari Vajpayee. During a trip to India, a senior State Department official delivered a *demarche* or official warning to the Indian government, but New Delhi still resisted the U.S. pressure.

Also in the summer of 2001, Enron was consolidating its influence at FERC. Ken Lay called White House aide Karl Rove to recommend Nora Mead Brownell, a member of the Pennsylvania Public Utility Commission, to be a new FERC commissioner, calling her "a strong force in getting the right outcome" in deregulating Pennsylvania's energy market, according to a July, 17, 2001, letter by Representative Henry Waxman, a California Democrat, to the White House counsel.

Then, in August 2001, FERC Chairman Hebert, who had broken with the White House over California price caps and had ordered the inquiry into Enron's arbitrage schemes, abruptly resigned only six months into his four-year term. He explained lamely that he desired "to seek other opportunities." Bush replaced Hebert with former Texas Public Utilities commissioner Pat Wood III. Lay had included Wood and Brownell on a list of his preferred FERC candidates.[23]

As Lay was flexing his political muscle in Washington, out of public view back in Houston, Enron's accounting house of cards was shaking. On August 15, 2001, Sherron Watkins, an Enron vice president, warned Lay that accounting irregularities, including the hedges tied to Enron stock, were threatening to undo the corporation.

10

Impending Disaster

George W. Bush, one of the least traveled presidents of modern times, adopted a foreign policy that combined a narrow concept of U.S. self-interest with a go-it-alone execution. Bush's backers hailed this "new unilateralism" as a bold reassertion of U.S. supremacy unencumbered by the sensibilities of other nations or by constraints of international law.

"After a decade of Prometheus playing pygmy, the first task of the new administration is precisely to reassert American freedom of action," wrote *Washington Post* columnist Charles Krauthammer. Toward this goal of reasserting U.S. power, Bush repudiated what Krauthammer called the "bizarrely self-flagellating" Kyoto global-warming agreement and made clear the administration's intent to junk the Anti-Ballistic Missile Treaty so the United States could fulfill Ronald Reagan's dream of a Star Wars missile defense.

"Rather than contain American power within a vast web of constraining international agreements, the new unilateralism seeks to strengthen American power and unashamedly deploy it on behalf of *self-defined* global ends," Krauthammer wrote.[1] (Emphasis in original.)

Bush's foreign policy defined itself as being what Bill Clinton's wasn't – a new term was even added to the political lexicon: Anything but Clinton. When it came to Bush's straightforward unilateralism, the counterpoint was Clinton's complex multilateralism. Clinton sought to understand the interests of other world actors and tried to defuse, with mixed success, intractable world conflicts from Northern Ireland to North Korea, from the Balkans to Israel-Palestine.

Bush was having none of that. What mattered was keeping America Number One by deploying the U.S. military and protecting the American Way of Life by ensuring an adequate supply of reasonably priced gasoline.

Europeans, in particular, were appalled by this new Leader of the Free World. They saw Bush as an arrogant cowboy-politician, heavy on ego, light on experience. They also were put off by his pride in having presided over scores of executions as Texas governor, whereas European countries had long since banned capital punishment.

Nat Parry had moved to Copenhagen, Denmark, in February 2001 to take a job at a European security organization, and he soon found that being an American in Europe was a difficult position to be in. Nearly everyone he met – whether colleagues at work, acquaintances at dinner parties, or total strangers at cafes – would begin the conversation by nervously asking, "So, what do you think of your President?"

Danes were especially puzzled by the U.S. Electoral College system, and would frequently ask how it was that a candidate who lost the popular vote could possibly be considered a legitimate President. Those sorts of perplexed queries gave way to outright hostility, however, when Bush announced U.S. withdrawal from the Kyoto Protocol on global warming. After that move, the polite questions of "What do you think of your President," gave way to hostile questions of "What is America *doing?!*"

Sam Parry was equally taken aback when he made a trip to Scandinavia in May 2001.

"I encountered blunt worries – if not outright disgust – about the Bush administration," he wrote. "On the ride from the airport in Copenhagen, Denmark, I commented to the driver about the many windmills that dotted the landscape. The driver responded that it was too bad the United States had such a 'fool' in the White House, or the U.S. might consider adopting a similar strategy for alternative energy. I had been in Denmark less than an hour and someone had already called my country's President a 'fool.'

"I encountered similar attitudes in meeting people along my travels through Sweden and Norway. When they recognized I was an American, they asked how Bush could have become President after losing the popular vote. They also seemed knowledgeable about the irregularities in Florida and were distressed about the complacency of Americans in not mounting stronger protests against the undemocratic outcome."

Indeed, these sentiments appeared to be widespread across Europe. Even in the United Kingdom, the European country considered most similar to the United States politically, a 2001 opinion poll found that Bush had only a 25 percent approval rating and a greater than 60 percent disapproval rating. The poll indicated that the European people, even more than European leaders, were concerned about Bush's unilateral decision to pull out of the Kyoto agreement and about his intentions to build a missile shield.

◆◆◆

In a two-part series on May 31 and June 1, 2001, *The Washington Post* finally acknowledged what critics of George W. Bush's election "victory" had long alleged – that his 537-vote margin in Florida benefited from a host of irregularities, many traceable to his brother's administration or to post-election Republican maneuvering.

The *Post* discovered that Bush's side padded its tiny lead with scores of absentee votes that were cast after Election Day or did not meet legal standards. Those votes were counted in heavily Republican counties, though not in Democratic strongholds. "Matthew Hendrickson, a sailor aboard the cruiser USS Ticonderoga, mailed his overseas absentee ballot from Puerto Rico on November 13, six days after the Election Day deadline," the *Post* reported. "He knew the presidential race was undecided and he wanted Bush to win. Records show that Duval County included his vote in its results."

Hendrickson's vote was not alone. The *Post* reported that "at least 17 ballots examined by the *Post* in four north Florida counties were counted despite bearing postmarks dated after November 7. Scores more were counted after arriving without postmarks in elections offices between November 8 and November 17."

Republican operatives had condemned Gore as unpatriotic for insisting that legal standards be met for these ballots, many coming from American soldiers stationed overseas. When Gore's side relented and let many of these ballots be included, "the result was a rout of the Democrats in the northern counties, where Bush picked up 176 votes that lacked postmarks and other required features," the *Post* said.

But the Bush forces followed a different strategy in counties of south Florida with high numbers of African-American, Hispanic and Jewish voters, according to the *Post*'s study. "Elsewhere, particularly in Democratic counties, canvassing boards saw things the opposite way – as did the Bush forces, who demanded that strict state rules be followed," the *Post* reported. "In overwhelmingly Democratic Broward County, elections officials rejected 304 overseas ballots for various technical reasons, including 119 because they lacked postmarks. Miami-Dade invalidated about 200; Volusia threw out 43 and Orange 117. All three counties voted Democratic."

Following up on groundbreaking work by BBC reporter Greg Palast, the *Post* also reported that "hundreds, perhaps thousands, of non-felons in

Florida" were improperly removed from Florida's voting rolls under an extraordinary effort by Governor Jeb Bush's administration to purge ex-felons. State officials specifically ordered that "false positives" – meaning voters whose names and other personal data did not match those of actual felons – still be put in lists sent to county canvassing boards.

"Obviously, we want to capture more names that possibly aren't matches and let the [county elections] supervisors make a final determination rather than exclude certain matches altogether," said Emmett "Bucky" Mitchell, Governor Bush's aide who headed the state purge, in a March 1999 e-mail to Database Technologies, the contractor hired to assemble the list.[2]

While complying with this state order, the contractors expressed concern about the obvious danger that the state's approach would remove non-felons from the voting rolls. "We warned them," said James E. Lee, spokesman for Database Technologies. The list "was exactly what the state wanted."[3]

The *Post* noted that "the impact of this botched felon purge fell disproportionately on black Floridians and, by extension, on the Democratic Party, which won the votes of nine out of every 10 African-American voters, according to exit polls."[4]

The *Los Angeles Times* reached similar conclusions. "A review ... of thousands of pages of records, reports and e-mail messages suggests the botched effort to stop felons from voting could have affected the ultimate outcome," the *Times* reported. "The reason: those on the list were disproportionately African-American. Blacks made up 66 percent of those named as felons in Miami-Dade, the state's largest county, for example, and 54 percent in Hillsborough County, which includes Tampa."[5]

The *Times* quoted Sandylynn Williams, a black Tampa resident and Gore supporter who was turned away after being wrongly identified as a felon. "I don't feel like it was an honest mistake," she said. "I felt like they knew most of the minorities was going to vote against Bush." Williams was restored to the voting rolls 10 days *after* the election, the *Times* said.[6]

In another examination of the Florida election, the U.S. Commission on Civil Rights concluded that the process was marred by "injustice, ineptitude and inefficiency," a combination of factors that depressed the votes of minorities, especially African-Americans. The report found that 54 percent of the rejected ballots in Florida were cast by African-Americans. That meant that an African-American was 10 times more likely to have a vote thrown out than was a white.

"Despite the closeness of the election, it was widespread voter disenfranchisement, not the dead-heat contest, that was the extraordinary feature in the Florida election," the commission concluded. "The disenfranchisement was not isolated or episodic. ... State officials failed to fulfill their duties in a manner that would prevent this disenfranchisement."

◆◆◆

President Bush found himself confronting another unexpected political obstacle when Senator James Jeffords of Vermont – a staunch environmentalist – switched from Republican to an independent, putting the Democrats back in control of the U.S. Senate.

As Bush's popular support waned and congressional resistance waxed, Bush began warning his followers that he was ready to "go back to Crawford" if he didn't get his way on his agenda. Conservative columnist Robert D. Novak reported that Bush issued one of his return-to-Crawford warnings on June 27 during a White House meeting with moderate House Republicans who were backing an alternative version of a Patients' Bill of Rights law. "Bush appeared to draw a line in the sand when he indicated he always could return to Crawford, Texas, if the liberal health juggernaut grinds him down," Novak wrote.[7]

Bush also found himself battling congressional momentum in favor of new campaign-finance restrictions. In that context, *Los Angeles Times* political writer Ronald Brownstein picked up word, too, of Bush issuing a "back to Crawford" threat. Bush "continues to send a signal that, 'I'm going to do what I want to do, and if nobody likes it, I'm going to go back to Crawford,'" Brownstein wrote, quoting a GOP lobbyist close to the administration.[8]

While these warnings sounded to some like a spoiled child vowing to take his ball and go home, Republican strategists spun the "back to Crawford" threats as a sign of Bush's principled leadership. Other admirers were discerning special skills in Bush, especially his confidence in making snap judgments.

"Gone is the tentativeness of 20 months ago, of the lost man of the early Republican debates," wrote Ronald Reagan's speechwriter Peggy Noonan in an article for *The Wall Street Journal*'s editorial page. "In its place seems an even-keeled confidence, even a robust faith in his own perceptions and judgments."

Exhibit One in Noonan's thesis was Bush's performance in his first overseas presidential trip, which she said he completed "with a deep feeling of satisfaction at how he'd done and who he'd been."[9] The trip had ended with Bush's claim that he had gauged the soul of Russian President Vladimir Putin, the autocratic former KGB officer.

"I looked the man in the eye," Bush said. "I found him to be very straightforward and trustworthy. We had a very good dialogue. I was able to get a sense of his soul."

Though Noonan similarly had looked into Bush's presidential demeanor and detected an "even-keeled confidence," other observers saw a continued unsteadiness. When Bush visited the Jefferson Memorial on July 2 and got the predictable question about what July Fourth meant to him, his response bordered on the incoherent:

"It's an unimaginable honor to be the President during the Fourth of July," Bush said. "It means what these words say, for starters. The great inalienable rights of our country. We're blessed with such values in America. And I – it's – I'm a proud man to be the nation based upon such wonderful values."

◆ ◆ ◆

July Fourth 2001 also was a time of increasing alarm inside the U.S. intelligence community. Electronic intercepts had picked up conversations suggesting that al-Qaeda, the Islamic terrorist group headed by Saudi militant Osama bin Laden, was planning a spectacular attack on U.S. soil. Yet, during the lazy summer of 2001, relatively few Americans had even heard of al-Qaeda, which in Arabic means "the base."

This organization of Islamic extremists had taken shape during the CIA-supported war against the Soviet occupation in Afghanistan in the 1980s. During those years of the late Cold War, CIA Director William J. Casey and other anti-Soviet hard-liners viewed Islamic fundamentalism as a tool to pry historically Muslim territories in the southern Soviet Union away from Moscow and its atheistic communist government. So, besides arming a multinational force of Islamists to fight in Afghanistan, the CIA printed thousands of copies of the Koran and smuggled them into the Soviet Union.

In another trade-off for the Afghan war, the CIA looked the other way while Pakistan was developing its nuclear bomb. The CIA wanted nothing to interfere with the vital cooperation that Pakistani intelligence was providing in funneling weapons to the anti-Soviet Afghan rebels and their Islamic allies, including bin Laden. But after the Soviets were driven from Afghanistan in 1989, many of the CIA-trained Islamist guerrillas turned their fury against other infidels encroaching on Muslim lands. The most obvious intruder was their old patron, the United States.

Bin Laden, the scion of a wealthy Saudi family which controlled much of the construction in the oil-rich kingdom, disdained the Saudi princes for their decadent ways and their reliance on the Americans for their security. The acetic and religious bin Laden grew more alienated from the Saudi power structure in 1990 when Iraqi dictator Saddam Hussein invaded Kuwait.

Bin Laden despised Hussein as a secular leader of an Arab country and wanted him driven from Kuwait, but bin Laden was disgusted at the thought of non-Muslims setting up military bases near Islamic holy sites in Saudi Arabia. He volunteered to raise an Islamic army of *mujahedeen* to push Hussein out of Kuwait. But the Saudi royals threw in their lot with the Americans, the British and a multinational force that succeeded in routing the Iraqi army in early 1991. But, just as bin Laden had feared, the Americans did not dismantle their military bases in Saudi Arabia. They made them more permanent.

In the early 1990s, bin Laden moved his fledgling al-Qaeda organization to Sudan and built up an array of interrelated businesses as a framework for his political activities. He reached out to other Islamic extremists from Saudi Arabia, Egypt, Jordan, Lebanon, Iraq, Oman, Algeria, Libya, Tunisia, Morocco, Somalia and Eritrea. Many were exiles from losing battles against the power structures in their home countries.[10]

During this transition period, bin Laden intensified his anti-American rhetoric and issued a *fatwa* – or religious order – in 1992 against U.S. "occupation" of Islamic lands. U.S. intelligence began to suspect that al-Qaeda was responsible for scattered attacks against U.S. targets in the Middle East and East Africa. By 1996, pressure from the United States and other countries persuaded the Sudanese government to expel bin Laden and his organization. Bin Laden left Sudan on May 19, 1996, and returned to his old sanctuary in Afghanistan.[11]

Though in a weakened position, bin Laden began reviving al-Qaeda in the mountains of Afghanistan, with the protection of the Pakistani intelligence services and the fundamentalist Taliban government in Kabul. Bin Laden rebuilt his financial structure, set up training camps and forged alliances with other extremist organizations, such as the Egyptian Islamic Jihad led by exile Ayman al-Zawahiri. On February 23, 1998, a resurgent bin Laden issued another *fatwa* against the United States, specifically authorizing his followers to kill Americans whether they were civilian or military.

"For over seven years," bin Laden declared, "the United States has been occupying the lands of Islam in the holiest of places, the Arabian Peninsula, plundering its riches, dictating to its rulers, humiliating its people, terrorizing its neighbors, and turning its bases in the Peninsula into a spearhead through which to fight the neighboring Muslim peoples. … These crimes and sins … are a clear declaration of war on God, his messenger, and Muslims."[12]

Five months later, on August 7, 1998, al-Qaeda militants struck at the U.S. embassies in Nairobi, Kenya, and Dar es Salaam, Tanzania. The bombing of the Nairobi embassy killed 12 Americans and 201 others. In Dar es Salaam, 11 people died. Bin Laden declared publicly that if inciting attacks intended to drive Americans and Jews from the Islamic holy lands is a crime, "let history be a witness that I am a criminal."[13]

After the embassy bombings in Kenya and Tanzania, President Bill Clinton ordered heightened attention on bin Laden and al-Qaeda, looking for ways of getting the terrorist leader expelled from Afghanistan or killed. On August 20, 1998, the United States launched a missile strike against bin Laden's Afghan base, killing about two dozen people but missing bin Laden, who was believed to have left the compound a few hours earlier.[14] Besides failing to kill bin Laden, Clinton earned the derision of Republicans and many Washington pundits, who accused him of a "wag-the-dog" attempt to distract attention from the scandal over his dalliance with Monica Lewinsky.

In the months that followed, as the U.S. government weighed additional countermoves, bin Laden's operatives prepared for another strike inside the United States, this one to coincide with the Millennium celebrations at the end of 1999. An intelligence report from the National Intelligence Council, which advises the President on emerging threats, warned that al-Qaeda should be expected to "retaliate in a spectacular way" for the 1998 cruise missile attack on Afghanistan. Such retaliation "could take several forms of terrorist attack in the nation's capital," warned the report, entitled "Sociology and Psychology of Terrorism."[15]

"Al-Qaeda could detonate a Chechen-type building-buster bomb at a federal building. Suicide bomber(s) … could crash-land an aircraft packed with high explosives (C-4 and Semtex) into the Pentagon, the headquarters of the Central Intelligence Agency, or the White House."[16] In fact, as it turned out, the principal attack was to be committed against Los Angeles Airport.

Tipped by Jordanian intelligence on al-Qaeda's plans, the Clinton administration ordered tightened security and got lucky when alert border guards at Port Angeles, Washington, apprehended Ahmed Rassam, who was on his way to Los Angeles to plant bombs at the airport.[17]

At the height of Campaign 2000, al-Qaeda took aim at another U.S. target, the destroyer USS Cole, as it docked in the port of Aden. On October 12, 2000, al-Qaeda operatives piloted a small boat laden with explosives against the Cole's hull, blasting a hole that killed 17 crew members and wounded another 40.[18]

Back in Afghanistan, bin Laden anticipated – and desired – a retaliatory strike. He hoped to lure the United States deeper into a direct conflict with al-Qaeda, which would enhance his group's reputation and – assuming a clumsy U.S. response – would radicalize the region's Muslim populations. Bin Laden evacuated al Qaeda's compound at the Kandahar airport and fled into the desert near Kabul and then to hideouts in Khowst and Jalalabad before returning to Kandahar where he alternated sleeping among a half dozen residences.[19]

But lacking hard evidence proving who was behind the Cole bombing, Clinton didn't order a retaliatory strike. Only during the transition to the Bush presidency did U.S. intelligence reach a conclusion that the attack was "a full-fledged al-Qaeda operation" under the direct supervision of bin Laden. However, Clinton left a decision on what do next up to the incoming administration – and it didn't agree with Clinton's assessment that al-Qaeda ranked at the top of the U.S. threat list.

From his opening days in office, Bush rebuffed the recommendations from almost anyone who shared Clinton's anxiety about terrorism. On January 31, 2001, just 11 days after Bush's Inauguration, a bipartisan terrorism commission headed by former Senators Gary Hart and Warren Rudman unveiled its final report, bluntly warning that urgent steps were needed to prevent a terrorist attack on U.S. cities.

"States, terrorists and other disaffected groups will acquire weapons of mass destruction, and some will use them," the report said. "Americans will likely die on American soil, possibly in large numbers." Hart specifically noted that the nation was vulnerable to "a weapon of mass destruction in a high-rise building."

The 9/11 Commission later wrote, "in February 2001, a source reported that an individual whom he identified as the big instructor (probably a reference to bin Laden) complained frequently that the United States had not yet attacked. According to the source, bin Laden wanted the United States to attack, and if it did not he would launch something bigger."[20]

By then, Muhamed Atta and other al-Qaeda operatives were moving into position for their next deadly operation. From safe houses in California and Florida, they enrolled in American flight schools and took lessons on how to fly commercial jetliners.

When congressional hearings on the Hart-Rudman findings were set for early May 2001, the Bush administration intervened to stop them.[21] The presumed reasoning was that the Bush administration didn't have much to show either in terms of accomplishments or plans of its own.

Instead of embracing the Hart-Rudman findings and getting to work on the recommendations, Bush set up a White House committee, headed by Vice President Dick Cheney, to examine the issue again and submit a report in fall 2001. Former Republican House Speaker Newt Gingrich, who had joined Clinton in creating the Hart-Rudman panel, acknowledged that Bush's actions delayed progress.

"The administration actually slowed down response to Hart-Rudman when momentum was building in the spring," said Gingrich in an interview cited by a later *Columbia Journalism Review* study of press coverage of the terrorism issue.[22]

By late spring 2001, other alarm bells were ringing, frequently and loudly. Credible evidence of an impending attack began pouring in to U.S. intelligence agencies. "It all came together in the third week of June," said Richard Clarke, who was the White House coordinator for counterterrorism. "The CIA's view was that a major terrorist attack was coming in the next several weeks."[23]

In late June, CIA Director George Tenet was reported "nearly frantic" about the likelihood of an al-Qaeda attack. He was described as running around "with his hair on fire" because the warning system was "blinking red." On June 28, a written intelligence summary to Bush's national security adviser Condoleezza Rice warned that "it is highly likely that a significant al-Qaeda attack is in the near future, within several weeks."[24]

On July 5, 2001, at a meeting in the White House Situation Room, counterterrorism chief Clarke told officials from a dozen federal agencies that "something really spectacular is going to happen here, and it's going to happen soon." But instead of sparking an intensified administration reaction to the danger, the flickering light of White House interest in the terror threat continued to sputter.

By July 10, senior CIA counterterrorism officials, including Cofer Black, had collected a body of intelligence that they presented to Director Tenet. "The briefing [Black] gave me literally made my hair stand on end," Tenet wrote in his memoir, *At the Center of the Storm*. "When he was through, I picked up the big white secure phone on the left side of my desk – the one with a direct line to Condi Rice – and told her that I needed to see her immediately to provide an update on the al-Qa'ida threat."

After reaching the White House, a CIA briefer, identified in Tenet's book only as Rich B., started his presentation by saying: "There will be a significant terrorist attack in the coming weeks or months!" Rich B. then displayed a chart showing "seven specific pieces of intelligence gathered over the past 24 hours, all of them predicting an imminent attack," Tenet wrote. The briefer presented another chart with "the more chilling statements we had in our possession through intelligence."

These comments included a mid-June statement by Osama bin Laden to trainees about an attack in the near future; talk about decisive acts and a "big event"; and fresh intelligence about predictions of "a stunning turn of events in the weeks ahead," Tenet wrote. Rich B. told Rice that the attack will be "spectacular" and designed to inflict heavy casualties against U.S. targets.

"Attack preparations have been made," Rich B. said about al-Qaeda's plans. "Multiple and simultaneous attacks are possible, and they will occur with little or no warning."

When Rice asked what needed to be done, the CIA's Black responded, "This country needs to go on a war footing *now*." The CIA officials sought approval for broad covert-action authority that had been languishing since March, Tenet wrote.

Despite the July 10 briefing, other senior Bush administration officials continued to pooh-pooh the seriousness of the al-Qaeda threat. Two leading neoconservatives at the Pentagon – Stephen Cambone and Paul Wolfowitz – suggested that the CIA might be falling for a disinformation campaign, Tenet recalled.

But the evidence of an impending attack continued to pour in. At one CIA meeting in late July, Tenet wrote that Rich B. told senior officials bluntly, "they're coming here," a declaration that was followed by stunned silence.[25]

◆◆◆

Through the sweltering heat of July, Bush turned his attention to an issue dear to the hearts of his right-wing base, the use of human embryos in stem-cell research. Medical scientists felt stem cells promised potential cures for debilitating and life-threatening injuries and illnesses, from spinal damage to Alzheimer's disease. Yet, despite this promise, the Christian Right objected on moral grounds to the extraction of cells from embryos, even if they were destined for destruction as waste at fertility clinics. Bush also was eyeing a month-long vacation at his ranch in Crawford, Texas.

While Atta and his team made final preparations, the U.S. press corps also missed the drama playing out inside the U.S. intelligence agencies. The hot stories that steamy summer were shark attacks and the mystery of a missing Capitol Hill intern Chandra Levy, who'd had an affair with Representative Gary Condit, a California Democrat. The news media pretended that its obsession with Levy's disappearance was a heartfelt concern to help her parents find their missing daughter; the sexual gossip about Levy and Condit proved to be a fortuitous byproduct.

The case also meant a return engagement for the cast of moralizing pundits who had become household names during the Clinton-Lewinsky scandal, the likes of Ann Coulter and William Bennett. In one interview, CNN's Larry King asked Bennett whether Republicans were being a bit hypocritical since they had embraced Condit as a conservative "Blue Dog" Democrat before the Chandra Levy scandal, but since then had disavowed him as another immoral Democrat. Bennett, author of the book, *The Death of Outrage*, explained this moral relativism: "Look, hypocrisy is better than no standards at all."[26]

As cable news played the Chandra Levy case 24/7, a far more significant life-or-death drama was playing out inside the FBI and CIA.

At the FBI's Phoenix field office, FBI agent Kenneth Williams noted the curious fact that suspected followers of bin Laden were learning to fly airplanes at schools inside the United States. Citing "an inordinate number of individuals of investigative interest" attending American flight schools, Williams sent a July 10, 2001, memo to FBI headquarters warning of the "possibility of a coordinated effort by Usama Bin Laden" to send student pilots to the United States. But the memo produced no follow-up.

National FBI officials seemed paralyzed at the thought of taking proactive measures. Instead they concentrated on what to do after an anticipated terror attack. Then-acting FBI Director Thomas Pickard later told the 9/11 Commission that he discussed the intelligence threat reports with FBI special agents from around the country in a conference call on July 19, 2001. But Pickard said the focus was on having "evidence response teams" ready to respond quickly in the event of an attack.

Pickard "did not task field offices to try to determine whether any plots were being considered within the United States or to take any action to disrupt any such plots," according to the 9/11 Commission's report.[27]

CIA officials encountered similar foot-dragging at the White House. At least two officials in the CIA's Counterterrorism Center were so apoplectic about the blasé reactions from the Bush administration that they considered resigning and going public with their concerns.[28] Instead, the CIA hierarchy made one more stab at startling Bush into action.

On August 6, 2001, the CIA dispatched senior analysts to brief Bush near the beginning of his month-long vacation at his Crawford ranch. They carried a highly classified report with the blunt title "Bin Laden Determined to Strike in US."

This Presidential Daily Brief summarized the history of bin Laden's interest in launching attacks inside the United States and ended with a carefully phrased warning about recent intelligence threat data: "FBI information ... indicates patterns of suspicious activity in this country consistent with preparations for hijackings or other types of attacks, including recent surveillance of federal buildings in New York. The FBI is conducting approximately 70 full field investigations throughout the US that it considers Bin Ladin-related. CIA and the FBI are investigating a call to our Embassy in the UAE in May saying that a group of Bin Ladin supporters was in the US planning attacks with explosives."[29]

Bush was not pleased by the CIA's intrusion on his vacation nor with the report's lack of specific targets and dates. He glared at the CIA briefer and snapped, "All right, you've covered your ass," according to an account in author Ron Suskind's *The One Percent Doctrine*, which relied heavily on senior CIA officials.[30]

Putting the CIA's warning in the back of his mind and ordering no special response, Bush returned to a vacation of fishing, clearing brush and working on a speech about stem-cell research. Yet, inside the FBI as the month wore on, there were more warnings that went unheeded. FBI agents in Minneapolis arrested Zacarias Moussaoui in August because of his suspicious behavior in trying to learn to fly commercial jetliners when he lacked even rudimentary skills.

FBI agent Harry Samit, who interrogated Moussaoui, sent 70 warnings to his superiors about suspicions that the al-Qaeda operative had been taking flight training in Minnesota because he was planning to hijack a plane for a terrorist operation. But FBI officials in Washington showed "criminal negligence" in blocking requests for a search warrant on Moussaoui's computer or taking other preventive action, Samit testified more than four years later at Moussaoui's criminal trial.

Samit's futile warnings matched the frustrations of other federal agents in Minnesota and Arizona who had gotten wind of al-Qaeda's audacious scheme to train pilots for operations in the United States. The agents couldn't get their warnings addressed by senior officials at FBI headquarters. Another big part of the problem was the lack of urgency at the top. Bush, who had been President for only half a year, shrugged off the growing alarm within the U.S. intelligence community.

Counterterrorism coordinator Clarke said the 9/11 attacks might have been averted if Bush had shown some initiative in "shaking the trees" by having high-level officials from the FBI, CIA, Customs and other federal agencies go back to their bureaucracies and demand any information about the terrorist threat. If they had, they might well have found the memos from the FBI agents in Arizona and Minnesota.

Clarke contrasted President Clinton's urgency over the intelligence warnings that preceded the Millennium events with the lackadaisical approach of Bush and his national security team. "In December 1999, we received intelligence reports that there were going to be major al-Qaeda attacks," Clarke said in an interview. "President Clinton asked his national security adviser Sandy Berger to hold daily meetings with the attorney general, the FBI director, the CIA director and stop the attacks.

"Every day they went back from the White House to the FBI, to the Justice Department, to the CIA and they shook the trees to find out if there was any information. You know, when you know the United States is going to be attacked, the top people in the United States government ought to be working hands-on to prevent it and working together. Now, contrast that with what happened in the summer of 2001, when we even had more clear indications that there was going to be an attack. Did the President ask for daily meetings of his team to try to stop the attack? Did Condi Rice hold meetings of her counterparts to try to stop the attack? No."[31]

In his book, *Against All Enemies,* Clarke offered other examples of pre-9/11 mistakes by the Bush administration, including a downgrading in importance of the counterterrorism office, a shifting of budget priorities, an obsession with Saddam Hussein's Iraq and an emphasis on conservative ideological issues, such as Reagan's missile defense program. A more hierarchical White House structure also insulated Bush from direct contact with mid-level national security officials who had specialized on the al-Qaeda issue.

The chairman and vice chairman of the 9/11 Commission – New Jersey's former Republican Governor Thomas Kean and former Democratic Indiana Representative Lee Hamilton, respectively – agreed that the 9/11 attacks could have been prevented. "The whole story might have been different," Kean said on NBC's "Meet the Press" on April 4, 2004. Kean cited a string of law-enforcement blunders including the "lack of coordination within the FBI" and the FBI's failure to understand the significance of Moussaoui's arrest in August while training to fly passenger jets.

Yet, as the clock ticked down to 9/11, the Bush administration continued to have other priorities. On August 9, Bush gave a nationally televised speech on stem cells, delivering his judgment permitting federal funding for research on 60 preexisting stem-cell lines, but barring government support for work on any other lines of stem cells that would be derived from human embryos. Scientists complained that the existing lines were too tainted with mouse cells and too limited to be of much value. But the national news media mostly hailed Bush's split decision as "Solomon-like" and proof that he had greater *gravitas* than his critics would acknowledge.

CIA Director Tenet said he made one last push to focus Bush on the impending terrorism crisis, but the encounter veered off into meaningless small talk. "A few weeks after the August 6 PDB was delivered, I followed it to Crawford to make sure the President stayed current on events," Tenet wrote in his memoir. "This was my first visit to the ranch. I remember the President graciously driving me around the spread in his pickup and my trying to make small talk about the flora and the fauna, none of which were native to Queens," where Tenet had grown up.[32]

Bush and his senior advisers continued their hostility toward what they viewed as the old Clinton phobia about terrorism and this little-known group called al-Qaeda. On September 6, 2001, Defense Secretary Donald Rumsfeld threatened a presidential veto of a proposal by Senator Carl Levin, Democrat of Michigan, seeking to transfer money from strategic missile defense to counterterrorism.

Also on September 6, former Senator Hart was still trying to galvanize the Bush administration into showing some urgency about the terrorist threat. Hart met with Condoleezza Rice and urged the White House to move faster. Rice agreed to pass on Hart's concerns to higher-ups.

11

The Attack

Under the clear blue sky of a late-summer morning on September 11, 2001, teams of al-Qaeda operatives seized four American commercial jetliners, slamming two into New York's Twin Towers, a third into the Pentagon and a fourth into a field in Pennsylvania after the passengers fought back. Three of the country's most notable landmarks – representing America's financial strength and its military might – lay in ruins or in flames as rescue workers dug through rubble looking for survivors and the remains of almost 3,000 people.

From the country's shock and anger emerged the recognition that George W. Bush might not be one of the more experienced or skilled presidents the nation has had in a time of crisis, but he was the only one at that desperate moment. The U.S. news media's priority in shielding Bush's fragile legitimacy after the Florida recount battle suddenly became a national imperative.

Not wanting to contribute to the crisis, the U.S. news media kept from the public many details about Bush's actions that horrible day. Still, what most Americans saw when Bush did appear in public wasn't exactly reassuring. In a rushed appearance before cameras in Florida, Bush jarringly referred to the mass murderers as "folks." Later, at a U.S. Air Force base in Louisiana, Bush appeared in a grainy videotape, looking nervous while declaring that "freedom itself was attacked this morning by a faceless coward."

None of Bush's early comments was an accurate description of the cold-blooded zealots who murdered civilians with military efficiency even in the face of their own certain death. They were neither "cowards" nor just "folks." Their target also wasn't "freedom" in any normal sense of the word. It was the rooting out of Western influence from the Islamic countries of the Middle East. One administration official conceded that the statement in Louisiana "was not our best moment."[1]

Bush next was flown to Offutt Air Force Base near Omaha, Nebraska, where he clambered into a cinder-block bunker and had a telephone conference with his national security advisers. With a fighter-jet escort, Bush finally returned to Washington at about 7 p.m., nearly 10 hours after the initial terrorist assault. At 8:30 p.m., Bush gave a brief televised speech declaring that now "we go forward to defend freedom and all that is good and just in our world." He looked shell-shocked and even his advisers acknowledged that the speech was a disappointment.

Over the next two days, the administration stiffened its rhetoric with talk of war and began to finger Osama bin Laden as the mastermind behind the attacks. But Bush continued to send mixed messages with shaky personal comments that sometimes slid into incoherence. In the Oval Office, Bush's lip quivered and his eyes welled with tears as he responded to a reporter's question: "I'm a lovin' guy. And I am also someone, however, who's got a job to do and I intend to do it."

By week's end, Bush began making sweeping promises of revenge, statements that struck a chord with the vast majority of Americans outraged over the terrorism. "Just three days removed from these events, Americans do not yet have the distance of history, but our responsibility to history is already clear: to answer these attacks and rid the world of evil," Bush said at a national prayer service. "Evil" had religious connotations that were particularly appealing to the President's Christian Right base.

As Bush regained his political footing by using tough talk to express the country's anger, the public's consciousness was soon flooded with the iconic picture of Bush holding a bullhorn with New York firefighters amid the rubble of the World Trade Center. Bush's approval ratings soared to about 90 percent.

Many facts from those initial days of the crisis would not become common knowledge for more than two years, until filmmaker Michael Moore released his controversial documentary, "Fahrenheit 9/11." Moore's movie featured footage of Bush's behavior in a second-grade classroom in Sarasota, Florida, after White House chief of staff Andrew Card told Bush that the second tower had been hit and that "America is under attack." Moore showed the scene with a superimposed clock counting the seconds. Bush sat frozen, pursing his lips and fiddling with a children's book, *My Pet Goat,* for seven excruciating minutes.

U.S. news crews were present filming Bush in the classroom, but few Americans got to see an extended version of the video until Moore's movie. The news media also played down the panic about Bush's safety as he was flown first to Louisiana and then to the military base in Nebraska. TV news executives and newspaper editors – apparently believing they were acting in the country's best interests – closed ranks around Bush, trying to protect the American people's faith in their shaky leader and give Bush the best chance to rise to the occasion.

In the weeks after the 9/11 attacks, Bush's aides further air-brushed the tale to enlarge the heroic myth growing around Bush as the decisive "war president." Rather than acknowledge that Bush sat frozen, Card claimed that "not that many seconds later, the President excused himself from the classroom, and we gathered in the holding room and talked about the situation." Later, explaining why Bush actually had remained seated for seven minutes, Card said Bush's "instinct was not to frighten the children by rushing out of the room."[2]

As for the panicky flight to Louisiana and Nebraska, White House officials insisted that Bush's decision was driven by a credible terrorist threat against Air Force One. Then, in explaining Bush's tardy return to Washington, political adviser Karl Rove said there were still reports about civilian jetliners aloft until 4 p.m. and thus still a threat to Air Force One.

But White House spokesman Dan Bartlett later acknowledged that there was no credible threat, only misunderstood rumors. Benjamin Sliney, the top Federal Aviation Administration official responsible for air-traffic control, said the agency informed the White House and the Pentagon at 12:16 p.m. that there were no more hijacked planes in the air and all commercial planes were out of U.S. airspace.[3]

◆ ◆ ◆

Still, the murderous 9/11 attacks offered Bush a true opportunity for command not just in guiding the United States but in leading the world. Hundreds of millions of people across the planet set aside their objections to Bush's earlier hostility to the Kyoto agreement and to other efforts at international cooperation.

In Copenhagen, Nat Parry joined a procession of Danes to the U.S. Embassy and saw a scene that was repeated on sidewalks in front of U.S. embassies everywhere – a sea of flowers, candles, sympathy notes and even a New York Yankees baseball cap. The flags of most nations flew at half-mast. Minutes of silence were observed all over the world on September 14. In Kenya, impoverished Africans offered cows to the U.S. Embassy. There was a hope that from the devastation of 9/11, there was a chance for multilateral cooperation to build a better and safer world.

Immediately after the attacks, the United Nations, the European Union and other multilateral organizations expressed solidarity with the United States. The Organization for Security and Cooperation in Europe condemned the slaughter in New York and outside Washington as "an attack on the whole of the international community." For the first time, the North Atlantic Treaty Organization invoked Article 5, which states that an attack on any member state is an attack on all. Even countries not natural U.S. allies, such as Uzbekistan in the former Soviet Union, offered help.

One of the first signs, however, that Bush might overplay his hand was his excessive rhetoric as he vowed to mount a "crusade" against "evildoers." While Bush and many Westerners perceive the word "crusade" as suggesting a noble undertaking by knights in shining armor, the word connotes to Muslims an aggressive invasion of their territory by Christian zealots. In 1099, the Crusaders massacred many of the inhabitants of Jerusalem, men, women and children. Bin Laden quickly exploited Bush's gaffe by releasing a typed statement calling the coming war "the new Christian-Jewish crusade led by the big crusader Bush under the flag of the cross."

Bush also appears to have viewed his new duties as a mission from God. "I think, in [Bush's] frame, this is what God has asked him to do," one close acquaintance told *The New York Times*. "It offers him enormous clarity." According to this acquaintance, Bush believes "he has encountered his reason for being, a conviction informed and shaped by the President's own strain of Christianity," the *Times* reported.[4]

But there was a more mundane explanation for Bush's behavior. It was a chance to expand and consolidate his political power. "The government may be justified in taking measures which in less troubled conditions could be seen as infringements of individual liberties," White House lawyer John Yoo wrote in a memorandum on September 21, ten days after the terror attacks. Yoo added that Congress has no authority to place "limits on the President's determinations as to any terrorist threat, the amount of military force to be used in response, or the method, timing and nature of the response."

As the son of a former President, Bush also understood how to use political power. Indeed, some insiders found the Bush administration subordinating everything to politics. "There is no precedent in any modern White House for what is going on in this one: a complete lack of a policy apparatus," said John DiIulio, who had run Bush's office of faith-based initiatives. "What you've got is everything – and I mean everything – being run by the political arm. It's the reign of the Mayberry Machiavellis."[5]

Yet, while Bush set off on his mission – whether inspired by the divine or the earthly – there remained an unsettling question: Was Bush up to this delicate, complex and dangerous task? In the weeks after 9/11, it was unclear whether he recognized the risks in the geopolitical tradeoffs involved in building an international coalition and the potential costs of an open-ended, ill-defined war against terrorism, which is defined as inflicting violence on civilians to achieve a political end, a tactic that is as old as warfare itself.

Bush's knowledge of recent history was sketchy, too. Repeatedly, he called this "war on terror" a new kind of conflict, the first war of the 21st century. Yet, his father was Vice President in the administration of Ronald Reagan that made combating terrorism a top priority of U.S. foreign policy, replacing Jimmy Carter's hallmark of human rights. Reagan committed his administration to the war on terrorism in the wake of the Islamic revolution in Iran and the radical Arab nationalism of Libya's Muammar Qaddafi.

Reagan created special counterterrorism task forces and authorized the CIA to hunt down suspected terrorists in preemptive attacks that included assassinations. Some administration hard-liners, such as CIA Director William J. Casey, sought to trace virtually all terrorism back to the Soviet Union, combining anti-communism with anti-terrorism. In Central America, wars between right-wing governments and left-wing guerrillas also were squeezed under the umbrella of counterterrorism, with Fidel Castro's Cuba listed as a chief sponsor of this "terrorism."

To wage a joint war against "terrorism" and "communism" in Central America, the Reagan administration armed and backed military repression in El Salvador, Guatemala and other countries. Tens of thousands of Central American civilians were slaughtered in army sweeps of areas considered sympathetic to guerrillas, including massacres of Mayan Indians in Guatemala that a truth commission later deemed genocide. The U.S.-backed armies also were linked to paramilitary "death squads" that murdered political dissidents, including labor leaders, academics, priests and nuns.[6]

To punish Nicaragua's leftist Sandinista government for aiding insurgents or "terrorists" elsewhere in Central America, the Reagan administration supported the Nicaraguan contra rebels, who earned a reputation for sabotage, torture, rape and murder as they swept through towns in northern Nicaragua. One former contra director, Edgar Chamorro, described the contras' practice of dragging captured government officials into town squares and executing them in front of other residents. American journalists also reported on contra massacres of peasants picking coffee, presumably to discourage economic activity.

As the Nicaraguan contras earned their own reputation as terrorists, the Reagan administration created special propaganda teams that engaged in "public diplomacy" to persuade editors, producers and bureau chiefs to stop their reporters from filing these kinds of stories and to remove journalists who continued resisting this pressure. Administration insiders called these aggressive – and largely successful – public relations efforts "perception management," with the goal of both curbing reporters and controlling how Americans perceived events.[7]

In George W. Bush's "war on terror," the nation could expect a similar contempt toward even mild forms of dissent or ambivalence. Anyone who saw subtleties in the new Middle East conflict would become an "Osama apologist," a practitioner of "moral equivalency," or simply "soft on terror." As Bush framed the coming battle between good and evil, you were either "with us" and thus worthy of U.S. friendship or you were "with the terrorists," deserving only condemnation, destruction and maybe death.

As Bush unveiled his post-9/11 counterterrorism doctrine, many U.S. allies were stunned by its continued reliance on unilateralism. "Close U.S. allies and many inside the administration itself are uncertain whether the doctrine really means what it appears to say – that the United States will be the unilateral judge of whether a country is supporting terrorism, and will determine the appropriate methods, including the use of military force, to impose behavioral change," wrote Karen DeYoung of *The Washington Post*.[8]

◆◆◆

Bush vowed to retaliate for 9/11 with a war against terrorism globally, starting with an offensive in Afghanistan to oust the Taliban government that was providing a safe haven for al-Qaeda. On the front lines of that new war were Pakistan and India, traditional enemies who were engaged in a sporadic conflict over Kashmir. The relationship with India also presented a test of whether Bush would put the interests of his "war on terror" ahead of the protection of a principal political benefactor, Enron.

Despite the post-9/11 need for strategic alliances in south-central Asia, Enron's Dabhol power plant stayed at the forefront of U.S. relations with India. On September 28 – just 17 days after 9/11 and only nine days before the start of war with Afghanistan – the NSC-led Dabhol Working Group was preparing "talking points" about the Enron business dispute for Vice President Dick Cheney to deliver in a meeting with India's Foreign Minister Jaswant Singh.

On October 9 – two days after the assault on Afghanistan began – the State Department was pressing Enron's case with the Indians again. Undersecretary of State Alan Larson "raised the Dabhol issue with both FM Singh and NSA [National Security Adviser Brajesh] Mishra and got a commitment to 'try' to get the government energized on this issue prior to the PM's visit to Washington on November 9," an October 23 NSC e-mail said. "Pls give me one/two bullets for the President to use during his meeting with [India's Prime Minister Atal Bihari] Vajpayee."

While the Bush administration twisted the arms of the Indians, Enron's intricately wound financial schemes continued to whirl out of control. Its credit rating was cut and its stock fell. On October 30, behind closed doors, the Securities and Exchange Commission approved a formal investigation of Enron's accounting. The Dabhol Working Group, however, continued to press for India to make concessions to Enron. On November 1, as the U.S. war in Afghanistan raged, the White House prepared a memo citing Dabhol talking points for Bush's meeting with Prime Minister Vajpayee during a state visit to Washington.

On November 6, Overseas Private Investment Corp. President Peter Watson sent a stern warning to Vajpayee's national security adviser Mishra. "The acute lack of progress in this matter has forced Dabhol to rise to the highest levels of the United States government," Watson said in a letter. The dispute "could have a negative effect regarding other U.S. agencies and their ability to function in India."

The Bush administration's pressure on India over Dabhol did not end until November 8, the day the SEC delivered subpoenas to Enron and the company announced that it was under formal SEC investigation. "President Bush can not talk about Dabhol," warned one internal e-mail timed off at 2:33 p.m. that same afternoon.

◆◆◆

The assault on Afghanistan was spearheaded by CIA paramilitary personnel and U.S. Special Forces, backed by American air power and local Afghan militias who opposed Taliban rule and who happily accepted millions of dollars from CIA officers. The war also got help from new allies in the region.

Though Bush said the 9/11 attacks had "changed everything" and his "war on terror" would be unlike any war fought by the United States, there were many similarities to past conflicts. One was that the United States built alliances with some very unsavory characters. An early case in point was the repressive government of Uzbekistan, a landlocked Central Asian nation of about 23 million people north of Afghanistan.

The Uzbek government, which operated much like the Soviet republic it once was, offered the United States use of Uzbek airspace and an airfield where about 1,500 American troops quickly set up shop. In an October 12 joint statement, the United States and Uzbekistan expressed their common "commitment to the elimination of international terrorism and its infrastructure." The statement cited a classified agreement between the two countries that established a "strong basis for bilateral cooperation" and a "qualitatively new relationship based on long-term commitment to advance security and regional stability."[9]

The Bush administration was not making an explicit promise to guarantee the security of the Uzbek government and its authoritarian leader Islam Karimov. But the policy sent a strong signal that Washington was prepared to protect Karimov much like the United States defended other authoritarian pro-U.S. leaders in the region. Bush identified the Islamic Movement of Uzbekistan – which opposed the Karimov government – as one of the targets of the U.S. anti-terrorist campaign. Bush's declaration treated the IMU as part of Osama bin Laden's international network of terrorist organizations.

Yet, that appeared to exaggerate the IMU's role. The Muslim fundamentalist group mainly had conducted small-scale armed attacks, including car-bombings, in Uzbekistan, aimed at destabilizing Karimov's repressive regime. While the group also was active in neighboring Kyrgystan and Tajikistan, there was no public evidence of the organization engaging in terrorism on a global scale. Its membership was estimated in the hundreds and its activities mostly were limited to remote mountain terrain and border areas.

Still, Bush's targeting of the IMU was welcomed by Karimov. For many of his 11 years in power, Karimov had been trying to defeat the IMU by employing increasingly harsh tactics, banning opposition parties since 1993 and forcing many political activists to go underground. Karimov targeted peaceful political dissidents, practicing Muslims, human rights activists and journalists who have criticized his policies.

One victim of Uzbek repression was Shobriq Rusimorodov, a former parliamentarian and activist with the Human Rights Society of Uzbekistan. Rusimorodov had criticized the government for convicting Uzbeks for allegedly collaborating with armed insurgents. He was arrested on June 15, 2001, and held incommunicado for three weeks. His body was delivered to his family on July 7. He was believed to have been tortured to death.

That case was not unique. Amnesty International, Human Rights Watch and other human rights organizations criticized the Uzbek government for persecuting Muslims as well as using "anti-terrorism" as a cover for crushing legitimate democratic opposition. There were thousands of political prisoners in Uzbekistan, serving sentences up to 20 years for "anti-state activity," according to human rights groups.

In the prisons, torture was used routinely and death in police custody was commonplace. The government even organized "hate rallies" to intimidate families of political prisoners. Under Karimov's crackdown, practicing Islam was enough to get individuals thrown into jail.

The Human Rights Society of Uzbekistan claimed that anyone accused of a crime who attempted to prove his or her innocence could be subjected to torture to extract a confession. Torture techniques included systematic beatings, hanging, electric shocks, suffocation, rape, cauterization – the use of hot irons – and pain inflicted through dentistry. The Human Rights Society documented cases of prisoners who died as a result of torture and other people who disappeared without a trace.

During the 1990s, the Clinton administration kept the Karimov government at arms length and criticized its human rights record, even as U.S. businesses invested in the energy-rich region. However, under the Bush-Karimov agreement, Washington backed off its human rights pressure. "Our government will get full support from the West to fight those our government declares terrorists," an Uzbek official said.

◆◆◆

In November 2001, the U.S. offensive in Afghanistan progressed toward a swift victory over the Taliban. Americans marveled at the images of U.S. Special Forces troops riding across rocky Afghan expanses on horseback and at the sights of American bombing raids blasting away at suspected al-Qaeda strongholds in the mountains.

Some military skeptics had feared the war might drag on into the harsh Afghan winter, but the Taliban's grip was already weakening by early November. On November 10, Taliban forces were routed from the northern strategic city of Mazar-e Sharif. On November 12, the Taliban began to abandon the capital of Kabul.

It was on that day, as Taliban fighters slipped out of Kabul, *The New York Times, The Washington Post,* CNN and five other major news outlets released their study of 175,010 disputed ballots in the Florida election and what might have happened if a statewide recount had gone forward. The study's completion had been delayed by the 9/11 crisis and came at a time when as many as nine out of 10 Americans were voicing approval of Bush.

On the surface, the new election stories represented more great news for the President. According to the headlines and the leads of the stories, Bush would have won Florida even if Al Gore had been permitted the recount he sought in several large Florida counties or if the five pro-Bush justices on the U.S. Supreme Court hadn't stopped the recount that had been ordered by the Florida Supreme Court.

"Study of Disputed Florida Ballots Finds Justices Did Not Cast the Deciding Vote," *The New York Times* declared. "Florida Recounts Would Have Favored Bush" exclaimed *The Washington Post*. The *Post*'s Page One findings were followed up by a sidebar article from media critic Howard Kurtz, who took the Bush-victory spin one cycle further, with a story headlined, "George W. Bush, Now More Than Ever." Kurtz ridiculed as "conspiracy theorists" those who had expected to learn that Gore had actually won.

"The conspiracy theorists have been out in force, convinced that the media were covering up the Florida election results to protect President Bush," Kurtz wrote. "That gets put to rest today, with the finding by eight news organizations that Bush would have beaten Gore under both of the recount plans being considered at the time."

Kurtz also mocked those who believed that winning an election fairly, based on the will of the voters, was all that important in a democracy. "Now the question is: How many people still care about the election deadlock that last fall felt like the story of the century – and now faintly echoes like some distant Civil War battle?" he wrote.

But, Kurtz's sarcasm aside, a close reading of the actual findings – buried by the big newspapers on inside pages or included as part of a statistical chart – revealed that the Page One stories were misleading, if not outright false. The reality was that Al Gore actually had been the choice of Florida's voters if all legally cast votes were counted. By any chad measure – hanging, dimpled or fully punched through – Gore would have won Florida and thus the White House.

Gore won even if one ignored the 15,000 to 25,000 votes that *USA Today* estimated Gore lost because of illegally designed "butterfly ballots," or the hundreds of predominantly African-American voters who were falsely identified by the state as felons and turned away from the polls. Gore won even if there were no adjustment for Bush's windfall of about 290 votes from improperly counted military absentee ballots where lax standards were applied to Republican counties and strict standards to Democratic ones.

Put differently, George W. Bush was not the choice of Florida's voters anymore than he had been the choice of the American people who cast a half million more ballots for Gore than Bush nationwide. Yet, possibly for reasons of patriotism or out of fear of criticism if they had written "Gore Won" leads, the news organizations that financed the Florida ballot study structured their stories on the ballot review to indicate that Bush was the legitimate winner.

In effect, the elite media's judgment was "Bush won, get over it." Only "Gore partisans" – as both *The Washington Post* and *The New York*

Times called critics of the official Florida election tallies – would insist on looking at the fine print.

While "Bush Won" was the short-hand theme of nearly all the stories on November 12, it was still a bit jarring to go beyond the Page One articles or CNN's headlines and read the actual results of the statewide review of 175,010 disputed ballots. "Full Review Favors Gore," *The Washington Post* stated in a box on Page 10, showing that under all standards applied to the ballots, Gore came out on top.

The New York Times' graphic revealed the same outcome. Counting fully punched chads and limited marks on optical ballots, Gore won by 115 votes. With any dimple or optical mark, Gore won by 107 votes. With one corner of a chad detached or any optical mark, Gore won by 60 votes. Applying the standards set by each county, Gore won by 171 votes.

The news organizations justified their pro-Bush leads by focusing only on two partial recounts that were proposed – but not completed – in the chaotic environment of November and December of 2000. The articles criticized Gore's decision to seek recounts in only four counties and the Florida Supreme Court's decision to examine only "under-votes," those rejected by voting machines for supposedly lacking a presidential vote. An undercurrent of the articles was that Gore was somehow to blame for his own defeat, even if he actually may have won the election.

"Mr. Gore might have eked out a victory if he had pursued in court a course like the one he publicly advocated when he called on the state to 'count all the votes,'" *The New York Times* wrote, with the suggestion that Gore was hypocritical and foolish. *The Washington Post* recalled that Gore "did at one point call on Bush to join him in asking for a statewide recount" and accepting the results without further legal challenge, but that Bush rejected the proposal as "a public relations gesture."

The November 12, 2001, news articles focused on two hypothetical cases in which Bush supposedly would have prevailed: the limited recounts of the four southern Florida counties – by 225 votes – and the state Supreme Court's under-vote order – by 430 votes. Yet, the newspapers made little or nothing of the fact that the U.S. Supreme Court's decision represented a third hypothetical.

Assuming that a brief extension had been granted to permit a full-and-fair Florida recount, the U.S. Supreme Court decision might well have resulted in the same result that the news organizations discovered: a Gore victory. The U.S. Supreme Court's proposed standards mirrored the standards applied in the news consortium's recount. However, the *Post* buried this important fact in the 22nd paragraph of its story.

"Ironically, it was Bush's lawyers who argued that recounting only the under-votes violated the constitutional guarantee of equal protection.

And the U.S. Supreme Court, in its December 12 ruling that ended the dispute, also questioned whether the Florida court should have limited a statewide recount only to under-votes," the *Post* wrote. "Had the high court acted on that, and had there been enough time left for the Florida Supreme Court to require yet another statewide recount, Gore's chances would have been dramatically improved."

In other words, if the U.S. Supreme Court had given the state enough time to fashion a comprehensive remedy or if Bush had agreed to a full recount earlier, the popular will of the American voters – both nationally and in Florida – might well have been respected and Al Gore would have been inaugurated President of the United States.

But the news media's treatment of the recount stories was not only slanted but quite likely dead wrong. It turned out that the major news organizations were mistaken in their assumption about which ballots would have been counted under the Florida Supreme Court's ruling.

While the court had referred to under-votes, the court also gave broad leeway to Circuit Court Judge Terry Lewis to decide which ballots ultimately should be tallied and he was leaning toward including over-votes, ballots where a presidential choice was both marked and written in. The over-votes broke decisively for Gore.

So, the five pro-Bush justices did stop a manual recount that almost surely would have tallied the ballots that, ironically, the justices ruled needed to be included for a fair recount. In other words, the U.S. Supreme Court ruling *had* altered the results of the presidential election.

Beyond getting the story wrong, the major U.S. newspapers acted as if it were their duty to convince the American people that Bush really was elected legitimately. On November 12, 2001, within one or two hours of posting a story at *Consortiumnews.com* challenging the big media's version of the recount, Robert Parry received an irate phone call from *New York Times* media writer, Felicity Barringer.

In an interview, which was more like a cross-examination, Barringer argued that Parry's story had unfairly impugned the journalistic integrity of then-*Times* executive editor Howell Raines. Barringer seemed to have been on the lookout for any deviant point of view that questioned the "Bush Won" conventional wisdom.

♦♦♦

The imperative of protecting the nation's pro-Bush unity seemed to extend into the editorial offices of every leading U.S. news organization. It had become almost un-American to criticize the President, post-9/11. As the Taliban regime collapsed in Afghanistan, the news coverage of

Bush crossed into the hagiographic. Even seasoned newsmen wrapped Bush in the glow of a natural leader who was divinely inspired and may have been divinely selected.

On December 23, 2001, NBC's Washington bureau chief Tim Russert joined New York Mayor Rudy Giuliani, Cardinal Theodore McCarrick and First Lady Laura Bush in ruminating about whether God had selected Bush for the White House so the President would be there to handle the 9/11 crisis. Russert asked Mrs. Bush if "in an extraordinary way, this is why he was elected."

Mrs. Bush disagreed with Russert's suggestion that "God picks the President, which he doesn't." Giuliani thought otherwise. "I do think, Mrs. Bush, that there was some divine guidance in the President being elected. I do," the mayor said.

McCarrick also saw some larger purpose. "I think I don't thoroughly agree with the First Lady. I think that the President really, he was where he was when we needed him," the cardinal said.

Theologically speaking, it was less clear why God didn't simply let Bush be elected, rather than making him get a U.S. Supreme Court ruling to stop the vote count in Florida – or why God didn't give Bush the foresight to act on the CIA's warnings and thus thwart the 9/11 terrorist attacks.

It was fuzzy, too, why God would have let Bush so mishandle the opportunity to capture or kill Osama bin Laden in mid-December 2001 when the terrorist leader was hiding out in caves at Tora Bora, the remote mountain region near the Afghan-Pakistani border. Bush failed to dispatch U.S. troops to block bin Laden's escape routes.

Instead, Bush relied on assurances from Pakistani leader Pervez Musharraf that his soldiers would seal off the area. But the Pakistani troops were not deployed quickly enough, possibly because many Pakistani officers still sympathized with their old allies in the Taliban and al-Qaeda.

Recognizing the danger, the CIA warned that "the back door is open." Bin Laden and a small band of followers fled Tora Bora by horseback, evading capture.[10]

12

Bush's Grim Vision

The day after the 9/11 attacks on the World Trade Center and the Pentagon, George W. Bush had assured Americans that "we will rally the world" in building a coalition to punish those responsible. The world did rally. Virtually every government on earth expressed outrage. For its slaughter of so many civilians, al-Qaeda stood politically isolated – and broadly condemned – across the Islamic world.

Most of this pro-U.S. international support held firm through the war against al-Qaeda and its Taliban hosts in Afghanistan. But by early 2002, as Nat Parry reported from his vantage point in Europe, the consensus was beginning to crack. Many U.S. allies were distraught when it became clear that the Bush administration was veering back to its pre-9/11 strategy of go-it-alone unilateralism, reasserting a studied contempt for international agreements and ignoring world opinion.[1]

Many Europeans were troubled by Bush's belligerent State of the Union address in January 2002 designating Iran, Iraq and North Korea as an "axis of evil" – when the three countries had little in common and, in the case of Iran and Iraq, were bitter enemies.

Bush alienated other friends with military tactics in Afghanistan that inflicted heavy collateral damage. Hundreds and possibly thousands of Afghan civilians were killed when U.S. warplanes dropped cluster bombs, devastating "daisy cutters" and other highly lethal ordnance on suspected enemy targets. But the final straw for many allies was Bush's decision to waive the Geneva Conventions as they pertained to Taliban and al-Qaeda prisoners who were captured in Afghanistan and were flown to the U.S. military base at Guantanamo Bay, Cuba.

Bush's spokesmen argued that the captives were not soldiers in the normal sense but dangerous criminals, though evidence of individual guilt was not presented. The administration coined a new category for the detainees, "unlawful enemy combatants," a concept not recognized in any international treaty. The detainees allegedly had not followed the rules of war as enumerated in Article 4 of the Geneva Conventions, that is, they lacked responsible command and didn't carry their arms openly, wear uniforms with distinct insignia or conduct their operations within the laws and customs of war.

So, the administration maintained the Geneva Conventions did not apply to the detainees, and the United States had no obligation to follow standards for handling the prisoners as POWs. Still, the administration said it was treating the detainees "humanely." The White House said "many POW privileges" would be provided, including water, medical care, shelter, showers and soap.

But an international outcry over Guantanamo's Camp X-Ray erupted when the living conditions of the prisoners were revealed, and particularly after photographs were released showing the detainees in open-air cages, their eyes covered, subjected to what looked like sensory deprivation techniques. Human rights groups and European leaders – notably the German and Dutch governments, British parliamentarians and the European Union – objected to the treatment.

Some of the loudest criticism came from the staunchest U.S. ally, the United Kingdom, where three cabinet ministers – Robin Cook, Patricia Hewitt and Jack Straw – expressed concern that international agreements about the treatment of prisoners of war were being breached.

The U.N. High Commissioner for Human Rights, Mary Robinson, also objected to the handling of the detainees and called on the Bush administration to follow the Geneva Conventions. Robinson argued that because the Afghanistan conflict was of an international nature, "the law of international armed conflict applies." She took issue with the Bush administration's assertion that the prisoners were "unlawful combatants" and thus outside the protections of the Geneva Conventions.[2]

In an article about Camp X-Ray, *The Mirror* of London admonished Prime Minister Tony Blair to "stop this brutality in our name," saying "these prisoners are trapped in open cages, manacled hand and foot, brutalized, tortured and humiliated."

Amnesty International expressed concern about the tactics being used and the secrecy surrounding the camp. "Keeping prisoners *incommunicado*, sensory deprivation, the use of unnecessary restraint and the humiliation of people through tactics such as shaving them, are all classic techniques employed to 'break' the spirit of individuals ahead of interrogation," the human rights group said.

British human rights attorney Stephen Solley said the treatment of the suspects was "so far removed from human rights norms that it [was] difficult to comprehend." Human Rights Watch said, "If there is doubt about anyone's status as a prisoner of war, the Geneva Conventions require that he be treated as such until a competent tribunal determines otherwise. To our knowledge, no tribunals have made any such determinations."

The issue of prisoner of war status was central to the debate. If detainees were deemed POWs, they would be accorded certain rights by the Geneva Convention Relative to the Treatment of Prisoners of War, which the United States had ratified. Those rights include – in Article 25 – being housed in quarters comparable to those of the "Detaining Power's" soldiers, which was clearly not happening at Guantanamo.

Also, "prisoners of war may not be held in close confinement except where necessary to safeguard their health and then only during the continuation of the circumstances which make such confinement necessary," according to Article 21. Since the United States was keeping the prisoners in 6-by-8-foot cells, with heights of only 8 feet, this too would seem to violate the Convention. It was hard to imagine conditions more confining than Camp X-Ray's cages.

There were other important protections of prisoners of war enumerated in the Geneva Conventions, including the right of detainees suspected of crimes to be informed of their rights, the right to have access to counsel of their choice, the right to silence without that silence being used against them, and the right not to be interrogated in the absence of their counsel.

But the Bush administration made clear that it would operate according to its own rules. The living conditions would not fully conform to those of traditional POWs. The detainees also would not be granted access to legal counsel, the right to remain silent or protection against maltreatment during interrogation. Defense Secretary Donald Rumsfeld said the "unlawful combatant" label was needed to permit interrogation about future terrorist operations, an indication that coercive methods might be used.

Under Article 17 of the Geneva Conventions, "every prisoner of war, when questioned on the subject, is bound to give only his surname, first names and rank, date of birth, and army, regimental, personal or serial number, or failing this, equivalent information." If prisoners refuse to give that prescribed information, they may have privileges taken away. Under no circumstances, however, are prisoners to undergo "physical or mental torture, nor any other form of coercion" in order to extract information.

"Prisoners of war who refuse to answer may not be threatened, insulted, or exposed to any unpleasant or disadvantageous treatment of any kind," the rule said. The United States itself cited this provision most notably in accusing North Vietnam of abusing U.S. pilots shot down while bombing targets during the Vietnam War.

Human rights advocates quickly came to suspect that the unstated reason for the Bush administration's avoidance of the Geneva Conventions was for the purpose of applying unlawful means to extract information from the detainees. One early worry was that the unusual and confining conditions at Camp X-Ray were a device to break the prisoners down in violation of the letter and the spirit of the Geneva Conventions. These suspicions proved to be very close to the mark.

◆ ◆ ◆

Inside the Bush administration, a secret debate was raging between neoconservatives who had little patience for international law and traditionalists who warned against the United States deviating from accepted norms of behavior on the battlefield. Many of the neocons were theorists with little or no experience in actual combat, while many of the traditionalists were former soldiers who knew the risks of eliminating rules of warfare.

On January 9, 2002, Justice Department lawyers John Yoo and Robert Delahuny – representing the neocon viewpoint – wrote a memo arguing that President Bush and the U.S. military were not obligated to abide by prohibitions against torture or to grant any POW rights to members of the Taliban or al-Qaeda.

"Any customary international law of armed conflict in no way binds, as a legal matter, the President or the U.S. Armed Forces concerning the detention or trial of members of al-Qaeda and the Taliban," the memo said.[3]

On January 22, 2002, Assistant Attorney General Jay S. Bybee offered more ammunition for the neocon side in a 37-page memo, sent to the White House and Pentagon counsels. Bybee's memo argued that President Bush was not bound by the Geneva Conventions or the War Crimes Act of 1984 because Afghanistan had been a "failed state."

On January 25, White House counsel Alberto Gonzales weighed in, advising Bush in another memo that it was up to him whether Geneva Convention rules on the treatment of POWs applied or not. Gonzales agreed with the Justice Department memo that the convention did not apply because the Taliban had a "militant, terrorist-like" nature.[4]

On January 26, Secretary of State Colin Powell, representing the traditionalists, entered the fray, albeit gingerly. He urged Bush to apply the Geneva Conventions. By upholding these rules of war, Bush would provide "the strongest legal foundation" for future military action, protect the "credibility and moral authority" of the United States, and shield U.S. soldiers and officials from possible criminal prosecutions, Powell wrote.[5]

On February 1, Attorney General John Ashcroft took a middle position, advising the President that the Geneva Conventions did not apply to al-Qaeda and the Taliban but still warning that U.S. officials might be subject to prosecution if, it turned out, U.S. and international laws did apply.[6]

On February 7, Bush tried to split the difference himself. He sent a memo to his national security advisers saying he accepted the Justice Department's position that the Geneva Conventions didn't apply to the Taliban and al-Qaeda. He added that he had "the authority under the Constitution" to decide that the Geneva Conventions did not apply, but he stopped short of exercising that authority. The same day, Assistant Attorney General Bybee declared that Bush "has reasonable factual grounds" for his decision.[7]

The broad outlines of Bush's decision were revealed to the public by his White House spokesman on February 7, but the announcement gave little sense of the behind-the-scenes legal drama or the constitutional significance.

"President Bush affirms our enduring commitment to the important principles of the Geneva Convention," White House spokesman Ari Fleischer said. "The United States will continue to treat all Taliban and al-Qaeda detainees in Guantanamo Bay humanely and consistent with the principles of the Geneva Convention. ... The Geneva Convention will apply to the Taliban detainees, but not the al-Qaeda international terrorists."

However, the Bush administration applied such a narrow interpretation of the Geneva Conventions that the concession seemed mostly rhetorical. Fleischer said Bush would decide on his own who was entitled to POW status, despite the Geneva Convention's provision that this decision can only be made by a "competent tribunal." At Guantanamo, regarding the treatment of the detainees, nothing of substance had changed.

The world community wasn't satisfied. On February 8, the International Committee of the Red Cross designated both the Taliban and al-Qaeda fighters prisoners of war fully protected by the Geneva Conventions. "They were captured in combat [and] we consider them prisoners of war," ICRC spokesperson Darcy Christen said. The ICRC and the U.N. High Commissioner on Human Rights also reiterated their position that any dispute over the status of a prisoner must be settled by a tribunal and not by one side of the conflict.

"This is international law *à la carte*, like multilateralism *à la carte*," one West European ambassador told the *International Herald Tribune*. "It annoys your allies in the war against terrorism, and it creates problems for our Muslim allies, too. It puts at stake the moral credibility of the war against terrorism."

This view held that Washington was asserting an American exceptionalism in which the United States could cite inviolable international legal principles when it wanted, such as after Iraq invaded Kuwait in 1990. But Washington could ignore the same rules when they proved inconvenient to U.S. interests. That selectivity came with a price, however. It eroded the world's respect for universal legal standards while spreading a cynicism that the only truly unalterable principle was that might makes right.

Iraqi dictator Saddam Hussein, widely condemned by the West for his human rights record, picked up on this theme of U.S. exceptionalism, as he criticized Washington for not adhering to its own strictures. "They used human rights and the rights of prisoners for propaganda purposes against other countries," Hussein said. "But when their turn came to uphold those rights, they openly violated them."

Besides undermining international law, the Guatanamo example reinforced the impression that Bush disdained multilateral agreements and would accept no constraints on his freedom of action. But there was another troubling signal that Camp X-Ray was sending, though in early 2002, few in the United States dared recognize what that message was. Bush seemed to be asserting his personal right to do whatever he wanted regardless of the law.

◆◆◆

In the United States – with Bush's popularity soaring – few national political leaders had the courage to question the wisdom of Bush's determination to go it alone or to rely excessively on military force. One exception was Bush's former rival, Al Gore, who cautioned against an overly simplistic approach to combating terrorism in ways that ignored the underlying causes.

"There is another axis of evil in the world: poverty and ignorance; disease and environmental disorder; corruption and political oppression," Gore said in a February 12 speech to the Council on Foreign Relations. "We may well put down terror in its present manifestations. But if we do not attend to the larger fundamentals as well, then the ground is fertile and has been seeded for the next generation of those born to hate us, who will hold these things up before the world's poor and dispossessed, and say that all these things are in our image, and rekindle the war we are now hoping to snuff out."

The former Vice President noted the difference between the Clinton-Gore attitude toward the world and the Bush-Cheney view.

"The administration in which I served looked at the challenges we faced in the world and said we wished to tackle these 'With others, if possible; alone, if we must.' This administration seems inclined to stand that on its head, so that the message is: 'With others, if we must; by ourselves, if possible,'" Gore said.

The prevailing view in Washington, however, was that Bush had attained an almost a mystical ability to make the correct decisions. Not only didn't the United States need the help of squabbling foreign leaders, but Bush didn't need the cautious advice of Democrats or, for that matter, his father's old guard.

As post-9/11 accolades continued to rain down on the President and his poll numbers stayed up, Bush increasingly bought into this view of his infallibility, proudly referring to himself a "gut player" who relied on his "instincts." According to author Bob Woodward, in *Bush at War*, "it's pretty clear that Bush's role as politician, President and Commander in Chief is driven by a secular faith in his instincts – his natural and spontaneous conclusions and judgments. His instincts are almost his second religion."[8]

But, as Sam Parry reported at *Consortiumnews.com* in March 2002, the swagger wasn't playing nearly as well with one crucial audience: the world's one billion Muslims, one-sixth of the human population. He wrote, "George W. Bush's depiction of the war on terrorism as an absolutist struggle of good versus evil is failing to win much popular support in the Islamic world, a warning sign that Bush's dispatch of more U.S. forces around the globe to fight 'evil-doers' could lead to a dangerous backlash."[9]

A Gallup poll of 9,924 residents from nine Islamic nations showed a two-to-one unfavorable opinion of the United States, five-to-one opposition to Bush and a 77 percent disapproval of the U.S. military actions in Afghanistan. The poll's findings matched extensive anecdotal evidence that Washington was losing the battle for the "hearts and minds" of the Islamic world.

The Gallup poll found strong anti-American sentiment among U.S. allies and adversaries alike. The countries surveyed included Indonesia, Iran, Jordan, Kuwait, Lebanon, Morocco, Pakistan, Saudi Arabia and Turkey. The lowest scores came from Pakistan, a principal U.S. ally in the Afghan war and a nuclear power. In Pakistan, only five percent of the respondents had a favorable opinion of the United States.

Gallup editor-in-chief Frank Newport said Muslims who were polled described the United States as "ruthless, aggressive, conceited, arrogant, easily provoked, biased." Newport added that "the people of Islamic countries have significant grievances with the West in general and with the United States in particular."

Some Arab experts said the Gallup poll revealed a dangerous chasm of distrust opening between the United States and the Islamic world. James Zogby, president of the Arab American Institute in Washington, told *ABCnews.com*, "The numbers overall as a whole are no doubt disturbing, but raise a clarion call: We have a problem; we don't understand each other."

The Gallup results suggested that a more treacherous path lay ahead for the "war on terror," with the possibility that short-term U.S. military successes might not solve the long-term problem. Force could swell the ranks of extremists willing to die for their cause.

"Military operations abroad and new security measures at home do nothing to address the virulent anti-Americanism of government-supported media, mullahs, and *madrassas* (Islamic schools)," wrote David Hoffman in the March/April issue of *Foreign Affairs*. "As the Israelis have discovered, terrorism thrives on a cruel paradox: The more force is used to retaliate, the more fuel is added to the terrorists' cause."[10]

Responding to the Gallup poll, Bush said the U.S. "must do a better job of telling the compassionate side of the American story."[11]

Earlier, Bush had tried to answer the question of "why do they hate us?" by asserting that the terrorists despised the United States because of its freedoms. Bush postulated that the motive for the 9/11 attacks was that Osama bin Laden and other Islamic extremists were trying to destroy the American Way.

"They hate what we see right here in this chamber – a democratically elected government," Bush said in a September 20, 2001, address to Congress. "They hate our freedoms – our freedom of religion, our freedom of speech, our freedom to vote and assemble and disagree with each other."[12]

Though that explanation played well domestically, it fell flat with many Middle East experts who recognized that bin Laden's goals were focused much more on Middle East politics and had little to do with American freedoms. Bin Laden's principal grievance was with the U.S. presence and influence in the Middle East, especially in his native land, Saudi Arabia. Another complaint was the Israeli-Palestinian conflict.

On these issues, bin Laden was far from alone. Muslims around the world have long protested U.S.-Middle East policies, including Washington's protection of undemocratic governments in Saudi Arabia, Kuwait and other oil-rich countries. The U.S. State Department's 2001 Human Rights Report acknowledged that the Saudi government's human rights record was "poor," adding that "citizens have neither the right nor the legal means to change their government. Security forces continued to abuse detainees and prisoners, arbitrarily arrest and detain persons, and hold them in *incommunicado* detention. In addition there were allegations that security forces committed torture."

Bush's anti-terror strategy also gave short shrift to an important precept of counterinsurgency warfare – that military action must address legitimate concerns of a population. Otherwise, military action can drive more recruits into the arms of the enemy and lead to an endless cycle of violence. The U.S. "hearts and minds" component required more than just pretty words dressed up by "public diplomacy" specialists, especially when the propaganda flew in the face of widespread public perceptions.

It was not enough, for instance, to tell the Islamic world that Bush did not consider the conflict a war against Islam. This rhetoric rang hollow to many Muslims who saw with their own eyes what they interpreted as a war against Islam – from the roundup of Arab men in the United States after 9/11 to locking Afghan war captives in cages at Guantanamo Bay, from U.S. bombing in Afghanistan that killed large numbers of civilians to Bush's support of Israeli Prime Minister Ariel Sharon's bloody crackdown on the Palestinians.

◆ ◆ ◆

Still, these warning flags didn't slow Bush's expansion of his "war on terror." Amid his favorable domestic poll ratings – still in the 70 and 80 percentiles – Bush acted like a man on a roll, deciding that now was the time to take on both stateless terrorists and a number of troublesome regimes. Widening the war beyond the initial goal of punishing the perpetrators of the 9/11 attacks, Bush sent U.S. troops into a variety of new countries, which had their own murky political and ethnic conflicts.

Bush's criteria for taking on "every terrorist group of global reach" – the justification for the expanded conflict – seemed to cover any irregular fighting force whose members might be able to pool their resources to buy an airplane ticket to the U.S., whether they were holed up on an island in the Philippines, in the mountains of Central Asia, in a desert in the Middle East or in the jungles of Colombia.

About 600 U.S. troops were sent to the Philippines to help prosecute a war against Muslim rebels. The administration was eager, too, to intervene against leftist rebels in Colombia. The Bush administration also planned to place several hundred more U.S. troops in Yemen, possibly Indonesia and the former Soviet republic of Georgia.

In the case of Georgia, the Bush administration justified the intervention as a strike against alleged al-Qaeda fighters who supposedly blended among Chechen rebels hiding out in Georgia's remote Pankisi Gorge in the Caucasus Mountains. Thousands of Chechens fled to the rugged terrain after Russia launched a brutal counterinsurgency war in the neighboring Russian province of Chechnya where Islamic rebels were fighting for independence from Moscow.

The Bush administration wanted U.S. troops to assist Georgian soldiers in hunting down and killing al-Qaeda fighters holed up among the Chechens in Pankisi Gorge. Yet, complicating matters was the fact that other rebels in Abkhazia and South Ossetia wanted to break away from Georgia, which was accused of engaging in ethnic cleansing in Abkhazia. Plus, the Chechen civil war had been the scene of widespread human rights abuses by both the Russians and the Chechens. So who were the good guys and who were the "evil-doers"?

Skewing the moral equation even more was the fact that the oil men around Bush wanted to pacify the region surrounding the oil-rich Caspian Sea basin so pipelines could be laid to extract an estimated $5 trillion in oil and natural gas to the West. One possible route for a pipeline was to go through Georgia, bypassing Russian territory.

Beyond the moral ambiguities, there were practical questions about Bush's "crusade." When would it end? Could it ever end?

"It will not end until every terrorist group of global reach has been found, stopped and defeated," Bush pledged in his speech nine days after 9/11. Then his "axis of evil" warning in the 2002 State of the Union address upped the ante to include possible action against Iraq, Iran and North Korea.

World leaders cautioned Washington. "You can't deal with the dark side of globalization – the terrorism, the financing of terrorism, the crime, the drugs, the trafficking of human beings, the relationship between environmental degradation and poverty and security," said Chris Patten, the European Union's external affairs commissioner, "unless you deal with them as a result of multilateral engagement."

World Bank President James Wolfensohn argued that to combat terrorism, global poverty and other international problems must be addressed. "We will not create a safer world with bombs or brigades alone," Wolfensohn said. Poverty "can provide a breeding ground for the ideas and actions of those who promote conflict and terror."[13]

But Bush seemed to read his initial success in Afghanistan and his domestic polls as *carte blanche* to spread the war wherever he chose, without significant debate in the United States or consultation with U.S. allies. Bush also ignored a difficult truth – that the plague of terrorism may be like a chronic illness that can be managed but not eradicated, that the best that can be done is to reduce terrorism through an intelligent mix of political and military strategies, attention to both security issues and root causes. A big part of waging the "war on terror" needed to be the amelioration of the despair and anger that otherwise turn young men and women into suicide bombers.

The poll results of the Muslim population reinforced that warning. By relying too heavily on military force and by going too far without international support, the administration risked starting new cycles of killing – creating a global version of the intractable Israeli-Palestinian conflict and ending up making the world an even more dangerous place.

Ironically, too, as Bush's broadened his vision toward a worldwide war against all forms of Islamic extremism, he lost sight of Osama bin Laden. At a March 13, 2002, press conference, a sullen Bush told reporters, "So I don't know where he is. You know, I just don't spend that much time on him ... to be honest with you."

◆◆◆

By the start of summer 2002, the shape of Bush's grim vision for the world's future was emerging vaguely and ominously as if from a deep fog. On June 21, 2002, Nat Parry compiled an early account of this troubling image for *Consortiumnews.com*. He wrote:

"In the nine months since September 11, George W. Bush has put the United States on a course that is so bleak that few analysts have – as the saying goes – connected the dots. If they had they would see an outline of a future that mixes constant war overseas with abridgement of constitutional freedoms at home, a picture drawn by a politician who once joked, 'If this were a dictatorship it would be a heck of a lot easier – so long as I'm the dictator.'

"The dots are certainly there. Bush's speech at West Point on June 1 asserted a unilateral U.S. right to overthrow any government in the world that is deemed a threat to American security, a position so sweeping that it lacks historical precedent. 'If we wait for threats to fully materialize, we will have waited too long,' Bush said in describing what he calls a 'new doctrine' and what some acolytes have dubbed the 'Bush Doctrine.'

"In a domestic corollary to this Bush Doctrine, Bush is asserting his personal authority to strip even U.S. citizens of due-process rights if he judges them 'enemy combatants.' With Vice President Dick Cheney and Attorney General John Ashcroft warning critics not to question Bush's policy, it's not too big a jump to see a future where there will be spying on dissenters and limits on public debate, especially now that Ashcroft has lifted restrictions on FBI surveillance activities. That possibility would grow if the Republicans succeed in regaining control of the Senate and place more of Bush's conservative political allies in the federal courts.

"Bush's grim vision is of a modern 'crusade,' as he once put it, with American military forces striking preemptively at 'evil-doers' wherever they live, while U.S. citizens live under a redefined Constitution with rights that can be suspended selectively by one man. Beyond the enormous sacrifices of blood, money and freedom that this plan entails, there is another problem: the strategy offers no guarantee of greater security for Americans and runs the risk of deepening the pool of hatred against the United States.

"With his cavalier tough talk, Bush continues to show no sign that he grasps how treacherous his course is, nor how much more difficult it will be if the U.S. alienates large segments of the world's population. One of the most stunning results of Bush's behavior over the past nine months has been the dissipation of the vast reservoir of goodwill that sprang up toward the United States in the days after September 11."[14]

Part of Bush's strategy was the silencing of dissent, both domestically and internationally. He especially went on the offensive against United Nations officials who had challenged his judgments – and they soon found themselves out of their jobs.

U.N. High Commissioner for Human Rights Mary C. Robinson was the first to experience this treatment. The former Irish president's efforts had won acclaim from human rights groups around the world. But her fierce independence, which surfaced in her criticism of Israel and Bush's "war on terror," rubbed Washington the wrong way. The Bush administration lobbied hard against her reappointment. Officially, she agreed to retire on her own accord.[15]

The Bush administration also forced out Robert Watson, the chairman of the U.N.-sponsored Intergovernmental Panel on Climate Change [IPCC]. Under his leadership, the panel had reached a consensus that human activities, such as burning fossil fuels, contributed to global warming Bush resisted this science, which also was opposed by oil companies such as ExxonMobil. The oil giant sent a memo to the White House asking the administration, "Can Watson be replaced now at the request of the U.S.?"[16]

The ExxonMobil memo, obtained by the Natural Resources Defense Council through the Freedom of Information Act, urged the White House to "restructure U.S. attendance at the IPCC meetings to assure no Clinton/Gore proponents are involved in decisional activities." On April

19, 2002, ExxonMobil got its wish. The administration succeeded in replacing Watson with Rajendra Pachauri, an Indian economist.

Commenting on his removal, Watson said, "U.S. support was, of course, an important factor. They [the IPCC] came under a lot of pressure from ExxonMobil who asked the White House to try and remove me."[17]

The next to go, on April 22, was Jose Mauricio Bustani, the head of the Organization for the Prohibition of Chemical Weapons [OPCW]. Bustani ran into trouble when he resisted Bush administration efforts to dictate the nationalities of inspectors assigned to investigate U.S. chemical facilities. Bustani also opposed a U.S. law allowing Bush to block unannounced inspections in the United States. Bustani came under criticism for "bias" because his organization had sought to inspect American chemical facilities as aggressively as it examined facilities of U.S.-designated "rogue states."[18]

The final straw for Bush apparently was Bustani's efforts to persuade Iraq to join the Chemical Weapons Convention, which would have allowed the OPCW to inspect Iraqi facilities. The Bush administration denounced this move as an "ill-considered initiative" and pushed to have Bustani deposed, threatening to withhold dues to the OPCW if Bustani remained.

Critics said Washington feared that Bush would be stripped of a principal rationale for invading Iraq and ousting Saddam Hussein if the Iraqi dictator agreed to join the international body designed to inspect chemical-weapons facilities, including those in Iraq. A senior U.S. official dismissed that interpretation of Bush's motive as "an atrocious red herring."

Accusing Bustani of mismanagement, U.S. officials called an unprecedented special session to vote Bustani out, only a year after he was unanimously reelected to another five-year term. The member states sacrificed Bustani to save the organization from the loss of U.S. funds.[19]

"By dismissing me," Bustani told the U.N. body, "an international precedent will have been established whereby any duly elected head of any international organization would at any point during his or her tenure remain vulnerable to the whims of one or a few major contributors." Bustani said that if the United States succeeded in removing him, "genuine multilateralism" would succumb to "unilateralism in a multilateral disguise."[20]

The Bush administration also took steps to insulate U.S. officials and soldiers from possible future prosecution by the International Criminal Court that was ratified on April 11, 2002, with the power to try people accused of genocide, crimes against humanity and war crimes. Amnesty International called the court "a historic development in the fight for justice." Human Rights Watch hailed it as "the most important new institution for enforcing human rights in 50 years."

But Bush reacted hostilely to the court's ratification, reiterating his opposition and repudiating President Clinton's decision to sign the accord. "The United States has no legal obligations arising from its signature on December 31, 2000," the Bush administration said in a May 6, 2002, letter to U.N. Secretary General Kofi Annan. "The United States requests that its intention not to become a party ... be reflected in the depositary's status lists relating to this treaty."[21]

While the "unsigning" was a remarkable snub at the world's diplomats and at principles of civilized behavior that the United States had long championed, it did not itself stop the court's creation. Still, the letter signaled Bush's intent to undermine the court at every turn. With administration support, the Republican-controlled Congress passed a bill that would allow U.S. armed forces to invade the Hague, Netherlands, where the court would be located, to rescue U.S. soldiers if they were ever prosecuted for war crimes.[22]

◆◆◆

Along with his rejection of international law, Bush quietly established a domestic corollary, that he could limit freedoms within the United States. The expansion of his police powers began immediately after 9/11 when Middle Easterners living in the U.S. were swept off the streets and jailed as "material witnesses" or for minor visa violations. The total number and the identities of those arrested were kept secret, though it was estimated that the number exceeded 1,100 people, mostly Middle Eastern-born men caught up in the dragnet. Yet, only one detainee was charged with a crime connected to 9/11, Zacarias Moussaoui, who was already in custody before the attacks.[23]

Next came the hundreds of combatants captured in Afghanistan and put in cages at the U.S. military base at Guantanamo Bay. Bush refused to grant the detainees protections under the Geneva Conventions and said they could be tried by a military tribunal established by his fiat. Initially, many Americans reconciled themselves to these detentions, believing they only affected foreigners and were a reaction to a short-term emergency. But that comfort level shrank when Jose Padilla, a 31-year-old U.S.-born citizen who had converted to Islam, was arrested on May 8, 2002, in Chicago.

Ashcroft announced the arrest at a dramatic news conference in Moscow more than a month later, on June 10. Ashcroft depicted Padilla's capture as a major victory in the "war on terror." Administration officials said Padilla had met with al-Qaeda operatives abroad and was in the early stages of a plot to develop a radiological "dirty bomb" that would be detonated in a U.S. city.

But Deputy Defense Secretary Paul Wolfowitz said later that the bomb plot amounted only to "some fairly loose talk."[24] Nothing concrete had occurred. Padilla had no bomb-making materials, no target, no operational co-conspirators, no plan. Beyond assertions, the administration offered no evidence of Padilla's guilt.

Bush described Padilla as an "enemy combatant" and ordered him detained indefinitely at a military prison in South Carolina. No trial, not even one before the military tribunal, was to be held. Attempting to justify this extra-constitutional detention, Bush explained that Padilla was a "bad guy" and "he is where he needs to be, detained." The Bush administration said Padilla would be jailed for as long as the "war on terror" continued, potentially a life sentence given the vague goals and indefinite timetable of the conflict.[25]

Even though the Clinton administration had succeeded in winning convictions against both Islamic and domestic terrorists in open court, Bush was demonstrating his Clint-Eastwood-style impatience with such legal niceties. Though many Americans felt little sympathy for Padilla, a street tough who allegedly consorted with al-Qaeda terrorists, the principle behind the case was clear: Bush was arrogating to himself the unilateral right to judge whether an American citizen was part of a terrorist cabal and should be stripped of all constitutional rights.

Under this precedent, a U.S. citizen could be denied his right to an attorney, his right to a speedy trial before a jury of peers, his right to confront accusers, his right against self-incrimination, even his right to have the charges against him spelled out and conceivably his protection against "cruel and unusual punishment." Simply on Bush's say-so, an allegation of conspiracy could become grounds for unlimited imprisonment, even without an overt act and without public evidence.

It no longer seemed so farfetched to think that George W. Bush would someday expand his extraordinary powers to silence those who asked difficult questions or criticized his judgment or otherwise gave "aid and comfort to the enemy." Within the administration, there was even anger about congressional fact-finding.

When some Democrats demanded to know what Bush knew about the terror threats before 9/11, Vice President Cheney delivered a blunt warning. "My Democratic friends in Congress," Cheney said, "they need to be very cautious not to seek political advantage by making incendiary suggestions, as were made by some today, that the White House had advance information that would have prevented the tragic attacks of 9/11."[26]

There was suddenly looming ahead the grotesque shape of a different kind of America, where people could disappear without public legal proceedings and possibly no legal proceedings at all, where senior government officials could casually issue warnings against anyone who dared to criticize or question the nation's leader, where all the terrifying force of American power was invested in the hands of one man.

In the nine months since 9/11, Bush had marched off in a political direction so troubling that American editorial writers didn't dare notice where he was heading. The President was moving toward a system in which the leader could decide what freedoms his people would be granted at home and what countries would be invaded abroad. Carried to its ultimate conclusion, Bush's grim vision was of an America without constitutional safeguards and with only a constrained politics of timid debate.

13

Rise of the Bush Doctrine

By mid-2002, a new conventional wisdom was taking hold in the newsrooms of Washington and New York – that Bush's lack of experience and knowledge might actually be an asset in handling the extraordinary challenges that America faced, that Bush's strong suits of decisiveness and instinct might fit the post-9/11 world perfectly.

Relying on his "moral clarity" and "gut," Bush had proved himself in his first test of war in Afghanistan, according to this thinking. Perhaps – despite the jokes about his limited intellect and his incurious personality – he really was the right man at the right time with the right stuff.

But toppling the Taliban and chasing out al-Qaeda was only to be the first step in the "global war on terror." Bush and his neoconservative advisers already were dreaming bigger dreams. Behind the scenes at the White House and at the Pentagon – not to mention inside Washington think tanks and among influential pundits – attention had locked on to what many considered a more important test and a more challenging target: Iraq and the troublesome Saddam Hussein.

In the thinking of Bush and his neoconservative advisers, the Taliban and al-Qaeda were only the *hors d'oeuvres*. The *entrees* would start with Iraq before moving on to Syria and Iran, with Lebanon's Hezbollah and the Palestinian Hamas as the dessert courses. At the banquet's end, if Bush and his foreign policy team had their way, their enemies in the Middle East would all be devoured or left begging for mercy.

But Iraq and Hussein had a special spot on the Bush family's menu. The Iraqi dictator had been their obsession for more than a decade. Hussein was the Arab leader whose existence itself amounted to an insult to American supremacy. Yet, during his four-plus decades on the Iraqi political scene, Hussein was not always a U.S. enemy. At times, he had played the role of a thuggish but useful U.S. asset.

Hussein's connection – and his debt – to American intelligence dated back to 1959 when he allegedly had CIA backing in an assassination attempt on Iraq's leader, Gen. Abdel Karim Qassim. After the plot failed,

Hussein fled Iraq and reportedly hid out in the early 1960s under the CIA's protection and sponsorship.[1]

By early 1963, Qassim had alienated Washington even more. He had pulled Iraq out of the pro-Western Baghdad Pact, was reaching out to Moscow, and had revoked oil exploration rights previously granted to a consortium of companies that included American oil interests. In February 1963, legendary CIA officer James Critchfield supported a *coup d'etat* spearheaded by Iraq's Baathist party. Qassim was killed along with scores of suspected communists who had been identified by the CIA.[2]

Five years later, Saddam Hussein emerged as a leader in another Baathist coup and, from there, elbowed and shoved his way to the top of the heap. After snagging the top job, however, Hussein confronted a formidable task. Iraq was a nearly ungovernable country whose borders had been capriciously set by the British after World War I, incorporating lands dominated by three rival sects: the Sunnis, the Shiites and the Kurds. Hussein soon gained a reputation as a ruthless leader who built up his own minority Sunni sect as Iraq's ruling class lording over the majority Shiites, who represented the bulk of Iraq's working class, and the Kurds, who were concentrated in the country's north.

Though Hussein's heavy-handed tactics drew criticism from human rights advocates, his iron fist ensured that Iraqi oil kept flowing to the world's economy. His formidable Soviet-supplied army also provided a useful shield to protect against the radical Shiite-led revolution that swept Iran in 1979, ousting the U.S.-backed Shah of Iran and sending shock waves through the ornate palaces of Saudi Arabia and the oil-rich Persian Gulf. Hussein suddenly found himself, if not popular with his Arab neighbors, at least useful. Serving as a bulwark against Iran's revolutionary zeal, Hussein went to war with Iran in September 1980.

◆ ◆ ◆

More than two decades later, it was still not clear to what degree Presidents Jimmy Carter, Ronald Reagan and George H.W. Bush joined with the Saudis and other pro-U.S. Arab leaders in encouraging and supporting Hussein's war machine. But substantial evidence has emerged that all three Presidents saw Hussein's secular regime as a valuable counterweight to Iranian-style Islamic extremism.

In 1980, as President Carter was running for re-election, Iran's radical Islamic government held 52 Americans hostage in Tehran. Ayatollah Ruhollah Khomeini's ascetic brand of Islam also was posing a strategic threat to the corrupt Persian Gulf's oil sheikhs who were famous for their extravagant playboy lifestyles. It was not an idle concern. Iran soon showed off its expansionist tendencies by putting pressure on Iraq through border clashes and by encouraging Iraq's Shiite and Kurdish populations to rise up. Iranian operatives also sought to destabilize Saddam's government by assassinating Iraqi leaders.[3]

On August 5, 1980, as tensions mounted on the Iran-Iraq border, Saudi rulers welcomed Saddam Hussein to Riyadh for the first state visit ever by an Iraqi president to Saudi Arabia. During meetings at the kingdom's palaces, the Saudis feted Hussein and urged him to take the fight to Iran's fundamentalist regime, advice that they said included a "green light" for the invasion from President Jimmy Carter.

Less than two months later, with Carter still frustrated by his inability to win release of the 52 Americans, Hussein's army invaded Iran on September 22, 1980. The war would rage for eight years and kill an estimated one million people. But did Carter really signal a "green light"? The claim was made by senior Arab leaders, including King Fahd of Saudi Arabia, to President Reagan's first Secretary of State, Alexander Haig, when Haig visited the Middle East in April 1981, according to "top secret" talking points that Haig used for a post-trip briefing of Reagan.

In the "talking points," Haig wrote that he was impressed with "bits of useful intelligence" that he had learned. "Both [Egypt's Anwar] Sadat and [Saudi then-Prince] Fahd [explained that] Iran is receiving military spares for U.S. equipment from Israel," Haig noted. "It was also interesting to confirm that President Carter gave the Iraqis a green light to launch the war against Iran through Fahd."[4]

Haig's "talking points" were first disclosed at *Consortiumnews.com* in 1995 after Robert Parry discovered the document amid records from a congressional investigation into the early history of the Reagan administration's contacts with Iran. Haig refused to answer questions about the "talking points," noting they were still classified. While not responding to direct questions about Haig's "talking points," Carter has pooh-poohed other claims that he encouraged Saddam to invade.[5]

During the Iran-Iraq war, as first one side and then the other gained the upper hand, the Reagan administration was officially neutral but behind the scenes tilted from one side to the other. When Iran appeared to be winning in 1982, Reagan and his advisers decided to secretly help Iraq's military, permitting shipments of dual-use technology that Iraq then used to build chemical and biological weapons, according to documents and witnesses. Tactical military assistance also was provided, including satellite photos of battlefields.

This covert support later took on the scandal name "Iraqgate." Over the years, congressional inquiries and press accounts have sketched out some of the Iraqgate facts. In September 2002, for example, *Newsweek* reported that the Reagan administration in the 1980s had allowed sales to Iraq of computer databases that Saddam Hussein could use to track political opponents and shipments of "bacteria/fungi/protozoa" that could help produce anthrax and other biological weapons.[6]

Senator Robert C. Byrd, a West Virginia Democrat, asked Defense Secretary Donald Rumsfeld about the *Newsweek* story at a Senate hearing on September 19, 2002. "Did the United States help Iraq to acquire the building blocks of biological weapons during the Iran-Iraq war?" Byrd inquired. "Are we, in fact, now facing the possibility of reaping what we have sown?"

"Certainly not to my knowledge," Rumsfeld responded. "I have no knowledge of United States companies or government being involved in assisting Iraq develop chemical, biological or nuclear weapons."

So, even the U.S. Secretary of Defense – who served the Reagan administration as a special envoy to the Middle East in 1983-84 and personally met with Saddam Hussein – claimed not to know about this secret history.

Beyond the "dual-use" supplies during the war, other unanswered Iraqgate questions related to whether then-Vice President George H.W. Bush urged Hussein to use greater ferocity in waging his war with Iran, advice that led the Iraqi air force to bomb civilian centers in Tehran and other Iranian cities in 1986.

A 1992 article by Murray Waas and Craig Unger in *The New Yorker* described the senior George Bush passing on advice to Hussein, through Arab intermediaries, for this more aggressive bombing campaign. Waas and Unger described the U.S. motive as a kind of diplomatic billiard shot. By getting Iraq to expand use of its air force, the Iranians would be more desperate for U.S.-made HAWK anti-aircraft missile parts, giving Washington more leverage with the Iranians.

Iran's need to protect its cities from Iraqi air attacks gave impetus to the Reagan administration's arms-for-hostage scheme, which involved selling U.S. missile parts to Iran with some profits going to the Nicaraguan contra rebels, a transaction that became known as the Iran-Contra Affair. Yet the historical issue of Bush's role was never officially settled. The senior Bush evaded any serious questioning on the topic, though it was known that Hussein did intensify his air campaign in 1986 after Bush's trip.[7]

That era's history of U.S. involvement with Iran and Iraq remained incomplete, in part, because the administrations of Bill Clinton and George W. Bush helped cover up the full story. Some Democratic sources said Clinton agreed to shelve the investigations into secret dealings with Iran and Iraq out of concern for national security and national unity.

Others suggested that Clinton was tricked by the wily elder Bush with promises that dropping the investigations might win Clinton some support for his domestic agenda from Republicans in Congress in 1993, a tantalizing prospect that never materialized.

Whatever the reasons, Clinton's Justice Department did bail out the Reagan-Bush team on Iraqgate. Clinton's lawyers issued a report in early 1995 declaring that the department "did not find evidence that U.S. agencies or officials illegally armed Iraq." But the review noted, curiously, that the CIA had withheld an unknown number of relevant documents that were contained in "sensitive compartments." Despite that denial of access, the Clinton investigators expressed confidence in their conclusions about Reagan-Bush innocence.

The Clinton administration then pressed ahead with a criminal arms-trafficking case against Teledyne Industries and a salesman named Ed Johnson. They had allegedly sold explosive pellets to Chilean arms manufacturer Carlos Cardoen, who used them illegally to manufacture cluster bombs for Iraq in the 1980s.

But, just two weeks after the Justice Department issued its report exonerating Reagan and Bush on Iraqgate, defense lawyers in the Teledyne case submitted an affidavit from Howard Teicher, who had served on Reagan's National Security Council staff. In this first sworn public account by a Reagan insider about the covert U.S.-Iraq relationship, Teicher traced the U.S. tilt to Iraq to a point in the war in 1982 when Iran had gained the offensive and fears swept the U.S. government that Iran's army might slice through Iraq to the oil fields of Kuwait and Saudi Arabia.

"In June 1982, President Reagan decided that the United States could not afford to allow Iraq to lose the war to Iran," Teicher wrote. Teicher said he helped draft a secret national security decision directive that Reagan signed to authorize covert U.S. assistance to Saddam Hussein's military. "The NSDD, including even its identifying number, is classified," Teicher wrote in 1995.

The effort to arm the Iraqis was "spearheaded" by CIA Director William Casey and involved his deputy, Robert Gates, according to Teicher's affidavit. "The CIA, including both CIA Director Casey and Deputy Director Gates, knew of, approved of, and assisted in the sale of non-U.S. origin military weapons, ammunition and vehicles to Iraq," Teicher wrote.

In 1984, Teicher said he also went to Iraq with Rumsfeld to convey a secret Israeli offer to assist Iraq after Israel had concluded that Iran was becoming a greater danger. "I traveled with Rumsfeld to Baghdad and was present at the meeting in which Rumsfeld told Iraqi Foreign Minister

Tariq Aziz about Israel's offer of assistance," Teicher wrote. "Aziz refused even to accept the Israelis' letter to Hussein offering assistance because Aziz told us that he would be executed on the spot by Hussein if he did so."

Another key player in Reagan's Iraq tilt was then-Vice President George H.W. Bush, according to Teicher's affidavit. "In 1986, President Reagan sent a secret message to Saddam Hussein telling him that Iraq should step up its air war and bombing of Iran," Teicher wrote. "This message was delivered by Vice President Bush who communicated it to Egyptian President [Hosni] Mubarak, who in turn passed the message to Saddam Hussein.

"Similar strategic operational military advice was passed to Saddam Hussein through various meetings with European and Middle Eastern heads of state. I authored Bush's talking points for the 1986 meeting with Mubarak and personally attended numerous meetings with European and Middle East heads of state where the strategic operational advice was communicated."

Teicher's affidavit represented a major break in the historical mystery of U.S. military aid to Iraq. But it complicated prosecution of the Teledyne case and made Clinton's Justice Department look foolish. So, the prosecutors took their fury out on Teicher, insisting that his affidavit was unreliable. But, paradoxically, they classified it as a state secret and placed it under court seal. They also threatened Teicher with possible prosecution for his disclosures.

Before the affidavit could be locked down, however, copies reached some journalists, including Robert Parry. Still, the remarkable document got little coverage from a national news media that was by then obsessed with "Clinton scandals." Since 1995, Teicher has refused to discuss his affidavit. With Republicans controlling Congress during nearly all the next 11 years, Teicher also was never offered a platform before a congressional committee to present his information.

After suppressing the Teicher affidavit, Clinton's prosecutors persuaded the judge presiding in the Teledyne-Johnson case to rule testimony about the Reagan-Bush policies in Iraq to be irrelevant. Unable to mount its planned defense, Teledyne agreed to plead guilty and accept a $13 million fine. Johnson, the salesman who had earned a modest salary in the mid-$30,000 range and dressed in inexpensive off-the-rack suits, was convicted of illegal arms trafficking and was sent to prison.

Some historians hoped that the mysteries of the Reagan administration's policies in the Middle East might finally be resolved in 2001 when a government-openness law required most records from that era to be made public. On January 20, 2001, however, George W. Bush made one of his first acts as President the issuance of an executive order blocking the release of the documents.

Then, after the 9/11 attacks, Bush issued an even more sweeping secrecy order. He granted former Presidents and Vice Presidents or their surviving family members the right to stop release of historical records, including those related to "military, diplomatic or national security secrets." Bush's order stripped the Archivist of the United States of the power to overrule claims of privilege from former Presidents and their representatives.[8]

By a twist of history, Bush's order eventually could give him control of both his and his father's records covering 12 years of the Reagan-Bush era and his own eight-year presidency, a 20-year swath of documentary evidence. The control of that history might eventually pass down to Bush's two daughters, Jenna and Barbara. In effect, that would mean that the American people might never get to know the truth of what happened regarding secret U.S. diplomacy with Iraq and Iran in the 1980s.

◆◆◆

In the early morning hours of August 2, 1990, Saddam Hussein ordered his army and tank columns to cross the Kuwaiti border. They quickly overwhelmed Kuwait's soft and undermanned defenses and began heading toward Kuwait City, the sheikhdom's capital. It soon became clear to the al-Sabahs, Kuwait's royal family, that the Iraqi invaders had no intention of halting in the disputed border area, as some had expected.

In a panic, the al-Sabahs had their servants pack the royal suitcases and load them into a long line of Mercedes limousines. With Iraqi forces only hours away, the white-robed al-Sabahs swept to the cars and the motorcade rushed off at high speeds through the deserted streets of Kuwait City. The limousines stopped briefly at the U.S. embassy where the emir, the crown prince and several other dignitaries alighted from the cars and scrambled aboard a U.S. helicopter, its blades already churning. The helicopter lifted off and bent toward the south. The rest of the royal entourage sped southward in the Mercedes caravan, traversing the 30 miles to the Saudi border.

The Kuwaiti royals departed so hastily they even failed to sound the warning sirens to alert other Kuwaiti citizens of the impending disaster. The al-Sabahs also left behind their dutiful servants to fend for themselves under Iraqi occupation. By contrast, the royals looked forward to a comfortable exile in Saudi Arabia. The emir, known for his piercing dark eyes and his womanizing, soon settled into Taif, the luxurious summer refuge of the Saudi royalty.

In those early hours of the invasion, Saddam Hussein's victory seemed total. His army had crushed Kuwait's defenders and literally sent the al-Sabahs packing. Overnight, Hussein had expanded his nation's already vast oil supplies. Including Kuwait's oil, Hussein controlled 20 percent of the world's total known oil reserves. But it would be the breathtaking scope of his oil conquest that would prove his undoing.

On August 5, three days after the invasion, President George H.W. Bush stepped from his Marine One helicopter onto the White House lawn and pronounced what would happen next. "This will not stand," Bush fumed. "This will not stand, this aggression against Kuwait." Bush ruled out any compromise and began assembling a powerful coalition army in the Persian Gulf.

To whip up public support for this war to restore the Kuwaiti royals to their palaces, Bush escalated his rhetoric against Hussein, comparing him to Adolf Hitler and hyping dubious propaganda claims, such as an apocryphal story about Hussein's henchmen ripping babies from hospital incubators and smashing the infants to the floor. In many ways, the propaganda build-up to the Persian Gulf War would become a modern model for stoking war fever in the United States.

With few exceptions, the U.S. press corps joined the stampede for war. "Look, Saddam Hussein is a big fat rat and he has been cornered," explained television pundit Morton Kondracke.[9] Other leading pundits saw the problem as the need to confront whiny, destructive Arabs. "Saddam's political 'strength' is built on a thirst for revenge by Arabs who blame the West for their vast problems and want payback," wrote *The Washington Post*'s Jim Hoagland. "It's a 'strength' that can create nothing. It can only destroy. Or be destroyed."[10]

U.S. warplanes were soon pounding Iraqi targets and pulverizing Hussein's army that was dug in along the Saudi border. In late February 1991, Bush followed the air campaign with a ground offensive that routed the Iraqi army and turned its hasty retreat into what became known as the "highway of death." After 100 hours, Bush called off the slaughter and – once U.S. soldiers reattached the gold fixtures in the palace bathrooms – the al-Sabahs were free to return to their palaces in Kuwait City.

But George H.W. Bush's propaganda blitz might have been too successful for his own good. After painting a black-and-white moral portrait of the evil Hussein, Bush slid back into his more comfortable grays of geopolitical realism when he stopped the U.S. expeditionary force from marching up the Euphrates River to Baghdad. After likening Hussein to Hitler, Bush decided that it wasn't worth hunting the dictator down and replacing him with an entirely new regime.

At first, amid the victory celebrations, there was little second guessing. Much of the American public was exhilarated by a U.S. military intervention won in a short time with a small number of American casualties. Neoconservative columnist Charles Krauthammer expressed the patriotic mood in a column announcing a new "Pax Americana" that disdained the frustrating compromises of international alliances.

"If we want relative stability and tranquility in the world, we are going to have to work for it," Krauthammer wrote. "It will come neither by itself nor as a gift from the [United Nations] Security Council. It will only come from an American foreign policy of 'robust and difficult interventionism.'" In the view of Krauthammer and other neoconservative thinkers, the United States acting unilaterally in a complex and dangerous world was both a strategic and moral imperative.[11]

Since the neoconservative power base was centered in the opinion circles of Washington – especially the op-ed pages and the TV chat shows – the neocons faced few real-world consequences when they talked tough and played to the crowd. The more bellicose the rhetoric the better when vanquishing rival pundits during Inside-the-Beltway debates. The neocons thrived in that role of armchair warriors – eschewing nuance, disdaining diplomacy and demanding war and more war.

So, while the neocons praised George H.W. Bush for routing the Iraqi army from Kuwait, they turned on him when he failed to send U.S. troops to Baghdad. The neocons mocked the President for his "prudence" in not finishing off Hussein. Before long, it became established wisdom in Washington's opinion circles that the elder George Bush had blundered by stopping the ground war after 100 hours. It was a pro-war consensus not lost on the younger George Bush.

◆◆◆

This notion of an unbridled America galloping off to right wrongs and slay villainous enemies helped give the neoconservatives their distinct political identity in the last decade of the 20th century and the first decade of the 21st. But the neocons and their philosophy had been emerging as a prominent school of thought since the mid-to-late 1970s. Many neocons were disaffected liberals and even leftists who had grown disgusted with the youth-dominated anti-Vietnam War movement.

Some neocons also disdained what they perceived as liberalism's coddling of African-Americans by seeking quotas for college admissions or demanding affirmative action in the work place. The neocons felt an even greater animus toward Muslims, in part, because of the neocons' high regard for Israel, which they admired as a beacon for Western modernity in a backward Middle East.

Many neocons saw themselves as intellectual followers of the late political philosopher Leo Strauss, who taught that some deception of a population was necessary in statecraft. So, as the neocons rose through the ranks of the U.S. government – most notably during the Reagan administration in the 1980s – they brought with them an appreciation for clever propaganda and the need to manage the perceptions of the American people. The neocons quickly learned that the key to this "perception management" was to play on the fears of the public.

In an important early lesson in 1976, a young neocon academic, Paul Wolfowitz, participated in the so-called "Team B" challenge to the CIA's assessment of the Soviet threat. At the time, the CIA's "Kremlinologists" were seeing cracks in the Soviet empire as it fell further behind the West both economically and technologically, with obvious implications for the competitiveness of the Soviet military.

However, Wolfowitz and other right-wing ideologues were granted extraordinary access to the CIA's secret data (by then CIA Director George H.W. Bush) and argued instead that the Soviets were on the rise and opening up a "window of vulnerability" that would put the United States in danger of a first-strike nuclear assault. Though the "Team B" analysis would ultimately be revealed as empty fear-mongering, it served its purpose in the late 1970s, discrediting Henry Kissinger's strategy of détente and undermining arms-control talks with Moscow.[12]

During the Reagan administration, neocons expanded and refined their "perception management" techniques, hyping threats to the United States from leftist movements in the Western Hemisphere. Even the tiny Caribbean island of Grenada and the poor Central American nation of Nicaragua were depicted as clear and present dangers to American security. Among the neocon propaganda stars were the likes of assistant secretary of state Elliott Abrams and Robert Kagan, who managed a special State Department Office of Public Diplomacy on Latin America.

After George H.W. Bush lost his reelection bid to Bill Clinton in 1992, many leading neoconservatives found themselves out of government. Yet they continued to organize for a comeback. Later in the 1990s, many coalesced around the Project for the New American Century, which promoted strategies for maintaining America's military supremacy and lobbied for aggressive policies against U.S. adversaries. Besides the aforementioned Wolfowitz, Abrams, Kagan and Krauthammer, important neocons included John Bolton, David Wurmser, Richard Perle, William Kristol, James Woolsey, I. Lewis Libby, Max Boot and Norman Podhoretz.[13]

By the mid-1990s, the neocons were pressing President Clinton to invade Iraq and finish the job left undone by George H.W. Bush. "The only acceptable strategy is one that eliminates the possibility that Iraq will be able to use or threaten to use weapons of mass destruction," said a letter prepared by the PNAC. "In the near term, this means a willingness to undertake military action as diplomacy is clearly failing." Along with prominent neocons, the letter was signed by more traditional conservatives, Donald Rumsfeld and Richard Armitage. Dick Cheney also joined the neoconservatives in some of their initiatives.[14]

Though considered more hard-line American nationalists than neocons, Cheney and Rumsfeld shared the neocon perspective on the need for unconstrained U.S. power. They "found that many of their deeply held beliefs about American exceptionalism and unilateralism parallel neoconservative thought," wrote conservative authors Stefan Halper and Jonathan Clarke in their book, *America Alone*.[15]

When George W. Bush restored the Republicans to power in January 2001, the neocons and their influential allies, Cheney and Rumsfeld, were ready to implement many of the policies they had espoused during their years out of power. Neocons assumed key positions in the National Security Council, the Vice President's Office, the Pentagon, the Justice Department and the State Department. The neocons blended their concepts of military power and political propaganda with Bush and Cheney's preoccupation with oil.

One of the few Executive Branch entities where the neocons were not dominant was the CIA. The steady assault from ideologues in the Reagan administration had worn down the CIA's once-vaunted analytical division, but there remained at least a faded commitment to objectivity and scholarship.[16]

But the Straussian neocons saw the relationship between information and policy differently. For them, truth was not the guiding light that led to the best policies; rather the policy goal was what mattered and the facts were then selected and arranged in the best possible way to support that grander purpose. Once information was shaped to create a favorable political climate, the neocons had the maximum latitude to pursue their policy goals.

Early in 2002, as the Bush administration refocused its attention on Iraq, the traditions of objectivity within the CIA's analytical division (along with similar attitudes at the State Department's Bureau of Intelligence and Research) were getting in the way of the more utilitarian approach toward information favored by the neocons. They had decided that the goal of achieving a new, more compliant Middle East required Saddam Hussein's removal and that, therefore, the government's job was to amass information that could be used to persuade the American people of the need for war.

In the wake of 9/11, it was obvious the best way to create a war fever was to exploit America's lingering fear and hunger for revenge. The neocons set about convincing Americans that Hussein possessed weapons of mass destruction and that he could be expected to share them with al-Qaeda terrorists. If the analysts at CIA and State were reluctant to make that case – because they had scant intelligence about the former point and had severe doubts about the latter – the neocons and their administration allies would set up *ad hoc* intelligence institutions that would.

Initially, Vice President Cheney tried to use repeated trips to CIA headquarters to persuade CIA analysts to get on board. Though Cheney achieved some success among CIA careerists and CIA Director George Tenet, the Vice President didn't gain the full cooperation that he wanted. So, more and more of the intelligence was handled at the White House or at a newly created Office of Special Plans at the Pentagon, under the guidance of Deputy Defense Secretary Paul Wolfowitz.

"They were using the intelligence from the CIA and other agencies only when it fit their agenda," a former Bush administration intelligence official told investigative reporter Seymour Hersh. "They didn't like the intelligence they were getting, and so they brought in people to write the stuff. They were so crazed and so far out and so difficult to reason with – to the point of being bizarre. Dogmatic, as if they were on a mission from God."[17]

In May 2002, Air Force Lt. Col. Karen Kwiatkowski was among the career military officers pulled into the war planning at the Office of Special Plans.

"I was 'volunteered' to enter what would be a well-appointed den of iniquity," Kwiatkowski wrote about her experiences. "The education I would receive there was like an M. Night Shyamalan movie – intense, fascinating and frightening. While the people were very much alive, I saw a dead philosophy – Cold War anti-communism and neo-imperialism – walking the corridors of the Pentagon. It wore the clothing of counter-terrorism and spoke the language of a holy war between good and evil."

Kwiatkowski said Bush's political appointees overwhelmed the judgments of career specialists and manipulated the fears of the American people. "Many of us in the Pentagon, conservatives and liberals alike, felt that this agenda, whatever its flaws or merits, had never been openly presented to the American people," she wrote. "Instead, the public story line was a fear-peddling and confusing set of messages, designed to take Congress and the country into a war of executive choice, a war based on false pretenses."[18]

14

March to War

By late summer 2002, George W. Bush's determination to invade Iraq had grown so obvious to the world that Nobel Peace Prize winner Nelson Mandela tried to contact the U.S. President in a desperate attempt to dissuade him from his course of action. If Mandela had been able to get Bush on the phone, the conversation might have been historic, the exchange of thoughts about war and reconciliation between two world leaders whose lives could not have stood in greater contrast.

Mandela, a well-educated and articulate lawyer, had spent more than two decades in prison for his resistance to the white-supremacist government of South Africa before gaining his freedom and becoming the country's first black president. To the surprise of many, the elegant Mandela then governed with a civility toward his long-time tormentors, enabling South Africa to avert the destructive cycles of violence that have afflicted other African states.

Twenty-eight years Mandela's junior, Bush had grown up a world away, both in geographic distance and personal experience. Bush's family personified the post-World War II privilege enjoyed by America's white upper classes. But Bush never took advantage of his opportunities to gain a sophisticated understanding of the world, nor did he master basic communication skills that would be expected of any politician without Bush's connections.

Yet, as Bush maneuvered the United States toward war in 2002, the 84-year-old Mandela wanted to share some of his life lessons with Bush about the threat to world order that Bush's doctrine of unilateral invasions represented. Bush, however, was on another extended vacation in Texas, which he interrupted only for occasional side trips around the country to raise money for Republican congressional candidates. Bush chose not to take Mandela's phone call.

Rebuffed by the White House, Mandela settled for speaking with the elder George Bush about his son's behavior. "We are really appalled by any country, whether a superpower or a small country, that goes outside the U.N. and attacks independent countries," Mandela said about the message he was delivering. "No country should be allowed to take the law into their own hands. ... What they are saying is introducing chaos in international affairs, and we condemn that in the strongest terms."[1]

As a person who lived through World War II, Mandela understood the practical reasons why international jurists had established universal principles prohibiting one country from invading another. It was Germany's wars of aggression against weaker nations that had set the world ablaze. The conflagration began in 1939 when Adolf Hitler trumped up an excuse to attack neighboring Poland. Before the war ended six years later, more than 60 million people were dead. From that devastation came the Nuremberg Principles and the United Nations Charter, which were formulated under American leadership and unequivocally banned aggressive wars.

While many Americans think of the Nuremberg trials after World War II as holding Nazi leaders accountable for genocide and other crimes against humanity, another major charge against Hitler's henchmen was their use of aggressive war. U.S. Supreme Court Justice Robert Jackson, who represented the United States as a prosecutor at the Nuremberg Tribunal, said the trials were not just about punishing the Nazis. Jackson wanted to establish a precedent for the future.

"Our position is that whatever grievances a nation may have, however objectionable it finds the status quo, aggressive warfare is an illegal means for settling those grievances or for altering those conditions," Jackson said, adding that the same rules would apply to the victors in World War II.

"Let me make clear that while this law is first applied against German aggressors, the law includes, and if it is to serve a useful purpose, it must condemn aggression by any other nations, including those which sit here now in judgment," Jackson said. "We are able to do away with domestic tyranny and violence and aggression by those in power against the rights of their own people only when we make all men answerable to the law. This trial represents mankind's desperate effort to apply the discipline of the law to statesmen who have used their powers of state to attack the foundations of the world's peace and to commit aggression against the rights of their neighbors."

But George W. Bush held such universal principles in contempt – at least when anyone sought to apply them to him. One of his favorite jokes, which he told when asked if his behavior violated international law, was to josh, "International law? I better call my lawyer," followed by a chuckle.

What Mandela and many other outside observers also didn't understand in 2002 was how little influence the elder Bush and his old-school advisers had on the younger Bush. When the elder Bush's National Security Adviser Brent Scowcroft weighed in on August 15, 2002, with a *Wall Street Journal* opinion piece warning against an invasion of Iraq, the younger Bush's National Security Adviser Condoleezza Rice gave her old mentor, Scowcroft, a tongue-lashing. Scowcroft subsequently stayed out of the debate.

"Neither Scowcroft nor Bush senior wanted to injure the son's self-confidence," Bob Woodward wrote in his post-invasion book *Plan of Attack*. When Woodward asked the younger Bush about his father's advice, the President responded petulantly, "I can't remember a moment where I said to myself, maybe he can help me make the decision."

His head inflated by the public adulation that followed his early military successes in Afghanistan, the younger Bush didn't even search for some words that might soften his deprecation of his father's influence.

"I'm not trying to be evasive," Bush said. "I don't remember. I could ask him and see if he remembers something. But how do you ask a person, What does it feel like to send somebody in and them lose life? Remember, I've already done so, for starters, in Afghanistan."[2]

Bush then added a line that played well with his Christian Right base but was viewed by many as another slight to his father. "You know, he is the wrong father to appeal to in terms of strength," Bush told Woodward. "There is a higher father that I appeal to."[3]

◆ ◆ ◆

Bush's divine guidance was pointing him toward invading Iraq whatever the opinions of his earthly father or the mandates of international law. During his State of the Union Address in January 2002, Bush had put Iraq into the "axis of evil." That was followed by a growing clamor among neoconservative intellectuals for a preemptive invasion of Iraq.

Kenneth Adelman, a military official from the Ford and Reagan administrations, penned an op-ed for *The Washington Post* mocking the opinion of two Brookings Institution experts who predicted that a war with Iraq would require 100,000 to 200,000 U.S. ground troops and cost the lives of thousands of American soldiers.

"I believe demolishing [Saddam] Hussein's military power and liberating Iraq would be a cakewalk," Adelman wrote. "Measured by any cost-benefit analysis, such an operation would constitute the greatest victory in America's war on terrorism."[4]

Bush was soon huddling with his advisers and his British allies to chart a secret timetable for war. The plans were later revealed in documents leaked to British lawyer and international law professor Philippe Sands for his book, *Lawless World*, and to foreign policy correspondent Michael Smith of the *London Sunday Times*. Other key British documents were revealed by Channel 4 in London. Together, these British records laid out a clandestine strategy for precipitating a conflict with Iraq while pretending that the United States and Great Britain really wanted a peaceful settlement.[5]

On March 14, 2002, Prime Minister Tony Blair's chief foreign policy adviser David Manning sent a memo to Blair reporting that Manning had explained over dinner with Condoleezza Rice how important it was to maneuver Saddam Hussein into a position where he would refuse to permit new United Nations weapons inspections. "This issue of weapons inspectors must be handled in a way that would persuade Europe and wider opinion that the U.S. was conscious of the international framework, and the insistence of many countries on the need for a legal basis," Manning wrote. "Renewed refusal by Saddam to accept unfettered inspections would be a powerful argument."

Manning also indicated to Rice that Blair needed this U.N. initiative because the British media and people weren't as easily persuaded as their American counterparts would be. "I said that you [Blair] would not budge in your support for regime change [in Iraq] but you had to manage a press, a Parliament and a public opinion that was different from anything in the States," Manning wrote.

On March 18, 2002, four days later, British Ambassador to the United States Christopher Meyer reported on a lunch with U.S. Deputy Defense Secretary Paul Wolfowitz at which they discussed how demands for weapons inspections might trip up Hussein.

Meyer told Wolfowitz that the United States could wage war on its own, "but if it wanted to act with partners, there had to be a strategy for building support for military action against Saddam. I then went through the need to wrong-foot Saddam on the inspectors and the [U.N. Security Council resolutions] … If all this could be accomplished skillfully, we were fairly confident that a number of countries would come on board."[6]

This concept of trying to "wrong-foot Saddam" was a recurring theme in the British memos. The next month, April 2002, Blair met with Bush in Crawford, Texas, to signal Blair's support for Bush's war plans. Publicly the two men still insisted they had not made the decision to invade. But the British documents from summer 2002 revealed that the invasion of Iraq was a done deal.

Three months after the Crawford summit, Blair's foreign policy team reconvened to hash out new plans for arranging a pretext for war. A July 21, 2002, briefing paper said it was "necessary to create the conditions" which would make an invasion legal. To achieve those conditions, the briefing paper proposed a U.N. Security Council resolution that would be insulting enough to goad the proud Hussein into rejecting inspections.

"It is just possible that an ultimatum could be cast in terms which Saddam would reject," the briefing paper said.

Though Blair and his advisers still hoped for some legal cover for invading Iraq, they already had accepted the war as inevitable. "In practice, much of the international community would find it difficult to stand in the way of the determined course of the U.S. hegemon," according to the briefing paper, which added: "U.S. views of international law vary from that of the UK and the international community."

The British found themselves caught between a rock and a hard place because Bush was determined to attack Iraq and would use British military facilities regardless of London's desires, the briefing paper said. "U.S. plans assume, as a minimum, the use of British bases in Cyprus and Diego Garcia," which meant that the issue of British complicity in an illegal American war "would arise virtually whatever option ministers choose with regard to UK participation," the briefing paper said.[7]

Two days later, on July 23, Blair met at his offices at 10 Downing Street with his top foreign policy advisers to review the Iraq situation. According to the minutes, which later became known as the "Downing Street Memo," Richard Dearlove, chief of the British intelligence agency MI6, described a recent trip to Washington at which he discussed Iraq with Bush's top national security officials.

"Bush wanted to remove Saddam, through military action, justified by the conjunction of terrorism and WMD. But the intelligence and facts were being fixed around the policy," Dearlove was quoted as saying. The minutes added, "It seemed clear that Bush had made up his mind to take military action, even if the timing was not yet decided. But the case was thin. Saddam was not threatening his neighbours, and his WMD capability was less than that of Libya, North Korea or Iran."

Again recognizing that an unprovoked invasion would violate international law, Blair favored first pursuing arms inspections with the hope that Hussein would say no.

"We should work up a plan for an ultimatum to Saddam to allow back in the U.N. weapons inspectors. This would also help with the legal justification for the use of force," the minutes read. "The Prime Minister said that it would make a big difference politically and legally if Saddam refused to allow in the U.N. inspectors."

The reality of the impending war also was setting in among senior American diplomats. Greg Thielmann, who monitored WMD issues for the State Department's bureau of intelligence, said he was unnerved in August 2002, when Vice President Dick Cheney declared that "there is no doubt that Saddam Hussein now has weapons of mass destruction" and that "we now know that Saddam has resumed his efforts to acquire nuclear weapons."

"That speech it seemed to me was basically a declaration of war speech," Thielmann said in a later interview with CNN. "That's when I, for the first time, became really alarmed about where we were going on this."[8]

♦♦♦

As Bush prepared to sell his new war to the public, his advisers understood the practical need to make sure that the American people were back from their summer vacations before the administration got serious about stirring up the necessary anger and spreading the requisite fear.

"From a marketing point of view," Bush's chief of staff Andrew Card explained to The New York Times, "you don't introduce new products in August."[9]

As his own vacation ended, Bush and his team were ready to begin the drumbeat to war, marching in line with friendly journalists who were eager for scoops that Saddam Hussein had moved to reconstitute his nuclear weapons program and was rebuilding his stockpiles of chemical and biological weapons. There would also be assertions that Hussein had closer relations than previously believed with Islamic terrorists who might use these weapons against the United States.

"This is not the way intelligence is done," former CIA analyst Ray McGovern told us in an interview. "You don't just decide to have a war and then arrange the intelligence."

That was, however, the way the Iraq War would be sold to the American people. Almost any scrap of information about Iraq's WMD, no matter how dubious, was grabbed by the administration and passed on to friendly reporters. For instance, when aluminum tubes were discovered heading to Iraq, one inexperienced CIA analyst came up with the shaky conclusion they must be for enriching uranium.

Nuclear experts at the State and Energy departments concluded otherwise, that the tubes matched the requirements for conventional Iraqi rockets and weren't suitable for nuclear enrichment. But the administration embraced the nuclear-tube argument.

"Why would you immediately jump to the conclusion that these were for their nuclear program?" asked Carl Ford, former assistant secretary of state running the department's Bureau of Intelligence and Research. "Once an analyst starts believing their own work and quits doubting themselves and starts saying, 'I'm going to prove to you that they've got nuclear weapons,' watch out."[10]

Next, the nuclear-tube story was leaked to a credulous *New York Times*, which put the article – co-authored by neoconservative favorite Judith Miller – on the front page of the September 8, 2002, editions under the headline, "U.S. Says Hussein Intensified Quest for A-Bomb Parts." The story focused on Iraq's purchase of aluminum tubes that the Bush administration claimed were for manufacturing nuclear weapons fuel.

Administration officials said there was no time to lose, warning that the United States couldn't let the "smoking gun" be a "mushroom cloud." Although there were hints in the *Times* story that the usefulness of the tubes in making nuclear fuel wasn't a sure thing, those *caveats* were buried deep, 1,700 words into a 3,600-word article.

Bush soon took his case for war to the international stage. Speaking to the United Nations the day after the first anniversary of 9/11, Bush raised the prospect that Iraq passing a nuclear bomb to terrorist allies would make the World Trade Center slaughter "a prelude to far greater horrors." Bush said, "to assume this regime's good faith is to bet the lives of millions and the peace of the world in a reckless gamble."

Bush's alarmist rhetoric gave many Americans the impression that Iraq already had a nuclear bomb or was close to getting one. But outside studies, including two British reports favorably cited by the Bush administration, offered a much less frightening analysis. A British intelligence assessment, released by Prime Minister Tony Blair on September 24, 2002, said the existing U.N. embargo against Iraq had succeeded in "hindering the import of crucial goods for the production of fissile material," such as highly enriched uranium needed for nuclear weapons. The British intelligence chiefs "judged that while sanctions remain effective, Iraq would not be able to produce a nuclear weapon."[11]

The London-based International Institute for Strategic Studies reached a similar conclusion. "Iraq does not possess facilities to produce fissile material in sufficient amounts for nuclear weapons," the IISS concluded. "It would require several years and extensive foreign assistance to build such fissile material production facilities."

In other words, these studies showed that a continued strategy of arms embargoes, backed by international inspections, would likely keep Iraq from developing a nuclear weapon for the foreseeable future. But the Bush administration argued that in the case of Iraq, inaction was a bigger risk than action. Bush's argument appealed to many can-do Americans who favored taking an adversary out rather than containing him.

As late summer turned to fall and congressional elections neared, Bush stepped up the drive to solidify political support for an invasion. "Iraq could decide on any given day to provide a biological or chemical weapon to a terrorist group or individual terrorists," Bush said in an October 7 speech in Cincinnati, Ohio. Reiterating the theme two days later, White House spokesman Ari Fleischer said, "If Saddam Hussein holds a gun to someone's head, while he denies he even owns a gun, do you really want to take a chance that he'll never use it?"[12]

But what Bush and his aides left out of their one-sided risk equation was the possibility that the administration's actions might increase the dangers to Americans, not reduce or eliminate the risks. Though Bush stressed the "clear evidence of peril" from Iraq giving chemical and biological weapons to terrorists, the CIA had a different view. The CIA judged the likelihood of Iraq attacking the United States without provocation as "low" but rising dramatically if the U.S. government prepared for a preemptive strike.

"Baghdad for now appears to be drawing a line short of conducting terrorist attacks with conventional or C.B.W. [chemical or biological warfare] against the United States," wrote CIA Director George Tenet in an October 7 letter to Congress. "Should Saddam conclude that a U.S.-led attack could no longer be deterred, he probably would become much less constrained in adopting terrorist actions."

Yet having succeeded in planting the seeds of fear about Saddam Hussein's nuclear and WMD programs, the Bush administration moved on to cultivate another necessary worry to justify an invasion – that Hussein's secular dictatorship was in league with al-Qaeda.

Again, the Bush administration brushed aside evidence that contradicted the desired rationale. Former CIA counterterrorism expert Michael Scheuer said a careful review of al-Qaeda intelligence information over nearly a decade "could find no connection in the terms of a state-sponsored relationship with Iraq ... but [the analysis] apparently didn't have any impact."[13]

Instead, National Security Adviser Rice denied any uncertainty. "Clearly, there are contacts between al-Qaeda and Iraq that can be documented. There clearly is testimony that some of these contacts have been important contacts and there's a relationship there," she said.

Bush requested authority from Congress to launch a preemptive war against Iraq, but he still had not ordered up a formal National Intelligence Estimate on Iraq's WMD. So, Congress took the unusual step of asking the CIA to prepare an NIE, which expresses the consensus view of the U.S. intelligence community.

Later, Senator Richard Durbin, Democrat of Illinois, said, "The agencies understand that if we're about to take a major military action or even consider one, you bring all your intelligence agencies together and say, 'what do you know, and what do you know for sure before we put our troops in harm's way, before we risk the reputation and treasure and bodies of our servicemen? What do we know?'"[14]

During the NIE process, Tenet defended the opinion of the inexperienced CIA analyst who had come up with the nuclear-tube theory. But the State Department's intelligence agency remained skeptical of the case being constructed about Iraq's supposed nuclear program. "We couldn't really buy on to any of the things being said so the State Department's intelligence bureau put in a very deliberate and strong and lengthy dissent," said State intelligence chief Ford.[15]

Still, with the dissenting views largely buried, the NIE helped solidify congressional support for Bush's war plans. Government leaders on the front lines of the Middle East, however, warned that a U.S. assault on Baghdad could set the region ablaze, spread Islamic fundamentalism, spark sectarian violence and endanger leaders who had supported the U.S. "war on terror."

More red flags were raised when the results rolled in from provincial and parliamentary elections in nuclear-armed Pakistan. Though the pro-U.S. dictator, General Pervez Musharraf, used heavy-handed tactics to guarantee victory for his supporters, both secular and Islamic opposition parties made strong showings. Islamic fundamentalists won at least 39 seats in the National Assembly – compared to four seats in 1997 – and gained control of the strategic North-West Frontier Province. That was where U.S. and Pakistani forces had been hunting al-Qaeda leaders and their Taliban allies from Afghanistan. The change in provincial leadership meant more trouble for the search.

"We will stop the ongoing pursuit of Taliban and al-Qaeda when we form the government," Munnawar Hasan, secretary general of the Islamic party, told Reuters. "Taliban and al-Qaeda members are our brothers."[16]

Bush's strategy risked boomeranging on the United States in another way. Watching how Bush exaggerated the threat from Iraq – moving to attack even when Iraq was trying not to threaten the United States – other candidates for forcible "regime change," such as Iran and North Korea, opted for a more belligerent course, embarking on crash programs for weapons of mass destruction with a readiness to use them.

Surviving al-Qaeda leaders also began to recover from their post-9/11 reversals by rallying Muslims against Bush's Iraq policy. "The campaign against Iraq has an objective that is far beyond Iraq to reach the Arab and Islamic world," said Osama bin Laden's top deputy Ayman al-Zawahiri.[17] A bombing of a nightclub in Bali, Indonesia, which killed more than 180 people, showed that al-Qaeda supporters or sympathizers were shifting back to the offensive.

Another problem for Washington was the broader international reaction to Bush's tone. While his tough-guy rhetoric played well with his right-wing base, it offended many others in the United States and elsewhere. Around the world, the pages of leading newspapers treated Bush as an arrogant bully, the archetypal Ugly American who knew little about other cultures and treated them with contempt.

Bush's unapologetic goal of achieving never-ending U.S. military domination – as unabashedly described in his "national security strategy" report on September 20 – added fuel to the growing fire. Anti-Americanism was emerging as a powerful political force in Europe and Latin America, as well as in the Middle East. German Chancellor Gerhard Schroeder reversed his political fortunes in Germany's parliamentary elections by opposing Bush's unilateral threats to attack Iraq.

International resistance to Bush was underscored again when the Nobel committee gave former President Jimmy Carter the Peace Prize and added a pointed rebuke to Bush's policy toward Iraq. "In a situation currently marked by threats of the use of power," the Nobel citation read, "Carter has stood by the principles that conflicts must as far as possible be resolved through mediation and international cooperation based on international law, respect for human rights and economic development."[18]

◆◆◆

Back home, Bush's strategy of "preemptive war" quickly developed a domestic corollary: silencing criticism through a kind of "politics of preemption." This disdainful treatment of dissent traced back to the weeks and months after 9/11. Attorney General John Ashcroft testified to Congress in December 2001 that those who object to "phantoms of lost liberty" only serve to "aid terrorists – for they erode our national unity and diminish our resolve." According to Ashcroft, those who questioned the administration's policies "give ammunition to America's enemies, and pause to America's friends."

By late summer and early fall 2002, Bush's allies had built a rapid-deployment force to counterattack any politician or public figure who questioned Bush's strategy or wisdom. In a test run, this pro-Bush SWAT team rushed out for rhetorical battle after former Vice President Al Gore on September 23 delivered a comprehensive critique of Bush's radical departure from decades of American support for international law.

In a speech at the Commonwealth Club in San Francisco, Gore laid out a series of concerns and differences that he had with Bush's preemption policy and specifically Bush's decision to refashion the "war on terror" into an immediate war with Iraq. Gore, who had supported the Persian Gulf War in 1990-91, criticized Bush's failure to enlist the international community as his father had. Gore also warned that alienating other nations was having a negative impact on the broader conflict against terrorists.

"I am deeply concerned that the course of action that we are presently embarking upon with respect to Iraq has the potential to seriously damage our ability to win the war against terrorism and to weaken our ability to lead the world in this new century," Gore said. "To put first things first, I believe that we ought to be focusing our efforts first and foremost against those who attacked us on September 11. ... Great nations persevere and then prevail. They do not jump from one unfinished task to another. We should remain focused on the war against terrorism."

Instead of keeping after al-Qaeda and stabilizing Afghanistan, Bush had chosen to jump to a new war against Iraq as the first example of his policy of preemption, Gore said. "He is telling us that our most urgent task right now is to shift our focus and concentrate on immediately launching a new war against Saddam Hussein," Gore said. "And the President is proclaiming a new uniquely American right to preemptively attack whomsoever he may deem represents a potential future threat."

Gore also objected to the timing of the vote on war with Iraq, just weeks before the congressional elections. "President Bush is demanding, in this high political season, that Congress speedily affirm that he has the necessary authority to proceed immediately against Iraq and, for that matter, under the language of his resolution, against any other nation in the region regardless of subsequent developments or emerging circumstances," Gore said.

The former Vice President staked out a position with subtle but important differences from Bush's broad assertion that the United States has the right to override international law on the President's command. Gore argued that U.S. unilateral power should be used sparingly, only in extreme situations.

"There's no international law that can prevent the United States from taking action to protect our vital interests when it is manifestly clear that there's a choice to be made between law and our survival," Gore said. "Indeed, international law itself recognizes that such choices stay within the purview of all nations. I believe, however, that such a choice is not presented in the case of Iraq."

Gore bemoaned, too, that Bush's actions had dissipated the international good will that surrounded the United States after the 9/11 attacks. "That has been squandered in a year's time and replaced with great anxiety all around the world, not primarily about what the terrorist networks are going to do, but about what we're going to do," Gore said. "Now, my point is not that they're right to feel that way, but that they do feel that way."

Gore also took aim at Bush's unilateral assertion of his right to imprison American citizens without trial or legal representation simply by labeling them "enemy combatants."

"The very idea that an American citizen can be imprisoned without recourse to judicial process or remedy, and that this can be done on the sole say-so of the President of the United States or those acting in his name, is beyond the pale and un-American, and ought to be stopped," Gore said.

Gore raised, too, practical concerns about the dangers that might follow the overthrow of Hussein, if chaos in Iraq ensued. Gore cited the deteriorating political condition in Afghanistan where the new central government exerted real control only in parts of Kabul while ceding effective power in the countryside to warlords.

"What if, in the aftermath of a war against Iraq, we faced a situation like that, because we've washed our hands of it?" Gore asked. "What if the al-Qaeda members infiltrated across the borders of Iraq the way they are in Afghanistan? ... Now, I just think that if we end the war in Iraq the way we ended the war in Afghanistan, we could very well be much worse off than we are today."

Gore's speech infuriated Bush supporters – radio talk show host Rush Limbaugh said he couldn't get to sleep after listening to it – but their responses sought to discredit Gore more than address what he said. Rather than welcome a vigorous debate on the merits and shortcomings of the "Bush Doctrine," right-wing and mainstream commentators alike treated Gore as dishonest, unpatriotic and even unhinged.

Gore was slapped around by Beltway political analysts, variously portrayed as seeking cheap political gain and committing political suicide. Helped by the fact that Gore's speech received only spotty television coverage – MSNBC carried excerpts live and C-SPAN replayed the speech later that night – pro-Bush commentators were free to distort Gore's words and then dismiss his arguments as "lies" largely because few Americans actually heard what he had said.

Some epithets came directly from Bush partisans. Republican National Committee spokesman Jim Dyke called Gore a "political hack." An administration source told *The Washington Post* that Gore was simply "irrelevant," a theme that would be repeated often in the days after Gore's speech.[19] Other broadsides were fired by right-wing opinion-makers on leading editorial pages, on talk radio and on television chat shows.

"Gore's speech was one no decent politician could have delivered," wrote *Washington Post* columnist Michael Kelly. "It was dishonest, cheap, low. It was hollow. It was bereft of policy, of solutions, of constructive ideas, very nearly of facts – bereft of anything other than taunts and jibes and embarrassingly obvious lies. It was breathtakingly hypocritical, a naked political assault delivered in tones of moral condescension from a man pretending to be superior to mere politics. It was wretched. It was vile. It was contemptible."[20]

"A pudding with no theme but much poison," declared another *Post* columnist, Charles Krauthammer. "It was a disgrace – a series of cheap shots strung together without logic or coherence."[21] At *Salon.com*, Andrew Sullivan entitled his piece about Gore's speech "The Opportunist" and characterized Gore as "bitter."

While some commentators depicted Gore's motivation as political opportunism, columnist William Bennett mocked Gore for sealing his political doom and banishing himself "from the mainstream of public opinion." In an op-ed piece for *The Wall Street Journal*, entitled "Al Gore's Political Suicide," Bennett said Gore had "made himself irrelevant by his inconsistency" and had engaged in "an act of self-immolation" by daring to criticize Bush's policy.

"Now we have reason to be grateful once again that Al Gore is not the man in the White House, and never will be," Bennett wrote.[22]

When the conservative pundits addressed Gore's actual speech, his words were bizarrely parsed or selectively edited to allow reprising of the news media's favorite "Lyin' Al" canard from the presidential campaign. The *Post*'s Kelly, for instance, resumed his editorial harangue with the argument that Gore was lying when the former Vice President said "the vast majority of those who sponsored, planned and implemented the cold-blooded murder of more than 3,000 Americans are still at large, still neither located nor apprehended, much less punished and neutralized."

To Kelly, this comment was "reprehensible" and "a lie." Kelly continued, "The men who 'implemented' the 'cold-blooded murder of more than 3,000 Americans' are dead; they died in the act of murder on September 11. Gore can look this up." Kelly added that most of the rest were in prison or on the run. Yet, Gore clearly was talking about the likes of Osama bin Laden and Ayman al-Zawahiri, who indeed had not been located. Plus, the Bush administration itself had expressed frustration at the failure of Afghan and Pakistani forces to cut off escape routes for al-Qaeda and Taliban leaders during the military offensive at Tora Bora.

The underlying theme running through the attacks against Gore and other critics of Bush's "preemptive war" policy was that a thorough debate would not be tolerated. Rather than confront arguments on their merits, Bush's supporters simply drummed Gore and fellow skeptics out of Washington's respectable political society.

In a speech in Trenton, New Jersey, on September 23, Bush attacked Democrats who opposed his demand for sweeping power to circumvent civil service rules at the new Department of Homeland Security. "The Senate is more interested in special interests in Washington, and not interested in the security of the American people," Bush declared.

Bush's assertion pushed the normally mild-mannered Senate Majority Leader Tom Daschle into a rage. He demanded an apology in the name of many Democrats who had fought for their country. In the U.S. Senate, Democratic Senator Daniel Inouye of Hawaii lost an arm in World War II and Senator Max Cleland of Georgia lost both legs and one arm in Vietnam. By contrast, both President Bush and Vice President Dick Cheney avoided military service in Vietnam, Bush by joining the Texas Air National Guard and Cheney by taking advantage of five separate draft deferments.

But Bush refused to apologize and the press corps turned on Daschle for his supposedly intemperate behavior. While Bush's comments were presumed to represent his penchant for speaking bluntly, Daschle's protest was analyzed for its political calculation or for its irrationality. Rev. Sun Myung Moon's newspaper, *The Washington Times*, pictured the South Dakota Democrat as headless in an editorial cartoon. Reprising the other media refrain of Lyin' Al, another *Washington Times* cartoon drew Gore as Pinocchio.

♦ ♦ ♦

The White House detailed the new "Bush Doctrine" in a report to Congress that justified the departure from traditional U.S. behavior by asserting that "the only path to peace and security is the path of action." The report added: "We must be prepared to stop rogue states and their terrorist clients before they are able to threaten or use weapons of mass destruction against the United States and our allies and friends."

What the doctrine of preemption meant, however, was that the U.S. government needed to analyze not only another country's capabilities but to read the minds of the country's leaders and to assess possible intentions and motives. Like some worldwide version of predictive crime, as in the movie "Minority Report," these evaluations then would become the basis for "defensive" action before any offensive action occurred.

Senator Robert Byrd, known for his scholarship on constitutional issues, argued in a Senate floor speech on October 3 that the "Bush Doctrine" represented a rewriting of the U.S. Constitution and augured a new era of international chaos. The West Virginia Democrat said Bush's resolution seeking broad powers to wage war in the Middle East was "a product of presidential hubris. This resolution is breathtaking, breathtaking in its scope. It redefines the nature of defense. It reinterprets the Constitution to suit the will of the Executive Branch. This Constitution, which I hold in my hand, is amended without going through the constitutional process of amending this Constitution."

Byrd said Bush's policy of preemptive war represented "an unprecedented and unfounded interpretation of the President's authority under the Constitution of the United States, not to mention the fact that it stands the Charter of the United Nations on its head." Other countries, Byrd noted, can be expected to cite the U.S. precedent in justifying strikes at their enemies which might be considered potential threats sometime off in the future.

Indeed, by definition, preemption could beget preemption. If one country explored the possibility of taking preemptive military action, as the U.S. had against Iraq, the logic of preemption would permit a country like Iraq to attack first, preemptively. If this new rule applied to all countries, it could usher in a cycle of military conflicts that would be self-sustaining and never-ending.

Of course, that was not what the "Bush Doctrine" envisioned. It asserted the notion of America's imperial exceptionalism, that the United States stood alone above other nations in its right to assess the intentions of other countries and attack preemptively.

As Sam Parry wrote at *Consortiumnews.com* on October 8, 2002, "Perhaps it should not be a surprise that as the Bush administration sets the United States on a course to become a modern-day Rome that many traditional notions of democracy, including the value of vigorous debate and the rule of law, also would require revision. ... As many in ancient Rome learned two millennia ago, it is difficult if not impossible to maintain a Republic within an Empire."[23]

15

Twisted Intelligence

In Tom Clancy's 2002 political thriller "Sum of All Fears," the United States and Russia are being pushed to the brink of nuclear war by neo-Nazi terrorists who have detonated a nuclear explosion in Baltimore and want the Americans to blame the Russians. CIA analysts have pieced together the real story but can't get it to the President. "The President is basing his decisions on some really bad information," analyst Jack Ryan (played by Ben Affleck) pleads to a U.S. general. "My orders are to get the right information to the people who make the decisions."

Though a bit corny, Ryan's dialogue captures the creed of professional intelligence analysts. Solid information, they believe, must be the foundation for sound decisions, especially when lives and the national security are at stake. In 2002, the battle over that principle was the dramatic but then-little-reported back story to the deadly politics of war. It was a story of how the CIA's once-vaunted analytical division was overwhelmed by ideologues who started with a decision to invade Iraq and then sought out information to help manufacture public consent.

This trend of corrupted – or "politicized" – intelligence could be traced back at least a quarter century. But unlike earlier battles in which CIA old-timers were around to resist the political pressures, there were fewer and fewer of those senior professionals left. They mostly had been replaced by careerists who put their salaries and status ahead of the integrity of the process.[1]

So, time and again, with only scattered resistance, Bush and his administration replaced the principle that good intelligence makes good policy with the near-opposite approach; you start with your end point and then distort all available information to sell the pre-ordained policy to an ill-informed and frightened people.

Instead of the U.S. intelligence community acting as a filter through which raw information flowed, allowing analysts to pick out the gems and wash away the dross, the pre-Iraq War filter operated in reverse, removing the good information – if it didn't fit with the policy – and keeping the junk that did.

It was as if the fictional CIA analyst Jack Ryan rushed to give the President not the truth of a terrorist provocation but instead hastened to reaffirm the false narrative that the neo-Nazis wanted the United States to believe.

◆◆◆

To gain public acceptance of an unprovoked invasion of Iraq, the Bush administration had to drive home two key points: first, the American people needed to think that Saddam Hussein had rebuilt his arsenal of chemical and biological weapons and was close to manufacturing a nuclear bomb, and second, there had to be a plausible case that Hussein's secular dictatorship had a secret relationship with Islamic terrorists, who might carry Hussein's weapons to the United States.

Otherwise, it was unlikely the American people would support sending an expeditionary force halfway around the world to attack a country that had not attacked or threatened to attack the United States. The key would be to overwhelm the American public with alarming intelligence about Iraq while keeping the handful of skeptics marginalized at the fringes of public discourse.

The official story of how the Bush administration succeeded in this undertaking would dribble out in bits and pieces over the next four years. But it was not until September 2006 that the Senate Intelligence Committee released a long-awaited assessment of how so much bad intelligence was injected into the decision-making process.

Over the objections of leading Republicans, the committee released two reports, one evaluating the false intelligence that buttressed the claims of cooperation between Saddam Hussein's government and al-Qaeda terrorists, and the other about the Iraqi National Congress, an influential group of exiles who worked with American neoconservatives to make the Iraq War happen.

The U.S. relationship with the Iraqi exiles dated back to 1991 as President George H.W. Bush won praise for routing Hussein's army from Kuwait but drew criticism from influential neoconservatives when he allowed the dictator to remain in power. Bush felt under pressure to take some action to keep up the pressure on Hussein.

In May 1991, the CIA approached Ahmed Chalabi, a secular Shiite who had not lived in Iraq since 1956. Chalabi was far from a perfect opposition candidate, however. Beyond his isolation from his homeland, Chalabi was a fugitive from bank fraud charges in Jordan. Still, in June

1992, the Iraqi exiles held an organizational meeting in Vienna, Austria, out of which came the Iraqi National Congress. Chalabi emerged as the group's chairman and most visible leader.

But Chalabi upset CIA officers who complained about the quality of his information, the excessive size of his security detail, his lobbying of Congress, and his resistance to working as a team player. For his part, Chalabi bristled at the idea that he was a U.S. intelligence asset, preferring to see himself as an independent political leader.

Nevertheless, he and his organization were not averse to accepting American money. With U.S. financial backing, the INC waged a propaganda campaign against Hussein and arranged for "a steady stream of low-ranking walk-ins" to provide intelligence about the Iraqi military, the Senate Intelligence Committee report said.[2]

The INC's mix of duties – propaganda and intelligence – would create concerns within the CIA as would Chalabi's "coziness" with the Shiite government of Iran. The CIA concluded that Chalabi was double-dealing both sides when he falsely informed Iran that the United States wanted Iran's help in conducting anti-Hussein operations.

"Chalabi passed a fabricated message from the White House to" an Iranian intelligence officer in northern Iraq, the CIA reported. According to one CIA representative, Chalabi used National Security Council stationery for the fabricated letter, a charge that Chalabi denied.[3]

In December 1996, Clinton administration officials decided to terminate the CIA's relationship with the INC and Chalabi. "There was a breakdown in trust and we never wanted to have anything to do with him anymore," CIA Director George Tenet told the Senate Intelligence Committee.[4]

However, in 1998, with the congressional passage of the Iraq Liberation Act, the INC was again one of the exile organizations that qualified for U.S. funding. Starting in March 2000, the State Department agreed to grant an INC foundation almost $33 million for several programs, including more propaganda operations and collection of information about alleged war crimes committed by Hussein's regime.

By March 2001, with George W. Bush in office and already focusing on Iraq, the INC was given greater leeway to pursue its projects, including an Information Collection Program.[5]

The INC's blurred responsibilities for both intelligence gathering and propaganda dissemination raised new concerns within the State Department. But Bush's National Security Council intervened against State's attempts to cut off funding. The NSC shifted the INC operation to the control of the Defense Department, where neoconservatives wielded more influence. To little avail, CIA officials warned their counterparts at the Defense Intelligence Agency about suspicions that "the INC was penetrated by Iranian and possibly other intelligence services, and that the INC had its own agenda," the Senate report said.[6]

"You've got a real bucket full of worms with the INC and we hope you're taking the appropriate steps," the CIA told the DIA.[7]

But the CIA's warnings did little to stop the flow of INC propaganda into America's politics and media. Besides irrigating the U.S. intelligence community with fresh propaganda, the INC funneled a steady stream of "defectors" to U.S. news outlets eager for anti-Hussein scoops.

The "defectors" also made the rounds of Congress where members saw a political advantage in citing the INC's propaganda as a way to talk tough about the Middle East. In turn, conservative and neoconservative think tanks honed their reputations in Washington by staying at the cutting edge of the negative news about Hussein, with human rights groups ready to pile on, too, against the brutal Iraqi dictator. The Bush administration found all this anti-Hussein propaganda fitting perfectly with its international agenda.

The INC's information program served the institutional needs – and biases – of Official Washington. And there were few counter-pressures to check any outrageous allegation against the widely despised Saddam Hussein. When Iraqi officials were allowed onto American news programs, it was an opportunity for the interviewers to show their tough side, pounding the Iraqis with hostile questions, but U.S. officials got a much easier ride.

In the months after 9/11, a war fever swept the United States – and the INC was doing all it could to spread the infection. The INC's "defectors" supplied primary or secondary intelligence on the two issues most important to the Bush administration, Iraq's supposed rebuilding of its unconventional weapons and its alleged training of non-Iraqi terrorists.

Sometimes, the INC "defectors" would slip into the secret world of U.S. intelligence with *entrées* from former U.S. government officials. For instance, ex-CIA Director James Woolsey referred at least a couple of these Iraqi sources to the DIA.

Woolsey, who was affiliated with the Center for Strategic and International Studies and other neoconservative think tanks, had been one of the Reagan administration's favorite Democrats in the 1980s because he supported a hawkish foreign policy. After Bill Clinton won the White House, Woolsey parlayed his close ties to Democratic neoconservatives into an appointment as CIA director.

In early 1993, Clinton's foreign policy adviser Samuel "Sandy" Berger explained to one well-placed Democratic official that Woolsey was given the CIA job because the Clinton team felt it owed a favor to the neoconservative-leaning *New Republic*, which had lent Clinton some cachet with the insider crowd of Washington.

Amid the more relaxed post-Cold War mood, the Clinton team seemed to view the CIA directorship as a patronage plum that could be handed out as a favor to campaign supporters. But new international challenges soon emerged and Woolsey proved to be an ineffective leader of the intelligence community. After two years, he was replaced.

As the 1990s wore on, the spurned Woolsey grew closer to Washington's fast-growing neoconservative movement, which turned openly hostile to President Clinton for his perceived softness in asserting U.S. military power, especially against Arab regimes in the Middle East.

On January 26, 1998, the neocon Project for the New American Century sent a letter to Clinton urging the ouster of Saddam Hussein by force if necessary. Woolsey was one of the 18 signers. By early 2001, he also had grown close to the INC, having been hired as co-counsel to represent eight Iraqis, including INC members, who had been detained on immigration charges.

So, Woolsey was well-positioned to serve as a conduit for INC "defectors" trying to get their stories to U.S. officials and to the American public. DIA officials told the Senate Intelligence Committee that Woolsey introduced them to the first in a long line of INC "defectors" who offered the DIA information about Hussein's WMD and his supposed relationship with Islamic terrorists. For his part, Woolsey said he didn't recall making that referral.[8]

The debriefings of "Source One" – as he was called in the Senate Intelligence Committee report – generated more than 250 intelligence reports. Two of the reports described alleged terrorist training sites in Iraq, where Afghan, Pakistani and Palestinian nationals were allegedly taught military skills at the Salman Pak base, 20 miles south of Baghdad.

"Many Iraqis believe that Saddam Hussein had made an agreement with Usama bin Ladin in order to support his terrorist movement against the U.S.," Source One claimed, according to the Senate report.[9]

After the 9/11 attacks, information from Source One and other INC-connected "defectors" began surfacing in U.S. press accounts, not only in the right-wing news media, but many mainstream publications. In an October 12, 2001, column entitled "What About Iraq?" *Washington Post* chief foreign correspondent Jim Hoagland cited "accumulating evidence of Iraq's role in sponsoring the development on its soil of weapons and techniques for international terrorism," including training at Salman Pak.

Hoagland's sources included Iraqi army defector Sabah Khalifa Khodada and another unnamed Iraqi ex-intelligence officer in Turkey.

Hoagland also criticized the CIA for not taking seriously a possible Iraqi link to 9/11.[10]

Hoagland's column was followed by a Page One article in *The New York Times*, which was headlined "Defectors Cite Iraqi Training for Terrorism." It relied on Khodada, the second source in Turkey (who was later identified as Abu Zeinab al-Qurairy, a former senior officer in Iraq's intelligence agency, the Mukhabarat), and a lower-ranking member of Mukhabarat. This story described 40 to 50 Islamic militants getting training at Salman Pak at any one time, including lessons on how to hijack an airplane without weapons. There were also claims about a German scientist working on biological weapons.[11]

In a *Columbia Journalism Review* retrospective on press coverage of U.S. intelligence on Iraq, writer Douglas McCollam asked *Times* correspondent Chris Hedges about the article, which was written in coordination with a PBS Frontline documentary called "Gunning for Saddam," with correspondent Lowell Bergman.

Explaining the difficulty of checking out defector accounts when they meshed with the interests of the U.S. government, Hedges said, "We tried to vet the defectors and we didn't get anything out of Washington that said, 'these guys are full of shit.'"

For his part, Bergman told *CJR*'s McCollam, "The people involved appeared credible and we had no way of getting into Iraq ourselves."

The journalistic competition for anti-Hussein exclusives was intensifying. Based in Paris, Hedges said he would get periodic calls from *Times* editors asking that he check out defector stories originating from Chalabi's operation.

"I thought he was unreliable and corrupt, but just because someone is a sleazebag doesn't mean he might not know something or that everything he says is wrong," Hedges said. Hedges described Chalabi as having an "endless stable" of ready sources who could fill in American reporters on any number of Iraq-related topics.[12]

The Salman Pak story was one of many products from the INC's propaganda mill that proved influential in the run-up to the Iraq War but was knocked down later by U.S. intelligence agencies. According to the Senate committee's *post mortem*, the DIA said in June 2006 that it found "no credible reports that non-Iraqis were trained to conduct or support transnational terrorist operations at Salman Pak after 1991."

Explaining the origins of the bogus tales, the DIA concluded that Operation Desert Storm in 1990-91 had brought attention to the training base at Salman Pak, so "fabricators and unestablished sources who reported hearsay or third-hand information created a large volume of human intelligence reporting. This type of reporting surged after September 2001."[13]

In the prelude to the Iraq War, however, U.S. intelligence agencies found it hard to resist the INC's "defectors" when that would have meant bucking the White House and going against Washington's conventional wisdom. Rather than take those career chances, many intelligence analysts found it easier to go with the flow.

Referring to the INC's Source One, a U.S. intelligence memorandum in July 2002 hailed the information as "highly credible and includes reports on a wide range of subjects including conventional weapons facilities, denial and deception; communications security; suspected terrorist training locations; illicit trade and smuggling; Saddam's palaces; the Iraqi prison system; and Iraqi petrochemical plants." Only analysts in the State Department's Bureau of Intelligence and Research were skeptical because they felt Source One was making unfounded assumptions, especially about possible nuclear research sites.[14]

Only after the invasion of Iraq would U.S. intelligence recognize the holes in Source One's stories and spot examples of analysts extrapolating faulty conclusions from his limited first-hand knowledge.

"In early February 2004, in order to resolve ... credibility issues with Source One, Intelligence Community elements brought Source One to Iraq," the Senate Intelligence Committee report said. "When taken to the location Source One had described as the suspect [nuclear] facility, he was unable to identify it.

"According to one intelligence assessment, the 'subject appeared stunned upon hearing that he was standing on the spot that he reported as the location of the facility, insisted that he had never been to that spot, and wanted to check a map' ... Intelligence Community officers confirmed that they were standing on the location he was identifying. ... During questioning, Source One acknowledged contact with the INC's Washington Director [redacted], but denied that the Washington Director directed Source One to provide any false information."[15]

The U.S. intelligence community had mixed reactions to other Iraqi "walk-ins" arranged by the INC. Some were caught in outright deceptions, such as "Source Two" who had talked about Iraq supposedly building mobile biological weapons labs. After catching Source Two in contradictions, the CIA issued a "fabrication notice" in May 2002, deeming him "a fabricator/provocateur" and asserting that he had "been coached by the Iraqi National Congress prior to his meeting with western intelligence services."

However, the DIA never repudiated the specific reports that had been based on Source Two's debriefings. So, Source Two continued to be cited in five CIA intelligence assessments and the pivotal National Intelligence Estimate in October 2002, "as corroborating other source reporting about a mobile biological weapons program," the Senate Intelligence Committee report said.

Source Two was one of four human sources referred to by Secretary of State Colin Powell in his United Nations speech on February 5, 2003. When asked how a "fabricator" could have been used for such an important speech, a CIA analyst who worked on Powell's speech said, "we lost the thread of concern ... as time progressed I don't think we remembered."

A CIA supervisor added, "Clearly we had it at one point, we understood, we had concerns about the source, but over time it started getting used again and there really was a loss of corporate awareness that we had a problem with the source."[16]

Part of the challenge facing U.S. intelligence agencies was the sheer volume of "defectors" shepherded into debriefing rooms by the INC and the appeal of their information to U.S. policymakers. "Source Five," for instance, claimed that Osama bin Laden had traveled to Baghdad for direct meetings with Saddam Hussein. "Source Six" claimed that the Iraqi population was "excited" about a U.S. invasion to topple Hussein. Plus, the source said Iraqis recognized the need for post-invasion U.S. control.

By early February 2003, as the final invasion plans were underway, U.S. intelligence agencies had progressed up to "Source Eighteen," who came to epitomize what some analysts still suspected – that the INC was coaching the sources.

As the CIA tried to set up a debriefing of Source Eighteen, another Iraqi exile passed on word to the agency that an INC representative had told Source Eighteen to "deliver the act of a lifetime." CIA analysts weren't sure what to make of that piece of news – since Iraqi exiles frequently badmouthed each other – but the value of the warning soon became clear.

U.S. intelligence officers debriefed Source Eighteen the next day and discovered that "Source Eighteen was supposed to have a nuclear engineering background, but was unable to discuss advanced mathematics or physics and described types of 'nuclear' reactors that do not exist. Source Eighteen used the bathroom frequently, particularly when he appeared to be flustered by a line of questioning, suddenly remembering a new piece of information upon his return. During one such incident, Source Eighteen appeared to be reviewing notes," according to the Senate Intelligence Committee report.

Not surprisingly, CIA and DIA case officers judged Source Eighteen to be a fabricator. But the sludge of INC-connected disinformation continued to ooze through the U.S. intelligence community and to foul the American intelligence product – in part because there was little pressure from above demanding strict quality controls.[17]

Other Iraqi exile sources – not directly connected to the INC – also supplied dubious information, including a source of a foreign intelligence agency who earned the code name "Curve Ball." He contributed important details about Iraq's alleged mobile facilities for producing agents for biological warfare. Tyler Drumheller, former chief of the CIA's European Division, said his office had issued repeated warnings about Curve Ball's accounts. "Everyone in the chain of command knew exactly what was happening," Drumheller said.[18]

Despite those complaints, Curve Ball earned a rating as "credible" or "very credible," and his information became a core element of the Bush administration's case for invading Iraq. Drawings of Curve Ball's imaginary bio-weapons labs were a central feature of Powell's presentation to the U.N. Even after the invasion, U.S. officials continued to promote these claims, portraying the discovery of a couple of trailers used for inflating artillery balloons as "the strongest evidence to date that Iraq was hiding a biological warfare program."[19]

Finally, on May 26, 2004, a CIA assessment of Curve Ball said "investigations since the war in Iraq and debriefings of the key source indicate he lied about his access to a mobile BW production product."[20]

The U.S. intelligence community also learned that Curve Ball "had a close relative who had worked for the INC since 1992," but the CIA could not resolve the question of whether the INC coached Curve Ball. One CIA analyst said she doubted a direct INC role because the INC pattern was to "shop their good sources around town, but they weren't known for sneaking people out of countries into some asylum system.[21]"

In September 2006, four years after the Bush administration began fanning the flames of war against Iraq, a majority of Senate Intelligence Committee members overrode the objections of the panel's senior Republicans and issued the report on the INC's contribution to the U.S. intelligence failures.

The report concluded that the INC fed false information to the intelligence community to convince Washington that Iraq was flouting prohibitions on WMD production. The panel also found that the falsehoods had been "widely distributed in intelligence products prior to the war" and did influence some American perceptions of the WMD threat in Iraq.[22]

But INC disinformation was not solely to blame for the bogus intelligence that permeated the pre-war debate. In Washington, there had been a breakdown of the normal checks and balances that American democracy has traditionally relied on for challenging and eliminating the corrosive effects of false data.

By 2002, that self-correcting mechanism – a skeptical press, congressional oversight, and tough-minded intelligence analysts – had collapsed. With very few exceptions, prominent journalists refused to put their careers at risk; intelligence professionals played along with the powers that be; Democratic leaders succumbed to the political pressure to toe the President's line; and Republicans marched in lockstep with Bush on his way to war.

Because of this systemic failure, the Senate Intelligence Committee concluded four years later that nearly every key assessment of the U.S. intelligence community as expressed in the 2002 National Intelligence Estimate about Iraq's WMD was wrong:

> Postwar findings do not support the [NIE] judgment that Iraq was reconstituting its nuclear weapons program; ... do not support the [NIE] assessment that Iraq's acquisition of high-strength aluminum tubes was intended for an Iraqi nuclear program; ... do not support the [NIE] assessment that Iraq was "vigorously trying to procure uranium ore and yellowcake" from Africa; ... do not support the [NIE] assessment that "Iraq has biological weapons" and that "all key aspects of Iraq's offensive biological weapons program are larger and more advanced than before the Gulf war"; ... do not support the [NIE] assessment that Iraq possessed, or ever developed, mobile facilities for producing biological warfare agents; ... do not support the [NIE] assessments that Iraq "has chemical weapons" or "is expanding its chemical industry to support chemical weapons production"; ... do not support the [NIE] assessments that Iraq had a developmental program for an Unmanned Aerial Vehicle "probably intended to deliver biological agents" or that an effort to procure U.S. mapping software "strongly suggests that Iraq is investigating the use of these UAVs for missions targeting the United States."[23]

It may be hard for future historians to comprehend how the largest and costliest intelligence system ever devised by man could get so much so wrong. For instance, how could the discovery that Iraq had tried to obtain U.S. mapping software lead to the absurd conclusion that Iraq was planning to use tiny remote-controlled planes to spray the United States with biological weapons? There was an obvious alternative explanation – that the Iraqis wanted to exploit the software and didn't care about the American maps.

But within a system in which punishments fell on those who didn't embrace the most alarmist explanations, the inevitable result was the acceptance of paranoid fantasies as fact. When one adds in the careerism that pervaded Washington media and government circles, the results – a kind of mass hysteria inside the Capital Beltway – were no longer surprising, but logical in a twisted sort of way.

◆◆◆

This institutional bias in favor of paranoia over reason was captured in the guidelines for a CIA paper produced in June 2002, entitled "Iraq and al-Qa'ida: Interpreting a Murky Relationship." The study was designed to assess the Iraqi government's links to al-Qaeda. But the analysts were given unusual instructions, told to be "purposely aggressive in seeking to draw connections, on the assumption that any indication of a relationship between these two hostile elements could carry great dangers to the United States."

A former CIA deputy director of intelligence told the Senate Intelligence Committee that the paper's authors were ordered to "lean far forward and do a speculative piece." The deputy director told them, "If you were going to stretch to the maximum the evidence you had, what could you come up with."[24]

In other words, the CIA analysts set out to put any evidence of links between Iraq and al-Qaeda in the harshest light. If some piece of information contained even a remote possibility of a connection, the assumption had to be that the tie-in was real and substantive. If Jordanian terrorist Abu Musab al-Zarqawi snuck into Baghdad for medical treatment, the assumption could not be that Iraqi authorities were unaware of his presence or couldn't find him; it had to be that Saddam Hussein knew all about it and was collaborating with Zarqawi.

This practice of assuming the worst – rather than attempting to gauge likelihoods as accurately as possible – guaranteed the kind of slanted intelligence reports that guided the United States to war in 2002-03.

In a 2006 book, *The One Percent Doctrine*, author Ron Suskind described how this worst-case bias evolved. He traced it to a theory espoused by Vice President Dick Cheney that if a terrorist threat was deemed even one percent likely, the United States had to act as if it were a certainty. Suskind described Cheney first enunciating his new approach when he heard about Pakistani physicists discussing nuclear weapons with al-Qaeda.

"If there's a one percent chance that Pakistani scientists are helping al-Qaeda build or develop a nuclear weapon, we have to treat it as a certainty in terms of our response," Cheney said. "It's not about our analysis, or finding a preponderance of evidence. ... It's about our response."[25]

Suskind reported that Cheney's new "standard of action ... would frame events and responses from the administration for years to come. The Cheney Doctrine. Even if there's just a one percent chance of the unimaginable coming due, act as if it is a certainty. ... This doctrine – the one percent solution – divided what had largely been indivisible in the conduct of American foreign policy: analysis and action. Justified or not, fact-based or not, 'our response' is what matters. As to 'evidence,' the bar was set so low that the word itself almost didn't apply."[26]

The one-percent risk threshold negated any serious analysis that sought to calibrate dangers within the complex array of possibilities that exist in the real world. In effect, it meant that any potential threat that crossed the administration's line of sight would exceed one percent and thus had to be treated as a clear and present danger.

The larger fallacy of the doctrine was that pursuing one-percent threats as if they were certainties was not just a case of choosing to be safe than sorry. Rather, it pulled the pursuer into a swollen river of other dangers, leading to a torrent of adverse consequences many of them far more dangerous than the original one-percent worry. It almost guaranteed that a country – while pursuing some phantom danger – would plunge over a waterfall, sooner or later.

So, while eradicating one unlikely nightmare scenario – Saddam Hussein's "mushroom cloud" in the hands of Osama bin Laden – the Bush administration might increase chances that other enemy states, such as North Korea and Iran, would resist pressure against them building their own nuclear weapons or that Pakistan's Islamic fundamentalists, already closely allied with bin Laden, would oust pro-U.S. dictator Pervez Musharraf and gain control of Pakistan's nuclear arsenal. Some analysts considered those possibilities much more likely than the original risk of Hussein developing a nuclear bomb and then giving it to bin Laden.

Acting on one-percent dangers also raised the strong possibility that the United States would turn out to be dead wrong, again and again. After all, a one-percent chance of being right could mean a 99-percent likelihood of being wrong.

That was what happened in the U.S. intelligence assessments of Saddam Hussein's alleged relationship with al-Qaeda. Though the bulk of the credible evidence went against believing that the secular dictator would throw in his lot with Islamic fundamentalists, there were enough shreds and shards of possibilities about a Hussein-al-Qaeda connection – many of them compiled in the CIA's "Murky" paper – that senior U.S.

officials went off in that direction although the preponderance of evidence pointed the opposite way.

As the CIA inspector general concluded in a December 21, 2005 report, "the data reveal few indications of an established relationship between al-Qa'ida and Saddam Hussein's regime before September 11, 2001." In June 2002, however, the "Murky" report sought to build the case for a Hussein-al-Qaeda relationship by assembling "a body of fragmented, conflicting reporting from sources of varying reliability." The report argued that the supposed relationship was "much like those between rival intelligence services, with each trying to exploit the other for its own benefit."[27]

But the CIA could only show that the two sides might have considered some cooperation regarding "safe-haven, training and reciprocal non-aggression," CIA Director George Tenet told the Senate Intelligence Committee on September 17, 2002. "There are several reported suggestions by al-Qa'ida to Iraq about joint terrorist ventures, but in no case can we establish that Iraq accepted or followed up on these suggestions."[28]

As explained by captured Iraqi officials after the invasion, the several contacts between Baghdad and al-Qaeda appeared to have been initiated by al-Qaeda and didn't lead to any cooperation from Iraq. Hussein was determined to keep the radical bin Laden at arm's length.

A senior Iraq Intelligence Service official, Faruq Hijazi, told American debriefers that he was picked by Hussein to meet with bin Laden in 1995 because Hijazi was secular and thus unsympathetic to bin Laden's fundamentalist message. Hussein also instructed Hijazi "only to listen" and promise nothing. Bin Laden requested permission to open an office in Iraq, to receive Chinese sea mines, and to obtain military training – all of which Hussein rejected, Hijazi said.[29]

Other al-Qaeda overtures met similar rebuffs from Hussein who disliked bin Laden, in part, because the Saudi exile had called Hussein an "unbeliever," according to a senior Iraqi official interviewed after the invasion. Hussein also ordered another al-Qaeda operative, who slipped into Iraq, to be apprehended and expelled.

Before the U.S. invasion, however, the CIA sought to prove an operational relationship by citing information obtained from captured al-Qaeda official Ibn al-Shaykh al-Libi. In June 2002, the "Murky" paper cited claims by al-Libi that Iraq had "provided" unspecified chemical and biological weapons training for two al-Qaeda operatives. Al-Libi's information went into a November 2002 National Intelligence Estimate, representing the consensus view of the U.S. intelligence community.[30]

In January 2003, another CIA paper expanded on al-Libi's claims of an Iraqi-al-Qaeda connection, saying that "Iraq – acting on the request of al-Qa'ida militant Abu Abdullah, who was Muhammad Atif's emissary – agreed to provide unspecified chemical or biological weapons training for two al-Qa'ida associates beginning in December 2000."

By February 11, 2003, as the countdown to the U.S. invasion progressed, CIA Director Tenet began treating al-Libi's assertions as fact. At a Senate Intelligence Committee hearing, Tenet said Iraq "has also provided training in poisons and gases to two al-Qa'ida associates. One of these associates characterized the relationship he forged with Iraqi officials as successful."[31]

But the CIA's professed certainty about al-Libi's information went against the suspicions voiced by the Defense Intelligence Agency. "He lacks specific details" about the supposed training, the DIA observed. "It is possible he does not know any further details; it is more likely this individual is intentionally misleading the debriefers."[32]

The DIA's doubts proved prescient. In January 2004, al-Libi recanted his statements and claimed that he had lied because of both actual and anticipated abuse, including threats that he would be sent to an intelligence service where he expected to be tortured. Al-Libi said he fabricated "all information regarding al-Qa'ida's sending representatives to Iraq to try to obtain WMD assistance," according to a February 4, 2004, CIA operational cable. "Once al-Libi started fabricating information, [he claimed] his treatment improved and he experienced no further physical pressures from the Americans."[33]

Despite his cooperation, al-Libi said he was transferred to another country that subjected him to beatings and confinement in a "small box" for about 17 hours. He said he then made up another story about three al-Qaeda operatives going to Iraq "to learn about nuclear weapons." Afterwards, he said his treatment improved.[34]

In September 2006, the Senate Intelligence Committee criticized the CIA for accepting al-Libi's claims as credible. "No postwar information has been found that indicates CBW training occurred and the detainee who provided the key prewar reporting about this training recanted his claims after the war," the committee report said.[35]

The Senate Intelligence Committee skirted making a conclusion about how al-Libi's statements were extracted. But the al-Libi case demonstrated one of the practical risks of coercing a witness to talk. To avoid pain, people often make stuff up.

◆◆◆

Beyond the claims about supposed Iraqi training of al-Qaeda, another key argument for invading Iraq was the alleged link between Hussein's government and Jordanian terrorist Abu Musab al-Zarqawi. While using an alias, Zarqawi obtained medical treatment in Baghdad in 2002. Although there was never any evidence of actual contact between the Iraqi government and Zarqawi, the suggestion persisted that Hussein's vaunted internal security apparatus must have known about Zarqawi's presence and thus must have been in league with Zarqawi.

However, after the invasion, U.S. intelligence agencies examined Iraqi government documents and interrogated captured officials. As it turned out, in spring 2002, the Iraq Intelligence Service had created a "special committee" to track down and arrest Zarqawi, but failed to find him, according to a CIA report dated October 25, 2005. "The regime did not have a relationship, harbor, or turn a blind eye toward Zarqawi and his associates," the CIA report concluded.[36]

The Senate Intelligence Committee determined that U.S. intelligence agencies "overestimated the Iraqi regime's capabilities to locate [Zarqawi and his associates]. Postwar information indicates that Saddam Hussein attempted, unsuccessfully, to locate and capture al-Zarqawi." Further, the Senate panel concluded that "no postwar information indicates that Iraq intended to use al-Qa'ida or any other terrorist group to strike the United States homeland before or during" the U.S. invasion.[37]

In effect, Cheney's "one-percent doctrine" for assessing danger had led the United States into a geopolitical version of "the little old lady who swallowed a fly." As the children's ditty goes, the little old lady next swallows a spider to catch the fly but soon finds that the spider "tickles inside her." So, she engorges other animals, in escalating size, to eliminate each previous animal. Eventually, she swallows a horse and "is dead of course." In this Iraq War case, however, it appears there was never a fly to begin with.

16

Selling the Product

After the one-sided U.S. intelligence reports on Iraq were assembled, some analysts grumbled about the pollution of the process, but their complaints received scant attention in the major U.S. news outlets, either the nation's premier newspapers or the 24/7 cable news programs. The story of the internal intelligence battle was told mostly in the foreign press, some second-tier U.S. newspapers and the Internet.

"Basically, cooked information is working its way into high-level pronouncements and there's a lot of unhappiness about it in intelligence, especially among analysts at the CIA," said Vincent Cannistraro, the former head of CIA's counter-intelligence office, according to an article published in *The Guardian*, a London newspaper.[1]

The Knight-Ridder newspaper chain also gave its readers a real-time sense of the behind-the-scenes drama..

"A growing number of military officers, intelligence professionals and diplomats ... charge that administration hawks have exaggerated evidence of the threat that Iraqi leader Saddam Hussein poses, including distorting his links to the al-Qaeda terrorist network, have overstated the amount of international support for attacking Iraq and have downplayed the potential repercussions of a new war in the Middle East," Knight-Ridder correspondents Warren Strobel and Jonathan Linday reported on October 8, 2002.

Besides exaggerating the Iraqi threat, the Bush administration is "squelch[ing] dissenting views," the article said. "Analysts at the working level in the intelligence community are feeling very strong pressure from the Pentagon to cook the intelligence books," said one official who spoke on condition of anonymity. Of a dozen other officials interviewed for the article, no one disagreed with that assessment.[2]

In a similar article three days later, the *Los Angeles Times* cited "an escalating war" within U.S. intelligence circles in which "senior Bush administration officials are pressuring CIA analysts to tailor their assessments of the Iraqi threat to help build a case against Saddam

Hussein." Top Pentagon officials, including Defense Secretary Donald Rumsfeld and his top deputy Paul Wolfowitz, "have bombarded CIA analysts with criticism and calls for revisions on such key questions as whether Iraq has ties to the al-Qaeda terrorist network, sources said," according to the *Los Angeles Times* article on October 11, 2002.

"The sources stressed that CIA analysts – who are supposed to be impartial – are fighting to resist the pressure. But they said analysts are increasingly resentful of what they perceive as efforts to contaminate the intelligence process," the newspaper reported. "Analysts feel more politicized and more pushed than many of them can ever remember," the *Times* quoted an intelligence official as saying.[3]

But this message of doctored intelligence never penetrated far into the conventional wisdom of Washington, especially given the lack of attention from two of the leading national newspapers, *The New York Times* and *The Washington Post*. On a day-to-day basis, Bush and his spokesmen had pretty much a clear field to make their case for war.

Still, some of their claims were ludicrous on their face. In his Cincinnati speech, Bush conjured up the image of Iraq sending unmanned aerial vehicles [UAVs] on chemical and biological warfare attacks against the United States. Bush said Iraq "is exploring ways of using these UAVs for missions targeting the United States," in which the UAVs "could be used to disperse chemical or biological weapons across broad areas."

Iraq indeed was developing drone aircraft, but the prospect of them somehow reaching the U.S. mainland was silly. "U.S. military experts … said that [the UAVs have] a maximum range of a few hundred miles" and are "no threat to targets in the U.S.," reported *The Guardian* in London. But that logical observation got little play in the United States.

The U.S. news media also gave short shrift to concerns that ousting Saddam Hussien could provoke sectarian violence between Iraq's Sunnis and Shiites, which, in turn, might destabilize the entire Middle East. "We are about to do something that will ignite a fuse in this region that we will rue the day we ever started," warned retired Marine Gen. Anthony Zinni, who had served as a Middle East envoy for Bush. But that warning, too, received inadequate attention.

Yet, while most major U.S. news outlets shied away from a thorough examination of Bush's case for war, a much more skeptical approach could be found at some Internet sites. On October 15, 2002, in a *Consortiumnews.com* article entitled "Misleading the Nation to War," Sam Parry observed how weak the administration's case was:

"Taken together, the evidence seems clear that the Bush administration doesn't want a full debate on the merits of the President's war policy. Bush and his aides simply want to twist whatever information they can to bring the American people into line. The irony of this manipulation of public opinion stands out against the glowing ideals expressed in Bush's 'national security strategy' report of September 20."

In that report, Bush declared that "the great struggles of the 20th century between liberty and totalitarianism ended with a decisive victory for the forces of freedom – and a single sustainable model for national success: freedom, democracy and free enterprise."

But, Sam Parry wrote, "that grand commitment to freedom and democracy apparently does not extend to the concept of a free and open debate in the United States, even about life-and-death issues such as whether the nation should send its soldiers off to war and potentially face greater dangers as a consequence."

One of the few senators who dared speak passionately against Bush's war resolution was Senator Robert Byrd, who argued that the Founding Fathers proscribed the war-making powers of the Executive out of clear-headed knowledge about the destruction that can befall a people when a misguided leader rushes a nation into war.

"We are at the gravest of moments," Byrd said in an op-ed piece in *The New York Times*. "We must not allow any President to unleash the dogs of war at his own discretion and for an unlimited period of time."[4]

Byrd lost the argument, as Congress – less than a month before congressional elections in November 2002 – gave Bush the powers he demanded. But the capitulation of many leading Democrats, including Senators Hillary Clinton and John Kerry, to Bush's demand for authorization to use military force in Iraq didn't buy them the political protection that many of them had expected.

Bush still urged voters to send him congressional allies who would stand shoulder to shoulder with him in the "war on terror." The Democrats were shocked at the Republican brazenness. But the strategy worked. Republicans swept to victory in key race after key race, ousting strong incumbents, such as Senator Max Cleland of Georgia. The Republicans got control of the Senate and retained control of the House.

◆◆◆

While consolidating his political power in Washington, Bush was quietly establishing the framework for what could be viewed as a new-age totalitarian society in which the people would have few secrets from the government and the President would possess almost unlimited authority. Nat Parry sketched the outlines on December 1, 2002, in a *Consortiumnews.com* article entitled "Richard Milhous W. Bush":

"Since the September 11, 2001, attacks, Bush has asserted broad powers to wiretap, spy on and imprison indefinitely people he deems a threat to national security – authority far beyond what was available to the famously paranoid [Richard Milhous] Nixon. Bush's executive powers are already so sweeping they may be unprecedented in U.S. history.

"While some of Bush's supporters cite prior suspensions of constitutional rights during the Civil War and World War II, those eras lacked today's technology to pry into the most personal details of the lives of Americans. Even in the late 1960s and early 1970s, President Nixon and his allies were forced to adopt relatively crude means for invading the privacy of Americans. Bugs were placed on phones; agents were infiltrated into political organizations; and burglars were sent into homes and offices searching for embarrassing or incriminating information.

"By contrast, today's modern technology can let Bush's team collect and analyze trillions of bytes of data on transactions and communications, the electronic footprints left in the course of everyday life: books borrowed from a library, fertilizer bought at a farm-supply outlet, X-rated movies rented at a video store, prescriptions filled at a pharmacy, sites visited on the Internet, tickets reserved for a plane, borders crossed while traveling, rooms rented at a motel, and hundreds of other examples.

"Bush's aides argue that their unrestricted access to this electronic data may help detect terrorists, but the data could prove even more useful in building dossiers on anti-war activists or blackmailing political opponents. Despite assurances that such abuses won't happen again, the capability will be a huge temptation for Bush, who has made clear his view that anyone not supporting his war on terror is siding with the terrorists.

"The technological blueprint for an Orwellian-style 'thought police' is already on the drawing board at the Defense Advanced Research Projects Agency, the Pentagon's top research and development arm. DARPA has commissioned a comprehensive plan for electronic spying that would track everyone in the world who is part of the modern economy."

According to the plan, "transactional data" was to be gleaned from electronic data on every kind of activity – "financial, education, travel, medical, veterinary, country entry, place/event entry, transportation, housing, critical resources, government, communications," according to the Web site for DARPA's Information Awareness Office. The program would then cross-reference this data with the "biometric signatures of humans," data collected on individuals' faces, fingerprints, gaits and irises. The project sought what it called "total information awareness."

The Information Awareness Office even boasted a logo that looked like some kind of clip art from George Orwell's *1984*. The logo showed the Masonic symbol of an all-seeing eye atop a pyramid peering over the globe, with the slogan, "scientia est potentia," Latin for "knowledge is power." Though apparently unintentional, DARPA's choice of a giant white pyramid eerily recalled Orwell's Ministry of Truth, "an enormous pyramidal structure of glittering white concrete, soaring up, terrace after terrace, 300 metres into the air." The all-seeing Masonic eye could be read as "Big Brother Is Watching."

Former Vice President Al Gore stepped out of the shadows again to point out the strange similarities both in style and substance with Orwell's totalitarian world. "We have always held out the shibboleth of Big Brother as a nightmare vision of the future that we're going to avoid at all costs," Gore said. "They have now taken the most fateful step in the direction of that Big Brother nightmare that any President has ever allowed to occur."[5]

Besides the parallels to *1984,* the assurances about respecting constitutional boundaries were undercut by the administration's provocative choice of director for the Information Awareness Office. The project was put under the control of President Reagan's former National Security Adviser John Poindexter, who was caught flouting other constitutional safeguards in the Iran-Contra scandal of the mid-1980s. Poindexter approved the sale of missiles to Iran and the transfer of profits to Nicaraguan contras, thus circumventing the Constitution's grant to Congress of war-making authority and the power of the purse.

In 1990, in federal court in Washington, Poindexter was convicted of five felonies in connection with the Iran-Contra scheme and the subsequent cover-up. But his case was overturned by a conservative-dominated three-judge appeals court panel, which voted 2-1 that the conviction was tainted by congressional immunity given to Poindexter to compel his testimony to Congress in 1987.

Though Poindexter's Iran-Contra excesses in the 1980s were viewed by some as disqualifying for a sensitive job overseeing the collection of information about everyone on earth, DARPA said it sought out committed characters to run its projects. "The best DARPA program managers have always been freewheeling zealots in pursuit of their goals," the agency's Web site said.

The Bush administration promised that this time there wouldn't be violations of constitutional protections like there had been in the Nixon era. But Bush actually faced fewer institutional obstacles to committing abuses of power. When Nixon was President, opposition Democrats held the congressional levers that permitted investigations into Nixon's domestic spying. The national news media also approached its duties with far more professionalism. The federal courts, too, were less partisan and less likely to rubber-stamp White House assertions of national security. In late 2002, with all those institutional checks and balances either gone or substantially weakened, there was little to interfere with Bush's return to Nixon-style abuses or worse.

♦ ♦ ♦

A year after the 9/11 attacks, Americans still didn't understand that there had been a fundamental change in the U.S. government and its relationship to the people. Short-term emergency actions that had followed the 9/11 attacks were solidifying into long-term ways of doing business.

Behind the scenes, Bush was operating under a theory that as Commander in Chief in a time of war, he held "plenary" – or unlimited – authority. That meant he could ignore domestic laws, international laws, treaties and even constitutional rights of citizens. In his view, his extraordinary powers – which rivaled the absolute authority of Medieval kings and queens – would stay with the President as long as the "war on terror" continued.

Amid the flush of overwhelming popular support in 2001 and 2002, Bush had begun seeing himself as the infallible leader whose judgments were beyond questioning. Bush had tasted the addictive nectar of presidential power.

When asked by author Bob Woodward if he ever explained his positions, Bush answered, "Of course not. I'm the commander – see, I don't need to explain why I say things. That's the interesting thing about being the President. Maybe somebody needs to explain to me why they say something, but I don't feel like I owe anybody an explanation."[6]

♦ ♦ ♦

By early 2003, Bush was putting the finishing touches on his war plans and his final pro-war propaganda push. At his State of the Union Address on January 28, Bush reprised the case against Iraq, throwing in one flourish that would later prove controversial. Citing a British "white paper," Bush said, "the British government has learned that Saddam Hussein recently sought significant quantities of uranium from Africa."

The claim, which became known as the "sixteen words," was intended to buttress the case about Hussein's nuclear weapons program by claiming that he had sought yellowcake uranium from Niger. But the

CIA doubted the allegation was true and struck the claim from an earlier presidential address. That prompted White House speechwriters to slip it back in by citing the reference to the British report.

While the United Kingdom had proved useful in that regard, Prime Minister Tony Blair still fretted about the absence of a specific U.N. Security Council resolution authorizing the war. A resolution would give Blair and the invasion some legal cover. Otherwise, Blair, Bush and their subordinates ran the risk of one day being hauled before an international tribunal and accused of war crimes.

According to the minutes of a January 31, 2003, meeting in the Oval Office between Bush and Blair, the U.S. President promised that "the US would put its full weight behind efforts to get another resolution and would 'twist arms' and 'even threaten'. But [Bush] had to say that if ultimately we failed, military action would follow anyway."

Bush and Blair also discussed the possibility of creating a pretext for war. According to Bush, "The US was thinking of flying U-2 reconnaissance aircraft with fighter cover over Iraq, painted in UN colours. If Saddam fired on them, he would be in breach" of U.N. resolutions. It was also possible that a defector could be brought out who would give a public presentation about Saddam's WMD, and there was also a small possibility that Saddam would be assassinated," Bush said, according to the minutes.

Bush and Blair acknowledged that no weapons of mass destruction had been found in Iraq by U.N. inspectors who had returned in fall 2002, nor was WMD likely to be found in the coming weeks, but that wouldn't get in the way of the U.S.-led invasion. But Blair still stressed the need for a second resolution from the U.N. Security Council that would authorize the use of force. Bush agreed to try but felt he had the authority to attack Iraq whether the U.N. approved or not. At the meeting, Bush added that after the invasion, he "thought it unlikely that there would be internecine warfare between the different religious and ethnic groups."[*]

In the early months of 2003, Bush faced another annoyance – those U.N. inspectors scurrying around Iraq, going from one suspected WMD site to another and coming up empty. By early 2003, the U.N. inspectors were reporting full cooperation from the Iraqi government in letting the inspectors go to any suspected WMD site. So, Bush and his allies turned the heat up on chief inspector Han Blix and his team.

Rather than conclude that the absence of any WMD discoveries might suggest the absence of WMD, Team Bush heaped ridicule and

---

[*] The minutes were obtained by human rights lawyer Philippe Sands for an edition of his book, *Lawless World*. The minutes were reviewed by British Channel 4 News.

contempt on the inspectors as incompetents. The flavor of this vitriol was captured in a TV routine by right-wing comic Dennis Miller who likened Blix and his inspectors to the cartoon characters in "Scooby Doo," racing around pointlessly in their vans. Meanwhile, pro-Bush news outlets carried accusations that Blix might be corrupt and possibly sympathetic to Saddam Hussein.

It was during this time frame that the Bush administration asked the British government to assist in a spying operation against U.N. officials in New York. While the motive for the spying has never been clarified, the operation fit the overall pattern of putting political pressure on U.N. officials. The spying was first revealed via a leak by British government translator Katharine Gun to the London *Observer* newspaper in early March 2003. Gun leaked a U.S. National Security Council memo, which described a "surge" in spying at the U.N. aimed "against" delegations from swing countries on the U.N. Security Council.

Gun was charged with violation of the British state secrecy laws, though the case was dropped in February 2004 when Tony Blair's government apparently concluded that the prosecution would require the disclosure of an internal debate about the legality of joining Bush's invasion of Iraq. After the Gun case collapsed, former British cabinet minister Clare Short said on BBC Radio that British spies had been instructed to carry out operations inside the U.N., including against Secretary General Kofi Annan. Short, who had resigned her position as International Development Secretary to protest the war, said she saw transcripts of Annan's conversations.[7]

Blix said he also suspected that his home and office in New York were bugged in the weeks before the Iraq War. The chief weapons inspector said a Bush administration official confronted him with photos that could only have been obtained from inside the U.N. weapons inspection office. When Blix asked the official how he had obtained the photos, the official wouldn't say. Blix suspected that his secure fax machine may have been penetrated to obtain the photos.[8]

In Bush's view, the United Nations needed to prove its "relevance" by endorsing war with Iraq. Some Bush supporters argued that the U.N. would be wise to sanction the conflict – to "board the train before it leaves the station" – rather than face the prospect of the world's only superpower acting in open violation of international law. In other words, it would be better to keep the U.S. within the framework of international law, even if that meant changing the rules, than to have the U.S. operating as a "super rogue state."

But acquiescence to Bush's demands carried the risk that the U.N. would look like a mere servant of U.S. interests, hypocritically setting aside its founding principles that rejected aggressive wars. For a half century, the U.N. Charter had stood as a beacon against war except in cases of national defense or when a menace to world stability was clear and immediate. Written in the historical shadow of World War II, the Charter was meant to avert exactly what Bush was proposing, a "preemptive" war when one powerful nation wanted to invade a weaker one because of some hazy threat.

The U.N. Charter's overriding goal was to avoid war if at all possible, "to save succeeding generations from the scourge of war." Peace – not some Orwellian concept of war in the name of peace – was the core principle behind the U.N. Not only was aggression shunned, but the Charter stated that acts of aggression must be opposed by "effective collective measures."

So, to go along with Bush's "preemptive" war against Iraq – when Iraq was making no overt threat against its neighbors – the U.N. would have to, in effect, accept Bush's assertion that he, as U.S. Commander in Chief, had the unfettered authority to apply international law as he saw fit. Rather than the U.N. intervening in an ongoing conflict to save lives, this would be the first war initiated by the U.N. against a nation and a people living in peace – if Bush got his way.

◆◆◆

To make his case before the U.N., Bush dispatched the most credible official in his administration, Secretary of State Colin Powell. By the time Powell was assigned to make the case for war, he counted himself among the growing list of officials nervous about the quality of the WMD intelligence. Indeed, Powell may have been one of the best positioned officials to know that the threat from Iraq was being exaggerated. In February 2001, Powell personally had cited the effectiveness of the U.N. sanctions in crippling Saddam Hussein's military capabilities.

"Frankly, they have worked," Powell said of the sanctions. "He [Hussein] has not developed any significant capability with respect to weapons of mass destruction. He is unable to project conventional power against his neighbors."

But Bush called on Powell to put his loyalty to the President first, over his own personal doubts. Col. Larry Wilkerson, Powell's longtime friend and chief of staff, said Powell was upset with the White House instructions about what to highlight in his speech.

"He came through the door that morning and he had in his hand a sheaf of papers and he said this is what I've got to present at the United Nations according to the White House and you need to look at it,"

Wilkerson later told CNN. "It was anything but an intelligence document. It was as some people characterized it later, some kind of Chinese menu from which you could pick and choose. ... There was no way the Secretary of State was going to read off a script about serious matters of intelligence that could lead to war when the script was basically unsourced."[9]

Powell's skepticism led to his "four day and four night" encampment at the CIA reviewing the intelligence. Despite assurances from CIA Director George Tenet, Powell recognized the shakiness of the case. Wilkerson said Powell "turned to the DCI, Mr. Tenet, and he [Powell] said, 'everything here, everything here, you stand behind?' And Mr. Tenet said, 'absolutely, Mr. Secretary.' And he [Powell] said, 'well, you know you're going to be sitting behind me. ... Right behind me. In camera."[10]

So, on February 5, 2003, Powell sat at the curved table of the U.N. Security Council – with CIA Director Tenet and U.S. Ambassador to the U.N. John Negroponte behind him. Revealing none of his internal doubts, Powell calmly presented what he claimed was a convincing factual case that "Saddam Hussein and his regime have made no effort – no effort – to disarm as required by the international community. Indeed, the facts and Iraq's behavior show that Saddam Hussein and his regime are concealing their efforts to produce more weapons of mass destruction."

Powell's speech was a classic case of persuading an audience of someone's guilt by piling on one suspicious incident after another. Even if no single example proved the point, the mind numbed to the volume of accusations and surrendered to the accumulation of pseudo-evidence. That's especially true if the target of the allegations is a figure of disdain and the person making the charges is respected. Rarely could that imbalance have been greater than Saddam Hussein versus Colin Powell. Even a determined skeptic, punching holes in one of Powell's dubious accusations after another, would grow weary offering innocent explanations of Hussein's suspicious behavior.

Powell's case to the U.N. was a collection of Bush's favorite accusations, albeit with some additions and omissions. For instance, Powell left out the uranium-from-Africa claim that Bush had cited in his State of the Union Address. But the strength of Powell's testimony came from his personal reputation and his presumption of credibility, much of it based on Powell's legend. Though conveying an image of integrity, Powell actually had compiled a long record of opportunism and obedience, not courage and principle.[11] But as he made his presentation to the U.N., Powell's legend was near its zenith.

Powell argued that Iraq's insistence that it didn't have WMD was itself proof of its defiance, even though the U.N. inspectors had failed to find anything. "This council placed the burden on Iraq to comply and disarm and not on the inspectors to find that which Iraq has gone out of its way to conceal for so long," Powell said. "Inspectors are inspectors; they are not detectives."

The Secretary of State then laid out the case that Iraq had a lot to hide. "The material I will present to you comes from a variety of sources," Powell said. "Some are U.S. sources. And some are those of other countries. Some of the sources are technical, such as intercepted telephone conversations and photos taken by satellites. Other sources are people who have risked their lives to let the world know what Saddam Hussein is really up to. I cannot tell you everything that we know. But what I can share with you, when combined with what all of us have learned over the years, is deeply troubling. What you will see is an accumulation of facts and disturbing patterns of behavior."

One of Powell's techniques was to play intercepted Iraqi telephone conversations in which the precise topic was unclear, but Powell assumed the worst. In one such conversation, an Iraqi official said, "we evacuated everything. We don't have anything left." So Powell added, "Note what he says: 'We evacuated everything.' We didn't destroy it. We didn't line it up for inspection. We didn't turn it into the inspectors. We evacuated it to make sure it was not around when the inspectors showed up." But Powell was speculating that the "everything" referred to WMD.

In another excerpt, Powell embellished an original State Department translation to cast more suspicion on the Iraqis. To prove that Iraqis were removing illegal weapons before a U.N. inspection team arrived, Powell read from one supposed transcript of an Iraqi official giving orders: "We sent you a message yesterday to clean out all of the areas, the scrap areas, the abandoned areas. Make sure there is nothing there."

What the original State Department transcript said, however, was: "We sent you a message to inspect the scrap areas and the abandoned areas." There was no order to "clean out all of the areas" and there was no instruction to "make sure there is nothing there."[*]

Powell used the doctored transcript to draw a powerful conclusion. "This is all part of a system of hiding things and moving things out of the way and making sure they have left nothing behind," he said. "They were trying to clean up the area to leave no evidence behind of the presence of weapons of mass destruction. And they can claim that nothing was there. And the inspectors can look all they want, and they will find nothing."

---

[*]Powell's apparent fabrication of the intercept was first reported by Gilbert Cranberg, a former editor of the *Des Moines Register*'s editorial pages, when he compared Powell's testimony with the original State Department translations.

Powell dismissed Iraq's U.N. submissions about its compliance with U.N. resolutions as bald-faced lies. "Everything we have seen and heard indicates that, instead of cooperating actively with the inspectors to ensure the success of their mission, Saddam Hussein and his regime are busy doing all they possibly can to ensure that inspectors succeed in finding absolutely nothing," Powell said.

Trying to remind the public of Adlai Stevenson's dramatic presentation of aerial reconnaissance during the Cuban Missile Crisis, Powell displayed photos of trucks and other items whose presence was given a sinister cast. Powell seemed to sense the weakness of this photographic evidence, so he prefaced the display by stressing the sophistication of U.S. photo analysts.

"The photos that I am about to show you are sometimes hard for the average person to interpret, hard for me," he said. "The painstaking work of photo analysis takes experts with years and years of experience, poring for hours and hours over light tables. But as I show you these images, I will try to capture and explain what they mean, what they indicate to our imagery specialists."

But what the photos often showed were simply bunkers that could be used for a variety of purposes and trucks that – while Powell insisted they were chemical contamination vehicles – were water trucks that could have multiple purposes. U.N. inspector Steve Allinson said some trucks spotted by U.S. satellites were fire trucks, while other vehicles were so neglected that they had cobwebs inside.

Powell then launched into a litany of claims made by various Iraqi "defectors," many of whom were fed to U.S. intelligence by the Iraqi National Congress. "One of the most worrisome things that emerges from the thick intelligence file we have on Iraq's biological weapons is the existence of mobile production facilities used to make biological agents," Powell said. "Let me take you inside that intelligence file and share with you what we know from eyewitness accounts. We have firsthand descriptions of biological weapons factories on wheels and on rails. ...

"In a matter of months, they can produce a quantity of biological poison equal to the entire amount that Iraq claimed to have produced in the years prior to the Gulf War. Although Iraq's mobile production program began in the mid-1990s, U.N. inspectors at the time only had vague hints of such programs. Confirmation came later, in the year 2000. The source was an eyewitness, an Iraqi chemical engineer who supervised one of these facilities. He actually was present during biological agent production runs. He was also at the site when an accident occurred in 1998. Twelve technicians died from exposure to biological agents. ...

"This defector [apparently Curve Ball] is currently hiding in another country with the certain knowledge that Saddam Hussein will kill him if he finds him. His eyewitness account of these mobile production facilities has been corroborated by other sources."

Powell provided a detailed account of how these mobile weapon labs supposedly worked, how many there were (18), and what dangerous toxins they could produce. "In fact, they can produce enough dry biological agent in a single month to kill thousands upon thousands of people," Powell intoned.

As for chemical weapons, Powell used another rhetorical technique, estimating a range for Iraq's alleged stockpiles and then taking the low end of the range to emphasize the careful reliability of his presentation. At one point, for dramatic effect, he held up a small vial to demonstrate how lethal some of Iraq's alleged poisons were.

"Our conservative estimate is that Iraq today has a stockpile of between 100 and 500 tons of chemical weapons agent," Powell said. "Even the low end of 100 tons of agent would enable Saddam Hussein to cause mass casualties across more than 100 square miles of territory, an area nearly five times the size of Manhattan. ... We have sources who tell us that he recently has authorized his field commanders to use [chemical weapons]. He wouldn't be passing out the orders if he didn't have the weapons or the intent to use them." Again, the alternative explanation that the sources were lying was not taken into account.

Then, Powell turned to the issue of nuclear weapons. Though Powell didn't reiterate Bush's claim about the uranium from Africa, he did play up the aluminum tubes that were supposedly for centrifuges although U.S. government experts in the Energy and State departments thought the tubes were more suitable for rocket launchers as the Iraqis said.

"There is controversy about what these tubes are for," Powell acknowledged before adding: "Most U.S. experts think they are intended to serve as rotors in centrifuges used to enrich uranium. ... I am no expert on centrifuge tubes, but just as an old Army trooper, I can tell you a couple of things: First, it strikes me as quite odd that these tubes are manufactured to a tolerance that far exceeds U.S. requirements for comparable rockets. Maybe Iraqis just manufacture their conventional weapons to a higher standard than we do, but I don't think so."

But Houston Wood, a consultant who worked on the Energy Department's Oak Ridge analysis of the aluminum tubes, later told CBS News that Powell's presentation was misleading, since the nuclear experts, who were concentrated in the Energy Department, knew the tubes were unsuited for uranium enrichment.

"I thought when I read that there must be some other tubes that people were talking about," Wood said. "I was just flabbergasted that people were still pushing that those might be centrifuges."[12]

U.N. inspector Allinson described the reaction of the U.N. team as it watched Powell's much ballyhooed address. "Various people would laugh at various times because the information he was presenting was just, you know, didn't mean anything, had no meaning," Allinson said, adding that the conclusion of the inspectors after Powell's speech was that "they have nothing."

After the speech, Colin Powell revealed his own doubts. He turned to his friend Wilkerson and "said words to the effect of, I wonder how we'll all feel if we put half a million troops in Iraq and march from one end of the country to the other and find nothing," Wilkerson said. For his part, Wilkerson added, "I look back on it and I still say it's the lowest point in my life. I wish I had not been involved in it."[13]

◆ ◆ ◆

Though many WMD experts didn't buy the Bush administration's case, Powell's speech worked wonders with the U.S. news media. American commentators and pundits – long enamored of Powell's glittering reputation – hailed Powell's evidence as overwhelming and unassailable.

The next day – February 6, 2003 – *The Washington Post*'s editorial pages stood as a solid phalanx behind Powell's presentation. The newspaper's editorial board judged Powell's WMD case "irrefutable" and added: "it is hard to imagine how anyone could doubt that Iraq possesses weapons of mass destruction."

That opinion was echoed across the *Post*'s op-ed page. "The evidence he [Powell] presented to the United Nations – some of it circumstantial, some of it absolutely bone-chilling in its detail – had to prove to anyone that Iraq not only hasn't accounted for its weapons of mass destruction but without a doubt still retains them," wrote *Post* columnist Richard Cohen. "Only a fool – or possibly a Frenchman – could conclude otherwise."

Post columnist Jim Hoagland demanded the surrender of any Bush-doubting holdouts: "To continue to say that the Bush administration has not made its case, you must now believe that Colin Powell lied in the most serious statement he will ever make, or was taken in by manufactured evidence. I don't believe that. Today, neither should you."

In the days leading up to war, Bush and his aides continued salting their speeches with bogus allegations, some of which had been disproved by the U.N. and even U.S. intelligence agencies. The International

Atomic Energy Agency debunked a key element of the U.S. case, that the famous aluminum tubes were meant for centrifuges to produce enriched uranium. The IAEA reported that the tubes would not serve that function.

The IAEA also reported that a document about Iraqi attempts to purchase uranium in Niger was a forgery. It later turned out that CIA analysts also had doubted the authenticity of the Niger document, but it was still included in Bush's State of the Union address in January 2003.[14]

IAEA director general Mohamed ElBaradei said inspections of Iraq had found "no indication of resumed nuclear activity."

Yet Iraq's alleged nuclear program remained a scary part of the case for war. On March 16, undeterred by the scientific and intelligence findings, Vice President Dick Cheney again trotted out the canard that Iraq had "reconstituted nuclear weapons."

◆◆◆

In the climate of fear and fawning that prevailed in late winter 2003, most U.S. government officials and journalists knew intuitively it wasn't safe for one's career to question Powell's truthfulness or Bush's leadership.

News organizations and individual journalists concluded that their corporate and personal financial interests were best served by waving the Red-White-and-Blue, instead of raising red warning flags. Competing with Fox News to "brand" its news product as super-patriotic, MSNBC fired host Phil Donahue because his show allowed on too many war critics. Also, reflecting its new direction, MSNBC devoted day-long coverage to a diner that renamed "French fries" as "freedom fries."

Bush and his friends stepped up pressure, too, on longtime allies, such as France and Germany, because they had urged caution. Pro-Bush activists launched boycotts of French and German products; some poured French wine into gutters; a Capitol Hill restaurant also renamed "French fries" as "freedom fries"; aboard Air Force One, "French toast" became "freedom toast"; Secretary of Defense Donald Rumsfeld denigrated France and Germany as part of "Old Europe"; and pro-Bush media outlets ridiculed anti-war Europeans as the "axis of weasels."

As the United States slid into full "war fever," both right-wing and mainstream news outlets veered between mocking anti-war demonstrators and ignoring them. When Bush was asked about the millions of demonstrators protesting the upcoming invasion, Bush dismissed them as a "focus group" and signaled to his backers that it was okay to intimidate Americans who questioned his case for war.

So conservative pundits saw no problem in painting former weapons inspector Scott Ritter as a "traitor" when the former Marine objected to

Bush's claims about Iraq's WMD. Actor Sean Penn lost work because of his Iraq War opposition, later prompting pro-Bush MSNBC commentator Joe Scarborough to chortle, "Sean Penn is fired from an acting job and finds out that actions bring about consequences. Whoa, dude!"

Bush backers flew into an especially ugly rage against the Dixie Chicks, a three-woman country-western band, after lead singer, Natalie Maines, criticized Bush. During a March 10, 2003, concert in London, Maines, a Texan, remarked, "we're ashamed the President of the United States is from Texas." Two days later – just a week before Bush launched the Iraq invasion – she added, "I feel the President is ignoring the opinions of many in the U.S. and alienating the rest of the world."

The right-wing attack machine switched into high gear, organizing rallies to drive trucks over Dixie Chicks CDs and threatening country-western stations that played Dixie Chicks music. For his part, Bush seemed to relish the punishment inflicted on those who dared criticize him. On April 24, 2003, barely a month after the Iraq invasion, NBC News anchor Tom Brokaw asked Bush about the boycott of the Dixie Chicks. The President responded that the singers "can say what they want to say," but he added that his supporters then had an equal right to punish the singers for their comments.

"They shouldn't have their feelings hurt just because some people don't want to buy their records when they speak out," Bush said. "Freedom is a two-way street."

So, instead of encouraging a full-and-fair debate, Bush made clear that he saw nothing wrong with his followers intimidating Americans who disagreed with him. Over the next three years, the Dixie Chicks were hounded by the boycott. Bush supporters even turned to threats of violence. During one tour, lead singer Maines was warned, "You will be shot dead at your show in Dallas," forcing her to perform there under tight police protection.[15]

Though shunned by many country-western stations, the Dixie Chicks remained defiant. Indeed, a new song in 2006 was entitled "Not Ready to Make Nice" and addressed the hatred and intolerance they faced for criticizing Bush and the Iraq War. The album, entitled "Taking the Long Way," received favorable reviews, but it struggled on the music charts as Bush supporters called up stations and demanded that it never be played.[*]

---

[*] In 2007, the Dixie Chicks's defiant music won five Grammys, including best album and best song.

17

'Day of Liberation'

Iraq's "Day of Liberation" – as George W. Bush called it – was supposed to begin with a bombardment consisting of 3,000 U.S. missiles delivered over 48 hours, ten times the number of bombs dropped during the first two days of the Persian Gulf War in 1991. Officials, who were briefed on the plans, said the goal was to so stun the Iraqis that they would simply submit to the overwhelming force demonstrated by the U.S. military. Administration officials dubbed the strategy "shock and awe."

In his 2003 State of the Union speech, Bush had addressed the "brave and oppressed people of Iraq" with the reassuring message that "your enemy is not surrounding your country – your enemy is ruling your country." Bush promised that the day that Saddam Hussein and his regime "are removed from power will be the day of your liberation."

But never before in history had a dominant world power planned to strike a much weaker nation in a preemptive war with such ferocity. It would be liberation through devastation. Many projections expected the deaths of thousands of Iraqi non-combatants, no matter how targeted or precise the U.S. weapons. For those civilians, their end would come in the dark terror of crushing concrete or the blinding flash of high explosives.

In the prelude to the invasion, the United Nations predicted possibly more than 500,000 civilians injured or killed during the war and its aftermath and nearly one million displaced from their homes. The International Study Team, a Canadian non-governmental organization, said the invasion of Iraq would cause a "grave humanitarian disaster," with potential casualties among children in "the tens of thousands, and possibly in the hundreds of thousands."

Assuming U.S. forces succeeded in eliminating Saddam Hussein and his army with relative speed, the post-war period still promised to be complicated and dangerous. At times, the Bush administration outlined plans to occupy Iraq for at least 18 months, installing a military governor in the style of Gen. Douglas MacArthur in Japan after World War II. But it was not clear how the United States would police a population that was certain to include anti-American militants ready to employ suicide bombings and other irregular tactics against an occupying force.

There was the risk, too, that the U.S. invasion would play into the hands of Osama bin Laden, who circulated a message portraying himself as the defender of the Arab people. "Anyone who tries to destroy our villages and cities, then we are going to destroy their villages and cities," the al-Qaeda leader said. "Anyone who steals our fortunes, then we must destroy their economy. Anyone who kills our civilians, then we are going to kill their civilians."[1]

Some U.S. military strategists saw Bush's war plan as the worst sort of wishful thinking. What if the Iraqi army – instead of making itself an easy target for the U.S. missiles – melted into urban centers and began coordinating with an armed civilian population to resist a foreign invasion? What if the Iraqi people chose to fight the American invaders, rather than shower them with rose petals? Already, Saddam Hussein had begun concentrating his troops in urban centers and passing out AK-47s to Iraqis, young and old, men and women.

But Bush's biggest gamble was whether the "shock and awe" bombardment from the air and the stunning American firepower during the ground invasion would intimidate the Iraqis into surrendering. The relatively light invading force of a couple hundred thousand troops would be enough to take Baghdad, most military analysts believed, but significant resistance during the invasion would be an early sign that the Army's chief of staff, Gen. Eric Shinseki, was right when he told Congress that the occupation could require "several hundred thousand troops." After that alarming estimate, Shinseki was pushed into early retirement and drew a public rebuke from Deputy Defense Secretary Paul Wolfowitz, who called Shinseki "wildly off the mark."

A similar dispute erupted over the cost of the war. White House economic adviser Lawrence Lindsay had estimated a figure as high as one or two percent of the gross national product or about $100 billion to $200 billion. To head off American worries about this high cost, Bush's budget director Mitch Daniels slapped down Lindsay's estimate as "very, very high," pegging it instead at between $50 billion and $60 billion.

As for reconstruction costs, Wolfowitz and other officials suggested that Iraq's oil revenues would pay for nearly all of that. Lindsay was soon headed for the door, fired in December 2002 along with Treasury Secretary Paul O'Neill, an even more outspoken Iraq War critic.

◆ ◆ ◆

There is the old cliché about war, that its first casualty is truth. But – as U.S. forces began the invasion of Iraq on March 20, 2003, still the evening of March 19 in Washington – an even more immediate casualty was the journalistic principle of objectivity. Many U.S. news outlets dropped even the pretense of trying to stay neutral and just report the facts. TV anchors were soon opining about what strategies "we" should follow in prosecuting the Iraq War.

"One of the things that we don't want to do is to destroy the infrastructure of Iraq because in a few days we're going to own that country," NBC's Tom Brokaw explained as he sat among a panel of retired generals on the opening night of "Operation Iraqi Freedom."

There was little sensitivity to the sensibilities of the region. U.S. networks used large floor maps of Iraq so American analysts could stride across the country to point out troop movements. They looked like giants towering over the Middle East.

When American troops faced resistance from Iraqi paramilitary fighters, Fox termed them "Saddam's goons." When Iraqi forces surrendered, they were paraded before U.S. cameras as "proof" that Iraqi resistance was crumbling. Some of the scenes showed Iraqi POWs forced at gunpoint to kneel down with their hands behind their heads as they were patted down by U.S. soldiers. Network executives apparently felt no sense of irony running these images over the words, "Operation Iraqi Freedom," the title for the coverage and the code name for the invasion.

Neither the Bush administration nor a single U.S. reporter covering the war for the news networks observed that these degrading scenes might violate the Geneva Conventions on treatment of prisoners of war. But several days into the invasion, five American soldiers were captured in the southern city of Nasiriyah. When their images were broadcast on Iraqi TV, Bush administration officials immediately denounced the brief televised interviews as a violation of the Geneva Conventions, a charge that was repeated over and over by outraged U.S. television networks.

"It's illegal to do things to POWs that are humiliating to those prisoners," said Defense Secretary Donald Rumsfeld.

In their collective outrage over Iraq's alleged violation of international law, the U.S. networks seemed to forget those earlier scenes of the Iraqi POWs. They also left out how President Bush had stripped POWs captured in Afghanistan of their rights under the Geneva Conventions. Prisoners at Guantanamo Bay were shaved bald and forced to kneel with their eyes, ears and mouths covered to deprive them of their senses. Their humiliation was broadcast widely for the world to see.

There also had been leaks to the news media that terrorist suspects were being subjected to "stress and duress" tactics, which in some cases could be considered forms of torture.[2] U.S. officials admitted to the use of sleep deprivation in their interrogations of prisoners.

But senior U.S. officials defended these tactics, with one official telling *The Washington Post*, "If you don't violate someone's human rights some of the time, you probably aren't doing your job." Virtually confirming the new U.S. policy of using forms of torture, Cofer Black, former head of the CIA Counterterrorist Center, told a joint hearing of the House and Senate intelligence committees that there was a new "operational flexibility" in dealing with suspected terrorists. "There was a before 9/11, and there was an after 9/11," Black said. "After 9/11 the gloves come off."

This background left many in the world shaking their heads over the U.S. outrage when Iraqi TV broadcast the videotapes of American POWs. The Bush administration – and the major American media – seemed to prefer their international law *a la carte*, picking and choosing when the rules should apply and when they shouldn't.

As the invasion – or "liberation" – proceeded, Fox News and MSNBC competed in the sweepstakes to be the network that demonstrated the greatest pro-war patriotism. Both Fox and MSNBC broadcast Madison Avenue-style montages of heroic American soldiers at war, amid thankful Iraqis and stirring background music. Fox News used a harmonica soundtrack of the "Battle Hymn of the Republic."

MSNBC brought even higher production values to its images of U.S. troops in Iraq. One segment ended with an American boy surrounded by yellow ribbons for his father at war, and the concluding slogan, "Home of the Brave." Another MSNBC montage showed happy Iraqis welcoming U.S. troops as liberators over the slogan, "Let Freedom Ring."

Left out of these "news" montages – and much of the American news coverage – were images of death and destruction. Rather than troubling Americans with gruesome pictures of mangled and dismembered Iraqis, including many children, the cable networks, in particular, edited the war in ways that helped avoid negativity, boost ratings and give advertisers the feel-good content that plays best around their products. Fox News may have pioneered the concept of casting the war in the gauzy light of heroic imagery, but the other U.S. networks weren't far behind.

Not to be completely out-foxed, CNN offered startlingly different war coverage to Americans on domestic CNN than what other viewers saw on CNN International. While domestic CNN focused on happy stories of American courage and appreciative Iraqis, CNNI carried more scenes of wounded civilians overflowing Iraqi hospitals.

"During the Gulf War in 1991, [CNN] presented a uniform global feed that showed the war largely through American eyes," the *Wall Street*

Journal reported. "Since then, CNN has developed several overseas networks that increasingly cater their programming to regional audiences and advertisers."[3]

Left unsaid by the *Journal*'s formulation of how CNN's overseas affiliates "cater" to foreign audiences was the flip side of that coin, that domestic CNN was freer to shape a version of the news that was more satisfying to Americans. Still, CNN – and MSNBC – lagged behind Fox in pulling in the viewers with super-patriotic war coverage, albeit not for lack of trying.

The U.S. networks fell over themselves to tell the glorious story of Pfc. Jessica Lynch, who was captured during the invasion's early days. Her rescue was filmed by the U.S. military in the fuzzy green of night-vision equipment and played over and over again. Only later was it revealed that the Lynch story had been embroidered for propaganda effect. The Iraqi doctors who had cared for Lynch said the rescue was staged, a kind of made-for-TV movie before it was destined to become a made-for-TV movie.

"They made a big show," said Haitham Gizzy, a doctor who treated Lynch. "It was just a drama" filmed after Iraqi fighters had fled the scene and with only doctors manning the hospital.[4]

◆ ◆ ◆

While Americans were fed a steady diet of cheerleading journalism, the stronger-than-expected resistance from Iraqi forces on the ground in the war's early days raised warning signs about trouble ahead. Robert Parry tracked down some of his longtime military and intelligence sources who painted for him a much grimmer picture than was appearing in the major U.S. news media. With the war less than two weeks old, he described their portents of disaster in a *Consortiumnews.com* article entitled "Bay of Pigs Meets Black Hawk Down." It read:

"Whatever happens in the weeks ahead, George W. Bush has 'lost' the war in Iraq. The only question now is how big a price America will pay, both in terms of battlefield casualties and political hatred swelling around the world. That is the view slowly dawning on U.S. military analysts, who privately are asking whether the cost of ousting Saddam Hussein has grown so large that 'victory' will constitute a strategic defeat of historic proportions. At best, even assuming Saddam's ouster, the Bush administration may be looking at an indefinite period of governing something akin to a California-size Gaza Strip.

"The chilling realization is spreading in Washington that Bush's Iraqi debacle may be the mother of all presidential miscalculations – an extraordinary blend of Bay of Pigs-style wishful thinking with a 'Black Hawk Down' reliance on special operations to wipe out enemy leaders as a short-cut to victory. But the magnitude of the Iraq disaster could be far worse than either the Bay of Pigs fiasco in Cuba in 1961 or the bloody miscalculations in Somalia in 1993.

"In both those cases, the U.S. government showed the tactical flexibility to extricate itself from military misjudgments without grave strategic damage. The CIA-backed Bay of Pigs invasion left a small army of Cuban exiles in the lurch when the rosy predictions of popular uprisings against Fidel Castro failed to materialize. To the nation's advantage, however, President John Kennedy applied what he learned from the Bay of Pigs – that he shouldn't blindly trust his military advisers – to navigate the far more dangerous Cuban missile crisis in 1962.

"The botched 'Black Hawk Down' raid in Mogadishu cost the lives of 18 U.S. soldiers, but President Bill Clinton then cut U.S. losses by recognizing the hopelessness of the leadership-decapitation strategy and withdrawing American troops from Somalia. Similarly, President Ronald Reagan pulled out U.S. forces from Lebanon in 1983 after a suicide bomber killed 241 Marines who were part of a force that had entered Beirut as peace-keepers but found itself drawn into the middle of a brutal civil war."

Robert Parry continued: "Few analysts today, however, believe that George W. Bush and his senior advisers, including Vice President Dick Cheney and Defense Secretary Donald Rumsfeld, have the common sense to swallow the short-term bitter medicine of a cease-fire or a U.S. withdrawal. Rather than face the political music for admitting to the gross error of ordering an invasion in defiance of the United Nations and then misjudging the enemy, these U.S. leaders are expected to push forward no matter how bloody or ghastly their future course might be.

"Without doubt, the Bush administration misjudged the biggest question of the war: 'Would the Iraqis fight?' Happy visions of rose petals and cheers have given way to a grim reality of ambushes and suicide bombs. But the Bush pattern of miscalculation continues unabated. Bush seems to have cut himself off from internal dissent at the CIA and the Pentagon, where intelligence analysts and field generals warned against the wishful thinking that is proving lethal on the Iraqi battlefields. ... Instead of recognizing their initial errors and rethinking their war strategy, Bush and his team are pressing forward confidently into what looks like a dreamscape of their own propaganda. ...

"While the Bush administration once talked about administering Iraq for a couple of years after victory, that timetable was based on the pre-war assumptions that the war would be a 'cakewalk' and that the Iraqi population would welcome U.S. troops with open arms. After that easy victory, a U.S. proconsul administration would weed out Saddam loyalists and build a 'representative' government, apparently meaning that the U.S. would pick leaders from among Iraq's various ethnic groups and tribes.

"However, now, with civilian casualties rising and a U.S. 'victory' possibly requiring a blood bath, the timeline for the post-war 'reconstruction' may need lengthening. Instead of a couple of years, the process could prove open-ended with fewer Iraqis willing to collaborate and more Iraqis determined to resist. A long occupation would be another grim prospect for American soldiers.

"Given what's happened in the past 11 days, U.S. occupation troops and Iraqi collaborators can expect an extended period of scattered fighting that might well involve assassinations and bombings. U.S. troops, inexperienced with Iraqi culture and ignorant of the Arabic language, will be put in the predicament of making split-second decisions about whether to shoot some 14-year-old boy with a backpack or some 70-year-old woman in a chador. ...

"Once the 'shock and awe' bombing failed to crack the regime and Iraqis showed they were willing to fight in southern Iraqi cities – such as Umm Qasr, Basra and Nasiriyah – where Saddam's support was considered weak, Bush's initial war strategy was shown to be a grave mistake. The supposedly decisive 'shock and awe' bombing in the war's opening days amounted to TV pyrotechnics that did little more than blow up empty government buildings, including Saddam's tackily decorated palaces. The U.S. had so telegraphed the punch that the buildings had been evacuated. ...

"Unwittingly, Bush may be applying all the wrong lessons from America's worst military disasters of the past 40-plus years. He's mixing risky military tactics with a heavy reliance on propaganda and a large dose of wishful thinking. Bush also has guessed wrong on the one crucial ingredient that would separate meaningful victory from the political defeat that is now looming. He completely miscalculated the reaction of the Iraqi people to an invasion. More and more, Bush appears to be heading toward that ultimate lesson of U.S. military futility. He's committed himself – and the nation – to destroying Iraq in order to save it."

◆ ◆ ◆

Despite the stiffer-than-expected resistance, the U.S. military continued to blast its way toward its goal of toppling Saddam Hussein. From the first days of the war, that violence took a heavy toll on Iraq's civilians.

The Bush administration's lack of sensitivity about civilian casualties was reflected in the hasty decision to bomb a residential restaurant where Hussein was thought to be eating. It turned out that the intelligence was wrong, but that wasn't discovered until after the restaurant was leveled and 14 civilians, including seven children, were killed. One mother hysterically sought her daughter and collapsed when the headless body was pulled from the rubble.

"When the broken body of the 20-year-old woman was brought out torso first, then her head," *The Associated Press* reported, "her mother started crying uncontrollably, then collapsed." The London *Independent* cited this restaurant attack as one that represented "a clear breach" of the Geneva Conventions ban on bombing civilian targets.

Hundreds of other civilian deaths were equally horrific. Saad Abbas, 34, was wounded in an American bombing raid, but his family sought to shield him from the greater horror. The bombing had killed his three daughters – Marwa, 11; Tabarek, 8; and Safia, 5 – who had been the center of his life. "It wasn't just ordinary love," his wife said. "He was crazy about them. It wasn't like other fathers."[5]

The horror of the war was captured, too, in the fate of 12-year-old Ali Ismaeel Abbas, who lost his two arms when a U.S. missile struck his Baghdad home. Ali's father, pregnant mother and siblings were all killed. As he was evacuated to a Kuwaiti hospital, becoming a symbol of U.S. compassion for injured Iraqi civilians, Ali said he would rather die than live without his hands. For its part, the Bush administration announced that it had no intention of tallying the number of dead Iraqi civilians.

On the battlefield, rather than throwing down their weapons, the Iraqi army sometimes fought heroically though hopelessly against the technologically superior U.S. forces. *Christian Science Monitor* reporter Ann Scott Tyson interviewed U.S. troops with the 3rd Infantry Division who were deeply troubled by their task of mowing down Iraqi soldiers who kept fighting even in suicidal situations.

"Even as U.S. commanders cite dramatic success in the three-week-old war, many look upon the wholesale destruction of Iraq's military and the killing of thousands of Iraqi fighters with a sense of regret," Tyson reported. "They voice frustration at the number of Iraqis who stood their ground against overwhelming U.S. firepower, wasting their lives and equipment rather than capitulating as expected."

"They have no command and control, no organization," said Brig. Gen. Louis Weber. "They're just dying."

Commenting upon the annihilation of Iraqi forces in one-sided battles, Lt. Col. Woody Radcliffe said, "We didn't want to do this. Even a brain-dead moron can understand we are so vastly superior militarily that there is no hope. You would think they would see that and give up."

In one battle around Najaf, U.S. commanders ordered air strikes to kill the Iraqis *en masse* rather than have U.S. soldiers continue to kill them one by one. "There were waves and waves of people coming at them with AK-47s, out of this factory, and they [the U.S. soldiers] were killing everyone," said Radcliffe. "The commander called and said, 'This is not right. This is insane. Let's hit the factory with close air support and take them out all at once.'"

This slaughter of young Iraqis troubled front-line U.S. soldiers. "For lack of a better word, I felt almost guilty about the massacre," one soldier said privately. "We wasted a lot of people. It makes you wonder how many were innocent. It takes away some of the pride. We won, but at what cost?"[6]

Bush seemed to share none of these regrets. Commenting about the Iraqi soldiers to his war council, Bush said they "fight like terrorists."[7]

Demonstrating overwhelming American might, Bush had made Iraq his Alderaan, the hapless planet in the original Star Wars movie that was picked to show off the power of the Death Star. "Fear will keep the local systems in line, fear of this battle station," explained Death Star commander Tarkin in the movie. "No star system will dare oppose the emperor now."

Similarly, the slaughter of the outmatched Iraqi military sent a message to other countries that might be tempted to resist Bush's dictates. At a Central Command briefing, Brig. Gen. Vincent Brooks took note of this awesome power on display as he described the "degrading" of Iraqi forces south of Baghdad. "They're in serious trouble," Brooks said. "They remain in contact now with the most powerful force on earth."

The enthusiasm of many Americans for the war in Iraq – and their lightly considered acquiescence to this crossover to imperial power – delivered another chilling message to the world. The message was that the American people and their increasingly enfeebled democratic process would not serve as a check on George W. Bush, at least in the near term.

◆◆◆

The fall of Baghdad after three weeks of fighting washed away the remaining doubts for most Americans. The iconic image of a U.S. soldier and tank helping Iraqis topple a statue of Hussein in Baghdad's Firdus Square on April 9 became Exhibit A to prove that Bush was right about "liberating" the Iraqis. After being pulled down by the U.S. tank, the toppled statue was set upon by dancing Iraqis who carried off the head.

For many Americans the scene was a catharsis, bringing relief that the war might end quickly and satisfaction that the Iraqis were finally acting like the grateful people that administration officials had said they would be. However, Americans seeking a fuller understanding of the moment needed to search the Internet or access foreign newspapers. Those who did found the victorious images were misleading.

Rather than a spontaneous Berlin Wall-type celebration by hundreds of thousands, the toppling of the statue was a staged event with a small crowd estimated in the scores, not even the hundreds. One photo from a distance showed the square ringed by U.S. tanks with a small knot of people gathered around the statue.

Indeed, given the political importance of the images, some intelligence experts expressed surprise that so few Iraqis were present. One CIA veteran told us that such images are never left to chance because of their psychological warfare potential. He said all U.S. battle plans include a "psy-war annex," a kind of public-relations script meant to influence the target population – in this case, the Iraqis – as well as the larger world public, including the American people.

Despite the scene's shortcomings, it served its purpose. The ouster of Hussein – and the apparent U.S. victory after a three-week campaign – solidified Bush's reputation as a decisive leader who wouldn't tolerate petty tyrants getting in America's way. For his neoconservative enthusiasts, the conquest of Iraq also marked an important step in establishing an American global empire that would punish any upstart who threatened U.S. interests and would send a message to potential American enemies everywhere.

As Hussein fled into hiding, Bush gained the political advantage over his domestic critics, too. The anti-empire side found itself pinned down by accusations that its opposition to the Iraq invasion had been naïve and even disloyal. The war skeptics still tried to warn their fellow citizens of the dangers from the neoconservative plan to transform the American Republic into a new-age empire. But many Americans were too caught up in the joy and excitement of military success to worry.

The Iraq War naysayers also were a scattered lot, a disorganized mix of political interests, including old-time conservatives and traditional liberals, from the likes of Pat Buchanan to Howard Dean. The anti-imperial groupings also emphasized different points.

For instance, Buchanan made the case to his conservative backers that neoconservative ideologues had won over Bush and were pushing their strategies in the interests of hard-liners in Israel's Likud Party who opposed ending Israel's occupation of Palestinian territories. "We charge that a cabal of polemicists and public officials seek to ensnare our country in a series of wars that are not in America's interests," Buchanan wrote in *The American Conservative.*[8]

Former Vermont Governor Dean, one of the few Democratic presidential contenders who opposed Bush's Iraq War resolution, stressed the damage Bush was doing to international cooperation needed to protect U.S. long-term interests. "This unilateral approach to foreign policy is a disaster," Dean wrote in explaining his opposition to the Bush Doctrine. "All of the challenges facing the United States – from winning the war on terror and containing weapons of mass destruction to building an open world economy and protecting the global environment – can only be met by working with our allies."[9]

Without doubt, Bush and the neoconservatives were on a roll. But there were early signs that not everything was going as well as the neocons had hoped. Chaos and looting followed the removal of the Hussein government. While U.S. Marines guarded offices associated with the oil industry, other unprotected government buildings were burned, including the central library where ancient Arabic texts were stored. The national museum – one of the prides of the Islamic world – was ransacked with many priceless antiquities stolen and others smashed.

"They lie across the floor in tens of thousands of pieces, the priceless antiquities of Iraq's history," wrote Robert Fisk of London's *Independent* newspaper. "The looters had gone from shelf to shelf, systematically pulling down the statues and pots and amphorae of the Assyrians and the Babylonians, the Sumerians, the Medes, the Persians and the Greeks and hurling them on to the concrete.

"Our feet crunched on the wreckage of 5,000-year-old marble plinths and stone statuary and pots that had endured every siege of Baghdad, every invasion of Iraq throughout history only to be destroyed when Americans came to 'liberate' the city."[10]

The CIA veteran told us that the post-combat chaos was partly the fault of inadequate Pentagon deployment of civil affairs personnel with the troops. The wishful thinking about capitulation immediately after the demonstration of "shock and awe" left U.S. forces without enough experts to deal with the breakdown of police operations, the need for riot control, and the lack of electricity, food and medicines, he said.

As Marines and other front-line combat troops sought to control anti-American demonstrations, killings of civilians resulted. In the northern city of Mosul, Marines fired into angry crowds, killing 17 Iraqis in the city's main square, the director of the city's hospital said. Marines said they had been fired upon, but Mosul residents denied those claims.[11]

"We must be united and support each other against the Anglo-American invasion," declared Sheik Ibrahim al-Namaa, who emerged as a rising leader in Mosul, where the looting of that city's ancient treasures also fed anger over the U.S. occupation. "We must try to put an end to this aggression."[12]

Thousands of Iraqis also demonstrated against the U.S. occupation in Baghdad, with nearly 100 Islamic leaders calling for the ouster of Americans and the creation of an Islamic state.

"You are the masters today," said Islamic leader Ahmed al-Kubeisy about the Americans. "But I warn you against thinking of staying. Get out before we kick you out."[13]

But in those heady days, after the collapse of Saddam Hussein's government, Bush was living the life of a conquering emperor.

18

Bush in Full

In April 2003, as Saddam Hussein's cult of personality collapsed across Iraq, George W. Bush's cult of personality surged in the United States. Pro-war pundits grew even more intolerant of criticism directed at the President. To question Bush's judgment was enough to earn banishment from respectable society if not reason to undergo observation at a psychiatric ward.

Fox News anchor Brit Hume chastised journalists who had doubted the ease with which the Iraq War would be won. "They didn't get it just a little wrong," Hume said. "They got it completely wrong."

Right-wing columnist Cal Thomas demanded that the words of the doubters be archived so they would be permanently discredited. "When these false prophets again appear, they can be reminded of the error of their previous ways and at least be offered an opportunity to recant and repent," Thomas wrote.

Washington Post columnist Charles Krauthammer declared that "the only people who think this wasn't a victory are Upper Westside liberals, and a few people here in Washington." MSNBC's Joe Scarborough singled out former U.N. weapons inspector Scott Ritter, who had doubted the existence of Iraqi WMD, as the "chief stooge for Saddam Hussein" and demanded that Ritter and other skeptics apologize.

"I'm waiting to hear the words 'I was wrong' from some of the world's most elite journalists, politicians and Hollywood types," Scarborough said. "Maybe disgraced commentators and politicians alike, like [Tom] Daschle, Jimmy Carter, Dennis Kucinich, and all those others, will step forward tonight and show the content of their character by simply admitting what we know already: that their wartime predictions were arrogant, they were misguided and they were dead wrong."

"We're all neocons now," chimed in MSNBC's Chris Matthews.

"The Tommy Franks-Don Rumsfeld battle plan, war plan, worked brilliantly, a three-week war with mercifully few American deaths or Iraqi civilian deaths," said Fox News commentator Morton Kondracke. "All the naysayers have been humiliated so far. ... The final word on this is hooray."

CNN's Lou Dobbs said, "Some journalists, in my judgment, just can't stand success, especially a few liberal columnists and newspapers and a few Arab reporters."[1]

Not only were the few doubting journalists chastised for their supposed failure to perceive Bush's geopolitical genius, but flag-waving journalism also paid dividends where it counted most – in the ratings race. While MSNBC remained in third place among U.S. cable news outlets, it posted the highest ratings growth in the lead-up to war and during the actual fighting, up 124 percent compared with a year earlier. Fox News, the industry leader, racked up a 102 percent gain and No. 2 CNN rose 91 percent.[2]

Some U.S. viewers seeking more objective war coverage switched to BBC or CNN's international channels, but large numbers of Americans clearly wanted the "feel-good" nationalism of Fox News, MSNBC and CNN's domestic service. Images of U.S. troops surrounded by smiling Iraqi children made for happier viewing than seeing the brutality of war, the slaughter of thousands of Iraqi civilians, the maiming of children. Journalistic objectivity also would have required revealing that many Iraqis reacted with coldness and even hostility to U.S. forces, a harbinger of the Iraqi insurgency to come. That was not what most Americans wanted to contemplate during the heady days of April 2003.

To some foreigners, the uniformity of the all-positive-all-the-time U.S. war coverage had the feel of a totalitarian state. "There have been times, living in America of late, when it seemed I was back in the Communist Moscow I left a dozen years ago," wrote Rupert Cornwell in the London-based *Independent*. "Switch to cable TV and reporters breathlessly relay the latest wisdom from the usual unnamed 'senior administration officials,' keeping us on the straight and narrow. Everyone, it seems, is on-side and on-message. Just like it used to be when the hammer and sickle flew over the Kremlin."

Cornwell traced this lock-step U.S. coverage to the influence of Fox News, which "has taken its cue from George Bush's view of the universe post-11 September – either you're with us or against us. Fox, most emphatically, is with him, and it's paid off at the box office. Not for Fox to dwell on uncomfortable realities like collateral damage, Iraqi casualties, or the failure of the U.S. troops to protect libraries and museums."[3]

Ironically, while a journalist questioning the supposed ease of the American victory or noting the surprising resistance from some Iraqi troops was faulted for disrupting the post-invasion glow, provoking readers to write angry letters to the editor or viewers to fire off furious e-mails, Bush himself acknowledged the reality.

"Shock and awe said to many people that all we've got to do is unleash some might and people will crumble," Bush said in an interview with NBC's Tom Brokaw. "And it turns out the fighters were a lot fiercer than we thought. ...The resistance for our troops moving south and north was significant resistance."[4]

But the near-universal acclaim of victory still went to Bush's head. His cult of personality literally took off on May 1, 2003, when Bush donned flight gear and hopped into the co-pilot seat of a Navy S-3B Viking jet. The plane flew from an airfield in California out over the Pacific and made a tail-hook landing on the deck of the aircraft carrier, USS Abraham Lincoln. The event was broadcast live on American TV. It was the first time a sitting President had landed on the deck of an aircraft carrier by plane.

The USS Abraham Lincoln, which had been at sea for 10 months, had been within helicopter range of the West Coast, but a helicopter landing wouldn't have offered the exciting visuals of a carrier landing, nor would it have made sense for Bush to have emerged from a helicopter in a flight suit. So, the ship slowed its pace and circled idly in the Pacific Ocean, shifting direction to guarantee the most favorable camera angles, while servicemen and women delayed their homecomings.

After the landing, Bush hopped out in his green flight suit, holding a white helmet. "Yes, I flew it," Bush said about handling the jet during the flight. "Yeah, of course, I liked it." He greeted the sailors with salutes and comments of "Thank you" and "'preciate it." Later, after changing into a suit and tie, Bush spoke to the nation under a "Mission Accomplished" banner. "Major combat operations in Iraq have ended," he said.

Though Bush's father had made great fun of Democrat Michael Dukakis when he rode in a tank in 1988 and the national news media had a field day in 1993 when President Bill Clinton got a haircut while Air Force One waited at a Los Angeles airport, the tone was different when Bush pulled off his Top Gun performance.

"U.S. television coverage ranged from respectful to gushing," observed *New York Times* columnist Paul Krugman. "Nobody seemed bothered that Mr. Bush, who appears to have skipped more than a year of the National Guard service that kept him out of Vietnam, is now emphasizing his flying experience."[5]

Indeed, the likes of MSNBC's Chris Matthews used the occasion of Bush strutting about the carrier's deck to praise Bush's manliness in contrast to Democratic presidential candidates, including Sen. John Kerry who earned war medals in Vietnam.

"Imagine Joe Lieberman in this costume, or even John Kerry," Matthews said. "Nobody looks right in the role Bush has set for the presidency-commander-in-chief, medium height, medium build, looks good in a jet pilot's costume or uniform, rather has a certain swagger, not too literary, certainly not too verbal, but a guy who speaks plainly and wins wars. I think that job definition is hard to match for the Dems."

There also was a lot of man-love from the TV tough guys. "We're proud of our President," Matthews said. "Americans love having a guy as President, a guy who has a little swagger, who's physical. ... Women like a guy who's President. Check it out. The women like this war. I think we like having a hero as our President."

Matthews was at least right about some women journalists who joined their male colleagues in cooing over the President's sea-swept performance. "Picture perfect," said PBS's Gwen Ifill. "Part Spider-Man, part Tom Cruise, part Ronald Reagan. The President seized the moment on an aircraft carrier in the Pacific."

"If image is everything, how can the Democratic presidential hopefuls compete with a President fresh from a war victory," commented CNN's Judy Woodruff.[6]

While Bush got the images he wanted in his carrier landing and the desired commentaries from the TV pundits, his aides mounted a mini-cover-up of the facts. In the days after the photo op, the White House lied about the reasons for the jet flight, insisting that it was necessary because the ship was outside helicopter range. That story fell apart when it became clear that the ship was only 30 miles offshore and slowing down to give Bush an excuse to use the jet.

A later *New York Times* article revealed that Bush collaborated in the jet landing idea and that the imagery was choreographed by a White House advance team led by communications specialist Scott Sforza, who arrived on the carrier days earlier. The carrier landing was just one scene in a deliberate pattern of images sought by the White House.

At an economic speech in Indianapolis, people sitting behind Bush were told to take off their ties so they'd look more like ordinary folks, WISH-TV reported. At a speech at Mount Rushmore in South Dakota, cameramen were given a platform that offered up Bush's profile as if he were already carved into the mountain with Washington, Jefferson, Lincoln and Theodore Roosevelt.[7]

But the TV pundits and the American people shrugged off concerns about whether Bush had used the USS Abraham Lincoln and its crew as political props. When Democrats demanded a cost accounting, MSNBC posed its question-of-the-day this way: "President Bush's Flight Flap. Much Ado About Nothing?"[8] A *New York Times*/CBS News poll found

59 percent of the American people agreeing that use of the carrier was appropriate and saying that Bush was not seeking political gain.

◆◆◆

For the few news outlets that had questioned the wisdom of the war, this high point in Bush's hero worship was a time of heightened ostracism. At *Consortiumnews.com*, our critical coverage of Bush's dubious case for war and our reporting about the risks of a prolonged and bloody conflict in Iraq brought hostile e-mails from Bush's triumphant supporters demanding apologies. The flow of e-mails would pick up whenever there were reports about U.S. forces discovering suspected sites for chemical or biological weapons.

To us, the layered complexity of the Iraq War deceptions – generated by the Bush administration and conveyed through the major U.S. news media – recalled the computerized fake reality in "The Matrix" movies. That sci-fi classic had returned to public attention in spring 2003 with the arrival of a sequel, "The Matrix Reloaded," providing a useful analogy for anyone trying to make sense of the chasm that had opened between what was real and what Americans perceived to be real. It was as if a false reality was being pulled daily over the eyes of the public through what they saw and heard on the TV screens.

Cartoonist Tom Tomorrow, whose real name is Dan Perkins, was another who perceived this Matrix-like quality of America, circa 2003. In his "This Modern World" cartoon, he depicted what he called "The Republican Matrix." Clueless Americans parroted back Bush administration talking points as the cartoon asked, "What is the Republican Matrix? It is an illusion that engulfs us all...a steady barrage of images which obscure reality. It is a world born anew each day...in which there is nothing to be learned from the lessons of the past ...a world where logic holds no sway...where up is down and black is white...where reality itself is a malleable thing...subject to constant revision. In short, it's their world."

The cartoon ended with a frame showing President Bush, Vice President Dick Cheney and Defense Secretary Donald Rumsfeld in sunglasses like those worn by the anti-human "agents" in "The Matrix." "What should we do today, fellas?" Bush asked. "Any damn thing we want, George," answered Cheney.

◆◆◆

Among U.S. politicians, the aging and ailing Senator Robert C. Byrd was one of the few voices addressing the dangers to democracy and to U.S. troops that came from pervasive government lying. "No matter to what lengths we humans may go to obfuscate facts or delude our fellows, truth has a way of squeezing out through the cracks, eventually," Byrd said on the Senate floor on May 21. "But the danger is that at some point it may no longer matter. The danger is that damage is done before the truth is widely realized."

His hands shaking, his voice quavering, Byrd continued, "Regarding the situation in Iraq, it appears to this senator that the American people may have been lured into accepting the unprovoked invasion of a sovereign nation, in violation of long-standing international law, under false pretenses. ... The run-up to our invasion of Iraq featured the President and members of his Cabinet invoking every frightening image they could conjure, from mushroom clouds, to buried caches of germ warfare, to drones poised to deliver germ-laden death in our major cities.

"The tactic was guaranteed to provoke a sure reaction from a nation still suffering from a combination of post-traumatic stress and justifiable anger after the attacks of 9/11. It was the exploitation of fear. It was a placebo for the anger. ... Presently our loyal military personnel continue their mission of diligently searching for WMD. They have so far turned up only fertilizer, vacuum cleaners, conventional weapons and the occasional buried swimming pool. They are misused on such a mission and they continue to be at grave risk," Byrd said.

But Byrd's voice was a lonely one in Washington. A far more vigorous examination of these questions was underway in Europe, where leading politicians and journalists questioned the pre-war claims of Bush and Blair. "We were told that Saddam had weapons ready for use within 45 minutes," said former British Foreign Minister Robin Cook, who resigned over Blair's pro-war policies. "It's now 45 days since the war has finished and we have still not found anything."

Paul Keetch, defense spokesman for the opposition Liberal Democrats, said, "No weapons means no threat. Without WMD, the case for war falls apart. It would seem either the intelligence was wrong and we should not rely on it, or the politicians overplayed the threat."[9]

BBC News quoted a senior British intelligence official as saying that a dossier that Blair's government compiled about Iraq's alleged WMD program was rewritten to make it "sexier," including the addition of the dubious claim that the Iraqis were prepared to launch a WMD strike within 45 minutes. "It was included in the dossier against our wishes because it wasn't reliable," the official said. "Most things in the dossier were double source but that was single source and we believe the source was wrong."[10]

By late May, Bush administration officials were grasping at straws to salvage the WMD claims. When the U.S. military located two Iraqi military trailers, a desperate CIA brushed aside evidence that they were for producing hydrogen to inflate artillery weather balloons and concluded instead that the trailers were the missing mobile biological weapons labs featured in Colin Powell's U.N. speech. The CIA joined with the Defense Intelligence Agency in putting out a quickie report touting the find.

"Those who say we haven't found the banned manufacturing devices or banned weapons are wrong," Bush declared, referring to the mobile labs. "We found them."[11]

Yet the CIA-DIA argument that the trailers were bio-labs didn't stand up to even casual scrutiny. The report read like one more example of selective intelligence, spurning plausible alternatives that didn't fit with Bush's political needs. In this case, the Bush administration, which had said for months that the Iraqi weapons secrets would be revealed once U.S. forces captured and questioned Iraq's top scientists, now rejected what those scientists were saying. When questioned, the captured scientists said the labs were used to produce hydrogen for artillery weather balloons.

In the CIA-DIA report, U.S. analysts agreed that hydrogen production was a plausible explanation for the labs. "Some of the features of the trailer – a gas collection system and the presence of a caustic – are consistent with both bio-production and hydrogen production," the CIA-DIA report said. "The plant's design possibly could be used to produce hydrogen using a chemical reaction."

The report also noted that "preliminary sample analysis results are negative for five standard BW agents, including *bacillus anthracis*, and for growth media for those agents." Also missing were companion mobile labs that would be needed "to prepare and sterilize the media and to concentrate and possibly dry the agent, before the agent is ready for introduction into a delivery system, such as bulk-filled munitions," the CIA-DIA report said.

In other words, U.S. intelligence analysts found no evidence that the trailers were used to make biological weapons nor that the trailers alone could produce weaponized BW agents. But that wasn't the politically expedient answer.

So, the CIA-DIA analysis veered off into an argumentative direction. The report asserted that the labs would be "inefficient" for producing hydrogen because their capacity is "larger than typical units for hydrogen production for weather balloons." Better systems are "commercially available," the CIA-DIA report said.

But the U.S. analysts didn't assess whether those more efficient systems would have been "commercially available" to Iraq, which had faced a decade of trade sanctions. What might be considered "inefficient" to U.S. scientists might be the best option available to Iraqis. Having made the inefficiency argument, the CIA-DIA analysis then concluded that hydrogen production must be a "cover story" and that "BW agent production is the only consistent, logical purpose for these vehicles."

The tendentious CIA-DIA conclusions were accepted by the major U.S. news media. But a June 2 article at *Consortiumnews.com* by Robert Parry questioned the CIA-DIA logic and explained why the trailers almost certainly were used to inflate weather balloons.[12]

Later, mainstream news organizations joined in the critique. "American and British intelligence analysts with direct access to the evidence are disputing claims that the mysterious trailers found in Iraq were for making deadly germs," *The New York Times* reported on June 7. The analysts "said the mobile units were more likely intended for other purposes and charged that the evaluation process had been damaged by a rush to judgment."[13]

The London-based *Observer* called the trailer flap another blow to Blair, who like Bush had cited the trailers as confirmation of pre-war WMD claims. "*The Observer* has established that it is increasingly likely that the units were designed to be used for hydrogen production to fill artillery balloons, part of a system originally sold to Saddam by Britain in 1987," the newspaper reported on June 8.[14]

The world's press also pounced on admissions by senior U.S. officials conceding that the pre-war WMD claims may have been hyped. In an interview with *Vanity Fair*, Deputy Defense Secretary Wolfowitz said the WMD allegation was stressed "for bureaucratic reasons" because "it was the one reason everyone could agree on."

By late spring 2003, some U.S. military analysts were detecting another dangerous trend – the emergence of a guerrilla war in Iraq. Roadside bombs, suicide attacks and ambushes were beginning to take their toll on U.S. occupation troops. "We're hanging on by our fingernails," one troubled military analyst told us.

Reality – or what Morpheus of "The Matrix" called the "desert of the real" – was about to reassert itself.

◆ ◆ ◆

"The United States is at a crossroads, with neither route offering an easy journey," Nat Parry wrote in a *Consortiumnews.com* article on June 17, 2003. "In one direction lies a pretend land – where tax cuts increase revenue, where war is peace, where any twisted bits of intelligence justify whatever the leader wants and the people follow. In the other direction lies a painful struggle to bring accountability to political forces that have operated with impunity now for years.

"The choice is so big, so intimidating, so important that many in politics, in the U.S. news media and on Main Street America don't want to believe that there is a crossroads or that there is a choice. They want to think everything's okay and go about their lives without making a choice. Or they hope someone else will do the hard work so they can stay on the sidelines as bemused observers.

"But more and more Americans have a sinking feeling that the institutions that they count on to check abuses – the Congress, the courts, the press – are no longer there as bulwarks. The dawning reality is, too, that what ultimately is at stake is not simply the fiscal stability of the United States or the relative comfort of the American people. Nor even the awful shedding of blood by U.S. soldiers and foreign inhabitants in faraway lands.

"What may be in the balance is an era of history that many Americans take for granted, an era that has lasted for a quarter of a millennium, an era that has given rise to scientific invention, to a flourishing of the arts and commerce, to modern democracy itself. There is a gnawing realization that the United States might be careening down a course leading to the end of the Age of Reason."[15]

The most glaring example of this dimming of rationality could be found in how effective the Bush administration's Iraq WMD deceptions had been. *New York Times* columnist Paul Krugman called taking the nation to war over a series of lies and distortions "the worst scandal in American political history." But in mid-2003, there were few signs that Bush's "feel-good" presidency was in any serious danger.

Bush subtly began shifting his argument about what constituted proof of his pre-war claims. Instead of talking about "vast stockpiles" of forbidden weapons, he predicted the United States will find evidence of "weapons programs," with the suggestion that proof of Iraq's capacity to make chemical and biological weapons – a very low threshold indeed – would suffice.

Even as the administration's case for Iraq possessing a trigger-ready stockpile of chemical and biological warfare collapsed, Bush's aides still didn't hesitate to go on the offensive against their critics. Some top Bush aides even had the audacity to accuse the critics of manipulating the historical record.

"There's a bit of revisionist history going on here," said National Security Adviser Condoleezza Rice on NBC's "Meet the Press" as she lashed out at former CIA analysts and others who questioned Bush's prewar WMD claims. "As I said, revisionist history all over the place."[16]

In this Brave New World, up was definitely down and black was clearly white. Those who didn't agree with Bush's false record were the "revisionists," which implied they – not Bush – were the ones playing games with facts and history.

Besides the WMD distortions, the Bush administration had pushed other pre-war hot buttons to get Americans ready for war. Bush and his aides repeatedly suggested that the Iraqi government and al-Qaeda were in cahoots, a theme used so aggressively that polls showed nearly half of Americans polled believed that Saddam Hussein was behind the 9/11 terror attacks.

Only after the Iraq invasion was it disclosed that the Bush administration knew – and hid – direct evidence contradicting its claims about Iraqi collaboration with al-Qaeda. Before the war began, the U.S. government had captured two senior al-Qaeda leaders, Abu Zahaydah and Khalid Sheik Mohammed, who in separate interrogations denied the existence of an alliance.

Abu Zahaydah told his U.S. interrogators in 2002 that the idea of cooperation was discussed inside al-Qaeda but was rebuffed by Osama bin Laden, who considered Saddam an infidel and his secular government anathema to al-Qaeda's Islamic fundamentalism. The Bush administration surely would have publicized an opposite answer, but the denial was kept under wraps. The al-Qaeda interrogations were not revealed until June 9, 2003, in *The New York Times*.

For the rest of the world, the American disconnect from reality was unnerving, given the awesome power of the U.S. military arsenal. What did it mean when the most powerful nation on earth chose fantasy over truth? For the American people, the price for believing in fictionalized facts was also about to become horribly expensive, in money and blood.

◆ ◆ ◆

"Political adviser Karl Rove may have envisioned George W. Bush in his Top Gun costume as a killer 30-second TV spot for Campaign 2004," Sam Parry wrote at *Consortiumnews.com* on June 25, 2003. "But the image of a swaggering Bush on the deck of the USS Abraham Lincoln is turning quickly into a political albatross as U.S. troops continue to die in what's becoming a nasty guerrilla war in Iraq.

"Bush's flight-suit scene could become a reminder of Bush's reckless over-confidence in declaring 'Mission Accomplished.' ... Having recognized this political danger, the White House pushed Bush out ... in a preemptive strike, laying the groundwork for accusing anyone who questions the open-ended occupation of Iraq as defeatist or unwilling to stand with 'the men and women of our military.' Former Republican National Committee Chairman Rich Bond warned that criticism from Democrats would reveal 'the huge disconnect between the liberals who control the Democratic Party and the rest of America.'"[17]

Sam Parry continued: "The prevailing conventional wisdom still holds that Bush is pretty much a shoo-in for a second term, a judgment that is more a testament to conservative domination of the U.S. news media than Bush's record. ... In recent weeks, the cable news networks have framed the central campaign debate with the headline: 'Bush – Is He Unbeatable?' They have shied away from asking: 'Bush – Does He Deserve a Second Term?' ...

"On domestic policy, Bush has left a lengthening trail of broken campaign promises. For instance, he had vowed to pay off the national debt while still affording tax cuts and claiming to set aside $1 trillion of the surplus for unforeseen calamities. Now, Bush's $3 trillion in tax cuts and the struggling economy are pushing the federal government deeper and deeper into the red. ...

"The ocean of red ink, which now stretches as far as the eye can see, also means the U.S. government won't have the resources to extend health benefits to the uninsured, fund education programs or pursue other popular policies such as fighting crime and protecting the environment. More likely, the swelling deficits will force deep cuts in existing programs, which has been a stated goal of conservative activists since the Reagan administration and the 1994 Gingrich Revolution. ...

"Politics was at the forefront, too, when the White House deleted from an environmental report a section that dealt with global warming. Despite the consensus of the scientific community about the threat, global warming doesn't fit with Bush's political spin. Though the news media mentions many of these facts in passing, the disclosures don't get anything like the traction that criticism of Bill Clinton or Al Gore did."[18]

19

Plame-Gate

George W. Bush's presidency reached a hinge point in June 2003, though the significance of the moment was not immediately apparent. From the outside, Bush remained the unquestioned master of his political domain, basking in national acclaim as the victorious "war president." He had large bipartisan majorities in Congress kneeling to kiss his ring, while most of the Washington press corps was lying prostrate before him. He could feel confident that his powerful right-wing attack machine would go after any dissenter who dared to challenge the conventional wisdom about his greatness.

On another level, however, Bush insiders were growing nervous that their principal argument for invading Iraq – the existence of hidden WMD stockpiles – was falling apart. They had leapt at the possibility that a couple of trailers used by the Iraqis for inflating artillery balloons might be the fabled mobile bio-weapons labs, but that hope quickly deflated. So, anxiety at the White House was deepening that the President might soon be challenged over his honesty and over his case for war.

The hinge – anchored on one side by Bush's seeming invincibility and on the other side by the emerging WMD-less reality in Iraq – was swung open by an unlikely historical figure, a dapper former U.S. ambassador named Joseph C. Wilson IV. Wilson had served in embassies in Africa and had been *chargé d'affaire* in Iraq at the time of Saddam Hussein's invasion of Kuwait in 1990. But nothing Wilson had done in his government career would match the notoriety that was in store for him when he emerged as the first Washington insider to directly challenge the honesty behind Bush's WMD claims.

The strange journey of Joe Wilson from obscure ex-diplomat to a leading *bete noire* of the Bush administration began in early 2002 as the case for invading Iraq was taking shape. Vice President Dick Cheney expressed interest in a dubious document that had surfaced in Italy purporting to show that Iraq had tried to buy yellowcake uranium from Niger, presumably for use in a revived nuclear program.

Given Cheney's obsession with the Iraq-WMD issue, senior officials in the CIA office known as Winpac – for weapons intelligence, nonproliferation and arms control – took the Vice President's interest seriously. As they looked around for someone for a fact-finding trip, one CIA officer in the unit mentioned to the attractive Valerie Plame that her husband's diplomatic experience fit many of the requirements. As an ex-diplomat, Wilson had experience in both Iraq and Niger. Plame's superiors asked her to pass on a message inviting her husband in for a meeting. While none of that might seem particularly unusual, Plame's peripheral role later would become an issue that would dominate internal White House discussions and permeate critical news reports.

"Apart from being the conduit of a message from a colleague in her office asking if I would be willing to have a conversation about Niger's uranium industry, Valerie had had nothing to do with this matter," Wilson later wrote in his memoir, *The Politics of Truth.* "Though she worked on weapons of mass destruction issues, she was not at the meeting I attended where the subject of Niger's uranium was discussed, when the possibility of my actually traveling to the country was broached. She definitely had not proposed that I make the trip."[1]

Wilson accepted the unpaid assignment with the CIA agreeing to pay his travel expenses. In February 2002, the ex-ambassador flew to Niger, discussed the Iraq suspicions with business and government officials, and returned with a conclusion that the allegations appeared to be false. In his oral report to the CIA, Wilson said he found no evidence that Iraq had sought yellowcake and – considering the international controls governing shipments of uranium – most of his sources doubted that a sale would even be possible.

Wilson did add a *caveat,* that one senior Nigerien, former Prime Minister Ibrahim Mayaki, said he had suspected that an Iraqi commercial delegation to Niger in 1999 might have been interested in buying yellowcake, but the uranium topic never came up at the meeting and nothing was sold to Iraq.

State Department intelligence analysts, who had already correctly concluded that the Iraq-Niger-yellowcake claims were baseless, reviewed Wilson's information and believed that it corroborated their judgment. But some CIA analysts, who then were pushing the Niger allegations, seized on Wilson's comment about Mayaki suspecting that Iraq might be in the market for yellowcake as corroboration for their position. In effect, they "cherry-picked" one inconsequential fact from Wilson's report that could be used to support their position.

Wilson's negative findings were backed up by other U.S. government reports from the field. Plus, the original Niger document, which had surfaced under mysterious circumstances in Italy, was viewed by many in the intelligence community as a crude forgery that used stationery stolen from the Nigerien embassy in Rome. Nevertheless, since the White House was scouring for any indication that Saddam Hussein might be reconstituting his nuclear program, the dubious Niger-yellowcake story proved hard to kill. U.S. intelligence agencies did get the allegation stripped out of at least one administration speech, but it kept returning, most notably when it was inserted into Bush's January 2003 State of the Union Address, attributed to the British.

"The British government has learned that Saddam Hussein recently sought significant quantities of uranium from Africa," Bush said in a sentence that became known as "the sixteen words."

In spring 2003, after the invasion of Iraq, as it became increasingly obvious that the administration's dire WMD warnings were hollow, Wilson began to speak privately with journalists about his trip. *New York Times* columnist Nicholas D. Kristof wrote an article that cited an unnamed former ambassador who had gone on a fact-finding mission to Africa and had returned discounting the suspicions of Iraqis buying uranium. Cheney grew curious about this mission that had been undertaken because of his expressed interest but that had not led to a formal report back to the Vice President.

After figuring out the identity of Kristof's source, the White House prepared to retaliate against Wilson, who was emerging as the first Washington establishment figure to accuse the administration of manipulating the WMD intelligence. The White House was determined to nip in the bud any "revisionist history" about the integrity behind the march to war. In his memoir, Wilson cited sources telling him that a meeting in Cheney's office led to a decision "to produce a workup" to discredit Wilson.

Lewis "Scooter" Libby, Cheney's chief of staff, asked Undersecretary of State Marc Grossman, a neoconservative ally in the State Department, to prepare a memo on Wilson. Dated June 10, 2003, Grossman's report included a paragraph, marked secret, that referred to CIA officer "Valerie Plame" as Wilson wife.[2]

On June 11, Libby also heard from CIA official Robert Grenier that Wilson's wife worked in the CIA unit that sent Wilson to Africa, Grenier later testified. CIA Director George Tenet also mentioned to Cheney that Wilson's wife worked for the CIA and had a hand in arranging Wilson's trip to Niger. Cheney passed that information on to Libby in a conversation on June 12, 2003, according to Libby's notes.[3]

While the senior officials who were bandying about the name of Valerie Plame might have had sufficient clearance to know Plame's identity as an undercover CIA officer, their behavior was highly unusual. Undercover officers in Plame's category, known as "NOCs" for "non-official cover," often operate in great danger outside the protections of the U.S. embassies. Normally, the CIA zealously protects their cover sharing the identities only on a strict need-to-know basis.

"The CIA is obsessive about protecting its NOCs," one former senior U.S. official told us. "There's almost nothing they care about more." But there was something the Bush administration seemed to care more about – stopping criticism of President Bush in its tracks.

On June 13, Deputy Secretary of State Richard Armitage – Grossman's boss – mentioned in an interview with *Washington Post* reporter Bob Woodward that Wilson's wife helped pick the ex-ambassador for the assignment. "Why would they send him?" Woodward asked. "Because his wife's a [expletive] analyst at the agency," Armitage responded. "She is a WMD analyst out there."[4]

Woodward didn't use the information, but Armitage's comment is believed to have been the first reference by an administration official to a reporter about Wilson's wife whose identity was a classified government secret. It was not clear, however, whether the tough-talking deputy secretary of state was just shooting off his mouth, trying to impress a famous journalist, or if Armitage was part of an emerging strategy by the White House to undermine Wilson's credibility by portraying his Niger trip as a case of nepotism.

When Armitage's early role was publicly revealed three years later, a conventional wisdom quickly took shape in Washington that Armitage was acting on his own, that he had no connection to the White House political machinations, and that he had been a dissenter on the Iraq War. But there was reason to believe otherwise.

A well-placed conservative source, who had been an early supporter of George W. Bush and who knew both Armitage and White House political adviser Karl Rove well, described a different reality to us. The source said Armitage and Rove were much closer than many Washington insiders understood.

Armitage and Rove developed a working relationship in the late 1990s when Bush was lining up Colin Powell to support a Bush presidential candidacy and to be his Secretary of State, the source said. In those negotiations, Armitage stood in for Powell and Rove represented Bush. After that, the two men provided a back channel for passing sensitive information between the White House and the State Department, the source said.

To illustrate the point, the conservative source recounted an incident early in the Bush administration when he warned Rove to be leery of

Armitage, whom the source regarded as untrustworthy. Shortly afterwards, the source got an angry call from Armitage who had been told by Rove about the warning. Though the source earlier had witnessed the Rove-Armitage connection over the Powell recruitment, he still was surprised that Rove felt so loyal to Armitage that he would immediately hop on the phone to alert Armitage about the criticism. Subsequently, the source said he was shut out of the White House. He blamed Rove and Armitage for the blackballing.

The significance of the Rove-Armitage friendship to the Wilson-Plame case was that it undercut the belief in Washington that Armitage had no link to Bush's inner circle and that therefore his comments about Wilson's wife must have been just gossip.

"Armitage isn't a gossip," the conservative source said, "but he is a leaker. There's a difference."

Also, although Armitage may have had doubts about invading Iraq in 2003, he was no dove, as some Washington journalists believed. In 1998, Armitage had been one of 18 signatories to a seminal letter from the neoconservative Project for the New American Century urging President Bill Clinton to oust Saddam Hussein by military force if necessary. Armitage joined a host of neoconservative icons, such as Elliott Abrams, John Bolton, William Kristol, Richard Perle and Paul Wolfowitz. Many signers became architects of Bush's Iraq War policy five years later.

◆◆◆

In mid-June 2003, as the White House fretted over the potential impact from Wilson's Niger-yellowcake criticism, Cheney and Libby began to pick out reporters who were considered friendly and likely would help in the anti-Wilson campaign. On June 23, 2003, Libby briefed *New York Times* reporter Judith Miller about Wilson and may have passed on the tip about Wilson's wife working at the CIA at that time.[5]

Other administration officials also reached out to journalists. About the same time as the Libby-Miller meeting, right-wing columnist Robert Novak got a surprise call from Armitage's office offering an interview.

"During his quarter of a century in Washington, I had had no contact with Armitage before our fateful interview," Novak wrote later. "I tried to see him in the first 2½ years of the Bush administration, but he rebuffed me – summarily and with disdain, I thought. Then, without explanation, in June 2003, Armitage's office said the deputy secretary would see me."

Novak dated the call from Armitage's office at about two weeks before Wilson went public with his article about the Niger story on July 6,

2003. In other words, Armitage's outreach to Novak and Libby's briefing of Miller came at virtually the same time.[6]

As the White House was setting its sights on Wilson, the ex-ambassador was deciding to attach his name directly to his charges of manipulated intelligence. In *The New York Times* opinion section on July 6, Wilson published his article, entitled "What I Didn't Find in Africa," in which he described his Niger mission and charged that the White House had "twisted" intelligence to justify war. Later the same day, he appeared on NBC's "Meet the Press" to expand on his charges.

As Cheney read Wilson's article, a perturbed Vice President scribbled in the margins the questions he wanted pursued. "Have they [CIA officials] done this sort of thing before?" Cheney wrote. "Send an Amb[assador] to answer a question? Do we ordinarily send people out pro bono to work for us? Or did his wife send him on a junket?"

Though Cheney did not write down Plame's name, his questions indicated that he was well aware that she worked for the CIA and was in a position (dealing with WMD issues) to have a hand in her husband's assignment to check out the Niger reports.

That same eventful day – July 6, 2003 – Armitage called Carl Ford, the assistant secretary of state for intelligence and research, at home and asked him to send a copy of Grossman's memo about Wilson to Secretary of State Powell. Since Powell was preparing to leave with Bush on a state visit to Africa, Ford forwarded Grossman's memo to the White House for delivery to Powell.[7]

The next day, July 7, Libby took the unusual step of inviting White House press secretary Ari Fleischer out to lunch. There, Libby told Fleischer that Wilson's wife worked in the CIA's counter-proliferation division. Libby "added that this was something hush-hush or on the QT, that not many people knew this information," Fleischer later testified.[8]

Giving this sensitive information to a press secretary suggested that Libby was looking for ways to disseminate the news to the media. Fleischer then joined the presidential party on a five-day state visit to African capitals.

Administration officials who stayed behind in Washington stepped up their efforts to counteract Wilson's op-ed. Libby later testified before a federal grand jury that he was told by Cheney that Bush had approved a plan in which Libby would brief a specific *New York Times* reporter about portions of a top-secret National Intelligence Estimate relating to the Niger uranium.

On July 8, Libby spoke again with *Times* reporter Judith Miller about the NIE and about the Wilsons. In a two-hour interview over breakfast at the elegant St. Regis Hotel near the White House, Libby told Miller that

Wilson's wife worked at a CIA unit responsible for weapons intelligence and non-proliferation. Miller wrote down the words "Valerie Flame," an apparent misspelling of Mrs. Wilson's maiden name.[9]

That same day, Novak had his interview with Armitage. Novak later recalled that Armitage divulged Plame's identity toward the end of an hour-long interview. Armitage "told me unequivocally that Mrs. Wilson worked in the CIA's Counter-proliferation Division and that she had suggested her husband's mission," Novak wrote, adding that Armitage seemed to want the information published. Armitage "noted that the story of Mrs. Wilson's role fit the style of the old Evans-Novak column – implying to me that it [the column] continued reporting Washington inside information," Novak wrote.[10]

Feeling encouraged by Armitage to disclose the Plame connection, Novak contacted Bush's chief political adviser Karl Rove, who confirmed the story as Novak's second source. "I didn't dig it out, it was given to me," Novak later told *Newsday*, adding that Bush administration officials "thought it was significant, they gave me the name."[11]

Meanwhile, to the administration's dismay, the Niger-yellowcake deceit was dogging Bush's Africa trip. At every stop, questions were asked about how the infamous "sixteen words" had ended up in the State of the Union speech. Fleischer was forced to concede that the yellowcake allegation was "incorrect" and should not have been included in the speech. On July 11, CIA Director Tenet took the fall for the State of the Union screw-up, apologizing for not better vetting the speech.

"This did not rise to the level of certainty which should be required for presidential speeches," Tenet said. The admission was one of the first times the Bush team had retreated on any national security issue. Administration officials were embarrassed, incensed and determined to punish Wilson.

In later court testimony about the Plame leak, Ari Fleischer said he decided to give the CIA-wife-sent-Wilson-to-Africa tip to two reporters, NBC's David Gregory and *Time* correspondent John Dickerson, as they strolled down a road in Uganda. "If you want to know who sent the ambassador to Niger, it was his wife; she works there," at the CIA, Fleischer said.[12]

Dickerson said Fleischer was one of two administration officials who urged him to pursue the seemingly insignificant question of who had been involved in arranging Wilson's trip. But Dickerson didn't recall Fleischer specifically identifying Wilson's wife at that time, only prodding him to look in that direction. Both officials urged him to "go ask the CIA who sent Wilson" and that "Wilson had been sent by a low-level CIA employee," Dickerson recalled.

"At the end of the two conversations I wrote down in my notebook: 'look who sent.'" Dickerson wrote. "What struck me was how hard both officials were working to knock down Wilson."[13]

Back in Washington on July 11, 2003, Dickerson's *Time* colleague, Matthew Cooper, was getting a similar earful from Rove, who tried to steer Cooper away from Wilson's information on the Niger deception and toward the notion that the Niger trip was authorized by "Wilson's wife, who apparently works at the agency [CIA] on WMD issues," according to Cooper's interview notes.[14]

Cooper later got the information about Wilson's wife confirmed by Cheney's chief of staff Libby, who was peddling the same information to Judith Miller. On July 12, in a telephone conversation, Libby and Miller returned to the Wilson topic. Miller's notes contained a reference to a "Victoria Wilson," apparently another misspelled reference to Wilson's wife, Valerie.[15] But Miller, who was on the defensive inside *The New York Times* for her credulous reporting on the administration's WMD claims, lacked the clout to push through the story about Wilson's wife.

Two days later, on July 14, Novak published a column, citing two unnamed administration sources (Armitage and Rove) outing Plame as a CIA officer and portraying Wilson's Niger trip as a case of nepotism. The disclosure of Plame's identity effectively meant the end of her CIA career and put the lives of her overseas contacts in jeopardy. But the White House counterattack against Wilson had only just begun.

On July 20, 2003, NBC's correspondent Andrea Mitchell told Wilson that "senior White House sources" had called her to stress "the real story here is not 'the sixteen words' but Wilson and his wife." The next day, Wilson was told by MSNBC's Chris Matthews that "I just got off the phone with Karl Rove. He says and I quote, 'Wilson's wife is fair game.'"

However, by September, CIA officials, angered by the damage done to Plame's spy network, struck back. They lodged a complaint with the Justice Department that the leaks may have amounted to an illegal exposure of a CIA officer. A White House official told *The Washington Post* that the administration had informed at least six reporters about Plame. The official said the disclosure was "purely and simply out of revenge."[16]

But the initial investigation was under the control of Attorney General John Ashcroft, considered a right-wing Bush loyalist. So, the President and other White House officials confidently denied any knowledge of the leak. Bush even vowed to fire anyone who leaked classified material.

"The President has set high standards, the highest of standards, for people in his administration," White House press secretary Scott

McClellan said on September 29, 2003. "If anyone in this administration was involved in it, they would no longer be in this administration."

Bush personally announced he wanted to get to the bottom of the matter. "If there is a leak out of my administration, I want to know who it is," Bush said on September 30. "I want to know the truth. If anybody has got any information inside our administration or outside our administration, it would be helpful if they came forward with the information so we can find out whether or not these allegations are true."

Yet, even as Bush was professing his curiosity and calling for anyone with information to step forward, he was withholding the fact that he had authorized the declassification of some secrets about the Niger uranium issue and had ordered Cheney to arrange for those secrets to be given to reporters. In other words, though Bush knew a great deal about how the anti-Wilson scheme got started – since he was involved in starting it – he uttered misleading public statements to conceal the White House role and possibly to signal others that they also should deny knowledge.

That was exactly what key White House officials did. In early October, press secretary McClellan said he could report that political adviser Karl Rove and National Security Council aide Elliott Abrams were not involved in the Plame leak. That comment riled Libby, who feared that he was being hung out to dry. Libby went to his boss, Dick Cheney, and complained that "they're trying to set me up; they want me to be the sacrificial lamb," Libby's lawyer Theodore Wells later said.

Cheney scribbled down his feelings in a note to press secretary McClellan: "Not going to protect one staffer + sacrifice the guy the Pres that was asked to stick his head in the meat grinder because of incompetence of others." In the note, Cheney initially was ascribing Libby's sacrifice to Bush but apparently thought better of it, crossing out "the Pres" and putting the clause in a passive tense. On October 4, 2003, McClellan added Libby to the list of officials who have "assured me that they were not involved in this."

So, Libby had a motive to lie to the FBI when he was first interviewed about the case. He had gone to the mat with his boss to get his name cleared in the press, meaning it would make little sense to then admit involvement to FBI investigators. "The White House had staked its credibility on there being no White House involvement in the leaking of information about Ms. Wilson," a federal court filing later noted. For his part, Libby began claiming that he had first learned about Plame's CIA identity from NBC's Washington bureau chief Tim Russert after Wilson's op-ed had appeared.

This White House cover-up might have worked, except in late 2003, Ashcroft recused himself because of a conflict of interest, and Deputy

Attorney General James Comey picked Patrick Fitzgerald – the U.S. Attorney in Chicago – to serve as special prosecutor. Fitzgerald pursued the investigation far more aggressively. Over the next three-plus years, the Plame-gate affair would become a slow-growing infection eating away at White House credibility, despite the best efforts of the President's political and media allies.

Rather than thank Wilson for undertaking a difficult fact-finding trip to Niger for no pay – and for reporting accurately about the dubious Iraq-Niger claims – Republicans were unrelenting in tearing down the former ambassador. The Republican-run Senate Intelligence Committee made derogatory claims about Wilson's honesty in a report issued about the WMD controversy on July 7, 2004.

Contradicting Wilson's assertion that he had found no evidence of an Iraqi-Niger uranium deal, the committee report said that "for most [intelligence] analysts, the information in the [Wilson] report lent more credibility to the original CIA reports on the uranium deal." That was a reference to the comment by former Prime Minister Mayaki that he had thought an Iraqi delegation might have been interested in yellowcake, although the topic was never raised and no negotiations were ever held.

The committee's reference to "most analysts" referred to the CIA officials who were then pushing the Niger story and had latched on to this one inconsequential point. The committee report noted that "State Department Bureau of Intelligence and Research analysts believed that the [Wilson] report supported their assessment that Niger was unlikely to be willing or able to sell uranium to Iraq."

After the Senate Intelligence Committee's report, Wilson's media enemies hurled the phrase "most analysts" against him, though it made no sense to blame Wilson for the fact that the CIA analysts who were wrong about the Niger-Iraq yellowcake suspicions outnumbered the State Department analysts who were right. Indeed, the fact that the committee's Republicans could push through this odd notion that a misguided majority somehow trumped an accurate minority showed how far the traditional concept of intelligence had drifted off course.

Committee chairman, Senator Pat Roberts, Republican of Kansas, stood out the most partisan leader to run the traditionally non-partisan intelligence oversight panel in its three-decade history. Not satisfied with the slap at Wilson in the full report, Roberts joined with two other right-wing Republicans, Christopher Bond and Orrin Hatch, to attach additional views to the report, asserting that Wilson's criticism of the administration's use of intelligence "had no basis in fact."

20

Rewriting History

In most cases in life, it wouldn't matter much that a 40-year-old long-time heavy drinker had refused to admit his alcoholism, nor that years later, he would play word games when asked about his alleged cocaine use. Doctors might say that denial isn't good for a person's recovery, but that wouldn't affect the rest of us. The difference in this case, however, was that the substance abuser somehow became President of the United States. And by hiding his earlier problems, George W. Bush learned a dangerous lesson – that his family and political connections could protect him from the truth.

Politicians with less powerful friends may pay dearly for their little lies or perceived exaggerations, as Bill Clinton and Al Gore learned. But the Bushes were not like lesser-born people. The Bushes asserted themselves as a kind of American royalty. When the rare question about their truthfulness did escape the cautious self-censorship of the mainstream media or slip past the political timidity of the Democrats, Bush's allies would step forward to spin the facts, bully the transgressor, or remind everyone that "we are a nation at war." On those even rarer occasions when intimidation didn't work, some subordinate would grudgingly take the fall.

Given the widespread (circa 2003) consensus about the "straight-shooting" George W. Bush – and the career damage that could come to anyone saying otherwise – the Washington press corps was appropriately silent on July 14, 2003, when Bush started altering key facts about why the war to oust Iraqi dictator Saddam Hussein had been necessary four months earlier.

"We gave him a chance to allow the inspectors in, and he wouldn't let them in," Bush said at the end of a brief press conference at the White House. "After a reasonable request, we decided to remove him from power."

With U.N. Secretary General Kofi Annan sitting next to him and a gaggle of White House reporters in front of him, Bush simply lied. As everyone knew during the march to war, Hussein did let U.N. inspectors in to scour the countryside for months before the U.S. invasion. Indeed, in early March 2003, U.N. inspectors were requesting more time for their work and noting that the Iraqis finally were filling in details about how they had destroyed earlier stockpiles of weapons. But Bush cut the inspections short and launched his invasion.

In mid-July 2003, however, Bush's old falsehoods about Iraq's WMD were collapsing. Just eight days before Bush's July 14 lie about Hussein barring U.N. inspectors, former Ambassador Joseph Wilson had accused the Bush administration of having "twisted" the Niger-uranium intelligence. On July 11, three days before Bush's U.N. inspectors remark, CIA Director George Tenet had agreed to take the blame for inclusion of the infamous "sixteen words" in Bush's State of the Union. Just that morning of July 14, Robert Novak had published his column outing Wilson's wife, Valerie Plame.

So, on that summer day, Bush was in the market for a new fiction to make the Iraq War more justifiable. Though citing Iraq's WMD threat was no longer tenable, Bush still behaved as if he could alter history and facts by sheer force of will. So he put the blame for the war on Saddam Hussein. If the Iraqi dictator had only let the U.N. inspectors in, Bush's new argument went, all this trouble could have been averted. It was Hussein who "chose war," not Bush.

Bush was asserting a kind of kingly right to say whatever he wished without contradiction. In a sense, he was the fabled emperor in his "new clothes," striding naked among the populace as they marveled at the finery of his wardrobe. Except in Bush's case, he was not an emperor deceived by his own vanity. Bush appeared confident that his lie would not be contradicted, at least not by anyone important. Who, after all, would be crazy enough to take up Hussein's side of the argument?

If that was Bush's thinking, he was right. The lie about the barred U.N. inspectors may have been brazen, but it worked. With Bush at the apex of his power, Washington journalists knew that the better part of valor was to show discretion by looking down at their shoes when the "war president" prevaricated. The smart choice was to act like nothing had happened. Washington journalists didn't even raise a peep when Bush attacked his critics as "historical revisionists" while he engaged in historical revisionism.

Bush's lie about Saddam Hussein barring the inspectors also wasn't a one-time lapse. It became a regular refrain in Bush's Iraq War speeches. In the following months, Bush repeated his claim in slightly varied forms. On January 27, 2004, Bush said, "We went to the United Nations, of course, and got an overwhelming resolution – 1441 – unanimous resolution, that said to Saddam, you must disclose and destroy your weapons programs, which obviously meant the world felt he had such programs. He chose defiance. It was his choice to make, and he did not let us in."

Defense Secretary Donald Rumsfeld argued the same false historical point in an op-ed article for *The New York Times* on March 19, 2004, the first anniversary of the Iraq invasion. "In September 2002, President Bush went to the United Nations, which gave Iraq still another 'final opportunity' to disarm and to prove it had done so," Rumsfeld wrote, adding that "Saddam Hussein passed up that final opportunity" and then rejected a U.S. ultimatum to flee. "Only then, after every peaceful option had been exhausted, did the President and our coalition partners order the liberation of Iraq," Rumsfeld wrote.

The repetition about Hussein refusing to let in the U.N. inspectors affected the memory and judgment of even experienced journalists like ABC's Ted Koppel. In a July 2004 interview with "Democracy Now" host Amy Goodman, Koppel explained why he thought the Iraq invasion was justified. "It did not make logical sense that Saddam Hussein, whose armies had been defeated once before by the United States and the Coalition, would be prepared to lose control over his country if all he had to do was say, 'All right, U.N., come on in, check it out,'" Koppel said.

In Bush's acceptance speech to the Republican National Convention on September 2, 2004, the President again felt confident that he could get away with spinning the history. He said: "We went to the United Nations Security Council, which passed a unanimous resolution demanding the dictator disarm, or face serious consequences. Leaders in the Middle East urged him to comply. After more than a decade of diplomacy, we gave Saddam Hussein another chance, a final chance, to meet his responsibilities to the civilized world. He again refused, and I faced the kind of decision no President would ask for, but must be prepared to make."

In this climate of deception and self-deception, Bush also felt confident enough to present his false version of history to the American people during a presidential debate with Senator John Kerry on September 30, 2004. "I went there [the United Nations] hoping that once and for all the free world would act in concert to get Saddam Hussein to listen to our demands," Bush said. "They [the Security Council] passed a resolution that said disclose, disarm or face serious consequences. I believe when an international body speaks, it must mean what it says.

"But Saddam Hussein had no intention of disarming. Why should he? He had 16 other resolutions and nothing took place. As a matter of fact, my opponent talks about inspectors. The facts are that he [Hussein] was systematically deceiving the inspectors. That wasn't going to work. That's kind of a pre-September 10 mentality, the hope that somehow resolutions and failed inspections would make this world a more peaceful place."

Bush's debate reference to the pre-invasion inspections and Hussein's supposed defiance was one of the rare times when a major news organization, in this case *The Washington Post*, actually mentioned the divergence between Bush's version and the facts, but not prominently. In the middle of an inside-the-paper fact-checking article about the debate, the *Post* mentioned Bush's assertion about Hussein having "no intention of disarming" and then politely noted that "Iraq asserted in its filing with the United Nations in December 2002 that it had no such weapons, and none has been found." But neither the *Post* nor any other big news organization made a serious issue out of Bush's prevarication.[1]

If the U.S. news media had asserted the kind of standards they used for, say, Al Gore, there would have been a week-long firestorm. Virtually every point in Bush's war justification had been wrong. Hussein had disarmed. The U.N. resolutions had achieved their goal of a WMD-free Iraq. The U.N. inspectors weren't finding WMD because the stockpiles weren't there. Bush's own post-invasion inspection teams didn't find the WMD either. But reporters exacted no meaningful penalty from Bush for his deceptive statements made to tens of millions of Americans.

◆◆◆

As Bush fought his rear-guard battles against the facts, he frequently reaffirmed his vision of the "war on terror" as a Manichean struggle between good and evil, a conflict that justified virtually any act.

Nat Parry wrote at *Consortiumnews.com* on September 3, 2003: "George W. Bush has declared 'no retreat' on Iraq even as that country descends into bloody anarchy and as Iraqi fighters pick off American soldiers by ones and twos almost daily. Instead, Bush is raising the stakes by refusing to rethink his Bush Doctrine of preemptive wars. 'Our only goal, our only option, is total victory in the war on terror, and this nation will press on to victory,' Bush told the American Legion convention in St. Louis on August 26, 2003, reiterating his strategy of waging war against any country or group that he says supports – or is likely to support – terrorism. ...

"Bush is leaving little doubt that his vision is one of endless warfare in which Washington will pick out nations that are judged threats to U.S. security and attack them. With Churchillian rhetorical flourishes, Bush's speech painted the world in black and white, with no sense of the gray that comes with indiscriminate killing whether from suicide bombers or from high-explosive rockets fired from the sky. In Bush's view, his side is all good, the other side is all bad, and there is no ambiguity.

"Bush's reference to 'total victory' over terrorism also suggests that he is still not listening to many national security analysts who warn that it is no more possible to eradicate 'terrorism' – an ill-defined concept throughout history – than it is to eliminate crime or drug use. To even approach 'total victory' would require draconian actions carried out by something akin to a permanent worldwide police state, which might only generate more desperation and more terrorism. ...

"His language was intentionally bellicose, almost defiant in the face of critics who have called for a mid-course correction in U.S. policy in Iraq. 'The terrorists have not seen America running,' Bush told the American Legion convention. 'They've seen America marching. They have seen the armies of liberation marching into Kabul and Baghdad. The terrorists have seen speeding tank convoys and roaring jets and Special Forces arriving in midnight raids – and sometimes justice has found them before they could see anything coming at all.'"

The article continued: "Bush's ideological vision of a world submitting to his desires is colliding with the reality that other countries will resist U.S. domination either politically – as the setbacks at the U.N. have shown – or militarily. That is most evident in Iraq where resistance to U.S. forces has been heavier than expected both during the three-week march to Baghdad and through almost five months of occupation. ...

"Increasingly, it looks like the fall of Saddam's government was not a victory after all, but only the start of a new phase of the war. In an interview with Newsday.com, an Iraqi militia fighter said, 'We have many more people and we're a lot better organized than the Americans realize. We have been preparing for this for a long time, and we're much more patient than the Americans. We have nowhere else to go.' As the U.S. death toll mounted this summer [2003], Bush kept up the macho rhetoric. American forces are 'plenty tough' to handle the situation, he said, as he taunted Iraqi fighters to 'bring 'em on.' ...

"But the lesson of the past several months is that whatever Bush's wishes, other governments and the people of the world will contest the notion of an all-dominant United States. Bush may want to pick and choose which countries must be invaded and which ones spared, but the world community is certain to organize a determined opposition to the Bush Doctrine."[2]

◆◆◆

As the WMD searches continued to come up empty and the Iraq insurgency claimed the lives of more U.S. soldiers, the Bush administration grasped for "turning points" and for new rationales that justified the war.

On July 22, 2003, U.S. forces killed Saddam Hussein's two sons – Uday and Qusay – in the northern Iraqi city of Mosul prompting a White House statement that "they can no longer cast a shadow of hate on Iraq." On December 13, the eight-month hunt for Saddam Hussein ended when the ousted leader was pulled from a "spider hole" near his former home town of Tikrit. "Now the former dictator of Iraq will face the justice he denied to millions," a triumphant Bush declared.

These dramatic events – complete with photos of the two corpses and video of an unkempt Hussein getting a medical exam – were public relations coups for Bush, but they also put the U.S. occupation in a tricky position. Before those events, the Bush administration could argue that the U.S. military was needed to prevent Hussein's return to power. Afterwards, if the Iraqi insurgency didn't collapse, U.S. soldiers would look more and more like occupiers battling a nationalist uprising.

Bush sought to counter the image of occupation by emphasizing another goal of the war: to bring "democracy" to Iraq and the Middle East. Bush and his advisers compared their policy to Harry Truman's democratic institution-building in Europe and Japan after World War II. According to this view, the U.S. occupation of Iraq was a modern-day Marshall Plan. Bush also argued that promotion of democracy was vital to overcome the appeal of terrorists, who had attacked the United States on 9/11 supposedly because they "hate" American freedoms.

"We're pursuing long-term victory in this war [against terror] by promoting democracy in the Middle East so that the nations of that region no longer breed hatred and terror," Bush said.

National Security Adviser Condoleezza Rice, an African-American, equated the administration's policies in Iraq to the struggles of blacks for civil rights in the United States. Rice said Americans "must never, ever indulge in the condescending voices who allege that some people in Africa or in the Middle East are just not interested in freedom, they're culturally just not ready for freedom or they just aren't ready for freedom's responsibilities."

Rice continued, "We've heard that argument before, and we, more than any, as a people, should be ready to reject it. The view was wrong in 1963 in Birmingham, and it is wrong in 2003 in Baghdad and in the rest of the Middle East." Rice's message suggested that anyone who questioned the wisdom of invading a country halfway around the world and killing thousands of its people for the ostensible purpose of establishing "democracy" was some kind of bigot.

There was also the question of Bush's hypocrisy. While attacking Iraq in the name of "democracy," Bush had based U.S. military operations in Persian Gulf sheikhdoms with few democratic freedoms. He enlisted allies who aggressively repressed their own people. Uzbekistan's authoritarian government, for instance, committed human rights abuses on par with Saddam Hussein's former government, but Uzbekistan hosted a U.S. military base in geo-strategically important Central Asia.

Yet, even while making these alliances of convenience, the Bush administration distanced itself rhetorically from past examples of the U.S. government compromising its principles. A disarming part of Bush's Iraq pitch was to admit past U.S. errors in the support of authoritarian states. In a speech on November 6, 2003, Bush acknowledged that the United States has too often put itself on the dark side of history by supporting repressive regimes and thwarting democratic development.

"Sixty years of Western nations excusing and accommodating the lack of freedom in the Middle East did nothing to make us safe because in the long run stability cannot be purchased at the expense of liberty," Bush said. That had now changed, Bush said, without addressing the contradictions in his own inconsistent policies.

Besides Bush's alliances with repressive regimes around the world, the "democracy" that his administration envisioned for Iraq looked like many past examples of colonial rule, relying on a handful of hand-picked locals to give the appearance of self-government. In the months after toppling Hussein's government in April 2003, U.S. authorities also found themselves challenged by grassroots political activism in Iraq seeking a quick end to the U.S. occupation and a rapid turnover of power to an elected Iraqi leadership.

Indeed, plans for rapid local elections were part of the original strategy devised by the first U.S. administrator, Jay Garner. But his replacement, Paul Bremer, decided that the first step would be U.S. appointment of Iraq's mayors and administrators. "Elections that are held too early can be destructive," Bremer said in June 2003, after the U.S.-run Coalition Provisional Authority canceled plans for the local elections.

Bremer promised that as soon as a constitution was written and a national census taken, elections would follow. But the U.S. occupation authority still preferred a limited form of democracy, indirect elections with representatives emerging from caucuses who would then pick Iraq's leaders. One effect of the two-stage process would be to avoid having a national leader arise who could claim a clear popular mandate. Also, the caucuses would leave the United States with greater control.

Besides the planned limits on elections, there were other missing features of democracy, such as freedom of speech, the right to assemble, and a free press. In U.S.-occupied Iraq, these fundamental freedoms were tightly constrained or virtually non-existent. Protests often were met with lethal force by American troops, occurrences that dated back to the first days of the occupation when Iraqis staged mass demonstrations against the U.S. presence in mid-April 2003. Time and again, claiming danger to U.S. troops, the Americans responded with gunfire.

After Hussein's capture, rallies in support of the captured leader sometimes turned violent. In one incident on December 15, four Iraqis were killed when U.S. soldiers fired indiscriminately into a protest in a Sunni district of Baghdad, according to an official from the Association of Muslim Ulama. "The only difference is that Saddam would kill you in private, where the Americans will kill you in public," commented Mohammad Saleh, a 39-year-old building contractor.

Freedom of the press also had arbitrary limits in the new Iraq. In June 2003, the Coalition Provisional Authority drafted a code of conduct for the press that prohibited "unsubstantiated news that will foment social unrest or hostility towards American troops." The code of conduct drew widespread criticism from press freedom advocates. The Iraqi operations of Dubai-based satellite news channel Al-Arabiyya were shut down in Iraq in November 2003 after the channel aired a tape recording of Hussein when he was still in hiding.

Freedom of speech also was limited, with Iraqis prohibited from making statements critical of the occupation. As Reuters reported on November 11, 2003, American troops arrested a man and placed masking tape over his mouth after he had criticized the occupation. When asked why they had arrested the man, the commanding officer told Reuters, "This man has been detained for making anti-coalition statements."

The Bush administration codenamed one crackdown on Iraqi rebels "Operation Iron Hammer," the same name used by a military operation carried out by Nazi Germany against the Soviet Union during World War II. In the German Operation Iron Hammer, Adolf Hitler tried to cripple the Soviet war industry through targeted bombing. In Iraq's Operation Iron Hammer, U.S. forces sought to intimidate the insurgents through bombing raids in the Sunni Triangle and other centers of resistance.

Besides bombing raids, U.S. officials employed a variety of other repressive measures intended to assert control over Iraq. Some of the strategies copied measures used by Israeli security forces in their occupation of the Palestinian territories. The techniques included surrounding entire villages with barbed wire and issuing identification cards – with information written in English – to inhabitants. Only by showing these cards could residents pass through the checkpoints. Also, U.S. forces destroyed the homes of suspected guerrillas and their families.

On a barbed wire fence surrounding the town of Abu Hishma, a sign was posted that read in English, "This fence is here for your protection. Do not approach or try to cross it, or you will be shot." A battalion commander explained the rationale: "With a heavy dose of fear and violence, and a lot of money for projects, I think we can convince these people that we are here to help them."[3]

Even more troubling to human rights advocates was the U.S. practice of abducting and detaining families of suspected insurgent leaders to coerce them into surrender. The wife and daughter of Izzat Ibrahim al-Douri, a former Saddam Hussein deputy, were arrested on November 26, 2003, and held, apparently to convince al-Douri to turn himself in.

Al-Douri has been accused of organizing guerrilla attacks on U.S. troops and one U.S. official said the prolonged detentions of his family members were "similar to [those of] a material witness," according to *Newsday*. Human rights groups said the detentions "violate international law and raise questions about the United States' ability to highlight human rights abuses by other countries," *Newsday* reported.[4]

Indiscriminate repression of an occupied people could be judged a violation of the Fourth Geneva Convention, which was established to protect the rights of civilians in times of conflict and occupation. The Convention states that collective punishments are strictly prohibited. Article 33 says, "No protected person may be punished for an offence he or she has not personally committed. Collective penalties and likewise all measures of intimidation or of terrorism are prohibited." Detaining family members as bargaining chips also can be seen as a form of hostage-taking, putting the Bush administration in violation of Article 34, which states, "The taking of hostages is prohibited."

But President Bush brushed aside questions about international law, and the U.S. news media didn't ask too many probing questions about Bush's sincerity in "promoting democracy" in Iraq or the broader Middle East. Never did Washington journalists ask questions like, "If Bush is so committed to democracy in Iraq, why did he stop the counting of votes in Florida?" Or "why – if Bush so cherishes democratic debate – didn't he rein in his supporters who repeatedly challenged the patriotism of Americans who questioned the factual basis of Bush's war on Iraq?"

The short answer might be that Bush's speeches about "democracy" and "freedom" were his biggest – and possibly most troubling – lie of all.

21

War for a Second Term

Campaign 2004 boiled down to whether George W. Bush could convince enough Americans that he was keeping them safe – and that the Iraq War wasn't the disaster it appeared to be. There also would be the usual tearing down of his Democratic opponent and the gamesmanship with voting. Plus, the Democratic contender was sure to stumble into a few unforced errors.

But the key element in Bush gaining a second term was to squeeze one more year out of the 9/11 unity, the rally-round-the-troops emotion at the start of the Iraq War, and the exaggerated fear of the "evil-doers."

"There is no neutral ground – no neutral ground – in the fight between civilization and terror, because there is no neutral ground between good and evil, freedom and slavery, and life and death," Bush said on March 19, 2004, the first anniversary of the Iraq invasion. "The terrorists are offended not merely by our policies; they're offended by our existence as free nations. No concession will appease their hatred. No accommodation will satisfy their endless demands."

The "war on terror," Bush said, was "an inescapable calling of our generation." The word "calling" had a powerful meaning to his fundamentalist Christian political base, suggesting a divine duty, much like Bush's earlier reference to a "crusade" against terrorism. It was a fight to the death. Eliminate everyone who would or might engage in terrorism before they could destroy civilization and impose slavery on the rest of us.

In Bush's strategy, there was almost nothing about a practical approach toward reducing tensions with the Muslim world. Bush's did the opposite: elevate a low-intensity conflict into a full-scale war in which the battlefield would be everywhere; set the bar at not just prevailing over a foe but eradicating "evil" itself.

The "war on terror" was shaping up into a worldwide version of the Hundred Years War in which the collateral damage would go far beyond the death and destruction in the Middle East and the loss of generations of young American soldiers. To carry out this virtually endless conflict, the

United States would have to undergo fundamental changes. Not only would the government have to borrow and spend trillions of dollars to sustain the war, but the U.S. political system would have to be transformed. Bush's vision of a warrior nation was incompatible with the old-fashioned notion of an American Republic that was based on inalienable rights of citizens. Sacrificing freedoms would be necessary to protect "freedom."

While some Americans saw these trade-offs as reasonable and even patriotic, Bush's vision was taking on the look of madness to many others across the United States and around the world. Still, Bush's grim vision was greeted with remarkably little criticism or even serious commentary, at least in the mainstream media. Most of the alarm was concentrated on the Internet where citizen bloggers warned about this descent into irrationality and authoritarianism.

To Bush's supporters, however, the President's vision of an all-for-one America in a black-and-white struggle against "evil" represented a reassuring "moral clarity." Their trust in the President bordered on the absolute and any sacrifice in civil liberties or democratic niceties was a small price to pay. A stirring slogan that rang out across the nation in song and bumper sticker was that "freedom isn't free." Though referring to sacrifices by soldiers in defense of "freedom," Bush's price tag for "freedom" included not just the blood of young warriors but eradication of many core principles that traditionally defined a free society.

By 2004, "freedom" in the United States had come to mean almost its classical opposite. Bush's "freedom" meant the right of the Executive to imprison enemies of the state indefinitely without charge and without even the centuries-old right of *habeas corpus*; "freedom" incorporated the concept of coercion, torture or what the Founders called "cruel and unusual punishment" to extract confessions from detainees; it countenanced surveillance of anyone – citizen and non-citizen alike – without a requirement for judicial review or evidence of probable cause that a crime was being committed; it saw no problem with the government and its private-sector allies teaming up to silence dissent.

"Freedom" also embraced the notion of an all-powerful leader. Bush could ignore domestic laws, international treaty commitments and even the Constitution when he deemed it necessary. In a way, Bush did George Orwell one better with a new definition of "freedom." The *1984* slogan that "freedom is slavery" was given a cynical new twist. By 2004, repression had been redefined as freedom.

◆◆◆

From the beginning of Campaign 2004, the "Democratic base" sent messages to the party leadership that stressed the urgency of the moment. The first message was embodied in the candidacy of former Vermont Governor Howard Dean, who soared in Democratic polls and rallied unprecedented grassroots financial support because he articulated a strong case against Bush, especially Bush's rush to war in Iraq. The "base," in effect, was repudiating a replay of the accommodating Democratic politics of 2002 and was insisting that the only hope for victory was to take Bush on.

The second message appeared in the later emergence of Massachusetts Senator John Kerry, a Vietnam War hero who adopted Dean's blunt criticism of Bush and defied the right-wing attack machine – challenging the Republicans to "bring it on" – but he did so within a political framework that was believed to offer a better chance of prevailing in November. By shifting to Kerry in Iowa and New Hampshire, the "base" showed a practical readiness to support a candidate who supposedly could win.

The mainstream U.S. news media and conservative pundits mischaracterized much of this urgency in the Democratic "base" as an irrational hatred of Bush. The alarm actually reflected a fairly rational sense of foreboding. These Americans perceived that Bush and the neoconservative ideologues who surrounded him were putting in place a radically different political system, one that supplanted facts and reasoned debate with bogus information and ideological rants, backed by punishments for those who dissented or who simply disagreed.

Bush's contempt for facts was the underlying warning from former Treasury Secretary Paul O'Neill as recounted to author Ron Suskind in *The Price of Loyalty*, which was published in early 2004. O'Neill described a range of administration policies – from Bush's "preemptive wars" to the rampaging budget deficit – that "were impenetrable by facts." O'Neill, who served in the Nixon and Ford administrations and later ran Alcoa, was startled to find the Bush administration making major decisions with little deliberation beyond Bush's tendency to embrace ideological certainties.

O'Neill said Bush was "clearly signing on to strong ideological positions that had not been fully thought through. But, of course, that's the nature of ideology. Thinking it through is the last thing an ideologue wants to do."

Besides O'Neill's portrait of a White House cavalierly sending soldiers off to war and blithely setting tax policy that pushed the nation to the brink of bankruptcy, the book corroborated the darkest fears of environmentalists. It confirmed that the White House was the captive of corporate special interests and had turned its back on the science behind the global-warming debate. During Campaign 2000, Bush tried to undercut Al Gore's edge as an environmentalist by pledging to regulate carbon dioxide. He also vowed to reduce other greenhouse gas emissions. The promises appealed to suburban soccer moms and burnished Bush's claim to be a "compassionate conservative."

Bush further promoted this reassuring image by selecting former New Jersey Governor Christie Whitman, a Republican moderate, to run the Environmental Protection Agency. However, less than two months after taking office, Bush reversed his position and abruptly pulled the rug out from under Whitman. Bush threw in his lot with the energy industry and conservative ideologues who disdained any recognition of the dangers from global warming.

When Whitman realized she was being blind-sided by the White House, she demanded a meeting with Bush, but he shut out her arguments. In *The Price of Loyalty*, Suskind reported that Whitman "started right in, talking about the importance of promoting international cooperation, the areas of scientific evidence that were indisputable, the issue of U.S. credibility. Bush cut her off, 'Chistie, I've already made my decision.'" Bush told a stunned Whitman that he not only would oppose the Kyoto agreement on global warming, but would renounce his promise to regulate carbon dioxide.

"Whitman just sat. It was a clean kill. She was running around the world, using her own hard-won, bipartisan credibility to add color and depth to his campaign pronouncements, and now she ended up looking like the fool," Suskind wrote.[1]

By 2004, Bush had earned a reputation as the worst environmental President in U.S. history. Environmentalist Robert F. Kennedy Jr., the son of assassinated Senator Robert F. Kennedy, catalogued more than 200 major rollbacks of environmental standards during the Bush administration.[2]

Yet Bush's signature position on environmental dangers was his neglect of the global warming issue. Though faced with scientific alarms about potential disasters to the world's ecosystems and possible economic and political devastation, Bush did little – other than confuse the issue.

"There is no scientific debate in which the White House has cooked the books more than that of global warming," Kennedy wrote in *Rolling Stone*. "In the past two years, the Bush administration has altered, suppressed or attempted to discredit close to a dozen major reports on the subject. These include a 10-year peer-reviewed study by the International Panel on Climate Change, commissioned by the President's father in

1993 in his own efforts to dodge what was already a virtual scientific consensus blaming industrial emissions for global warming."[3]

Meanwhile, the evidence of the global warming threat continued to grow. Ice was melting near the poles at alarming rates. Icebergs the size of small states were breaking off from the Antarctic continent with regularity. The Alaskan tundra was thawing, forcing indigenous human populations to move and resettle. Coral reefs were bleaching; forests were changing; weather patterns were growing more extreme.

The ecological journal *Nature* published a report predicting up to 37 percent of all species could become extinct by 2050 as a result of global warming. A report in Great Britain warned that climate change could redirect the Gulf Stream, which moderates the temperatures of the U.S. East Coast and much of Europe. Without the Gulf Stream, some heavily populated areas along the Atlantic Ocean could experience much colder winters, even as other parts of the planet heat up.

The science was solid enough for the U.S. military to start gaming out scenarios to deal with imminent climatic changes. An unclassified report prepared for the Pentagon by Defense Department planner Andrew Marshall described ominous climate events within the next two decades that could lead to global chaos with some parts of the world scorched by severe droughts and other regions flooded by huge storms and rising sea levels. According to *Fortune* magazine, the report proved that "at least some federal thought leaders may be starting to perceive climate change less as a political annoyance and more as an issue demanding action."[4]

But hostility to facts and disdain for logical analysis had become the norm of the Bush administration. From O'Neill's previous government service and his work in the private sector, the Treasury Secretary was accustomed to facts shaping policy. In the Bush administration, ideology shaped "facts." When Bush wasn't following his gut judgments, he was letting himself be guided by partisans and ideologues – from political adviser Karl Rove to the neoconservative foreign policy crowd. O'Neill was surprised, too, that Vice President Cheney, who had served with O'Neill in the Ford administration, had re-emerged a quarter century later as a hard-right ideologue.

Another little-mentioned issue on the ballot in 2004 was whether the American people would sign off on historic budget deficits, an ocean of red ink that stretched over the horizon. Bush had inherited a projected 10-year budget surplus that had prompted talk about a possible elimination of America's entire national debt. But the situation deteriorated quickly in the wake of the stock market bubble bursting in 2000. Yet, instead of adjusting his planned tax cuts or putting in triggers tied to continued surpluses – as O'Neill favored – President Bush pressed ahead, effectively abandoning the careful budget-balancing policies promoted during the Clinton years. The results of Bush's tax-cut policies, combined with higher military and security spending, was a nightmare for traditional Republican fiscal conservatives like O'Neill.

As Treasury Secretary, the top U.S. economic official, O'Neill said he was staggered not just by Bush's fiscal policy but by the disorganized way it was decided. After Republican congressional victories in 2002, for instance, the Bush administration made plans to push through a new round of tax cuts. O'Neill described the intellectually sloppy discussion during which the key decisions were made with minimal preparation and analysis. Bush led the chaotic discussion in the Roosevelt Room at the White House, siding with tax-cut ideologues against O'Neill's position that the exploding deficit would cripple plans to address Social Security and other budget priorities.

In the days after the meeting, "O'Neill thought often of that extraordinary meeting in the Roosevelt Room, its haphazard, improvised quality, the way portentous issues had been raised and spun and tossed about, untethered from the weight of their consequences," author Suskind wrote in *The Price of Loyalty*.

"I think of a meeting like that, with so much at stake," O'Neill said. "It's like June bugs hopping around on a lake."[5]

Beyond a disdain for careful policy formulation, some Bush administration officials voiced contempt for reason itself. Author Suskind had a conversation with a senior Bush aide who taunted Suskind for coming from "what we call the reality-based community." The Bush aide said this "reality-based community" consisted of people who "believe that solutions emerge from your judicious study of discernible reality."

The chastised Suskind nodded and muttered some praise for the principles of the Enlightenment, only to be cut off. "That's not the way the world really works anymore," the Bush aide told the journalist. "We're an empire now, and when we act, we create our own reality. And while you're studying that reality – judiciously, as you will – we'll act again, creating other new realities, which you can study too, and that's how things will sort out. We're history's actors ... and you, all of you, will be left to study what we do."[6]

Suskind, a former *Wall Street Journal* reporter, quoted other Republicans who concluded that Bush believed – or at least gave the impression he believed – that his judgments were directed by God.

"I think a light has gone off for people who've spent time up close to Bush: that this instinct he's always talking about is this sort of weird, Messianic idea of what he thinks God has told him to do," said Bruce Bartlett, a domestic policy adviser to Ronald Reagan and a Treasury official in the first Bush administration. "He truly believes he's on a mission from God. Absolute faith like that overwhelms a need for analysis. The whole thing about faith is to believe things for which there is no empirical evidence."

Because Bush was convinced of his rightness, he often snapped at aides who questioned his "gut" judgments, according to Republicans who watched Bush in action. "This is why he dispenses with people who confront him with inconvenient facts," Bartlett said.[7]

◆◆◆

On May 4, 2004, at *Consortiumnews.com*, Nat Parry compared the excesses of Bush's Iraq War with the insanity that had seeped into the Vietnam War almost four decades earlier, as fictionalized in Francis Ford Coppola's classic movie about irrationality in a time of war:

"Marlon Brando's Col. Kurtz character in 'Apocalypse Now' applied crystal logic to the madness of the Vietnam War, concluding that what made sense was to descend into barbarism. The U.S. military hierarchy, judging Kurtz's tactics to be 'unsound,' ordered the colonel eliminated to keep at least a façade of civilization.

"A reprise of that tragedy – a kind of 'Apocalypse Again' – is now playing out in Iraq, with U.S. soldiers sent halfway around the globe to invade and occupy a country supposedly with the goal of protecting the world from violence and introducing democratic freedoms. As in Vietnam, there is a widening gap between the uplifting rhetoric and the ugly facts on the ground.

"On April 30, for instance, with previous claims about Iraqi weapons of mass destruction and Saddam Hussein's supposed links to al-Qaeda no longer tenable, George W. Bush touted a humanitarian justification for the invasion. 'There are no longer torture chambers or rape rooms or mass graves in Iraq,' Bush told reporters as he retreated to this latest line of defense. But now even those minimal standards don't appear to be true.

"The year-long occupation of Iraq – like the war in Vietnam – has led some U.S. troops to engage in behavior that much of the world views as madness or war crimes. The U.S. assault on Fallujah in April transformed a soccer field into a fresh mass grave for hundreds of Iraqis – many of them civilians – killed when U.S. forces bombarded the rebellious city with 500-pound bombs and raked its streets with cannon and machine-gun fire. There were so many dead that the soccer field became the only place to bury the bodies. Supposedly avenging Saddam Hussein's old mass graves of the 1980s and 1990s, Bush's policies have opened up new ones.

"Even Bush's oft-repeated assertion about closing Hussein's torture chambers and rape rooms no longer can draw a sharp line of moral clarity. As Bush spoke, worldwide press attention was focusing on evidence that U.S. guards had tortured and sexually abused Iraqi prisoners held at the Abu Ghraib prison, the same prison that Saddam Hussein's henchmen used. U.S. guards photographed repulsive scenes of naked Iraqis forced into sexual acts and humiliating postures while a U.S. servicewoman gleefully gestured at their genitalia, according to pictures first shown on CBS News's '60 Minutes II.'"

Investigative journalist Seymour Hersh disclosed in *The New Yorker*'s May 10 issue that a 53-page classified Army report concluded that the prison's military police were urged on by intelligence officers seeking to break down the Iraqis before interrogation. The abuses, occurring from October to December 2003, included use of a chemical light or broomstick to sexually assault one Iraqi, the report said. Witnesses also told Army investigators that prisoners were beaten and threatened with rape, electrocution and dog attacks. At least one Iraqi died during interrogation.

"Numerous incidents of sadistic, blatant and wanton criminal abuses were inflicted on several detainees," said the report written by Maj. Gen. Antonio M. Taguba.[9] In other words, Iraq's torture and rape rooms were open for business, only under new U.S. management.

One victim who faced torture at Abu Ghraib under both Saddam Hussein's regime and the U.S. occupation said the physical abuse from Hussein's guards was preferable to the sexual humiliation employed by the Americans. Dhia al-Shweiri told *The Associated Press* that the Americans were trying "to break our pride."[8]

After the publication of the Abu Ghraib photos, Bush said he "shared a deep disgust that those prisoners were treated the way they were treated." He added that "their treatment does not reflect the nature of the American people."

But, as Nat Parry observed, "Bush's protest was reminiscent of the senior officers in 'Apocalypse Now' condemning Kurtz's atrocities and extrajudicial killings, when Kurtz's barbarism was only the logical extension of that war's excessive violence.

"The generals created Kurtz and then had to disavow him. In a similar line of argument about Iraq, many people around the world are asking whether Bush should be held accountable for the policies that led to war crimes. Bush ordered the invasion in defiance of the United

---

[9] After encountering hostility from the Bush administration to his report, Gen. Taguba was forced into retirement in 2007.

Nations, deemed his Iraqi enemies to be 'evil,' and brought to bear massive firepower against both military and civilian targets.

"As the official who ordered the invasion, Bush also must bear ultimate responsibility for excesses blamed on U.S. troops who were put in an extraordinarily difficult and dangerous position of both conquering and then occupying a country with a different language and an alien culture."[9]

♦ ♦ ♦

Domestically, too, Bush was putting himself above the law. While elements of Bush's grand self-image were previously known, a fuller picture slowly came into focus in 2004. In an appearance before the Senate Judiciary Committee on June 8, 2004, Attorney General John Ashcroft balked at showing Congress the administration's memos arguing that Bush had the inherent authority to order torture whenever he deemed it necessary.

The Wall Street Journal, which obtained a draft of the torture memo, summarized its contents this way: "The President, despite domestic and international laws constraining the use of torture, has the authority as Commander in Chief to approve almost any physical or psychological actions during interrogation, up to and including torture." The *Journal* also reported that "a military lawyer who helped prepare the report said that political appointees heading the working group sought to assign to the President virtually unlimited authority on matters of torture – to assert 'presidential power at its absolute apex,' the lawyer said."[10]

Still, the U.S. media's analysis of the Bush Doctrine – both foreign and domestic – concentrated on its various parts, not its larger meaning. Putting those pieces together created a troubling mosaic of a leader who disdained legal limits, trusted his personal instincts and considered himself guided by the Almighty.

At best, it seemed that by placing the emphasis on extracting information, regardless of the rules of interrogation, Bush created the atmosphere in which the Abu Ghraib abuses were allowed to take place. As Kenneth Roth, executive director of Human Rights Watch, put it, "The horrors of Abu Ghraib were not simply the acts of individual soldiers. Abu Ghraib resulted from decisions made by the Bush administration to cast the rules aside."

But Bush's defenders saw matters differently, arguing that Bush was a historic figure confronting special challenges with insight and resolve. National Security Adviser Condoleezza Rice predicted that George W.

Bush would go down in history as a world leader on par with Franklin Delano Roosevelt and Winston Churchill.

"When you think of statesmen," Rice said, "you think of people who seized historic opportunities to change the world for the better, people like Roosevelt, people like Churchill, and people like Truman, who understood the challenges of communism. And this President has been an agent of change for the better – historic change for the better."

However, the Bush administration's internal debate about loosening the rules on torture was more likely to bring back memories of Adolf Hitler than Roosevelt and Churchill, since it was Hitler who was blamed for reviving the practice in Europe.

On the Continent, the use of torture to extract confessions had been condemned since the Enlightenment when rationality and the rule of law replaced the divine right of kings. The practice was resurrected in Germany when the Nazis rose to power and legitimized "third degree" interrogations. The Nazis used torture extensively, particularly in the nations Germany invaded and occupied to obtain information about anti-occupation resistance activities.

At the end of World War II, as the atrocities of war were examined, torture was perceived to be an aberration that must not be allowed to recur, leading to requirements for humane treatment of prisoners to be inserted in the Geneva Conventions. In the official commentary on the text, the International Committee of the Red Cross wrote that the motivation behind these standards was to prevent "acts which world public opinion finds particularly revolting – acts which were committed frequently in the Second World War."[11]

In the decades that followed World War II, the practice of torture re-emerged in the waging of so-called "dirty wars" mostly in Third World countries and authoritarian states. Sometimes, Western intelligence agencies would be implicated in the teaching of torture or even engaging in its practice, but officially, developed countries decried these barbarities. The United States often led the way, rebuking offending nations through diplomatic channels and in the State Department's annual human rights report.

In the wake of Guantanamo and Abu Ghraib, however, Washington's lectures looked more and more like rank hypocrisy.

22

Kerry as Caricature

Much like Al Gore was defined by the national news media in 2000 as a liar and an exaggerator, the "conventional wisdom" on John Kerry in 2004 was that he took two sides on nearly every issue. In a *New York Times* front-page article on March 6, 2004, entitled "Kerry's Shifts: Nuanced Ideas Or Flip-Flops," reporter David M. Halbfinger helped establish that consensus by dissecting Kerry's statements on issues, such as gay marriage, just the way the Republican National Committee drew it up: portraying the Massachusetts Democrat as a waffler.

Nowhere in the piece, however, was there any reference to Bush's history of flip-flopping on issues of grave consequence, such as his promises to curb carbon dioxide and other greenhouse gases; his pledges to maintain a balanced federal budget and keep his hands off the Social Security trust fund; and his assurances that he would run a "humble" foreign policy that wouldn't stretch U.S. forces with "nation-building." Yet, whatever the reality of Bush speaking out of both sides of his mouth, he remained – as far as the major U.S. news media was concerned – a straight-talker.

Without doubt, Kerry, a two-decade veteran of the U.S. Senate, brought on some of his flip-flopping image himself through his comfort level with the convoluted voting that the U.S. Congress is famous for. Members often favor one version of a bill while opposing another, opening them to campaign attack ads in which their nuanced positions are pulled out of context and made to look contradictory.

Kerry fell into that trap while trying to explain why he had favored one form of an $87 billion war appropriation bill but had opposed another. Kerry had been part of a losing effort to pay for the Iraq War spending by repealing Bush's tax cuts. When the Republicans beat back that amendment, Kerry demonstrated his anger over what he saw as fiscal irresponsibility by opposing the bill on final passage.

"I actually did vote for the $87 billion before I voted against it," Kerry said in one exchange with voters, a sentence that would haunt him for the rest of the campaign.

John Kerry's larger political problem, however, may have been that he had two distinct sides to his personality – and never reconciled them. On one side, Kerry felt part of the Establishment. The son of a diplomat, he attended Yale, joined the exclusive Skull and Bones secret society, and enlisted in the Navy though he opposed the Vietnam War. When he followed the contrarian side of his character, however, he veered into rebellion. He was a leader of Vietnam Veterans Against the War, testifying eloquently before a Senate committee with his other famous quote, "How do you ask a man to be the last man to die for a mistake?"

This dichotomy continued during his political career, as he tried to balance his cautious ambition to be part of the political club with his rebellious idealism. Only a year after entering the Senate, the rebel side led Kerry into one of the most challenging issues of the day, opposing the excesses from Ronald Reagan's secret policy of aiding the Nicaraguan contra rebels despite a congressional ban on military assistance. Not only had Reagan secretly authorized one of his National Security Council aides, Marine Lt. Col. Oliver North, to spearhead a clandestine effort to circumvent the law, but some contra units turned to drug smuggling as a means of supporting themselves.

In December 1985, while working at *The Associated Press*, Robert Parry and his colleague Brian Barger wrote a groundbreaking story about this contra-cocaine connection. At the time, the contras were President Reagan's favorite "freedom fighters," hailed as "the moral equals of the Founding Fathers." Like the *mujahedeen* in Afghanistan, the contras were billed as courageous front-line fighters battling the Soviet empire, only the contras were fighting an enemy closer to the U.S. homeland. As Reagan famously warned, Nicaragua was only "two days' driving time from Harlingen, Texas."

For years, however, contra units had gone on bloody rampages through Nicaraguan border towns, raping women, torturing captives and executing civilian officials. In private, Reagan referred to the contras as "vandals," according to Duane Clarridge, the CIA officer in charge of the operation, in his memoir, *A Spy for All Seasons*.[1] But in public, the Reagan administration attacked anyone who pointed out the contras' corruption and brutality.

In 1984, Congress barred U.S. military assistance to the contras, forcing the rebels to search for new funding sources. Drug money became an easy way to fill their depleted coffers. Contra units both in Costa Rica and Honduras opened or deepened ties to Colombian cartels and other regional drug traffickers. The White House also scrambled to find other ways to keep the contras afloat, turning to third countries, such as Saudi Arabia, and eventually to profits from clandestine arms sales to Iran.

The contra-funding secrets began to seep out in the mid-1980s. In June 1985, AP reporter Parry wrote the first story mentioning Oliver North's secret contra supply operation. By that fall, Parry and Barger had stumbled onto evidence that some contras were helping traffickers transship cocaine through Central America to the United States. Eventually, it became clear that the drug connection implicated nearly all major contra organizations.

The AP published the story on December 20, 1985, describing contra units "engaged in cocaine smuggling, using some of the profits to finance their war against Nicaragua's leftist government." The story provoked little coverage elsewhere in the U.S. press corps, but it pricked the interest of 42-year-old first-term Senator John Kerry.

A former prosecutor, Kerry also heard about contra law violations from a Miami-based federal public defender named John Mattes, who had been assigned a case that touched on contra gunrunning. Mattes's sister had worked for Kerry in Massachusetts. By spring 1986, Kerry had begun a limited investigation deploying some of his personal staff in Washington. Kerry's chief investigators were Ron Rosenblith, Jonathan Winer and Dick McCall.

Rosenblith, a Massachusetts political strategist from Kerry's 1984 campaign, braved both political and personal risks as he traveled to Central America for face-to-face meetings with witnesses. Winer, a lawyer also from Massachusetts, charted the inquiry's legal framework and mastered its complex details. McCall, an experienced congressional staffer, brought Capitol Hill savvy to the investigation.

Kerry's staff inquiry advanced against withering political fire. The Reagan administration went to great lengths to thwart Kerry's investigation, including attempting to discredit witnesses and stonewalling the Senate when it requested evidence.

On April 10, 1986, Barger and Parry followed up on their original story by reporting on the AP wire that the U.S. Attorney's office in Miami was examining allegations of contra gunrunning and drug trafficking. The AP story rattled nerves inside the Reagan administration. On an unrelated trip to Miami, Attorney General Edwin Meese pulled U.S. Attorney Leon Kellner aside and asked about the existence of this contra probe.

Back in Washington, other major news organizations began to sniff around the contra-cocaine story but mostly went off in wrong directions. On May 6, 1986, *The New York Times* relied for its story on information from Meese's spokesman Patrick Korten, who claimed "various bits of information got referred to us. We ran them all down and didn't find anything. It comes to nothing."

But that wasn't the truth. In Miami, Assistant U.S. Attorney Jeffrey Feldman and FBI agents were corroborating many of the allegations. On May 14, 1986, Feldman recommended to his superiors that the evidence of contra crimes was strong enough to take the case to a grand jury. U.S. Attorney Kellner agreed, scribbling on Feldman's memo, "I concur that we have sufficient evidence to ask for a grand jury investigation."

But on May 20, less than a week later, Kellner reversed that recommendation. Without telling Feldman, Kellner rewrote the memo to state that "a grand jury investigation at this point would represent a fishing expedition with little prospect that it would bear fruit." Kellner signed Feldman's name to the mixed-metaphor memo and sent it to Washington on June 3.

The revised "Feldman" memo was then circulated to congressional Republicans and leaked to conservative news media outlets, which used it to discredit Kerry's investigation. The right-wing *Washington Times* denounced the probe as a wasteful political "witch hunt" in a June 12, 1986, article. "Kerry's anti-contra efforts extensive, expensive, in vain," blared another headline on August 13, 1986. Back in Miami, Kellner reassigned Feldman to unrelated far-flung investigations, including one to Thailand.

Mattes, the federal public defender in Miami, watched as the administration ratcheted up pressure on Kerry's investigation. "From a political point of view, … Kerry had every reason to shut down his staff investigation," Mattes said. "There was no upside for him doing it."

The Kerry that Mattes witnessed at the time was the ex-prosecutor determined to get to the bottom of serious criminal allegations even if they implicated senior government officials. "As an investigator, he had a sense it was there," said Mattes. "Kerry was a crusader. He was the consummate outsider, doing what you expect people to do. … At no point did he flinch."

Years later, a document surfaced in the National Archives showing that the CIA was keeping tabs on Kerry's investigation. Alan Fiers Jr., who served as the CIA's Central American Task Force chief, told independent counsel Lawrence Walsh's Iran-Contra investigators that the AP and Feldman's investigations had attracted the hostility of the Reagan administration. Fiers said he "was also getting a dump on the Senator Kerry investigation about mercenary activity in Central America from the CIA's legislative affairs people who were monitoring it."

Negative publicity about the contras was particularly unwelcome to the Reagan administration in spring and summer 1986 as the White House battled to restore U.S. government funding to the contras. In the politically charged atmosphere, the administration sought to smear anti-contra witnesses who were talking to Kerry.

In a July 28, 1986, memo, initialed as read by President Reagan, North labeled onetime contra mercenary Jack Terrell as a "terrorist threat" because of his "anti-contra and anti-U.S. activities." North said Terrell had been cooperating "with various congressional staffs in preparing for hearings and inquiries regarding the role of U.S. government officials in illegally supporting the Nicaraguan resistance."

In August 1986, FBI and Secret Service agents hauled Terrell in for two days of polygraph examinations on suspicion that Terrell intended to assassinate President Reagan, an allegation that proved baseless. But Terrell said later that the investigation of him had chilled his readiness to testify about the contras. "It burned me up," he said. "The pressure was always there."

Beyond intimidating some witnesses, the Reagan administration systematically worked to frustrate Kerry's investigation. Years later, one of Kerry's investigators, Jack Blum, complained publicly that the Justice Department had actively obstructed the congressional probe. Blum said William Weld, who took over as assistant attorney general in charge of the criminal division in September 1986, was an "absolute stonewall" blocking the Senate's access to evidence on contra-cocaine smuggling.

Inside the Justice Department, senior career investigators worried about the administration's failure to turn over information requested by the Senate. "I was concerned that we were not responding to what was obviously a legitimate congressional request," Mark Richard, one of Weld's top deputies, testified in a deposition.

On September 26, 1986, Kerry tried to spur action by presenting Weld with an 11-page "proffer" statement from a 31-year-old FBI informant who had worked with the Medellin cartel and had become a witness on cartel activities. The woman, Wanda Palacio, had approached Kerry with an account about Colombian cocaine kingpin Jorge Ochoa bragging about payments he had made to the Nicaraguan contras.

As part of this Contra connection, Palacio said pilots for a CIA-connected airline, Southern Air Transport, were flying cocaine out of Barranquilla, Colombia. She said she had witnessed two such flights, one in 1983 and the other in October 1985, and quoted Ochoa saying the flights were part of an arrangement to exchange "drugs for guns." According to contemporaneous notes of the Weld-Kerry meeting, Weld chuckled that he was not surprised at allegations about corrupt dealings by "bum agents, former and current CIA agents." He promised to give serious consideration to Palacio's allegations.

After Kerry left Weld's office, however, the Justice Department concentrated on poking holes in Palacio's account. Though Palacio had been considered credible in her earlier testimony to the FBI, she was judged to lack credibility when she made accusations about the contras and the CIA. On October 3, 1986, Weld's office told Kerry that it was rejecting Palacio as a witness on the grounds that there were some contradictions in her testimony. The discrepancies apparently related to such minor points as which month she had first talked with the FBI.

Two days after Weld rejected Palacio's contra-cocaine testimony, other secrets about the White House's covert contra support operations suddenly crashed – literally – into view. On October 5, a quiet Sunday morning, an aging C-123 cargo plane rumbled over the skies of Nicaragua preparing to drop AK-47 rifles and other equipment to contra units in the jungle below. Since the Reagan administration had recently won congressional approval for renewed CIA military aid to the contras, the flight was to be one of the last by Oliver North's ragtag air force.

The plane, however, attracted the attention of a teenage Sandinista soldier armed with a shoulder-fired surface-to-air missile. He aimed, pulled the trigger and watched as the Soviet-made missile scored a direct hit on the aircraft. Inside, cargo handler Eugene Hasenfus, an American mercenary working with the contras, was knocked to the floor, but managed to crawl to an open door, pushed himself through, and parachuted to the ground, where he was captured by Sandinista forces. The pilot and other crew members died in the crash.

As word spread about the plane crash, Barger – who had left the AP and was working for a CBS News show – persuaded Parry to join him on a trip to Nicaragua with the goal of getting an interview with Hasenfus, who turned out to be an unemployed Wisconsin construction worker and onetime CIA cargo handler. Hasenfus told a press conference in Managua that the contra supply operation was run by CIA officers working with the office of Vice President George H.W. Bush. But administration officials, including Bush, denied any involvement with the downed plane.

The interview with Hasenfus didn't pan out for Barger and Parry, but Sandinista officials did offer up flight records and other documents they had recovered from the plane. The flight logs of copilot Wallace "Buzz" Sawyer listed hundreds of flights with the airports identified by their four-letter international codes and the planes designated by tail numbers. Upon returning to Washington, Parry began deciphering Wallace's travels and matching the tail numbers with their registered owners.

Meanwhile, in Kerry's Senate office, witness Wanda Palacio was waiting for a meeting when she noticed Sawyer's photo flashing on a TV screen. Palacio began insisting that Sawyer was one of the pilots whom she had witnessed loading cocaine onto a Southern Air Transport plane in Barranquilla, Colombia, in early October 1985. Her identification of Sawyer struck some of Kerry's aides as a bit too convenient, causing them to have their own doubts about her credibility.

In the AP story about Sawyer's logs, however, the last paragraph noted that Sawyer's logs revealed that he had piloted a Southern Air Transport plane on three flights to Barranquilla on October 2, 4, and 6, 1985. Shortly after the AP story moved, Parry got a call from Rosenblith at Kerry's office. Sounding shocked, the Kerry investigator asked for more details about the last paragraph of the story, but he wouldn't say why he wanted to know. Palacio also passed a polygraph exam on her statements. But Weld and the Justice Department still refused to accept her testimony as credible.

On November 25, 1986, the Iran-Contra scandal was officially born when Oliver North was fired and Attorney General Meese announced that profits from secret U.S. arms sales to Iran had been diverted to help fund the Nicaraguan contras. The Washington press corps scrambled to get a handle on the dramatic story of clandestine operations, but still resisted the allegations that the administration's zeal had spilled over into sanctioning or tolerating contra-connected drug trafficking.

Though John Kerry's early warnings about White House-aided contra gunrunning had proved out, his accusations about contra drug smuggling would continue to be rejected by much of the press corps as going too far. On January 21, 1987, the right-wing *Washington Times* attacked Kerry's contra drug investigation again; his alleged offense this time was obstructing justice because his probe was supposedly interfering with the Reagan administration's determination to get at the truth. "Kerry's staffers damaged FBI probe," the headline read.

The mainstream press also continued to publish stories that denigrated Kerry's investigation. On February 24, 1987, a *New York Times* article quoted "law enforcement officials" saying that the contra drug allegations "have come from a small group of convicted drug traffickers in South Florida who never mentioned contras or the White House until the Iran-Contra Affair broke in November."

The article made Kerry out to be something of a dupe. His contra-cocaine witnesses were depicted as simply convicts trying to get lighter prison sentences by embroidering false allegations onto the Iran-Contra scandal. But the *Times* story was untrue. The AP's original contra-cocaine story had run in December 1985, almost a year before the Iran-Contra story broke. The witnesses also weren't helping themselves with Reagan's Justice Department by talking about contra drug smuggling.

But the parameters for a "responsible" Iran-Contra investigation were being set. On July 16, 1987, *The New York Times* published another story that discredited the contra drug charges. It reported that except for a few convicted drug smugglers from Miami, the contra-cocaine "charges have not been verified by any other people and have been vigorously denied by several government agencies."

Four days later, the *Times* added that "investigators, including reporters from major news outlets, have tried without success to find proof of ... allegations that military supplies may have been paid for with profits from drug smuggling." (The *Times* was inaccurate again. The original AP story had cited a CIA report describing the contras buying a helicopter with drug money.)

The joint Senate-House Iran-Contra committee also averted its eyes from the contra-cocaine allegations. The only time the issue was raised publicly was when a demonstrator interrupted one hearing by shouting, "Ask about the cocaine," before being dragged out by police.

In one of those perverse judgments of Washington, Kerry was excluded from the joint committee because of his pioneering work on Oliver North's network. The Massachusetts senator was judged as biased on the topic. The Democratic ranks were filled instead mostly with centrist and even pro-contra Democrats.

Despite official denials and press hostility, Kerry and his investigators pressed ahead. In 1987, with the arrival of a Democratic majority in the Senate, Kerry also became chairman of the Senate subcommittee on terrorism, narcotics and international operations. He used that position to pry loose facts proving that the official denials were wrong and that contra units indeed were involved in the drug trade.[2]

Kerry's report was issued two years later, on April 13, 1989. Its stunning conclusion: "On the basis of the evidence, it is clear that individuals who provided support for the contras were involved in drug trafficking, the supply network of the contras was used by drug trafficking organizations, and elements of the contras themselves knowingly received financial and material assistance from drug traffickers. In each case, one or another agency of the U.S. government had information regarding the involvement either while it was occurring, or immediately thereafter."

The report discovered that drug traffickers gave the contras "cash, weapons, planes, pilots, air supply services and other materials." Moreover, the U.S. State Department had paid some drug traffickers as part of a program to fly non-lethal assistance to the contras. Some payments occurred "after the traffickers had been indicted by federal law enforcement agencies on drug charges, in others while traffickers were under active investigation by these same agencies."

Although Kerry's findings represented the first time a congressional report explicitly accused federal agencies of willful collaboration with drug traffickers, the major news organizations chose to bury the startling findings. Instead of front-page treatment, *The New York Times*, *The Washington Post* and the *Los Angeles Times* all wrote brief accounts and stuck them deep inside their papers. For his tireless efforts, Kerry earned a reputation as a reckless investigator. *Newsweek*'s "Conventional Wisdom Watch" dubbed Kerry a "randy conspiracy buff."

One of the best-read political reference books, the *Almanac of American Politics*, gave this account of Kerry's investigation in its 1992 edition: "In search of right-wing villains and complicit Americans, [Kerry] tried to link Nicaraguan contras to the drug trade, without turning up much credible evidence." Thus, Kerry's reward for his strenuous efforts to get to the bottom of a difficult case of high-level government corruption was to be largely ignored by the mainstream press and to have his reputation besmirched.

But the contra-cocaine story didn't entirely go away. In 1991, in the trial of former Panamanian dictator Manuel Noriega for drug trafficking, federal prosecutors called as a witness Medellin cartel kingpin Carlos Lehder, who testified that the Medellin cartel had given $10 million to the contras, a claim that one of Kerry's witnesses had made years earlier. "The Kerry hearings didn't get the attention they deserved at the time," a *Washington Post* editorial on November 27, 1991, acknowledged.

Kerry's full vindication on the contra drug issue did not come until 1998, when the inspectors general at the CIA and the Justice Department reviewed their files in connection with allegations published by the *San Jose Mercury News* that the contra-cocaine pipeline had contributed to the crack epidemic that ravaged inner-city neighborhoods in the 1980s. (Ironically, the major national newspapers only saw fit to put the contra-cocaine story on their front pages in criticizing the *Mercury News* and its reporter Gary Webb for taking the allegations too far.)

The CIA and Justice Department reports confirmed that the Reagan administration knew from almost the outset of the contra war that cocaine traffickers permeated the CIA-backed army but the administration did next to nothing to expose or stop these criminals. The reports revealed example after example of leads not followed, witnesses disparaged and official law-enforcement investigations sabotaged. The evidence indicated that contra-connected smugglers included the Medellin cartel, Noriega's government, the Honduran military, the Honduran-Mexican smuggling ring of Ramon Matta Ballesteros, and Miami-based anti-Castro Cubans.[3]

CIA inspector general Frederick Hitz found that some contra-connected drug traffickers worked directly for Reagan's National Security Council staff and the CIA. In 1987, Cuban-American Bay of Pigs veteran Moises Nunez told CIA investigators that "it was difficult to answer questions relating to his involvement in narcotics trafficking because of the specific tasks he had performed at the direction of the NSC."

CIA Task Force Chief Alan Fiers said the Nunez-NSC drug lead was not pursued then "because of the NSC connection and the possibility that this could be somehow connected to the Private Benefactor program [Oliver North's fundraising]. A decision was made not to pursue this matter."

Another Cuban-American who had attracted Kerry's interest was Felipe Vidal, who had a criminal record as a narcotics trafficker in the 1970s. But the CIA still hired him to serve as a logistics officer for the contras and covered up for him when the agency learned that he was collaborating with known traffickers to raise money for the contras, Hitz reported. Fiers had briefed Kerry about Vidal on October 15, 1986, without mentioning Vidal's drug arrests and conviction in the 1970s.[4]

Hitz found that a chief reason for the CIA's protective handling of contra drug evidence was the agency's "one overriding priority: to oust the Sandinista government ... [CIA officers] were determined that the various difficulties they encountered not be allowed to prevent effective implementation of the contra program." According to Hitz's report, one CIA field officer explained, "The focus was to get the job done, get the support and win the war."

In 1998, perhaps a handful of Iran-Contra experts realized that Kerry's earlier findings had been corroborated, but that reality never penetrated into Washington's conventional wisdom. The lesson that Kerry learned was that going too much against the grain didn't make for smart politics. Kerry didn't even try to claim any credit for the contra-cocaine investigation in 1998 or later. By then, the senator had surrounded himself with world-weary consultants who urged him to forget about his rebellious behavior as a young senator and to concentrate on sculpting his image as a former war hero who would never again wander too far from the insider crowd.

It was that over-coached John Kerry that most Americans saw in Campaign 2004, a politician who appeared to have a very thin record between his medal-winning heroism in Vietnam and the night he arrived at the Democratic National Convention, snapped off a salute and declared, "Reporting for duty."*

◆◆◆

As Sam Parry observed in a *Consortiumnews.com* article on August 19, 2004, "This year's general election campaign is taking on the trademark stamp of every Bush national campaign since 1988: attack politics that tear down the Bush opponent while a compliant Washington press corps can't believe the Bush family would play dirty.

"In 1988, Massachusetts Governor Michael Dukakis faced Republican attacks suggesting he had undergone psychiatric care, favored dangerous criminals and lacked patriotism. In 1992, the Republicans went on a search for a 'silver bullet' against Arkansas Governor Bill Clinton, which included searching his passport file and leaking false rumors that he had tried to renounce his U.S. citizenship.†

"In 2000, Senator John McCain confronted whispers about his sanity after five years in a North Vietnamese prisoner-of-war camp and mysterious phone calls about his 'black' baby (a child he had adopted from Bangladesh). Vice President Al Gore saw his words so twisted that they were used to justify Republican claims that he was 'delusional' and thus unfit to serve as President.

"Now, it's Senator John Kerry's turn. On one level, the Bush campaign presents Kerry as confused and inconsistent about his ability to make decisions on war and other issues. In a parallel operation, a conservative group of Vietnam veterans accuses Kerry of lying about his war record as the Bush campaign neither condemns nor discourages the smears.

"This two-pronged strategy again echoes back to 1988 when another 'arms-length' group produced the infamous Willie Horton ad that blamed Dukakis for a furloughed black inmate who had raped a white woman. At the same time, George H.W. Bush's campaign stressed similar themes but kept its fingerprints off the more racially provocative ad.

"Though this historical pattern is both obvious and well-documented, the Washington press corps acts as if every day is a new day for the Bush

---

* After coming under intense attack from the major U.S. newspapers for his contra-cocaine series, Gary Webb lost his job at the *Mercury News* and could not find a decent-paying job in journalism. The largely corroborative findings of the CIA's internal investigation didn't help Webb either, since they got scant coverage in the U.S. press. With his career and his personal life in ruins, on the night of December 9, 2004, Webb used his father's pistol to commit suicide.

† For details on these Bush campaign tactics, see Robert Parry's *Secrecy & Privilege*.

"Though this historical pattern is both obvious and well-documented, the Washington press corps acts as if every day is a new day for the Bush family. At best, the voters are confused by the charges and counter-charges, which leave a residue of doubt and disdain for whatever politician got in the way of the Bush family political machine."

Sam Parry continued, "This pattern also goes beyond political campaigns explaining, in part, why the national news media found itself so thoroughly bamboozled on the Iraq War. If there's one overriding principle in today's American politics, it appears to be that the Bushes always get the benefit of the doubt. A growing number of major news organizations – now including *The Washington Post* – have admitted to an overly credulous acceptance of George W. Bush's case for war. ...

"In comments to *Post* media critic Howard Kurtz for his internal review of the newspaper's WMD coverage, senior *Post* editors expressed only mild self-criticism for their lack of pre-war skepticism. *Post* Executive Editor Leonard Downie Jr. even used the occasion to take another slap at the war critics for presumably lacking in realism."

"People who were opposed to the war from the beginning and have been critical of the media's coverage in the period before the war have this belief that somehow the media should have crusaded against the war," Downie said. "They have the mistaken impression that somehow if the media's coverage had been different, there wouldn't have been a war."

Downie's disparaging tone against the Iraq War skeptics represented another odd phenomenon at the highest levels of the U.S. news media, the continued contempt heaped on those who were right in questioning the administration's case for war. Rather than give these people their due – whether American citizens or European allies – many U.S. journalists simply dismissed the skeptics as "ideologues" who approached the war with a closed mind. In this view, those who followed the pro-Bush herd were the free-thinkers.

Also, contrary to Downie's comment, very few Iraq War skeptics were naïve enough to expect the major U.S. news media to "have crusaded against the war," nor did many war opponents think that Bush could have been dissuaded from war. But the skeptics might have expected the news media at least to perform in a professional manner, taking a hard look at the administration's evidence before thousands of American and Iraqi lives were put at risk.

Other comments by senior *Post* journalists also were revealing. "We are inevitably the mouthpiece for whatever administration is in power," said Karen DeYoung, a former assistant managing editor who covered the prewar diplomacy. "If the President stands up and says something, we report what the President said."

In his August 19 article, Sam Parry observed, "That *The Washington Post*, which still boasts about its Watergate scandal coverage three decades later, now considers itself an administration 'mouthpiece' may be shocking enough, but the admission doesn't tell the whole story. It was certainly not true during the Clinton administration when the *Post* aggressively promoted virtually every Clinton 'scandal' story, including the Whitewater real estate deal and the Travel Office firings that ended up being much ado about almost nothing.

"The truth is that the *Post*, like much of the national news media, has been trending neoconservative for the past couple of decades. Bush's case for war was not seriously vetted in large part because many of the senior editors and news executives agreed with his neoconservative policies. Others may have simply feared the career consequences of challenging Bush, especially if some of his claims proved true."

Top *Post* reporters acknowledged the imbalanced coverage. "Administration assertions were on the front page," said the *Post*'s Pentagon correspondent Thomas Ricks. "Things that challenged the administration were on A18 on Sunday or A24 on Monday. There was an attitude among editors: Look, we're going to war, why do we even worry about all this contrary stuff?"

Even the U.S. intelligence community, which historically has been hostile to the news media's revelations about CIA wrongdoing, expected the *Post* and other news outlets to be far more skeptical, according to Kurtz's article. A group of intelligence officers peppered *Post* national security reporter Dana Priest with tough questions after a speech. She said they wanted to know, "Why didn't the *Post* do a more aggressive job? Why didn't the *Post* ask more questions? Why didn't the *Post* dig harder?"[5]

◆ ◆ ◆

So, in such a media climate, it shouldn't have come as too much of a surprise that John Kerry, who won the Bronze Star and the Silver Star for heroism in the Vietnam War, would have his war record challenged and face accusations of cowardice. A well-financed front group called Swift Boat Veterans for Truth spearheaded these attacks with assistance from operatives close to George W. Bush's campaign. The pro-Bush veterans called Kerry a liar over his account that he turned his Swift boat around and braved enemy fire to pull a Special Forces soldier out of the water. The Kerry critics also accused him of fabricating an account of a firefight with a Vietcong soldier. They claimed instead that Kerry had shot a loin-cloth-clad youngster in the back.

As these anti-Kerry veterans presented their version of Kerry as a conniving coward, much of the national press corps fell into line. CNN competed with Fox News to promote the dubious Swift Boat claims as serious news. Eventually – belatedly as far as Kerry's reputation was concerned – several major newspapers, including *The New York Times* and the *Los Angeles Times*, examined the historical record and exposed the Swift Boat Veterans for Truth's accusations as deceptive and contradictory.

For instance, many of the anti-Kerry veterans were not in a position to know what the circumstances were on Kerry's boat when he rushed back to pull Jim Rassmann of the Special Forces out of the water. Rassmann said Kerry's boat was taking small-arms fire, an account that matched what others on board said and what the Navy's contemporaneous records showed.

Reporters for ABC News' "Nightline" traveled to the villages of Tran Thoi and Nha Vi on the Bay Hap River in Vietnam to check out the claim that Kerry had shot a Vietnamese youngster in the back and that the official records of Kerry's heroism were false. Though the villagers didn't know about the controversy raging in the United States, they confirmed the wartime accounts of Kerry, his crew and the official U.S. records – that there had been heavy firing in a clash between Kerry's Swift boat and Vietcong cadre on February 28, 1969.

The villagers also identified the Vietcong killed by Kerry as Ba Thanh, a man in his mid-20s who was dressed in the Vietcong's characteristic black pajamas. He had been sent to the village by his Vietcong superiors with a B-40 rocket launcher as part of a special 12-man unit targeting Swift boats, the villagers said.[6]

Beyond the details of the engagements – which reaffirmed Kerry's personal heroism – there also should have been no question that Kerry and other Swift boat pilots put themselves at extraordinary risk while patrolling the Mekong Delta. Their service in Operation Sealords was one of the most dangerous assignments in the Vietnam War.

In effect, Swift boats were the bait for drawing Vietcong fire so other American forces could swoop in on the targets. Vice Admiral Elmo Zumwalt, Navy commander in Vietnam, estimated that sailors in Operation Sealords suffered a 75 percent casualty rate.

But the conservative news media and many mainstream news outlets, such as CNN, let themselves be used to promote the dubious Swift Boat Veterans for Truth charges. These pro-Bush veterans also accused Kerry of exaggerating war wounds that led to his three Purple Hearts. Even after many of the Swift boat accusations were shown to be lies, the perpetrators were not taken to task by CNN or other outlets that had given the stories such currency. The impact on Kerry's reputation was devastating, sending him into freefall in some national polls and making him the subject of public derision.

For his part, President Bush refused to specifically denounce the attacks on Kerry, saying only that all political advertising from independent groups should be banned. In effect, Bush was equating the spurious attacks on Kerry's war record with questions raised by some liberal groups about how Bush slipped past better-qualified candidates to get a position in the Texas Air National Guard and then failed to fulfill even those duties.

◆◆◆

At their national party conventions in summer 2004, the Democrats bent over backwards not to criticize Bush harshly and often not at all, excising his name from many speech drafts. Some of the consultants around Kerry apparently feared that attacks on Bush would open the Democrats to accusations that they had staged an anti-Bush "hatefest" and would invite comparisons to Michael Moore's anti-Bush documentary, "Fahrenheit 9/11." The Democratic keynote address by Illinois Senate candidate Barack Obama didn't even mention Bush's name, stressing instead a positive message about America's traditions and potential to become an even greater nation.

By contrast, the Republicans showed no hesitancy to bash Kerry. Speaker after speaker laid into Kerry as unfit to serve while delegates waved rubber flip-flops or pointed to purple-heart band-aids pasted to their bodies to mock Kerry's war wounds. The GOP convention's keynote address was delivered by disaffected Democratic Senator Zell Miller, who attacked Kerry by name 16 times, twice the number of times he mentioned Bush. Miller accused Kerry of wanting to "outsource" America's national security and to "let Paris decide when America needs defending."

Though many of the Republican punches were below the belt, they were effective. The Democrats, who had shied away from negativity about Bush, got virtually no poll bounce out of their convention. The Republicans, who relished their anti-Kerry derision, got a double-digit bounce, according to some national polls.

23

Eking It Out

Despite the shortcomings of John Kerry's campaign, the U.S. presidential race tightened considerably in fall 2004. Public doubts continued to grow about progress in the Iraq War and about George W. Bush's overall competence. Bush himself highlighted those concerns with clunky debate performances during which he was out-dueled by Kerry, who finally seemed to be hitting his stride and shifting onto the offensive.

So, with Bush's poll numbers slumping, his campaign turned to Plan B, a coordinated strategy to suppress the vote in battleground states like Ohio and especially in Democratic strongholds. The heart of the plan was to swarm the polls with Republican activists who would challenge individual voters to tie up the process, lengthen voting lines and cause time-strapped voters to give up and go home. To some political historians, the scheme had the smell of Jim Crow tactics used during the days of the segregationist South to keep African-Americans from voting.

Ironically, Ohio's Secretary of State J. Kenneth Blackwell, a black Republican, was responsible for overseeing the election in that key swing state. By late October, Republicans had challenged the eligibility of 35,000 voters in closely contested Ohio. The Republicans also disclosed that they would send activists into 8,000 Ohio polling places to contest newly registered voters.[1]

There were also concerns among some Democrats that Republicans were planning high-tech voter fraud. Much of the suspicion centered on touch-screen electronic voting machines made by Ohio-based Diebold, which had more than 75,000 electronic voting stations operating across the United States. Diebold's chief executive Walden O'Dell was a major Bush fundraiser who stated in one invitation to a Bush fundraising event at his mansion in Columbus that he was "committed to helping Ohio deliver its electoral votes for the President." He later expressed regret at his choice of language.[2]

While Republicans were making plans to counter the expected surge in voters who were newly registered by pro-Democratic groups, Bush was employing an unusual stump strategy for an incumbent. The President ran what amounted to an insurgent campaign, tearing down his opponent rather than emphasizing his own administration's accomplishments. In speech after speech, Bush told cheering crowds that Kerry "can run, but he can't hide" from his Senate voting record. In another applause line, Bush said Kerry had entered "the flip-flop hall of fame."

By contrast, Kerry generally employed a less negative tone. Though Kerry sharpened his criticism of Bush in the campaign's final weeks, the Democrat stressed a variety of policy initiatives, such as reducing health care costs, protecting American jobs, strengthening environmental protections, reversing federal budget deficits, and enlisting more international cooperation in both the Iraq War and the fight against terrorism.

◆◆◆

As the campaign headed into its final weekend with the polls tightening and Bush's dream of a second term suddenly in doubt, a surprising visage showed up on American television screens, the bearded face of Osama bin Laden. On October 29, 2004, the al-Qaeda terrorist leader ended nearly a year of silence and took the risk of releasing a videotape denouncing and ridiculing President Bush.

"He [Bush] was more interested in listening to the child's story about the goat rather than worry about what was happening to the [twin] towers," bin Laden said, mockingly. "So, we had three times the time necessary to accomplish the events."

Some of Bush's supporters quickly spun bin Laden's attack on Bush as "Osama's endorsement of John Kerry." They pitched the videotape as evidence that al-Qaeda was frightened of Bush and wanted the American people to elect Kerry. Two last-minute tracking polls by TIPP and *Newsweek* detected a surge in Bush support from a virtual dead-heat to a lead of five and six points, respectively.

However, behind the locked doors of CIA headquarters, senior CIA analysts concluded that bin Laden's real intent was to ensure a second term for Bush. "Bin Laden certainly did a nice favor today for the President," said deputy CIA director John McLaughlin in opening a meeting to review secret "strategic analysis" after the videotape had dominated the day's news, Ron Suskind reported in *The One Percent Doctrine*.

Suskind wrote that CIA analysts had spent years "parsing each expressed word of the al-Qaeda leader and his deputy, [Ayman al-] Zawahiri. What they'd learned over nearly a decade is that bin Laden speaks only for strategic reasons. ... Today's conclusion: bin Laden's message was clearly designed to assist the President's reelection."

Jami Miscik, CIA deputy associate director for intelligence, expressed the consensus view that bin Laden recognized how Bush's heavy-handed policies were serving al-Qaeda's strategic goals for recruiting a new generation of jihadists. "Certainly," Miscik said, "he would want Bush to keep doing what he's doing for a few more years," according to Suskind's account.

As their internal assessment sank in, the CIA analysts were troubled by the implications of their own conclusions. "An ocean of hard truths before them – such as what did it say about U.S. policies that bin Laden would want Bush reelected – remained untouched," Suskind wrote.[3]

Bush himself recognized that bin Laden's diatribe likely brought in a rush of last-minute votes. "I thought it was going to help," Bush said in a post-election interview. "I thought it would help remind people that if bin Laden doesn't want Bush to be the President, something must be right with Bush."[4]

Republican National Chairman Ken Mehlman agreed that bin Laden's videotape helped Bush. "It reminded people of the stakes," Mehlman said. "It reinforced an issue on which Bush had a big lead over Kerry."[5]

But what was apparent to Bush and Mehlman also was probably clear to bin Laden, a well-educated Saudi who was a longtime student of U.S. politics. Bin Laden recognized that he was widely despised by American voters, so he could be confident that a last-minute attack on Bush would help the President, just as the CIA analysts had concluded.

Many American baby-boomers grew up watching Walt Disney's "Song of the South," featuring Uncle Remus tales which included how the clever Brer Rabbit escaped one famously tight spot by pretending that what he feared most was to be hurled into the briar patch – when that was exactly where he wanted to go. It appeared that the wily bin Laden was trying out the old Brer Rabbit briar-patch trick, pretending that the last thing he wanted was another four years of Bush when that was exactly what al-Qaeda did want.

◆ ◆ ◆

On Election Day 2004, a record 122 million Americans went to the polls. Some polling stations were overloaded simply because of the extraordinary numbers of voters. Other polling places, like one at liberal Kenyon College in Ohio and at many inner-city locations, appeared to have been shorted on machines. At Kenyon, students waited in line for up to 10 hours. Their experience, while extreme, was repeated in hundreds of other polling stations across the country with Democrats complaining that their strongholds suffered the most. There were also anecdotal accounts from Democratic voters who would touch a computer screen to vote for Kerry and the vote would be marked for Bush.

Despite these scattered signs of trouble, the Kerry people still felt reasonably optimistic, especially when the early exit polls came in. Exit polls, which are regarded as generally very accurate, showed Kerry leading in almost all the swing states, including Florida and Ohio, and holding a margin of about three percentage points nationally. As *The New York Times* reported later, "The presumption of a Kerry victory built a head of steam late in the day, when the national survey showed the senator with a statistically significant lead, one falling outside the survey's margin of error."

Washington Post managing editor Steve Coll wrote in an online chat that "the last wave of national exit polls we received ... showed Kerry winning the popular vote by 51 percent to 48 percent – if true, surely enough to carry the Electoral College."[6]

During the day, Bush's aides informed the President that he was losing the election by about three percentage points, according to a source with access to information inside the White House. But Bush's political adviser Karl Rove reportedly voiced confidence that the vote would turn around. "Our vote comes in late," Rove assured the President, according to the source.

Most of the exit polls also showed Republicans carrying the bulk of the tight Senate races. However, when the official results were tallied that night, the presidential exit polls proved wrong – as Bush squeaked past Kerry in most of the battleground states – while the Senate polls showing likely Republican victories proved right.

Republican pollster Dick Morris said the pattern of mistaken exit polls favoring Kerry in six battleground states – Florida, Ohio, New Mexico, Colorado, Nevada and Iowa – was virtually inconceivable. "Exit polls are almost never wrong," Morris wrote. "So reliable are the surveys that actually tap voters as they leave the polling places that they are used as guides to the relative honesty of elections in Third World countries. ... To screw up one exit poll is unheard of. To miss six of them is incredible. It boggles the imagination how pollsters could be that incompetent and invites speculation that more than honest error was at play here."

But instead of following his logic that the discrepancy suggested vote tampering – as it would in Latin America, Africa or Eastern Europe – Morris postulated a bizarre conspiracy theory that the exit polls were part of a scheme to have the networks call the election for Kerry and thus discourage Bush voters on the West Coast. Of course, none of the networks did call any of the six states for Kerry, making Morris's conspiracy theory nonsensical. Nevertheless, some Democrats agreed with Morris's bottom-line recommendation that the whole matter deserved "more scrutiny and investigation."[7]

The official excuse from the architects of the exit polls boiled down to their assumption that the Kerry voters were simply more willing than Bush voters to answer the exit pollsters' questions. But this "chattiness thesis" seemed more like a *post facto* rationalization, especially given the accuracy of the Senate exit polls, than a serious argument. The late vote turnaround for Bush immediately sparked suspicions among Democrats who had witnessed hardball political strategies from the Republicans for decades and especially from the Bush family.

On November 3, after the TV networks finally called the pivotal state of Ohio for Bush, some Democrats wanted Kerry to live up to a campaign promise and make sure that every vote was counted before conceding. But other Kerry advisers urged him to issue a graceful concession, thus avoiding the label "sore loser," and protecting his "political viability" for another run at the presidency in 2008. Concluding that the uncounted ballots were not sufficient to overturn Bush's lead in Ohio, Kerry agreed to concede.

Kerry's quick concession probably guaranteed that no one will ever know conclusively if the Bush campaign had augmented its Plan B for holding down the Democratic turnout by adding in computer manipulation of vote counts. Since many new touch-screen voting machines lacked a paper backup, it was doubtful that even a diligent recount could have ascertained whether computer coding or hacking had falsified the numbers.

One Kerry insider told us that Democratic suspicions had been raised by Republican resistance to implementing any meaningful backup system for checking the results on Diebold and other electronic-voting machines. For its part, Diebold denied that its systems were vulnerable to computer hacking and called such allegations "fantasy." But some of the numbers did look fishy.

As Sam Parry reported at *Consortiumnews.com*, "George W. Bush's vote tallies, especially in the key state of Florida, are so statistically stunning that they border on the unbelievable. While it's extraordinary for a candidate to get a vote total that exceeds his party's registration in any voting jurisdiction – because of non-voters – Bush racked up more votes than registered Republicans in 47 out of 67 counties in Florida. In 15 of those counties, his vote total more than doubled the number of registered Republicans and in four counties, Bush more than tripled the number.

Statewide, Bush earned about 20,000 more votes than registered Republicans.

"By comparison, in 2000, Bush's Florida total represented about 85 percent of the total number of registered Republicans, about 2.9 million votes compared with 3.4 million registered Republicans. Bush achieved these totals [in 2004] although exit polls showed him winning only about 14 percent of the Democratic vote statewide – statistically the same as in 2000 when he won 13 percent of the Democratic vote – and losing Florida's independent voters to Kerry by a 57 percent to 41 percent margin. In 2000, Gore won the independent vote by a much narrower margin of 47 to 46 percent.

"Similar surprising jumps in Bush's vote tallies across the country – especially when matched against national exits polls showing Kerry winning by 51 percent to 48 percent – have fed suspicion among rank-and-file Democrats that the Bush campaign rigged the vote, possibly through systematic computer hacking. ... In Ohio, election officials said an error with an electronic voting system in Franklin County gave Bush 3,893 extra votes in suburban Columbus, more than 1,000 percent more than he actually got."[8]

Across the nation, Bush garnered 62 million votes, a stunning total that shattered Ronald Reagan's old record of 54.5 million from his landslide victory in 1984. What made Bush's numbers even more difficult to comprehend was that he got this vote total while Kerry also was surpassing Reagan's record by totaling 59 million votes. Comparing Election 2004 to Election 2000 was equally remarkable. In four years, Bush increased his total vote by about 22 percent, even as Kerry topped Al Gore's margin by about 15 percent. In earlier presidential elections when one party has managed to boost its vote by 20 percent or so, the other party has suffered widespread defections.

◆◆◆

At *Consortiumnews.com*, Nat Parry looked at the message that Election 2004 delivered to people around the globe. He wrote, "On the surface, the world's reaction to George W. Bush's victory has been one of disbelief and revulsion. But underneath, the lesson may be even more troubling, as authoritarian regimes are tempted to cite flaws in the U.S. electoral process to justify their own anti-democratic impulses.

"The day after the election, the British *Daily Mirror* asked plaintively, 'How can 59,017,382 people [Bush's total at the time] be so dumb?' Not to be outdone, Russia's *Pravda* asserted that 'America was betrayed and murdered on November 2, 2004. Also killed during this time of madness were the following virtues: truth, justice, integrity, freedom, compassion, brotherhood, tolerance, faith, hope, charity, peace, and respect for other cultures and nations.' ...

"I also witnessed the reaction of European parliamentarians who came to the U.S. as part of the Election Observation Mission of the Organization for Security and Cooperation in Europe (OSCE), which includes the United States as a member. I helped coordinate the mission, and on Election Day, I escorted about 10 observers to polling stations in Northern Virginia. While the observers were strictly neutral during the election, it was clear that many of them worried about four more years of Bush.

"Besides Bush's policies, some of the parliamentarians felt that questionable U.S. election tactics, including voter intimidation, undermined the image of popular rule in the nation that had long been considered the world's leading democracy. One Albanian told me that she had struggled for democracy for much of her life and suffered beatings by state security forces for speaking out for freedom. During those dark days, the United States had been the brightest beacon of hope, inspiring activists to keep fighting, she said.

"But now, in the United States, she was learning about voter intimidation and other irregularities during a briefing at the national call center of the Election Protection Coalition in Arlington, Virginia. Her voice shook as she recounted reports of black voters being challenged by Republican lawyers at polling places, of minorities asked for two forms of identification when only one was needed, of polling places moved to police stations in minority precincts, of hundreds of electronic voting malfunctions, and of polling stations lacking enough provisional ballots.

"The Albanian parliamentarian, flipping through page after page of her notes, was stunned by the bigger picture of disenfranchisement aimed at minority voters. 'How could this happen here?' she asked me. 'How could this happen in America?' She also was concerned about the worldwide consequences for democracy in Albania and elsewhere. When anti-democratic abuses happen in the United States, they encourage anti-democratic forces everywhere, she said.

Nat Parry continued, "This lesson was not missed by the OSCE observer delegation from Belarus. As I heard from numerous sources, the primary reason the Belarusians were so interested in observing the U.S. election was so they could cite flaws in the American electoral system to excuse their own lack of transparency. Belarus is among the least democratic countries in Europe with one of the worst human rights records. For months, Belarus had been making statements at the OSCE's

Permanent Council in Vienna condemning the U.S. for its lack of democracy and its failure to respect human rights. ...

"The Permanent Representative of Belarus to the OSCE issued a harsh statement about the U.S. electoral system, asserting that it 'does not meet present-day requirements, is archaic, unwieldy, frequently complicated and bureaucratic in nature and, in the final analysis, does not guarantee the holding of genuinely democratic elections.' ...

"From its observation mission, the OSCE concluded that the U.S. 'mostly' met its international commitments for holding free and fair elections. But the mission cited a number of 'significant issues,' particularly around implementation of the 'Help America Vote Act,' electoral fraud and voter suppression, as well as problems relating to the use of electronic voting machines. ... 'Significant delays at the polling station are likely to deter some voters from voting and may restrict the right to vote,' the OSCE said."[9]

◆◆◆

In another *Consortiumnews.com* article, Robert Parry looked at the plausibility that computer hacking could have played a role in the unusual vote totals. He reported that theoretically at least, it was conceivable that sophisticated CIA-style computer hacking – known as "cyber-warfare" – could have let the Bush campaign transform a three-percentage-point defeat, as measured by exit polls, into an official victory of about the same margin.

Whether such a scheme was actually feasible, however, was another matter, since it would have required penetration of hundreds of local computer systems across the country, presumably from a relatively small number of remote locations. The known CIA successes in "cyber-war" have been far less ambitious, targeting a specific bank account or shutting down an adversary's computer system, not altering data simultaneously in a large number of computers.

To achieve that kind of result, cyber-war experts say, a preprogrammed "kernel of brain" would have to be inserted into election computers beforehand or teams of hackers would be needed to penetrate the lightly protected systems, targeting touch-screen systems without a paper backup for verifying the numbers. Though there was no solid proof of such a cyber-attack, suspicions continued to grow that the U.S. presidential election results were manipulated to some degree.

By 2004, the highly secretive practice of cyber-warfare had advanced far more than many Americans understood, with U.S. intelligence agencies pioneering methods for surreptitiously entering enemy computer systems. Through the 1990s, the CIA and the U.S. military aggressively expanded cyber-war capabilities, bringing online powerful computer systems and recruiting some of the nation's best hackers, intelligence sources told us. During the CIA's recruitment rush, some hackers were hired despite criminal records and questionable backgrounds.

By the mid-1990s, cyber-war – also known as "information warfare" – was such a hot topic within the U.S. military that the Pentagon produced a breezy 13-page booklet called "Information Warfare for Dummies." The primer said information warfare at one level could mean using more traditional methods for targeting an enemy's battlefield command-and-control structure to "decapitate" senior officers from their fighters, thereby "causing panic and paralysis." But the primer added that "network penetrations" – or hacking – "represents a new and very high-tech form of warfighting."

Indirectly, the booklet acknowledged secret U.S. capabilities in these areas. The manual described these info-war tactics as "fairly ground-breaking stuff for our nation's mud-sloggers. ... Theft and the intentional manipulation of data are the product of devilish minds." The primer also gave hints about the disruptive strategies in the U.S. arsenal. "Network penetrations" include "insertion of malicious code (viruses, worms, etc.), theft of information, manipulation of information, denial of service," the primer said.

The booklet also recognized the sensitivity of the topic. "Due to the moral, ethical and legal questions raised by hacking, the military likes to keep a low profile on this issue," the primer explained. Despite the Pentagon's nervousness about the topic, the booklet said the cyber-war tactics do have advantages over other military operations. "The intrusions can be carried out remotely, transcending the boundaries of time and space," the manual said. "They also offer the prospect of 'plausible deniability' or repudiation."

The booklet indicated that U.S. intelligence had found it relatively easy to cover its tracks. "Due to the difficulty of tracing a network penetration to its source, it's difficult for the adversary to prove that you are the one responsible for corrupting their system," the primer said. "In fact, viral infections can be so subtle and insidious that the adversary may not even know that their systems have been attacked."

U.S. intelligence sources described to us one case study of a CIA high-tech "dirty trick" that worked in the mid-1990s. After learning of a drug lord's plan to bribe a South American government official, the spy agency waited for the money to be transferred and then accessed the bank records to remotely delete the bribe. Besides stopping the bribe, the money's disappearance spread confusion within the cartel. The recriminations that followed – with the corrupt official and the drug lord complaining about the lost money – led eventually to the execution of a hapless bookkeeper, according to the story.

During the war over Kosovo in 1999, U.S. government hackers tried to expand on these strategies, targeting Serbian computer systems and government bank accounts. By most accounts, the cyber-war attacks on Serbian targets achieved only limited success.

While avoiding clear confirmation of a U.S. offensive cyber-war capability, American officials occasionally have discussed the topic in the third person, as if the United States were not a participant in this new arms race.

On February 2, 1999, for instance, CIA Director George Tenet said "several countries have or are developing the capability to attack an adversary's computer systems." He added that "developing a computer attack capability can be quite inexpensive and easily concealable." Left unsaid in Tenet's statement was that the U.S. government, with the world's most powerful computers and the most sophisticated software designs, has led the way both in offensive cyber-war strategies and defensive countermeasures.

As questions lingered about discrepancies between the November 2 exit polls and Bush's final victory margin, some Democrats wondered whether the intelligence community's cyber-war capabilities may have come home to roost.[10]

◆ ◆ ◆

Whatever the ultimate truth behind Election 2004, the outcome – a continuation of Republican control of the White House and Congress – put Karl Rove and the American Right within reach of a top political goal, long-term domination of the U.S. political system. The prophecy that George W. Bush would be the "transformational" leader forever banishing liberals and Democrats from power seemed close to fulfillment.

Over the next two years, simply with the luck of the actuarial tables, Bush looked forward to appointing new justices to the U.S. Supreme Court. Rove and his aides also were setting their sights on replacing independent-minded Republican U.S. Attorneys with "loyal Bushies."

That would give the President greater legal leverage over which prosecutions might be brought against political enemies and which cases involving friends might be left to languish. Combined with Bush's view of his own unlimited powers as Commander in Chief at a time of the "war on terror," Bush had in his sights a new form of authoritarian state with global ambitions.

Beyond the immense powers of the U.S. government, leaders on the Right worked to consolidate their already strong bonds with major corporations. Their strategy called for starving Democrats of political resources through operations like the "K Street Project," which pressed industry associations and lobbying firms to hire only Republicans. The Right's leaders also sought to solidify their influence over public opinion by expanding the right-wing media and eliminating any residual resistance within the mainstream press.

By pulling these various levers, Republicans thought they could assure victories far into the future. The concept was similar to the "managed democracy" that President Vladimir Putin was building in Russia, with his opposition kept around to maintain the trappings of democracy but never within reach of real power.

As right-wing activist Grover Norquist explained after Election 2004, the way for Democrats to fit in to this new Republican-run Washington was to accept their permanent lot as a marginalized minority party.

"Once the minority of House and Senate are comfortable in their minority status, they will have no problem socializing with the Republicans," Norquist said in an interview with *The Washington Post*. "Any farmer will tell you that certain animals run around and are unpleasant, but when they've been fixed, then they are happy and sedate. They are contented and cheerful. They don't go around peeing on the furniture and such."

Norquist, president of Americans for Tax Reform and a close ally of White House political adviser Rove, said he didn't mean for his comments to be taken literally; the Democrats only needed to be "psychologically" neutered.[11]

When political analysts started mining Election 2004 for lessons learned, they reached a conclusion that the original Swift Boat smears against John Kerry had been a remarkable bargain. Costing only $546,000, the ads changed the course of the campaign.

"The Swift Boat Veterans eventually would raise and spend $28 million, but the first ad was exceptionally cost effective: most voters learned about it through free coverage in mainstream media and talk radio," wrote *Washington Post* reporters Thomas B. Edsall and James V. Grimaldi.[12]

Post columnist E. J. Dionne Jr. marveled that "the sheer negative genius of the Bush campaign is worthy of close study."

◆ ◆ ◆

On January 6, 2005, as the new Congress convened, Representatives John Conyers, Maxine Waters and other members of the Congressional Black Caucus announced that they would file a motion demanding an investigation of Election 2004, particularly the widespread allegations of voting fraud in the pivotal state of Ohio. If signed by at least one senator, the motion would temporarily delay the acceptance of Bush's victory and force a floor debate about the fairness of the election.

The Black Caucus had offered a similar motion in 2001, challenging the validity of Bush's victory in Florida. In one of the most painful scenes featured in Michael Moore's "Fahrenheit 9/11," African-American congressional representatives rose one after another to protest the disenfranchisement of voters in Florida. But they were ruled out of order by Vice President Al Gore (who was presiding in his constitutional role as president of the Senate) because not a single senator would sign on to the motion.

In 2005, even if the Black Caucus's motion did get a senator's signature and was ruled to be in order, the Republican congressional majority would be sure to block a full-scale investigation and instead just certify Bush's election. Still, the challenge would mark a new determination among the Democrats to fight the Republicans over principles of democracy.

The pressure on Senator John Kerry was that he would have to decide whether to sign the motion and take the chance of being tagged a "sore loser" or refuse to sign and run the risk of the black members of Congress being gaveled out of order, this time by Vice President Dick Cheney. If that happened, the Democratic "base" would be livid.

Many of these grassroots Democrats were already furious with Kerry for failing to wage a more aggressive campaign after taunting the Republicans to "bring it on." They complained that Kerry's political advisers, such as consultant Bob Shrum, held the candidate back from making a forceful case that a second Bush term would be a national catastrophe.

Rank-and-file Democrats also were angry over what they saw as a Bush campaign that relied on dirty tricks, voter suppression, vote tampering and stonewalling of recount demands. Indeed, a large number of Democrats nationwide appeared convinced that Bush had stolen a second presidential election.

On the eve of Congress convening, John Kerry made his decision. Though outside the country traveling in the Middle East, he released a letter opposing the Black Caucus challenge. He also urged his followers to call on the Republican leadership to hold later hearings on electoral reform. The letter read like it was written by the caricature of Kerry that

Bush had portrayed during the campaign: the indecisive, flip-flopping politician who wanted to be on every side of an issue.

"I will not be taking part in a formal protest of the Ohio Electors," Kerry wrote in an e-mail to three million supporters. "Despite widespread reports of irregularities, questionable practices by some election officials and instances of lawful voters being denied the right to vote, our legal teams on the ground have found no evidence that would change the outcome of the election."

Kerry then called on his supporters to renew the fight for fair elections in the future. "If you want to force real action on election reform, we've got to demand that congressional leaders hold full hearings," Kerry wrote. "Make sure they hear from you and help hold them accountable." He then listed the office phone numbers for Republican House Speaker Dennis Hastert and Senate Majority Leader Bill Frist.

Kerry's recommendation – to avoid a high-profile clash with the Republicans now in favor of some unlikely bipartisan hearings in the future – sealed the senator's fate with much of the Democratic "base." At the time, Sam Parry wrote, "John Kerry may have written his own political obituary with a pathetic letter to his supporters saying he won't back a protest by African-American House members against voting fraud in Ohio."

At least, however, Kerry was spared the scene of Cheney gaveling down black Democrats. Senator Barbara Boxer of California signed the motion forcing a brief floor debate before Bush's election was formalized.

◆◆◆

Nearly a year after Election 2004, Kerry let slip his private concerns about what had happened. Mark Crispin Miller, a New York University professor and author of a book about the 2004 election entitled *Fooled Again*, said he discussed the voting issue with Kerry on October 28, 2005, when he encountered the senator at a public event. A week later on Amy Goodman's "Democracy Now," Miller described giving Kerry a copy of *Fooled Again*, which prompted Kerry to make some comments.

"He told me he now thinks the election was stolen," Miller said. "He said he doesn't believe that he is the person who can go out front on the issue because of the sour grapes … question. But he said he believes it was stolen. He says he argues about this with his Democratic colleagues on the Hill. He had just had a big fight with Christopher Dodd."

Miller said Kerry suspected possible tampering with electronic voting machines, but was persuaded by his campaign's top advisers, including Bob Shrum, that contesting the results only would damage Kerry's public image. Miller said Kerry bent to the will of his advisers, even though his vice presidential running mate, John Edwards, favored holding out until more information was in. Based on reporting for *Fooled Again*, Miller said Kerry told Edwards in a phone call that Shrum and other advisers insisted that a concession was the best course.

"They say that if I don't pull out, they (Kerry's political opponents) are going to call us sore losers," Miller said, recounting the substance of Kerry's phone call to Edwards. Miller said Edwards responded, "So what if they call us sore losers?" But Kerry pressed ahead with his decision to concede.

After learning of Miller's account, Robert Parry contacted longtime Kerry adviser Jonathan Winer who confirmed that Kerry did hold doubts about the election when the two discussed the issue in November and December of 2004. "Kerry heard all the disquieting stories" about voting irregularities in Ohio and other states, Winer said. "But he didn't have the evidence to do more."

Winer said the "disquieting stuff" that troubled Kerry included reports that touch-screen systems had malfunctioned in such a way that voters who tried to vote for Kerry saw their votes switched to Bush. Kerry also was upset with reports that Ohio's Republican election officials shorted Democratic strongholds on voting machines, Winer said.

But Winer said Kerry never asserted "outright" that the election was stolen, nor did Kerry believe the evidence existed to prove systematic tampering with the vote. Kerry also was certain that he would face withering criticism if he challenged the election results without strong evidence.

"The powers in place would have smashed him," Winer said.

24

Freedom/Liberty

Despite lingering questions about Election 2004, George W. Bush treated his victory as something akin to an absolution for all he had done in the previous four years and a blessing for whatever he would do in the future. "We had an accountability moment, and that's called the 2004 elections," Bush declared. "The American people listened to different assessments made about what was taking place in Iraq, and they looked at the two candidates, and chose me."[1]

Some neoconservative legal theorists around Bush suggested that the election had cleansed Bush of any guilt for torture or other abuses that had occurred during his first term. John C. Yoo, the former deputy assistant attorney general who had developed many of the legal theories behind Bush's expansive view of executive power, said Bush's election victory had made the question of other accountability moot. "The issue is dying out," Yoo said. "The public has had its referendum."[2]

It wasn't clear how – under any normal theory of international law – an election in one country could obviate war crimes committed in another country, but Bush's victory did bring a new wave of good feelings toward Bush at least from Washington insiders and the national press corps. During the quadrennial celebration of American democracy surrounding a presidential inauguration, there was nary a negative word spoken about the misdeeds of Bush's first term. The news media was in the President's thrall once more, especially on January 20, 2005, when he dedicated his second Inaugural Address to his promise that he would bring "freedom" and "liberty" to all corners of the globe.

In a reprise of his earlier vows to eradicate "evil," Bush focused on what he called the "ultimate goal of ending tyranny in our world." At points, his speech sounded like a list of platitudes about freedom that Bush liked so much that he didn't want to strike any from the drafts. "In the long run, there is no justice without freedom, and there can be no human rights without human liberty," Bush said. "We do not accept the existence of permanent tyranny because we do not accept the possibility of permanent slavery."

Other times, Bush sounded like a high school graduation speaker who locked in on a trite metaphor: "As hope kindles hope, millions more will find it. By our efforts, we have lit a fire as well as a fire in the minds of men. It warms those who feel its power; it burns those who fight its progress. And one day this untamed fire of freedom will reach the darkest corners of our world."

Bush also sought to warm the hearts of his listeners with rhetoric about America's innate goodness. "Americans move forward in every generation by reaffirming all that is good and true that came before, ideals of justice and conduct that are the same yesterday, today, and forever," he said. "In America's ideal of freedom, the exercise of rights is ennobled by service, and mercy, and a heart for the weak. Liberty for all does not mean independence from one another. Our nation relies on men and women who look after a neighbor and surround the lost with love."

At other junctures, the speech crossed over into the nonsensical. "Liberty will come to those who love it," Bush said. "Self-government relies, in the end, on the governing of the self." Then, there were the strange truisms: "America will not pretend that jailed dissidents prefer their chains, or that women welcome humiliation and servitude, or that any human being aspires to live at the mercy of bullies."

Some longtime listeners of Inaugural Addresses might argue that one or two corny aphorisms can be expected as a President tries to grab for immortality with a phrase that catches the public's fancy. But Bush's speech was unusual in that his bromides about freedom represented virtually the entire structure and content. Bush also used the banalities to set up straw men of opposition, as if anyone who didn't agree with his unilateralist foreign policy or his autocratic treatment of his adversaries was dishonest and craven. Bush was the brave leader who stood up for all that was good, while his imaginary opponents thought dissidents preferred their chains, women welcomed humiliation, and human beings aspired to be bullied.

Through the speech, Bush uttered the words "freedom" and "liberty" 27 and 15 times respectively. And the Washington journalists – despite their self-image as worldly cynics – ate it up. Just as during the previous four years, the major U.S. news media couldn't look past Bush's words to the reality. No prominent journalist gave voice to the thought that Bush might be just mouthing noble words to cloak an ignoble record, or that he was hiding an autocratic reality under a cloak of democratic rhetoric. Though some columnists questioned the feasibility of Bush's "freedom" enterprise, almost no one doubted Bush's sincerity.

The Washington Post's David S. Broder, known as the "dean" of the national press corps, wrote a glowing tribute to Bush's "eloquent" speech, which Broder cited as proof that Bush was holding steadfast to his goal of achieving "the worldwide realization of the ideals of freedom and democracy."[3]

Another *Post* columnist E.J. Dionne Jr. chimed in that "every American will cheer the President's repeated reference to the U.S. obligation to hold high the torch of freedom." Dionne, a supposed liberal, gushed further, "I love what the President said about our obligation to dissidents around the world." Dionne's only doubts were about "whether the President has been candid about the costs of his all-embracing vision, about how to pay for it and raise the troops to fight it."[4]

While the lavish praise of his Inaugural Address gave Bush a bump in his domestic popularity, his rhetoric fed into the anti-Americanism growing in the rest of the world. Bush's perceived hypocrisy about "freedom" and "liberty" especially undercut U.S. strategies for winning "hearts and minds" in the Islamic world. Many Muslims snickered at Bush's concepts of freedom, liberty and democracy. To them, those words meant subjugation to the West.

As former CIA analyst Michael Scheuer wrote in his book, *Imperial Hubris*, U.S. policies over the past half century have "moved America from being the much-admired champion of liberty and self-government to the hated and feared advocate of a new imperial order, one that has much the same characteristics as 19th century European imperialism: military garrisons; economic penetration and control; support for leaders, no matter how brutal and undemocratic, as long as they obey the imperial power; and the exploitation and depletion of natural resources."[5]

In Scheuer's view, Bush also misrepresented the struggle that the United States faced against Islamic militants in the Middle East. "Their goal is not to wipe out our secular democracy, but to deter us by military means from attacking the things they love," including their religion and their territory, Scheuer wrote.

"Bin Laden *et al.* are not eternal warriors; there is no evidence they are fighting for fighting's sake." Rather, Scheuer wrote, the resistance to the United States is part of what many Muslims regard as a "defensive jihad," a principled struggle against a foreign power seeking to re-impose a form of colonialism on the Arab world.[6]

Domestically, even as Bush professed his love of democracy, his hostility toward dissent continued. Bush declined to join Senator John Kerry in seeking explanations for the disenfranchisement of voters in Election 2004. Meanwhile, Bush's supporters denounced challenges to voting irregularities as "conspiracy theories." In Ohio, Republican

Attorney General James Petro sought fines and court sanctions against four Election Protection attorneys who filed a lawsuit seeking an investigation of the Ohio balloting.

When reporters examined Bush's Middle East policies, they met with other kinds of attacks. Pro-Bush pundits, such as *The Washington Times'* Tony Blankley, suggested that veteran journalist Seymour Hersh be investigated for espionage for writing an article in *The New Yorker* about the Bush administration's secret military operations in Iran and elsewhere. "Federal prosecutors should review the information disclosed by Mr. Hersh to determine whether or not his conduct falls within the proscribed conduct of the [espionage] statute," Blankley wrote.[7]

As his second term began, Bush also narrowed his circle of advisers. He continued the purge of dissident CIA analysts and ousted heavyweight skeptics, such as Secretary of State Colin Powell and retired Gen. Brent Scowcroft, who had chaired the President's Foreign Intelligence Advisory Board. Still, the Washington commentariat joined Bush for a long bath in his warm rhetoric of "freedom" and "liberty." It was as if the one freedom most fundamental to Bush and his admirers was freedom from reality.

◆◆◆

Bush's second inauguration was followed ten days later by a widely praised election in Iraq. To the major U.S. news media, the sizable voter turnout in the war-torn country was further evidence that Bush indeed was the visionary of a democratic future for the Middle East. *New York Times* foreign policy columnist Thomas L. Friedman penned a column entitled "A Day to Remember" and pronounced himself "unreservedly happy" about Iraq's January 30 election. He told any holdouts that "you should be, too."[8]

However, Robert Parry reported at *Consortiumnews.com* on February 3, 2005, that "there is a dark potential to those pleasing images of Iraqis voting in the face of violence. Rather than pointing toward an exit for the United States from Iraq, the election may be just another mirage leading U.S. troops deeper into Iraq's long and bloody history of sectarian violence between Sunnis and Shiites.

"Indeed, if the Sunni-based insurgency doesn't give up in the months ahead, American soldiers could find themselves enmeshed in a long and brutal civil war helping the Shiite majority crush the resistance of the Sunni minority. The Sunnis, who have long dominated Iraq, find themselves in a tight corner and may see little choice but to fight on.

"The U.S. invasion of Iraq in March 2003 started the Sunnis' reversal of fortune by ousting the Sunni-run government of Saddam Hussein.

Since then, the armed resistance, based in the so-called Sunni Triangle, has represented the Sunnis' reaction to their sharply diminished status as well as their resentment of the U.S.-led military occupation. Now, the election has hardened this new reality of the Sunnis' secondary role, leaving them a painful choice of either accepting Shiite domination of the country's political system or challenging the powerful U.S. military in a guerrilla war that could turn many Sunni communities into smoking ruins like Fallujah.

"Those troubling prospects represent a scenario that the U.S. news media has largely ignored amid the effusive coverage of the Iraqi election. As Iraqis raised fingers stained with voting ink, American journalists scrambled over each other to climb on board George W. Bush's bandwagon. Just as the U.S. press corps feared challenging Bush during the WMD hysteria in fall 2002 or after the toppled Saddam Hussein statue in spring 2003, the press corps treated the Iraqi election as an unquestioned success story."

Robert Parry continued, "In retrospect, the election followed what should have been an anticipated course. The long-oppressed Shiite majority, expecting to gain the bulk of national power, voted in fairly large numbers, as did Kurds, who want either autonomy or outright independence. The Sunnis, the powerful minority who had the most to lose from the election, either boycotted it or voted in fairly low numbers.

"Turnout was 'quite low' in Sunni communities, according to a Western diplomat quoted by *The New York Times*. Even in the ethnically diverse city of Mosul, the citywide turnout was estimated at barely more than 10 percent.[9]

"Now, the question is whether the Sunnis will seek some post-election accommodation with the Shiites or will continue resisting the new U.S.-backed power structure. If they choose the latter, the election may end up locking the U.S. military into a long-term role as the military arm of a Shiite-dominated government given legitimacy by the ballot. A second question is whether the Bush administration will interpret the relatively successful election in Iraq as reason to revive the neoconservative dream of spreading democracy by force throughout the Middle East.

"If the Iraqi election ends up pushing the Bush administration into new foreign-policy adventures or keeps the U.S. military fighting in Iraq for the foreseeable future, the American people may look back at January 30, 2005, as 'a day to remember,' though not as columnist Friedman had in mind."[10]

◆◆◆

Those early weeks of Bush's second term represented a high water mark for American neoconservatives. The tide certainly looked to be surging in for the President's "freedom" initiative, at least as far as the Washington press corps was concerned. The pundits were seeing progress everywhere.

After two years of bloody war in Iraq – with some 1,500 U.S. soldiers dead and tens of thousands of Iraqis killed – the neocons were claiming vindication citing several developments in the Middle East: the Iraqi election, tentative progress in Israeli-Palestinian negotiations, Lebanese demands for a full Syrian withdrawal, even some modest gestures toward democracy in Egypt.

This triumphal moment was noted by *New York Times* columnist Friedman, who hailed the developments as historical "tipping points" possibly foreshadowing "incredible" changes in the Middle East.[11] A lead editorial in the *Times* expanded on Friedman's thesis. "The Bush administration is entitled to claim a healthy share of the credit for many of these advances," the editorial said.[12]

Editorialists at *The Washington Post* picked up the same point. "Could it be that the neocons were right and that the invasion of Iraq, the toppling of Hussein and the holding of elections will trigger a political chain reaction throughout the Arab world?" marveled *Post* columnist Richard Cohen.[13]

Another influential *Post* columnist, David Ignatius, was swept up in the excitement, too. "The old system [in the Middle East] that had looked so stable is ripping apart, with each beam pulling another down as it falls," Ignatius wrote. Crediting the U.S. invasion of Iraq for the "sudden stress" that started this collapse, Ignatius wrote, "It's hard not to feel giddy, watching the dominoes fall."[14]

However, there was an alternative explanation for each of these Middle East developments that was rooted in local circumstances. In Iraq, the Shiites and the Kurds turned out in large numbers – not to endorse principles of democratic tolerance – but because the election let them consolidate control of the country at the expense of their longtime tormentors, Iraq's formerly dominant Sunni minority.

Similarly, slight cracks in the Palestinian-Israeli stalemate related far more to the death of longtime Palestinian leader Yasser Arafat – and to aging Israeli Prime Minister Ariel Sharon's quest for a positive legacy – than to the U.S. invasion of Iraq. But even if Sharon felt he could negotiate with new Palestinian leader Mahmoud Abbas, long-term peace prospects were threatened by a stubborn Sharon legacy, his "facts-on-the-ground" strategy that put about 230,000 Jewish settlers in the West Bank.

In Lebanon, popular resistance to Syrian troops has been growing for years, especially since Israel withdrew its troops from southern Lebanon in 2000. The assassination of former Lebanese Prime Minister Rafik Hariri on February 14, 2005, was the catalyst for the renewed public demands for a complete Syrian withdrawal, but there was no evidence that the Lebanese protests had anything to do with the Iraq War.

Nevertheless, the *Post*'s Ignatius argued that the only appropriate U.S. policy reaction to what he called "the Middle East's glorious catastrophe" was to accelerate it. "We are careening around the curve of history, and it's useful to remember a basic rule for navigating slippery roads: Once you're in the curve, you can't hit the brakes. The only way for America to keep this car on the road is to keep its foot on the accelerator," Ignatius wrote.[15]

Other commentators who supported Bush's Iraq invasion cited the several small steps toward democracy as vindication and an excuse for self-pity. "The last couple of years have not been easy for anyone, myself included, who hoped that the Iraq War would produce a decent, democratizing outcome," wrote *New York Times* columnist Friedman.[16]

The Washington Post's neoconservative columnist Charles Krauthammer sounded like a combination of Trotsky and Robespierre as he proclaimed that this was the time to escalate Bush's policies in the Arab world. "Revolutions do not stand still," Krauthammer wrote. "They either move forward or die."[17]

This Washington conventional wisdom of an all-wise George W. Bush also permeated the news pages. "A powerful confluence of events in the Middle East in recent weeks has infused President Bush's drive to spread democracy with a burst of momentum, according to supporters and critics alike," reported *The Washington Post* in a Page One article on March 8, 2005.

Of course, the celebratory talk of the neocons was always backed up by someone else's blood or the blood of someone else's kid. Not only had 1,500 U.S. soldiers died two years into the Iraq War but thousands more U.S. veterans had suffered lost limbs or other severe injuries. Some experienced psychological crises that were left unattended by a suddenly overburdened veterans' health system.

Jeffrey Michael Lucey, a 23-year-old lance corporal in the Marine Reserves, returned from Iraq to his home to Belchertown, Massachusetts, suffering from post-traumatic stress disorder and relegated to a waiting list for psychological care. On June 22, 2004, he went down to the cellar of his family's home and hanged himself with a garden hose. Months later, speaking for many mothers who have lost their children because of the Iraq War, Joyce Lucey said of her son, "He wasn't an important person, but he was very important to us."[18]

◆◆◆

One of the political dangers that still faced the high-riding Bush and his fellow Republicans was the temptation to overreach. Bush demonstrated that hubris by making the partial privatization of Social Security his signature domestic issue of his second term. Congressional Republicans also altered the ethics process to protect House Majority Tom DeLay from growing questions about his financial dealings. But the event that brought home to many Americans the Republican arrogance of power was passage of emergency legislation that brought Congress and Bush together to prevent the removal of life support for a severely brain-damaged woman in Florida named Terri Schiavo.

As Sam Parry wrote at *Consortiumnews.com* on April 1: "The media frenzy surrounding the Terri Schiavo case is new evidence of the American Right's ability to dominate national news cycles, a power that has become possibly the most intimidating force in modern U.S. politics. In the Schiavo case, however, the Right has discovered that even its impressive message machinery sometimes can push the envelope too far.

"In the Schiavo tragedy, leaders of the Christian Right and the Republican Party marketed themselves as the defenders of life and painted their liberal adversaries as intellectual elitists lacking compassion for a defenseless woman. Conservative leaders also hoped to rally their base around the need for more conservative judges who would defend the so-called 'culture of life.'

"With stunning bravado, the Right played on the Schiavo story's appeal as a round-the-clock cable TV drama: a life-or-death countdown; grieving parents; a husband who could be made into the heavy; supposedly insensitive judges; Republican leaders rushing to the rescue, including both Jeb and George W. Bush.

"But then the results of early opinion polls rolled in. Those samplings of public opinion suggested that – at least this time – the religious Right, congressional Republicans and the Bushes may have overreached, looking more ghoulish than godly. The conservatives may have underestimated the risk of exploiting a crisis that touches on the personal experiences of too many Americans.

"It is one thing to whip up outrage against a foreign leader, such as Iraq's Saddam Hussein, or to focus anger at an individual politician, like Senator John Kerry. Few Americans have much knowledge of foreign affairs or have much sympathy for a politician whom they know mostly through televised images. In both situations, it's easy to get the U.S. public to think the worst.

"But the Schiavo case featured an issue that thousands of Americans face every year: how to deal with painful end-of-life decisions for their loved ones – and whether they themselves would want to continue living with severe brain damage, kept alive in a semi-vegetative state with tubes coming out of their bodies. People who have been forced to contemplate such matters know that there are no easy answers, only hard choices."[19]

The Republican excesses on the Schiavo case had a secondary effect of giving the Democrats new courage. After four years of mostly cowering in the corner, the Democrats began to reemerge and started taking the fight to the Bush administration. The development was so surprising that *The Washington Post* put the story on Page One with the headline, "Unexpectedly, Capitol Hill Democrats Stand Firm."

The *Post* story said, "Democrats were supposed to enter the 109th Congress meek and cowed, demoralized by November's election losses and ready to cut deals with Republicans who threatened further campaigns against 'obstructionists.' But House and Senate Democrats have turned that conventional wisdom on its head."[20]

While part of the answer to the mystery of the Democrats' new spine was the Republican bumbling, another part was the emergence of some friendly media outlets, most notably progressive AM talk radio which expanded rapidly in early 2005. Democratic leaders found they could go on sympathetic radio shows and make their case directly to listeners. Before, Democrats usually found themselves speaking in unfriendly territory. Faced with hostile questioning, national Democrats often sought a safe middle ground, which made them look weak or indecisive, opening them to other attacks for "flip-flopping" or "lacking conviction."

That dynamic began to change as more U.S. cities got "progressive talk radio" stations, rising to more than 50, many affiliated with Air America Radio. Though still far fewer than the hundreds of conservative talk radio outlets, this "left side of the dial" began reaching critical mass in early 2005, altering the political psyche both of rank-and-file Democrats and their leaders. With humor and without deference, progressive hosts – the likes of Stephanie Miller, Randi Rhodes and Al Franken – gave voice to the outrage that many liberals felt over what they regarded as years of conservative highhandedness – a stolen election in 2000, a deceptive case for war in Iraq in 2002-03, and the smearing of Kerry's war record in 2004.

After more than a decade of the Right's near monopoly of AM talk radio, listeners on the Left took pleasure in hearing the conservatives get a taste of their own medicine. Leading Democratic politicians from the

House and Senate were soon lining up as guests to address an audience that expected tough talk against the Republicans, not mushy rhetoric designed not to offend. In effect, a political market emerged that rewarded courageous Democrats and punished wimpy ones.

Liberalism also gained media traction through the emergence of irreverent Internet sites, distribution of progressive documentaries on DVDs, and the satire of Comedy Central's "The Daily Show with Jon Stewart," which poked fun at both the Bush administration and the national news media. For the first time in memory, many Americans were hearing coherent and consistent arguments from progressives. It was suddenly cool to stand up to Bush and to recognize the phoniness of the mainstream news media.

◆◆◆

Spring 2005 brought to light many details about how George W. Bush had misled the United States to war, but the key documents emerged primarily from scholars and journalists in the United Kingdom. For instance, leaked minutes of a July 2002 meeting at 10 Downing Street between Prime Minister Tony Blair and his top intelligence officials revealed that the Bush administration was determined to make a case for war with Iraq regardless of the actual evidence.

"Intelligence and facts were being fixed around the policy," British intelligence chief Richard Dearlove was quoted as saying. The papers, known as the "Downing Street Memo," surely would have warranted front-page coverage in the big U.S. newspaper in a different era.

Instead, the British documents were largely ignored by major U.S. news outlets, both mainstream and right-wing. But Big Media suddenly was finding it harder to brush aside unwelcome news. The "Downing Street Memo" became a phenomenon on the Internet and on progressive talk radio, the news spreading by e-mail and word of mouth.

Despite this pressure to address the startling admissions of "fixed" intelligence, *The Washington Post* and other leading news outlets weren't about to surrender. So, in a lead editorial on June 15, 2005, the *Post* assured its readers that "the memos add not a single fact to what was previously known about the administration's prewar deliberations. Not only that: They add nothing to what was publicly known in July 2002."

But that wasn't really true. While some people were alleging what the secret British documents confirmed – that Bush had acted in bad faith and was just going through the motions of taking his Iraq case to the United Nations – those people had been vocal opponents of the invasion and were granted almost no voice by the *Post* and other U.S. news outlets.

In early 2003, editorialists at *The Washington Post*, *The New York Times* and other major newspapers praised Bush for going to the U.N. on the advice of supposed moderates such as Secretary of State Colin Powell and Prime Minister Tony Blair. Indeed, looking back to that time frame, it would be hard to find any "reputable" commentary in the mainstream U.S. press calling Bush's actions fraudulent, which is what the British evidence indicated they were.

In June 2005, as the grassroots pressure over the Downing Street Memo continued to build, mainstream journalists exploded in annoyance. On June 12, *The Washington Post* carried an opinion column by *Los Angeles Times* editorial page editor Michael Kinsley, lashing out at those who thought the memo was "proof positive that President Bush was determined to invade Iraq the year before he did so" or who thought "the whole 'weapons of mass destruction' concern was phony from the start, and the drama about inspections was just kabuki: going through the motions." Kinsley then added mockingly, "Although it is flattering to be thought personally responsible for allowing a proven war criminal to remain in office, in the end I don't buy the fuss."[21]

When the Republican congressional majority refused to hold hearings on the Downing Street Memo, Representative John Conyers, a Michigan Democrat, held his own rump hearing, which the Republicans allowed to take place only in a basement room. Instead of seeing this slight as an abuse of majority power by the Republicans, the *Post*'s political correspondent Dana Milbank chose to pile on the Democrats.

"In the Capitol basement yesterday, long-suffering House Democrats took a trip to the land of make-believe," Milbank wrote. "They pretended a small conference room was the Judiciary Committee hearing room, draping white linens over folding tables to make them look like witness tables and bringing in cardboard name tags and extra flags to make the whole thing look official. [Conyers] banged a large wooden gavel and got the other lawmakers to call him 'Mr. Chairman.'"[22]

◆ ◆ ◆

While the major U.S. news media continued to poke fun at war critics, the situation on the ground in Iraq worsened and the impact on the larger U.S. standing in the Middle East was growing catastrophic.

CIA analysts concluded that Iraq was emerging as a far more effective training ground for Islamic terrorists than Afghanistan ever was. Not only was Iraq more central to the Arab world, but the conflict offered an opportunity for hands-on experience in bomb-making, kidnapping, assassination and conventional attacks on military targets. Battle-hardened terrorists later could turn their skills on American targets around the world or on pro-U.S. governments in the Middle East, such as Saudi Arabia and Jordan, according to an internal CIA analysis written in May 2005.[23]

A drawn-out Iraq War also threatened America's volunteer military. Some of the nation's best warriors were being killed, wounded or embittered after repeated tours in Iraq. Recruiters struggled to meet quotas, and many current GIs stayed in the military only because the Bush administration invoked so-called "stop-loss" orders that prevented soldiers from leaving when their tours of duty were up.

Another sign of how poorly "Operation Iraqi Freedom" was going was that one of the mission's new goals was a major expansion of Iraq's prison system. In other words, Saddam Hussein's old police state would be followed by a new government that would lock up even more people.

25

History & Hatred

"In a dark and musty bar in Stirling, Scotland, a working-class fellow named Colin reminded me why wars – especially invasions – are to be avoided, lest they engender hatreds that can divide people and lands for generations and even centuries," Robert Parry wrote in summer 2005 at *Consortiumnews.com*. "Americans with shorter historical perspectives tend to underestimate this fact, unless they were part of some ethnic or regional group that has borne the brunt of a military occupation, such as Native Americans or old-time Southerners, who still call the Civil War 'the War of Northern Aggression.'

"For many people in the world, grievances of past centuries can be as real as the events of last week and often more powerful. Animosities born of brutality and perceived injustice can distort relations even between countries with strong economic and cultural ties. Which is what Colin, with his close-cropped hair and strong Scottish accent, recalled to me as we sat in the bar on the night of July 4, 2005, talking about the bloody wars waged against Scotland and Wales by Edward I, the ruthless and cunning English monarch of the late 13th century.

"My conversation with Colin and his spike-haired friend David was the sort of serendipity that comes with foreign travel. Off-duty guides from the nearby Stirling Castle, both were mildly intrigued by my reason for being in their gritty, central Scottish city of Stirling: My wife and I were taking my 16-year-old son, Jeffrey, and one of his friends on what I had dubbed the 'Edward I/William Wallace tour' of the United Kingdom. (Yes, it is that much fun to be one of my kids.)

"Our tour had started four days earlier in London, after we had arrived from Washington. We began our little quest at the end for the two historical figures. First, we searched through Westminster Abbey for Edward I's tomb, upon which Scots are reputed to spit even seven centuries later. We found its location, although access to the tomb itself was cordoned off to the general public.

"Later, we toured the Tower of London, a castle best known as a prison for political enemies, many of whom met the grisly fate that Edward I and other English monarchs meted out to traitors. While victims of royal blood faced relatively quick death from beheading, lesser-born victims were dragged through the streets, partially hanged, castrated and disemboweled – before their hearts were cut out. Then they were decapitated and their bodies chopped into quarters.

"It was that fate that awaited Scottish hero William Wallace – also known as 'Braveheart' – who led the Scottish resistance to Edward I's military campaigns against Scotland in the 1290s. Wallace was captured in 1305 and taken to London for a show trial at Westminster before being condemned. Edward I ordered Wallace's torture to be especially deliberate with his entrails to be pulled out inch by inch as a warning to Scots to cease all rebellion. On August 23, 1305, Wallace was dragged some four miles through London streets to a market area called Smithfield, where his public torture and execution were carried out.

"After completing our visit to the Tower of London, we took the Underground to the Barbican station and then walked to the Smithfield market area in search of a plaque that marks the location where Wallace was drawn and quartered. Following directions I got from a gentleman who sang in the choir at the Medieval-era St. Bartholomew's Church, we walked 20 paces beyond the church grounds, looked to our left and found Wallace's plaque on the wall of an adjacent hospital building. In front of the plaque, someone had left a display of fresh flowers.

"A few days later, another part of our U.K. trip took us to northern Wales, which Edward I had subdued with his usual ferocity, before turning on Scotland. In Wales, Edward I – known as 'Longshanks' because of his height – had imposed his dominion over the Celtic population by constructing a network of mammoth castles in important towns, a strategy that strangled Welsh resistance but drained the English treasury. We visited two of Edward's castles – one at Conwy and another at Caernarfon (near where our Parry ancestors had lived).

"After throttling Wales, Edward I turned his attention to Scotland, where Gaelic tribes had resisted external control for a thousand years, since the days of the Roman Empire. In 1297, Edward's army – without him in command – marched north to crush Scottish rebels led by Wallace. That campaign brought the English army to the strategic Scottish town of Stirling. There, English commanders, including Edward's treasurer for Scotland, Hugh Cressingham, rashly decided to cross a narrow bridge, giving Wallace his opportunity.

"Though outnumbered, the Scottish soldiers charged down a slope and set upon the half of the English army that had made its way across the bridge. Amid the chaos, the rest of the English force couldn't cross and the wooden bridge collapsed. The Scots slaughtered half the English army, driving many into the river where they drowned. Among the dead was Cressingham, whose skin was cut off and sliced into Scottish battle ribbons. The rout at Stirling Bridge forced the English into retreat. Wallace's army marched south after them, taking the war to towns in northern England before withdrawing back to Scotland as winter weather set in.

"The next year, Edward personally led a fearsome new campaign against the Scots. Aided by dissension within the Scottish ranks and using the devastating longbow developed by Welsh archers, Edward crushed Wallace's army at the Battle of Falkirk. Gradually, Edward tightened his grip on Scotland as Wallace went into hiding and exile. Seven years later, after Wallace returned to Scotland, he was betrayed by a fellow Scot, taken prisoner by Edward's forces and paraded before mocking crowds in English towns *en route* to his grisly fate in London.

"After Wallace was drawn and quartered, Edward ordered Wallace's head put on a spike on London Bridge and his severed limbs displayed over the sewers in the Scottish towns of Newcastle, Berwick-upon-Tweed, Perth and Aberdeen. Edward's goal was to make Wallace's suffering and humiliation a warning to the Scots.

"Instead, Edward created a martyr who has inspired the Scottish independence movement to this day. After actor Mel Gibson portrayed Wallace in the 1995 movie 'Braveheart,' new impetus was given to the cause of Scottish nationalism. In the decade since the movie, the Scots have pursued what they call the 'devolution' of their ties to England. With their own parliament and control over many domestic policies, many Scots now regard their land as an independent country only in loose confederation with Great Britain.

"On July 4, 2005, our 'Wallace/Edward tour' brought us to Stirling, where we met Colin and David, who were drinking beers at the bar after finishing their day's work as guides at Stirling Castle. It was hard to tell if they were more bemused or impressed that some Americans had bothered to visit the site of Wallace's execution in London.

"Colin especially held Wallace in deep reverence as the archetypal Scottish hero who never bent to the will of England, even in the face of a horrible death. There were other Scottish heroes, Colin said, but none measured up to Wallace. After Edward I's own death in 1307, as he was preparing another military campaign against Scotland, Robert the Bruce led the Scots to a major victory over Edward II at Bannockburn in 1314. But Colin said the memory of Robert the Bruce was tainted by his on-again-off-again collaboration with Edward I.

"Colin leaned toward me at the bar. 'You know a bunch of us Scots are going down to London on the 700th anniversary of Wallace's death,' he said. 'We're going to follow the route that Wallace took through London, to where he was executed in Smithfield.'

"It struck me that the calm commitment on Colin's face was a lesson that should not be lost on George W. Bush and other politicians of today. However justified they might regard their military operations in other lands, those wars carry the heavy risk of creating martyrs and enflaming hatreds that could outlast any short-term objectives, just as Edward I's brutality against Scotland did. That is one reason why leaders with deep historical perspective really do treat war as a last resort, rather than a casual means for achieving some geopolitical end."[1]

◆ ◆ ◆

Back in London at the end of the trip, there would be another more modern historical lesson. As Robert Parry wrote at *Consortiumnews.com*, "At about 9:30 a.m. on July 7, an overcast Thursday, I left a hotel in the Kensington section of London and walked – with my wife and 16-year-old son – toward the Earl's Court subway station, planning to take the Piccadilly line to Heathrow Airport to catch a noontime flight back to Washington.

"When we reached the Underground, we encountered a surge of people moving away from the entrance. We were told that the station was being evacuated because of some emergency elsewhere in the system, possibly an electrical explosion. With little prospect for finding a cab and unclear how widespread the problem was, we began trudging off – luggage in hand – toward the next stop on the line, at Barons Court. Many Londoners were doing the same, some in their business suits with cell phones to their ears trying to glean the latest detail of what was happening.

"The sorry parade had the feel of a disaster film in which people are suddenly denied the transportation that they so casually rely on. When we finally reached Barons Court, guards barred the door to that station, too, informing us that multiple explosions had forced the closing of the entire London Underground. It was becoming clear that this incident wasn't just the result of a malfunctioning electrical grid.

"At the advice of one security guard, we double-backed about a quarter mile and found a store-front office of a 'mini-cab' company. We secured the services of its last available car, which for the price of 40 pounds took us – and an elderly chap on his way to Belfast – to Heathrow Airport. By the time we boarded our flight and departed for Washington

early in the afternoon, news reports were describing how four bombs –
three on subway cars and a fourth on a double-decker bus – had killed an
undetermined number of people in London. Suspicions were already
focused on an al-Qaeda connection.

"Several hours later, after we landed at Dulles Airport, we climbed
into a cab for the last leg of our trip back to Arlington, Virginia. The cab
driver was listening to a right-wing radio station that was already drawing
lessons from the London bombings. George W. Bush's wisdom and
resolve were vindicated again, the radio voices told us, while American
liberals were cowards and traitors for wanting to coddle terrorists.

"We were back in the USA."

Robert Parry's article continued: "But what are the real lessons of the
London bombings – and what do those lessons mean for the Iraq War, the
'war on terror' and the shaky future of American democracy? First, there
is the forensic evidence, the relatively crude nature of the four bombs.
That could be viewed as a negative or a positive.

"On the one hand, ... their simplicity could suggest a declining
terrorist capability. On the other hand, the bombs indicate that even
amateurish terrorist cells can disrupt the functioning of a sophisticated
city like London and kill scores of people. The London bombings
suggest, too, that al-Qaeda may be evolving into a diffused movement,
more an inspiration to disaffected Muslim youth on how to wage war
against the West than a centralized organization that hatches complex
plots and dispatches operatives to carry out the attacks.

"Second, ... the London bombings undercut one of Bush's primary
arguments for continuing the war in Iraq – that fighting the 'terrorists'
there somehow prevents them from attacking elsewhere. As Bush said in
a June 18 radio address, 'Our troops are fighting these terrorists in Iraq so
you will not have to face them here at home.' This argument has always
flown in the face of both logic and U.S. intelligence analyses, which have
concluded that hatreds stirred up by the invasion of Iraq have been a
recruiting boon for al-Qaeda, strengthening Islamic extremism, not
weakening it.

"Plus, it made no sense to think that fighting extremists in Iraq
precluded other extremists from launching attacks in Europe or the United
States. Rather, the opposite would almost certainly be true, that hardened
veterans of the Iraq conflict – or sympathetic Muslims already living in
the West – were more likely to avenge the deaths of Iraqi civilians by
killing civilians in countries that have sent troops to Iraq, such as Great
Britain.

"But Bush's case for the Iraq War was never strong on logic. It's
always been about pushing America's 'hot buttons' – whether

exaggerating threats from Saddam Hussein's supposed weapons of mass destruction or juxtaposing references to Iraq and the September 11 attacks despite the lack of evidence linking the two. ... Just last month, facing deepening criticism over his Iraq War policies, Bush returned to this approach, unleashing his deputy chief of staff Karl Rove to mock 'liberals' for supposedly demonstrating a cowardly naivety in the face of the September 11 terrorism.

"'Conservatives saw the savagery of 9/11 in the attacks and prepared for war; liberals saw the savagery of the 9/11 attacks and wanted to prepare indictments and offer therapy and understanding for our attackers,' Rove said in a speech to the Conservative Party of New York State on June 22. 'I don't know about you, but moderation and restraint is not what I felt when I watched the Twin Towers crumble to the ground, a side of the Pentagon destroyed, and almost 3,000 of our fellow citizens perish in flames and rubble.'

"Although Bush spoke after the London bombings about the need for an 'ideology of hope,' he has shown little willingness to rethink a counterterrorism strategy based on the prospects of endless war. Indeed, a chilling subtext of Rove's speech is the demonization of anyone who suggests that conventional warfare may be a clumsy and even counter-productive tool to employ against terrorism. To recommend scaling back the level of violence – away from war toward a police operation or, in Rove's scoffing words, 'to prepare indictments' – is deemed proof of weakness.

"Typical of Bush's backers, radio talk show host Kevin McCullough used the London bombings as another opportunity to denounce American liberals as cowards whose very existence endangers the nation. 'What none of the Left in America understand is that this life can't be lived by sheer moral relativism,' McCullough said, according to a text of his comments distributed by the Christian Wire Service. 'They are afraid of this because they don't wish to be forced to curb their own behavior to actually become moral people. But their fears aside, the unwillingness to look at the face of Satan and call it what it is jeopardizes all of us. These people can not be trusted with national security because they have no sense of the difference between good and evil.' ...

"A third lesson from the London bombings," Robert Parry wrote, "appears to be that the world does face a growing risk that the tit-for-tat violence between the warring sides will spread geographically, worsening fears and deepening hatreds. Further, a simplistic black-and-white view of the enemy is not helpful in winning this kind of conflict. As counterinsurgency experts have taught for decades, effective strategies to quell rebellions require multilayered responses aimed at winning hearts and minds, not just killing all possible enemies. These military experts note that success requires identifying legitimate grievances, taking concrete steps to address these problems, and then isolating the hard-core enemies. ...

"Yet, given how deeply Bush has dug himself in to his 'with-us-or-with-the-terrorists' strategies, it is difficult to envision how the United States might clamber out of the hole, especially the one in Iraq, in the near future. But the restoration of rational – and even respectful – discourse about realistic options might be a good place to start."[2]

◆ ◆ ◆

On the domestic front in the United States, Nat Parry also was drawing lessons from the past and present: "Three years ago, I wrote an article entitled 'Bush's Grim Vision.' It began with the observation that since the September 11, 2001, terror attacks, 'George W. Bush has put the United States on a course that is so bleak that few analysts have – as the saying goes – connected the dots. If they had they would see an outline of a future that mixes constant war overseas with abridgement of constitutional freedoms at home.'

"Since then, the dots have not only been connected, but many of the shapes have been colored in. The immediate fear and anger following the September 11 attacks have given way to the grinding permanence of a never-ending state of emergency. In many ways, the reality has turned out worse than the article's expectations. For the last two-plus years, the bloody war in Iraq has raged with no end in sight, as more evidence emerges daily that the Bush administration misled the nation into the invasion through a mix of false intelligence on weapons of mass destruction and clever juxtapositions that blurred Iraq's Saddam Hussein with al-Qaeda's Osama bin Laden.

"The war – and the animosities it engendered – have, in turn, added to the likelihood of terrorist attacks, like the July 7 bombings in London, which provide further justification for more security and greater encroachments on individual liberties. Already, the Iraq War has deformed the democratic process in the United States, even as Bush claims that his goal is to spread democracy in the Middle East. At home, his operatives have demonstrated that when fear-mongering isn't enough to scare the American people into line, bare-knuckled bullying is in store for those who speak out. ...

"Bush's 'grim vision' always recognized that the 'war on terror' abroad would require restricted freedoms at home – as well as expanded powers for the police and military. So, just as in 2002, when the Bush

Doctrine on preemptive wars laid the intellectual groundwork for invading Iraq, new doctrines are now being promulgated to justify the creation of a full-scale 'security state' inside the United States.

"One Defense Department document, called the 'Strategy for Homeland Defense and Civil Support,' sets out a military strategy against terrorism that envisions an 'active, layered defense' both inside and outside U.S. territory. As a kind of domestic corollary to the Bush Doctrine, the Pentagon strategy paper also has a preemptive element, calling for increased military reconnaissance and surveillance to 'defeat potential challengers before they threaten the United States.' The plan 'maximizes threat awareness and seizes the initiative from those who would harm us.'

"Besides lifting the traditional limits on military operations on U.S. soil, the document makes clear that global warfare will be the reality for at least the next decade. 'The likelihood of U.S. military operations overseas will be high throughout the next 10 years,' the document said, adding that the Pentagon fully expects terrorists to carry out 'multiple, simultaneous mass casualty (chemical, biological, radiological, nuclear and explosive) attacks against the U.S. homeland.' The primary response will be 'projecting power across the globe ... in ways that an enemy cannot predict,' the paper said, promising 'an unpredictable web of land, maritime, and air assets that are arrayed to detect, deter, and defeat hostile action.'

"For any American suspected of collaborating with terrorists, Bush has already revealed what's in store. In May 2002, the FBI arrested U.S. citizen Jose Padilla in Chicago on suspicion that he might be an al-Qaeda operative planning an attack. Rather than bring criminal charges, Bush designated Padilla an 'enemy combatant' and had him imprisoned indefinitely without benefit of due process.

"Now, Bush is asking the federal courts to recognize the President's sole right to strip American citizens of their constitutional protections. 'In the war against terrorists of global reach, as the Nation learned all too well on September 11, 2001, the territory of the United States is part of the battlefield,' Bush's lawyers have argued in briefs to the federal courts."[3]

Nat Parry continued, "The Republican-controlled Congress is moving toward rubber-stamping Bush's 'security state' plans both at home and abroad. Beyond the expanded domestic role for the Pentagon, the powers of the FBI are increasing. ... Congress is not only reauthorizing many of those stop-gap powers but adding new ones.

"'Administrative subpoena' authority, for instance, would allow the FBI to execute its own search orders for intelligence investigations, without judicial review. The legislation also would give agents the authority to seize personal records from medical facilities, libraries, hotels, gun dealers, banks and any other businesses without any specific facts connecting those records to any criminal activity or a foreign agent.

"Bush also recently ordered the creation of a domestic spy service within the FBI, called the National Security Service. Intended to centralize authority and remove barriers between the FBI and the CIA, the NSS will combine the Justice Department's intelligence, counterterrorism and espionage units. The NSS will have the authority to bypass traditional due-process when seizing assets of people or companies thought to be aiding the spread of weapons of mass destruction.

"The new police powers come on top of guidelines for intelligence-gathering that Attorney General John Ashcroft established in 2002 when he loosened restrictions that were put on the FBI after the COINTELPRO political-spying scandal of the 1970s. Under the Ashcroft guidelines, the FBI must only have a reasonable indication that 'two or more persons are engaged in an enterprise for the purpose of ... furthering political or social goals wholly or in part through activities that involve force or violence and a violation of federal criminal law.' The investigation does not need to be approved by FBI headquarters, but rather, may be authorized by a special agent in charge of an FBI field office.

"Critics argue that the authority to investigate domestic terrorism invites political abuses because the Patriot Act adopted a broad definition of terrorism. Section 802 of the law defines terrorism as acts that 'appear to be intended ... to influence the policy of a government by intimidation or coercion,' which could include confrontational protests and civil disobedience. Civil libertarians have warned that rather than improving security or combating terrorism, the new laws and guidelines may be more useful in silencing critics of the Bush administration and chilling political dissent.

"One early indication of how the government might use its expanded powers came in 2003, when the FBI sent a memorandum to local law enforcement agencies before planned demonstrations against the war in Iraq. The memo detailed protesters' tactics and analyzed activities such as the recruitment of protesters over the Internet. The FBI instructed local law enforcement agencies to be on the lookout for 'possible indicators of protest activity and report any potentially illegal acts to the nearest FBI Joint Terrorism Task Force.' (JTTF)

"Since then, there have been many stories about the JTTF harassing and intimidating political activists engaged in lawful protests. Before last summer's demonstrations at the Democratic and Republican national conventions, for instance, the JTTF visited the homes of activists, while

FBI agents in Missouri, Kansas and Colorado spied on and interrogated activists. One target of these visits, Sarah Bardwell of Denver, Colorado, said, 'The message I took from it was that they were trying to intimidate us into not going to any protests and to let us know that, 'hey, we're watching you.'[4]

"Over the past few years, the FBI also has collected thousands of pages of internal documents on civil rights and antiwar protest groups," Nat Parry's article continued. "Another group singled out by the FBI was United for Peace and Justice, which facilitated last summer's protest at the Republican convention.

"Leslie Cagan, the national coordinator for the coalition, said she was particularly concerned that the FBI's counterterrorism division was discussing the coalition's operations. 'We always assumed the FBI was monitoring us, but to see the counterterrorism people looking at us like this is pretty jarring,' Cagan said.

"But even as people around the world call for rethinking the U.S. strategy on terrorism, the Bush administration is calling for more of the same – increased police powers at home and intensified war abroad."[5]

◆◆◆

Though more Americans were shifting into opposition to George W. Bush's policies, Washington's conventional wisdom remained steadfastly behind the original wisdom of the Iraq invasion. A split was growing, however, between two camps in Washington. One camp was solidly behind Bush and wanted to "stay the course" – while the other questioned the administration's execution of the war but felt "we must get it right" because "failure is not an option."

Both groups ruled out a prompt U.S. military withdrawal because that supposedly would turn Iraq into a "failed state" and a "breeding ground for Islamic terrorism." Therefore, the thinking went, U.S. troops must remain while Iraq builds a democracy that can stop the extremists.

But, as Robert Parry wrote at *Consortiumnews.com* on August 17, 2005, there was "a case to be made for U.S. withdrawal as the best option for both resolving the conflict and neutralizing the foreign Islamic extremists in Iraq. A corollary of this thinking holds that the continued U.S. military presence does more harm than good.

"The logic of withdrawal goes like this: First, a distinction must be made between the Sunni-led insurgency, which is fighting out of a sense of Iraqi nationalism and to protect the Sunni minority's interests in Iraq, and the al-Qaeda-linked terrorist network of Jordanian Abu Musab al-Zarqawi. It is engaged in a jihad to drive Americans and other Westerners out of the Middle East. While the interests of the Sunni-led insurgency and the Zarqawi-led terrorists may overlap under the present circumstances, that is primarily because an American force of 138,000 troops remains inside Iraq.

"The Sunni insurgents see the U.S. army as the enemy because it invaded Iraq and is now protecting a government dominated by Iraq's Shiite majority. Zarqawi's group has made itself somewhat useful to the Sunnis by recruiting Islamic extremists to come to Iraq and undertake suicide bombings that kill Americans and wreak havoc. If the Americans and other Western forces weren't in Iraq, however, two changes would likely occur: first, the draw for radicalized Islamic youth to infiltrate into Iraq and become suicide bombers would have disappeared; second, Zarqawi's limited usefulness to the Sunnis would soon dissipate.

"There would no longer be Americans for Zarqawi and his terrorist band to target and the loss of new recruits would minimize any value his organization would have in battling the Shiites. Zarqawi's remaining terrorists would quickly become more a liability than an asset – and thus a target of Iraqis from all religious sects.

"Many Sunnis and Shiites in Iraq already are fed up with the indiscriminate devastation inflicted by Zarqawi's militants. Despite religious differences, which date back 1,400 years, there even have been reports of Iraqi Sunnis turning their guns on Zarqawi's fighters to protect Shiite neighbors. For instance, on August 13, 2005, in the western city of Ramadi, Sunni members of the Dulaimi tribe set up protective perimeters around their Shiite neighbors and reportedly fought Zarqawi's forces who were trying to dislodge the Shiites from the Sunni-dominated city.[6]

"Without the presence of U.S. troops, Zarqawi could lose his *raison d'etre*, his manpower and his protection from Sunni insurgents who tolerate him now only because they're in a desperate struggle against both the powerful American military and the Shiite majority.

"But the Bush administration's political strategy," Robert Parry continued, "has been to treat the Sunni-led insurgents and the Zarqawi-led terrorists as the same enemy. Few distinctions are made even though the two groups employ different tactics. The Iraqi insurgents fight primarily with small arms and roadside bombs aimed at U.S. troops, while the foreign terrorists rely heavily on suicide bombers to kill Iraqi civilians and police as well as American soldiers.

"By lumping the two forces together as 'terrorists,' Bush again has shaped the Washington debate much as he did in 2002 and early 2003 when he and Vice President Dick Cheney morphed Iraq's secular dictator Saddam Hussein into al-Qaeda leader Osama bin Laden. ...

"Another argument for American withdrawal is that it could push the Shiites and their Kurdish allies into compromising with the Sunni minority on an overall settlement. As the current impasse over a new constitution shows, the Shiites and Kurds see little reason to make significant concessions to the Sunnis because the American military continues to tilt the power balance in favor of the Shiite-Kurdish side. The Shiites and Kurds want broad autonomy over the oil riches of Iraq's south and north, respectively, and feel they can get that. ...

"In part, that's because Bush has left himself little maneuvering room for pressuring the Shiites and Kurds, since he has effectively ruled out any sudden U.S. military withdrawal. Rather than looking for an exit, which might at least worry the Shiites and Kurds, Bush continues to paint himself – and the United States – into a corner.

"'Pulling the troops out now would send a terrible message to the enemy,' Bush declared on August 11, 2005, at his ranch in Crawford, Texas. By tying American 'credibility' to the outcome in Iraq, Bush has locked the United States in even tighter. ...

"It still can't be ruled out that a messy civil war in Iraq will follow [a U.S. withdrawal], but that could happen whether U.S. forces stay or go. It already appears that a civil war is underway, with militias and death squads from various factions eliminating perceived enemies. Now, however, the Shiites can rely on Americans to do much of the hard fighting in Fallujah and other Sunni strongholds. ...

"A U.S. withdrawal also would free up Special Forces to concentrate on tracking down and eliminating al-Qaeda's leadership, an operation that was disrupted by Bush's hasty decision to focus on Iraq in 2002."[7]

26

Drowning Accountability

On August 27, 2005, as a powerful hurricane named Katrina surged through the Gulf of Mexico and took aim at New Orleans, most Americans still had confidence in their government's ability to respond to crises and natural disasters with efficiency and speed. The country prided itself on its ability to rescue people in danger, to dispatch resources, to rebuild after the worst was over.

Many Americans considered the United States unparalleled in its ability to fly disaster specialists to the far corners of the globe when catastrophe struck, to oversee the delivery of food, water, medicines and other necessities. It was part of America's can-do spirit; it was part of the national self-image.

There was also a belief that technology had gone a long way in taming the threats of nature, that the types of disasters that had plagued the country in its earlier days were like yellowed newspaper articles. They were tales from grandparents, like the stories of World War II or the Great Depression, mildly interesting but no longer very relevant. Modern catastrophes – at least as they affected most Americans – were confined to Hollywood disaster movies with big-budget special effects that brought the audience right into the middle of the danger but without any real threat of harm.

That was the frame of reference for many Americans as they concentrated on the news of Katrina's approach to New Orleans. There was a fascination with the possibility of danger; there was awareness that many experts warned about flood waters breaching the levees and inundating the low-lying city; but there were few expectations that those alarms would prove true or that serious harm would befall New Orleans.

On another long vacation in Crawford, Texas, President Bush treated the gathering threat to New Orleans in a similar vein. He responded to the alarm among government weather experts with little more than cheerleading, praise for and confidence in the federal, state and local officials on the front lines. Like many Americans watching on TV, Bush acted like a spectator expecting whatever damage did occur would be neatly cleared away and everything would quickly be put back in order.

Newsmen and network anchors also behaved with more excitement than trepidation. They flew to New Orleans expecting some dramatic scenes of themselves in rain gear leaning into the wind to shout live reports into a microphone. They would bemoan the property damage and some loss of life, before packing up and flying back to New York or on to another assignment.

But that wasn't how Hurricane Katrina played out. Instead the storm and its devastation brought a national awakening – or at least the beginning of one – with large numbers of Americans finally catching on to the gap between Bush's rhetoric and reality. Before Katrina, the mix of Bush's folksy charm, the lasting emotions from 9/11 and the powerful right-wing media/political apparatus had kept most Americans under the President's spell.

In a way, Bush's ability to mesmerize so many people fit with a different type of thriller movie, one in which a harrowing truth dawns slowly on a community although the recognition of danger may have come too late.

◆◆◆

There had been plenty of warnings about the precarious topographical situation facing New Orleans, one of the nation's best-known and best-loved cities, the home of jazz, Cajun cooking and Mardi Gras. Government experts and journalists knew that a severe hurricane could force a storm surge that would push the waters of Lake Pontchartrain over the levees and flood large sections of the city that sat below sea level. New Orleans was often compared to a saucer that would quickly fill if liquid began pouring over the edges.

In a report prior to the 9/11 attacks, the Federal Emergency Management Administration had listed a hurricane inundating New Orleans as one of the three most likely catastrophes hitting the United States, along with a terrorist assault on New York City and a San Francisco earthquake. A series of articles in the New Orleans *Times-Picayune* in 2004 had detailed the looming threat, which was made worse by budgetary neglect of the sinking levee system and an incomplete reconstruction.

"It appears that the money has been moved in the President's budget to handle homeland security and the war in Iraq, and I suppose that's the price we pay," said Walter Maestri, emergency management chief for Jefferson Parish, Louisiana. "Nobody locally is happy that the levees can't be finished, and we are doing everything we can to make the case that this is a security issue for us."[1]

A possible breach of the levees also was a major topic of discussion on news and weather channels as Katrina churned through the Gulf. Yet, when Katrina crashed ashore, wreaking devastation along the coasts of Louisiana, Mississippi and Alabama, government officials – local, state and federal – seemed taken aback, at times almost paralyzed.

The flood broke through the levees protecting New Orleans Ninth Ward, filling block after block with muddy fetid water. Tens of thousands of residents were trapped; hundreds drowning in their homes; others seeking refuge in emergency shelters at the Superdome and at the Convention Center. On August 30, 2005, the *Times-Picayune* posted a story at its Web site saying "no one can say they didn't see it coming."

It took a while for the magnitude of the New Orleans disaster to become clear. The big-name newscasters who had pre-positioned themselves in the storm's path – the likes of NBC's Brian Williams and CNN's Anderson Cooper – sounded more shocked at first than horrified. After the storm passed, they looked out their hotel windows at the strange sight of city streets covered in water.

Then, as the summer heat returned, the journalists moved out around the city, often by boat, to witness a scene more befitting the Third World than the world's superpower. Bloated bodies floated in the water or rotted in the hot sun. Hundreds of residents, trapped in their homes, frantically tore through attic ceilings to climb out onto roof tops and to wave their arms for help. Others drowned in steamy attics as the water kept rising.

The Superdome, which had hosted Super Bowl games and other national sporting events, quickly became infamous as a scene of unspeakable living conditions as New Orleans residents sweltered inside amid overflowing toilets and urine-soaked artificial turf.

The U.S. government along with local and state authorities appeared powerless to respond quickly. Instead, federal, state and local officials descended into rounds of acrimonious finger-pointing. The Katrina crisis also brought to light some of Bush's leadership weaknesses that had been hidden behind White House P.R. curtains during his first term.

In a retrospective on the Katrina disaster, *Newsweek*'s Evan Thomas reported that "it's a standing joke among the President's top aides: who gets to deliver the bad news? Warm and hearty in public, Bush can be cold and snappish in private, and aides sometimes cringe before the displeasure of the President of the United States."[2]

On August 30, after Hurricane Katrina overwhelmed the New Orleans levees, the White House staff was in full cringe mode. Someone was going to have to tell Bush that he needed to cut short his five-week vacation by a couple of days. Though Bush did agree to return to Washington, he remained in a protective bubble about how bad the Katrina news really was. Before devoting his attention to the catastrophe, he fulfilled speaking commitments in San Diego and Phoenix – even clowning with a gift guitar – before heading back to Washington.

Since Bush famously shuns reading newspapers or watching the news, his staff decided that the best way to clue Bush in on how bad things were was to burn a special DVD with TV footage of the flood so he could watch the DVD on Air Force One, *Newsweek*'s Thomas reported. "How this could be – how the President of the United States could have even less 'situational awareness,' as they say in the military, than the average American about the worse natural disaster in a century – is one of the more perplexing and troubling chapters in a story that, despite moments of heroism and acts of great generosity, ranks as a national disgrace," Thomas wrote.[3]

The Katrina debacle also represented the first significant test of whether the marginal inroads that American progressives had made in talk radio and the Internet would have any measurable effect. Certainly, pro-Bush right-wing talk radio was doing the best it could to divert blame from the Bush administration onto New Orleans' black mayor Ray Nagin, Louisiana's Democratic Governor Kathleen Blanco and the mostly black survivors of New Orleans who had been trapped by the storm.

Some right-wing AM radio talkers said "able-bodied" people who lacked transportation should simply have walked out of New Orleans. In other words, if these folks weren't so lazy and stupid, they would have used their own two feet. But the idea of trying to out-walk a hurricane with 150-mile-per-hour winds would seem nutty to anyone who's ever lived through even a milder storm. Still, the argument gave Bush's base another reason not to blame the President or his team.

But for once, there was another side of the story reaching listeners on the AM dial. As the seriousness of the Katrina crisis sank in on August 31, Robert Parry was driving north from Washington to Montreal. He wrote at *Consortiumnews.com* that "while on the road, I also got a taste of how valuable progressive talk radio could be for arming American liberals with facts and for persuading Middle Americans that the nation needs new leadership.

"As I drove past New York City, I picked up an Air America Radio station where the hosts explained how Bush's spending in Iraq had diverted money needed to strengthen New Orleans' levees and how deployment of National Guard troops in Iraq had undermined the Guard's ability to respond to the disaster.

"What was even more striking was the anger and passion in the voices of Air America listeners who called in from all over the country. They were furious over the national disgrace that was unfolding in New Orleans, as Bush vacationed in Texas and then responded haltingly to the crisis.

"But the radio signal of the New York City station faded as I reached upstate New York. The only AM talk radio I could get then was the far more pervasive conservative variety. On those stations, the New Orleans crisis either was treated as not that big a deal or as something to blame on anybody but Bush."[4]

When Bush finally made his belated trip to the Gulf Coast on September 2, the DVD strategy did not appear to have worked. He still seemed disconnected from the human tragedy and more interested in suggesting that the catastrophe was unforeseen. "I don't think anyone anticipated the breach of the levees," Bush told ABC's Diane Sawyer, although the threat to the levees had been recognized for years.

As tens of thousands of mostly poor and black citizens endured squalor in flooded New Orleans, Bush slid into his role of peppy cheerleader and consoled friends like Senator Trent Lott, a Mississippi Republican, who had lost one of his homes. "Out of the rubbles of Trent Lott's house – he's lost his entire house – there's going to be a fantastic house," Bush joshed. "And I'm looking forward to sitting on the porch."

Bush also had some encouraging words for his hapless FEMA director, Michael Brown. "Brownie, you're doing a heck of a job," Bush said.

Before boarding a flight back to Washington, Bush continued to banter amid the suffering. Playing for laughs, Bush recalled his past hard partying in New Orleans, which he called "the town where I used to come … to enjoy myself, occasionally too much."

That night during a televised fundraiser for hurricane relief, rapper Kanye West veered off script to criticize the media for its perceived bias against African-Americans and George Bush for his lackadaisical response to the disaster.

"I hate the way they portray us in the media," he said. "If you see a black family it says they are looting [but] if you see a white family it says they are looking for food." Summing up the President's attitude, West said, "George Bush doesn't care about black people." The remark sent NBC executives into a panic that led them to censor West's comments from the show's rebroadcast in the Pacific time zone.

On Saturday, September 3, driving back toward Washington, Robert Parry reported that "I reached the New York City area and again tuned in the Air America station. But I was disappointed to hear only the broadcast of pre-recorded 'best-of' content, some of it predating Hurricane Katrina. Air America appeared to lack the resources to dispatch correspondents to the scene and offer special live weekend coverage of the crisis. I did, however, find live right-wing talk radio, including more blame being heaped on the trapped New Orleans residents for not using their feet and walking out of the city before the hurricane hit."

For once, however, the right-wing media couldn't dictate the terms of a national story. Not only had the New Orleans levees broken, but the dams protecting George W. Bush's image were cracking, too. This time when Bush fumbled a national crisis, many leading newscasters were on scene to witness the debacle and other journalists echoed their first-hand assessments of the chaos and ineptitude.

More and more Americans were waking up to how they had been lulled to sleep by the clever political operatives who surrounded Bush. With New Orleans turned into a giant cesspool – and with bloated remains of American citizens left for days to rot in the sun – the nation was finally shaking itself alert and finding the nightmare all too real.

Facing a suddenly critical news media and a sharp decline in poll numbers, Bush revised his approach to the crisis. He ordered up more trips to the region; posed with more African-Americans; and vowed a vast rebuilding project on par with what he promised for Iraq.

But his mother stepped on Bush's new compassion. During a visit to Katrina evacuees in Houston's Astrodome, former First Lady Barbara Bush expressed her discomfort over "what I'm hearing which is sort of scary is they all want to stay in Texas. ... So many of the people in the arena here, you know, were underprivileged anyway, so this – this (she chuckles) is working very well for them."

Bush, the *ersatz* populist, looked like a phony to many Americans when he gave a nationally televised speech in shirt sleeves in New Orleans' Jackson Square with special generators and lighting that had been flown in to give him a dramatic backdrop. "We will do what it takes; we will stay as long as it takes," Bush declared on September 15, 2005, in phrasing reminiscent of his pledges about Iraq.

But many prominent figures in the mainstream U.S. news media weren't buying Bush's P.R. offensive this time. *New York Times* columnist Frank Rich wrote that the Katrina disaster had exposed, once and for all, Bush's incompetence and phoniness.

"Once Toto parts the curtain, the Wizard of Oz can never be the wizard again," Rich wrote. "He is forever Professor Marvel, blowhard and snake-oil salesman. Hurricane Katrina, which is likely to endure in the American psyche as long as L. Frank Baum's mythic tornado, has similarly unmasked George W. Bush. The worst storm in our history proved perfect for exposing this President because in one big blast it illuminated all his failings: the rampant cronyism, the empty sloganeering of 'compassionate conservatism,' the lack of concern for the 'underprivileged' his mother condescended to at the Astrodome, the reckless lack of planning for all government operations except tax cuts, the use of spin and photo-ops to camouflage failure and to substitute for action."[5]

Political moderates also were having second thoughts. *Times* columnist Thomas L. Friedman, who supported the Iraq War and other parts of Bush's foreign policy, concluded that Katrina had left Bush's ship of state adrift.

Friedman wrote: "Katrina deprived the Bush team of the energy source that propelled it forward for the last four years: 9/11 and the halo over the presidency that came with it. The events of 9/11 created a deference in the U.S. public, and media, for the administration, which exploited it to the hilt to push an uncompassionate conservative agenda on tax cuts and runaway spending, on which it never could have gotten elected. That deference is over."[6]

"There's nothing more pathetic than watching someone who's out of touch feign being in touch," observed another *New York Times* columnist, Maureen Dowd. "On his fifth sodden pilgrimage of penitence to the devastation he took so long to comprehend, W. desperately tried to show concern. He said he had spent some 'quality time' at a Chevron plant in Pascagoula and nattered about trash removal, infrastructure assessment teams and the 'can-do spirit.'

"'We look forward to hearing your vision so we can more better do our job,' he said at a briefing in Gulfport, Mississippi. ... The more the President echoes his dad's 'Message: I care,' the more the world hears 'Message: I can't.'"[7]

But the overriding question remained: Did this American awakening arrive too late? Was there still time to stop Bush and his allies from consolidating their political control over the federal government? Already holding the White House and Congress, the conservatives saw the final key as gaining a firm grip on the federal courts. That way Bush's assertion of nearly unlimited presidential power could be rubber-stamped and any electoral disputes – like the one that put Bush in office in 2000 – could be settled in the Republicans' favor.

With that goal in mind, the White House pressed for quick confirmation of John Roberts, Bush's nominee to succeed the late William Rehnquist as chief justice of the U.S. Supreme Court. Next would come another conservative to fill the vacancy from Sandra Day O'Connor's retirement.

◆◆◆

As Nat Parry wrote at *Consortiumnews.com*, "What's at stake with the Supreme Court confirmation of John Roberts, especially with George W. Bush poised to name a second justice, is not only how the United States deals with abortion and other social issues but whether the President will be granted broad authoritarian powers over the nation's future and the civil liberties of people worldwide. ...

"Roberts's deference to presidential power is a strand that has run through his entire career as special assistant to Ronald Reagan's attorney general, a legal strategist for Reagan's White House counsel, a top deputy to George H.W. Bush's solicitor general Kenneth W. Starr, and a federal appeals court judge accepting George W. Bush's right to deny due-process rights to anyone deemed an 'enemy combatant.'"[8]

Roberts sided with executive power on both foreign policy issues and on bureaucratic disputes. For instance, during the Reagan administration in 1983, he said it was time to "reconsider the existence" of independent regulatory agencies, such as the Federal Communications Commission and the Federal Trade Commission, and to "take action to bring them back within the Executive Branch." Roberts called these agencies a "constitutional anomaly," which should be rectified by putting them under direct presidential control.

That, however, could let an unscrupulous President have a White House-run FTC look the other way when accusations of unfair business practices are lodged against a corporate contributor. Putting the FCC under tighter White House control would let the President pull the strings of communication policy to reward his media allies and punish anyone using the broadcast media to criticize him, much as Richard Nixon tried to do during the Watergate scandal of the 1970s.

In the 1980s, Roberts also provided legal advice to the Reagan administration on how to pick its way around the legal obstacles erected by Congress to limit military and other assistance to the Nicaraguan contra rebels who were fighting to overthrow Nicaragua's leftist Sandinista government. Reagan's evasion of those legal restrictions gave rise to the Iran-Contra scandal in 1986.

Even more troubling to civil libertarians has been Roberts's readiness to cede almost total power to the President at a time of conflict, even a vaguely defined one like the indefinite "war on terror." In Roberts's job as a U.S. Appeals Court judge, he endorsed an extreme view of executive power claimed by the Bush administration, the right to designate anyone in the world an "enemy combatant" and thus deny these people basic legal protections under international or U.S. law. On July 15, 2005, just four days before George W. Bush nominated him to the U.S. Supreme Court, Roberts ruled as part of a three-judge appeals court panel against judicial review for Salim Ahmed Hamdan, a detainee in the prison camp at Guantanamo Bay.

Hamdan was labeled an "enemy combatant" because he allegedly was the personal driver of al-Qaeda leader Osama bin Laden. While not accused of a specific crime against U.S. citizens, Hamdan, like all Guantanamo detainees, was denied access to U.S. courts and stripped of rights guaranteed to prisoners of war under the Geneva Convention of 1949. Roberts sided with George W. Bush in ruling that the Geneva Convention "does not confer upon Hamdan a right to enforce its provisions in court."

The panel ruled that the Geneva Convention would not apply to Hamdan because it covers only nation-states and not terrorist organizations like al-Qaeda. But the court went even further, asserting that presidential action cannot be constrained by "judicially enforceable rights" in treaties approved by the U.S. government. The court also endorsed Bush's proposed military commissions for trying and possibly executing those designated "enemy combatants."

Essentially, the appeals court endorsed all of the Bush administration's legal rationales and accepted at face value its factual assertions about Hamdan and the other Guantanamo detainees, particularly the White House claim that they are members of al-Qaeda. Under Bush's theory of presidential authority, a designated person can't contest any of the facts, including whether he actually is an al-Qaeda "member" or whether it might be a case of mistaken identity.

Roberts also endorsed Bush's legal arguments stemming from Bush's Military Order No. 1 issued as Commander in Chief on November 13, 2001, defining people whom he could detain at will. "The President decided that he was no longer running the country as a civilian President," civil rights attorney Michael Ratner explained in *Guantanamo: What the World Should Know.* "He issued a military order giving himself the power to run the country as a general."

◆◆◆

The little accountability there was for the Bush administration's human rights abuses was usually meted out to the lowest-level personnel. For instance, on September 27, 2005, federal authorities "frog-marched" Private Lynndie England in handcuffs and shackles off to prison to serve three years for her role in abusing and humiliating Iraqi detainees at Abu Ghraib prison.

The 22-year-old single mother from West Virginia was one of nine reservists punished for mistreating Iraqis, some of whom were stripped naked and forced to pose in mock sexual positions. England appeared in photos, pointing at a prisoner's penis and holding a naked Iraqi by a leash.

Lynndie England's sentencing at Fort Hood, Texas, came as new evidence surfaced that the abuse of Iraqi prisoners was not just the work of some deviant prison guards on the night shift at Abu Ghraib. Army Capt. Ian Fishback and two sergeants alleged that prisoners were subjected to similar treatment by the 82nd Airborne at a camp near Fallujah and that senior officers knew. Fishback blamed the pattern of abuse on the Bush administration's vague orders about when and how Geneva Convention protections applied to detainees.

"We did not set the conditions for our soldiers to succeed," said Fishback, 26, who had served tours in Afghanistan and Iraq. "We failed to set clear standards, communicate those standards and enforce those standards."[9]

Yet, as the U.S. military death toll headed toward 2,000 and Iraqis were dying in far greater numbers, the U.S. news media continued to avert its gaze from the central question: Should senior Bush administration officials most responsible for the bloody debacle in Iraq join Lynndie England in the dock of accountability?

27

Why We Fight

For the first two years of the Iraq War, the Bush administration's narrative was that al-Qaeda terrorists and some "dead-enders" from Saddam Hussein's regime were threatening the peace-loving people of Iraq. The Iraqis and their young democracy, therefore, needed the protection of U.S. forces – and an American withdrawal would both betray the Iraqis and invite al-Qaeda to turn Iraq into a central base for projecting terrorism and destabilizing the region.

By fall 2005, however, there was a widening gap between that narrative and the analysis of the CIA and U.S. military. They were seeing a far more complex conflict in which Sunni insurgent groups were fighting both U.S. forces and the Shiite-dominated government; Shiite radicals and "death squads," with shadowy ties to the Interior Ministry, targeted Sunnis; and a fairly small contingent of non-Iraqi *jihadists* – estimated at about five percent of the armed fighters – was killing Americans, their Iraqi collaborators and many innocent bystanders.

The *jihadist* faction had coalesced under Abu Musab al-Zarqawi, the Jordanian terrorist who had affiliated his group with al-Qaeda but still had strained relations with its leadership holed up along the Afghan-Pakistani border. U.S. intelligence analysts were seeing an incipient civil war and a descent into chaos.

Under pressure from the U.S. intelligence community, President Bush finally began to shift how he talked about the war. Though famously unwilling to admit errors, Bush also conceded that mistakes had been made about the WMD. "It is true that much of the intelligence turned out to be wrong," Bush said in one speech. He also acknowledged that most of the Iraqi insurgency was being waged by Iraqis themselves with the foreign al-Qaeda element the smallest group in the armed resistance. Responding to Bush's revamped speeches, the U.S. news media praised the President for his new "candor."

But Bush still wasn't leveling with the American people. He continued his tactic of scaring the public by warning of cataclysmic consequences if his policies weren't followed. Bush likened al-Qaeda leaders to historic tyrants, such as Adolf Hitler and Josef Stalin, suggesting that anyone opposed to the Iraq War was inviting slaughter on a massive scale and world domination by an unrelenting enemy. But Hitler and Stalin were totalitarian leaders in charge of powerful countries. Al-Qaeda in 2005 remained a rag-tag movement with no state-sponsorship and with leaders in hiding or on the run.

Still, Bush understood the value of a frightened American public. So, as he had once claimed that failure to remove Saddam Hussein would open the United States to "mushroom clouds" or other WMD attacks from Iraq, Bush warned that failure to win in Iraq would open the path for al-Qaeda to achieve its "grand strategy" of creating a global "caliphate" that would surround, attack and ultimately isolate the United States.

"Their stated objective is to drive the United States and coalition forces out of the Middle East so they can gain control of Iraq and use that country as a base from which to launch attacks against America, overthrow moderate governments in the Middle East, and establish a totalitarian Islamic empire that stretches from Spain to Indonesia," Bush said.

"Hear the words of the terrorists. In a letter to the terrorist leader Zarqawi, the al-Qaeda leader [Ayman al] Zawahiri has outlined plans that will unfold in several stages. These are his words: 'Expel the Americans from Iraq. ... Establish an Islamic authority over as much territory as you can to spread its power in Iraq... Extend the *jihad* wave to secular countries neighboring Iraq.' End quote," Bush said.

But intercepted al-Qaeda communiqués revealed that the organization's position in Iraq – and in its Afghan-Pakistani hideouts – was much more fragile than Bush wanted the American people to know. Though strengthened by new recruits rallying to the cause of fighting the United States, al-Qaeda's leadership struggled to get out its message and enforce discipline on Zarqawi in Iraq. Far from envisioning some unified "caliphate" spanning the globe, Osama bin Laden and his top lieutenants worried that a prompt U.S. pullout from Iraq might lead to the disintegration of their forces there.

For instance, the so-called "Zawahiri letter," dated July 9, 2005, didn't actually mention an Islamic empire stretching from the Atlantic to the Pacific. Instead, it raised the notion of a much more limited Islamic "caliphate" along the eastern coast of the Mediterranean Sea, known as the Levant. Zawahiri also pitched the idea as a ploy to keep the young *jihadists* from simply giving up and returning home once the United States departed Iraq.

The letter stated that the "caliphate" was mentioned "only to stress ... that the *mujahedeen* must not have their mission end with the expulsion of the Americans from Iraq, and then lay down their weapons, and silence the fighting zeal."

Assuming the "Zawahiri letter" was real – al-Qaeda denied its authenticity – it also portrayed al-Qaeda as a struggling organization under financial and political strain, holding out hope for limited successes in Iraq rather than dreaming of global domination. According to the letter, al-Qaeda remained so disorganized that it even lacked a reliable means for getting out its messages.

According to the letter, Zawahiri complained that six of his audio statements "were not published for one reason or another." Al-Qaeda's leaders also were so short of cash that they asked their embattled operatives in Iraq to send $100,000.

Al-Qaeda leaders had deep differences, too, with Zarqawi over his brutality and attacks on Shiite religious targets. The letter noted that many Muslims were offended by the beheadings of Western captives and the bombings that have killed hundreds of Shiites. "Many of your Muslim admirers amongst the common folk are wondering about your attacks on the Shia," the letter said. "The sharpness of this questioning increases when the attacks are on one of their mosques."

Several months later, on December 11, 2005, al-Qaeda's leadership sent another letter to Zarqawi, again urging him to behave in a more respectful and politic manner toward Iraqis. This letter, written by a senior al-Qaeda operative known as "Atiyah," faulted Zarqawi for attacks on fellow Muslims that had alienated key elements of the Sunni-led opposition to the U.S. occupation. In a long and rambling lecture, Atiyah warned Zarqawi that he must show patience and that al-Qaeda would benefit most if the war against the Americans in Iraq was dragged out.

"The most important thing is that the *jihad* continues with steadfastness and firm rooting, and that it grows in terms of supporters, strength, clarity of justification, and visible proof each day," Atiyah wrote. "Indeed, prolonging the war is in our interest."

The Atiyah letter represented further proof that Bush's refusal to consider a prompt U.S. military withdrawal from Iraq was playing into al-Qaeda's hands, just the opposite of Bush's statements to the American people. Al-Qaeda did not want the United States to withdraw despite some of its public posturing to that effect; instead, the terrorists had concluded privately that "prolonging the war is in our interest."

Their goal was to keep the Americans bogged down in Iraq so al-Qaeda could continue rebuilding its operations along the Afghan-Pakistani border and keep on using the U.S. occupation of Iraq as a recruitment tool.* While al-Qaeda applied the reverse psychology of Brer Rabbit's briar patch ploy – publicly hoping for America's humiliating departure from Iraq – its real goal was to trap the United States in another Brer Rabbit escapade, when the character rashly started a fight with a "tar baby," one punch after another until Brer Rabbit was hopelessly stuck.

While the United States continued to thrash around in Iraq, Atiyah urged Zarqawi to recognize the vulnerability of al-Qaeda's position in Iraq and to mend fences with angry Iraqis. "Know that we, like all *mujahedeen*, are still weak," Atiyah told Zarqawi. "We have not yet reached a level of stability. We have no alternative but to not squander any element of the foundations of strength or any helper or supporter."

The letter strongly instructed Zarqawi that "it is highly advisable to be polite and to show complete respect, regret, compassion, and mercy and so forth. You must incline yourself to this, and be humble to the believers, and smile in people's faces, even if you are cursing them in your heart, even if it has been said that they are 'a bad tribal brother.'"

Beyond the significance of Atiyah's wish for "prolonging" the war, the letter underscored how tenuous al-Qaeda's position in Iraq was, especially when contrasted with Bush's alarmist rhetoric. Indeed, the "Atiyah" and "Zawahiri" letters suggested that one of al-Qaeda's biggest fears was that the United States would pull out of Iraq before the terrorist organization had built the necessary political infrastructure to turn the country into a future base of operations. In other words, Bush was creating exactly the conditions that he was claiming to prevent.

◆◆◆

The United States and the new Shiite-dominated Iraqi government reacted to the frustration of grappling with an elusive and brutal enemy with an escalation of what military strategists would call "counter-terror" that targeted Iraq's Sunni minority. Retaliating against Sunni bombings and other attacks on Shiite targets, Iraq's Shiite-controlled security forces began rounding up, torturing and executing Sunni men.

"Hundreds of accounts of killings and abductions have emerged in recent weeks, most of them brought forward by Sunni civilians, who claim that their relatives have been taken away by Iraqi men in uniform without warrant or explanation," *New York Times* correspondent Dexter Filkins reported from Baghdad on November 29, 2005. "Some Sunni

---

* The "Atiyah letter," which was discovered by U.S. authorities at the time of Zarqawi's death on June 7, 2006, was translated by the U.S. military's Combating Terrorism Center at West Point.

males have been found dead in ditches and fields, with bullet holes in their temples, acid burns on their skin, and holes in their bodies apparently made by electric drills. Many have simply vanished."[1]

In November 2005, a secret bunker – where Sunni captives were mistreated and apparently tortured – was discovered in an Interior Ministry building in Baghdad. The Shiite-dominated government denied responsibility for the abuses and the murders. But human rights groups and other investigators blamed many of the Sunni killings on the Badr Brigade, an Iranian-backed Shiite militia associated with a leading element of the Iraqi government, the Supreme Council for the Islamic Revolution in Iraq. The Council maintained close ties to the fundamentalist Shiite government of Iran.

U.S. officials acknowledged that hard-line Shiite militiamen, who had penetrated the government's security forces, were operating "death squads" to terrorize Sunnis. The killings and disappearances were reminiscent of the bloodshed in Central America in the 1980s when right-wing regimes in Guatemala and El Salvador unleashed security forces to round up, torture and kill suspected leftists.[2]

◆ ◆ ◆

The drawn-out legal battle that followed the Bush administration's retaliation against former Ambassador Joseph Wilson in 2003 over President Bush's famous "sixteen words" alleging that Iraq sought uranium in Africa reached a head in fall 2005. Special prosecutor Patrick Fitzgerald finally succeeded in forcing many of the reporters who had received administration leaks about Wilson's wife, CIA officer Valerie Plame, to divulge what they knew.

Though Judith Miller of *The New York Times* never wrote about Plame's identity, her conversations with I. Lewis Libby, Vice President Dick Cheney's chief of staff, became central to Fitzgerald proving that Libby lied when he told FBI investigators that he first learned of Plame's identity from NBC's Tim Russert. After 85 days in jail for her refusal to reveal her source, Miller received from Libby what she regarded as an adequate waiver of her pledge of confidentiality.

Even Libby's waiver, however, suggested a conspiratorial relationship between the journalist and her source. Libby's friendly letter read like an invitation to testify but also to stick with the team. "Out West, where you vacation, the aspens will already be turning," Libby wrote. "They turn in clusters, because their roots connect them."

Before the Iraq invasion, Miller had written or co-written five of the six articles that the *Times* singled out as overly credulous of the U.S.

government's point of view in an extraordinary self-criticism. "In some cases, information that was controversial then, and seems questionable now, was insufficiently qualified or allowed to stand unchallenged," the *Times* editor's note said.[3]

On October 28, 2005, after securing the reluctant testimony of Judith Miller, special prosecutor Fitzgerald obtained a five-count indictment of Libby for lying to the FBI, perjury before the grand jury, and obstruction of justice. Fitzgerald opted for a narrow criminal case centered on run-of-the-mill charges rather than daring to run the potential legal gauntlet of the largely untested Intelligence Identities Protection Act of 1982.

That law had been enacted with the goal of punishing CIA enemies, the likes of rogue CIA agent Philip Agee and others who blew the cover of covert agents to sabotage U.S. intelligence activities In writing the law, Congress never anticipated the facts of the Plame case, that senior U.S. government officials would divulge the identity of a covert CIA officer as a way to discredit a spouse in a political dispute.

Despite those unusual circumstances, the law did seem to apply to the facts of the Plame case. Many of the Bush administration participants were aware of Plame's covert status and knew that the U.S. government had classified her identity. Arguably, Fitzgerald could have used the law to build a conspiracy case against some of the top administration officials, including Vice President Cheney, political adviser Karl Rove, Deputy Secretary of State Richard Armitage and conceivably Bush himself.

But Fitzgerald surely would have encountered a ferocious political counterattack, not to mention daunting legal obstacles. For instance, there would be constitutional issues about a President's inherent authority to declassify information and whether that power could be delegated to the Vice President. If Libby, Rove and possibly Armitage were operating under instructions from Cheney or Bush, would that authorization constitute a defense? Could defense lawyers sabotage the case by demanding classified White House documents and then have Bush refuse to release the material? Might legal challenges over these issues tie up the case for years?

During the Iran-Contra scandal of the 1980s, special prosecutor Lawrence Walsh had faced similar problems when former White House aide Oliver North and other defendants identified documents needed for the defense while their old friends in the White House knew that by refusing to declassify the documents they could frustrate and kill the case. Eventually, Walsh was forced to jettison his more ambitious criminal charges related to arms trafficking and money-laundering and focus only on narrower issues, such as North's lying to Congress and accepting an illegal gift.

Rather than follow Walsh's trail – starting out with ambitious charges and then retreating to more mundane ones – Fitzgerald started with the garden-variety crimes of perjury and obstruction, and only indicted Libby. At a post-indictment press conference, Fitzgerald splashed cold water on the notion that his investigation might unravel a larger government conspiracy. However, one of his subsequent court filings asserted that the White House had engaged in a "concerted" effort to "discredit, punish or seek revenge against" Wilson because of his criticism of the administration.

While the White House suffered some political damage from the Libby case, the price exacted from the Wilson-Plame family turned out to be steep. Valerie Plame, who had been sidetracked at the CIA because of her blown identity, gave up her intelligence career, quitting the spy agency on December 9, 2005. (Exactly one month earlier, Judith Miller announced that she had negotiated an agreement to leave the *Times*.)[*]

---

[*] On March 6, 2007, a federal jury in Washington convicted Lewis Libby on four of five perjury and obstruction counts. He was sentenced to 30 months in jail but President Bush commuted the sentence on July 2, 2007, sparing Libby any jail time.

28

Listening In

Over the four years after the 9/11 attacks, a careful analyst could have pieced together scattered clues about George W. Bush's expansive vision of his executive powers: detention without trial of "enemy combatants," coercive techniques to extract information and confessions, the "total information awareness" program to compile detailed dossiers on enemies at home and abroad, assertion of the President's right to wage war with or without congressional approval, the notion that the Commander-in-Chief authority for the "war on terror" knew no limits either in place or time because the endless conflict's battlefield was both in the United States and around the world.

Though partly obscured by secrecy, the outlines of this panorama were visible to the discerning eye, a terrifying image for Americans who believed in a constitutional Republic where citizens possessed inalienable rights and even the highest government officials were subordinate to the rule of law.

But it was not until December 2005 when some of the key details of Bush's vision emerged. Some of this information actually was known by members of the U.S. news media for more than a year but was kept from the American people.

Before Election 2004, *The New York Times* had prepared a story about Bush's secret decision to waive the law on electronic spying within the United States. The President had authorized warrantless wiretaps of hundreds of Americans communicating abroad. But *Times* publisher Arthur Ochs Sulzberger Jr. bent to White House claims that publication would endanger national security. So, the *Times* agreed to withhold the story, even though the disclosure might have affected the outcome of Election 2004. The *Times* chose to keep the American voters in the dark.

More than a year later, the issue reemerged. James Risen, one of the reporters on the spiked story, was publishing a book due out in January 2006 which would reveal Bush's secret decision. The *Times* executives had to decide: would they look worse if they belatedly defied Bush's censorship demand or if they got beat by their own reporter's book on a scoop they had been sitting on? The *Times* editors concluded that they would look worse if Risen's book appeared before their story did.

So, on December 16, 2005, the *Times* published its blockbuster story, which revealed that Bush had been violating the Foreign Intelligence Surveillance Act since shortly after 9/11. He had signed a secret executive order authorizing the National Security Agency to eavesdrop on Americans and others inside the United States without warrants from a special court that the FISA law had established to oversee domestic spying. On Bush's orders, the NSA monitored the international telephone calls and international e-mails of hundreds and possibly thousands of people inside the United States.

Some NSA officials considered the Bush-authorized spying program illegal and refused to participate, according to an ex-Bush administration official. "Before the 2004 election, the official said, some NSA personnel worried that the program might come under scrutiny by congressional or criminal investigators if Senator John Kerry, the Democratic nominee, was elected President," the *Times* reported. "In mid-2004, concerns about the program expressed by national security officials, government lawyers and a judge prompted the Bush administration to suspend elements of the program and revamp it."

But the *Times* article offered few insights into why the newspaper had held the story in 2004 or why it was revived more than a year later. The article simply said, "The White House asked *The New York Times* not to publish this article, arguing that it could jeopardize continuing investigations and alert would-be terrorists that they might be under scrutiny. After meeting with senior administration officials to hear their concerns, the newspaper delayed publication for a year to conduct additional reporting."[1]

The administration's claim about alerting would-be terrorists made little sense, however. Presumably, al-Qaeda terrorists were aware that their communications were vulnerable to intercepts, explaining why the 9/11 attackers were careful to limit telephonic contact with their handlers abroad, often using couriers and face-to-face meetings. Plus, the terrorists would have no way to know whether any electronic eavesdropping they did confront had a warrant or didn't have a warrant. So, it was hard to comprehend how disclosure of the warrantless aspect of the wiretaps made any difference.

Rather, the *Times*' delay had the look of another timid concession from the nation's premier newspaper to the Bush administration. By withholding the wiretap story, the *Times* also had let Bush get away with lying to the voters when he told them that he always obtained warrants for wiretaps. For instance, during a speech in Buffalo, New York, on April 20, 2004, Bush called for renewal of the USA Patriot Act and then veered off into a broader discussion of wiretaps.

"By the way, any time you hear the United States government talking about wiretap, it requires – a wiretap requires a court order," Bush said. "Nothing has changed, by the way. When we're talking about chasing down terrorists, we're talking about getting a court order before we do so." Several months later, the *Times* had evidence that the President was lying but bowed to White House demands that the newspaper keep quiet.

Bush, however, was not appreciative that he got more than a year of silence. On December 17, 2005, the day after the wiretapping story appeared, an angry Bush used his weekly radio address to confirm the story but rip into the *Times* for the disclosure.

"As a result, our enemies have learned information they should not have, and the unauthorized disclosure of this effort damages our national security and puts our citizens at risk," Bush said, though it wasn't clear why that would be true. Still, Bush's rhetoric stoked the right-wing talk shows, which heaped abuse on the *Times* and the "liberal media."

The Bush administration floated another argument: that Bush's order saved time when a quick wiretap was needed, such as when a foreign terrorist was captured and his phone records were seized. But the FISA court could clear warrants in a few hours and almost never said no – or Bush could exercise emergency powers under the law to conduct wiretaps for 72 hours before obtaining approval from the court. So, again, it wasn't clear why Bush's waiver of the law was so vital.

But Bush's assertion of his unilateral right to wiretap anyone he wished did raise questions about whether some eavesdropping might have been aimed at political opponents or journalists, rather than at terrorists. Was Bush nervous that some of the wiretaps were so out of bounds that they might raise the eyebrows of even the compliant FISA court?

In late 2005, there were other disclosures about the Bush administration asserting extraordinary executive power. For instance, it was learned that the Defense Department was moving into domestic spying and law enforcement, seemingly in violation of the Posse Comitatus Act, passed in 1878 to prohibit federal military personnel from acting in a law enforcement capacity within the United States, except where expressly authorized by the Constitution or Congress.

NBC News revealed that the Pentagon had been conducting surveillance of antiwar groups such as the Quakers and campus-based counter-recruitment organizations. A secret 400-page document obtained by NBC listed 1,500 "suspicious incidents" over a 10-month period, including dozens of small antiwar demonstrations that were classified as a "threat." *The Washington Post* also reported that the Defense Department had been expanding its domestic surveillance activities since 9/11, including creating new agencies that gathered and analyzed intelligence within the United States.[2]

The White House moved to broaden the power of the Pentagon's Counterintelligence Field Activity (CIFA), created three years earlier to consolidate counterintelligence operations. The White House sought to transform CIFA into an office that had authority to investigate crimes such as treason, terrorist sabotage or economic espionage. The Pentagon pushed, too, for legislation in Congress that would create an intelligence exception to the Privacy Act, allowing the FBI and others to share information about U.S. citizens with the Pentagon, CIA and other intelligence agencies.

"We are deputizing the military to spy on law-abiding Americans in America," said Senator Ron Wyden, Oregon Democrat. "This is a huge leap without even a [congressional] hearing."

While there were a few voices of protest on Capitol Hill, the Republican-controlled Congress mostly went along, often with substantial Democratic support. In December 2005, Congress essentially overturned the U.S. Supreme Court ruling that guaranteed *habeas corpus* access to U.S. courts for the detainees held in the legal black hole of Guantanamo Bay. Senators Lindsey Graham, a South Carolina Republican, and Carl Levin, a Michigan Democrat, crafted an amendment that barred inmates from having further access to the courts. Human rights groups criticized the measure, noting that it reversed long-standing *habeas* and due-process principles.

The Justice Department promptly filed notice in federal courts that the administration would seek to dismiss 186 pending motions by detainees. Levin protested that his legislation was meant to apply only to future cases, not pending petitions. But it seemed senators once again had placed inordinate faith in the Bush administration's willingness to respect the will of Congress.

◆◆◆

On the Sunday before Christmas 2005, a fidgety George W. Bush interrupted regular programming on U.S. television networks to deliver an address to the nation that painted the Iraq War and the "war on terror" in the same black-and-white colors he always favored. The old canards were still there – Saddam Hussein choosing war by rejecting United Nations weapons inspectors; blurred distinctions between Iraqi insurgents and non-Iraqi terrorists; intimations that Bush's critics were "partisan" while he embodied the national interest. Plus, there was the same old stark choice between success and failure.

"There are only two options before our country – victory or defeat," Bush declared.

Bush also baited his critics ascribing to them ridiculous notions. "If you think the terrorists would become peaceful if only America would stop provoking them, then it might make sense to leave them alone," Bush said describing the purported belief of Americans who opposed him. "Defeatism may have its partisan uses," Bush said, "but it is not justified by the facts."

In the Oval Office speech, Bush broke with the tradition of a President sitting with folded hands; Bush took to waving his hands as he delivered the speech. "Grim-faced, yet with a trace of anxiety in his eyes, Bush delivered the remarks seated rigidly at a desk, making a variety of hand gestures," observed *Washington Post* TV critic Tom Shales.[3]

Some of Bush's strange body language might have been explained by the fact that even he must have realized by the end of 2005 that the nation increasingly doubted his leadership. Indeed, it appeared the American people finally had begun to understand the cost in blood, money and freedoms that Bush's "war on terror" was exacting from them.

Bush also may have grasped that his accretion of power that had progressed mostly under the cover of 9/11 fear and secrecy in the previous four-plus years was finally emerging into the sunlight. Bush and his administration would have to defend more openly their belief that it was time for the nation to surrender its romantic notions about the workings of a democratic Republic; that it was time for an autocrat to lead the country through dangerous times.

As Vice President Cheney told reporters aboard Air Force Two on December 20, 2005, "I do believe that especially in the day and age we live in, the nature of the threats we face, the President of the United States needs to have his constitutional powers unimpaired, if you will, in terms of the conduct of national security policy."[4]

From the mid-1970s and his days as Gerald Ford's White House chief of staff through his years in Congress in the 1980s and his service as Defense Secretary in the early 1990s, Cheney had been a powerful advocate for expansive presidential powers. He gave the reporters on Air Force Two a brief tour of how he saw that history.

"Watergate and a lot of the things around Watergate and Vietnam both during the 70's served, I think, to erode the authority I think the President needs to be effective, especially in the national security area," Cheney said. "Part of the argument in Iran-Contra was whether or not the President had the authority to do what was done in the Reagan years. And those of us in the minority wrote minority views that were actually authored by a guy working for me, one of my staff people,[*] that I think was very good at laying out a robust view of the President's prerogatives with respect to the conduct of especially foreign policy and national security matters."

Cheney also warned Democrats who rejected his assertion of "robust" presidential powers that they could expect to be punished politically. "Either we're serious about fighting the war on terror or we're not," Cheney said.[5]

As the year ended, the choice was becoming clear to many American citizens. Either they must accept the Imperial Presidency and bow to Bush's right to do whatever he wanted in the name of fighting terrorism or they would have to stand up to him.

The battle lines were forming. On one side were the White House legions arrayed with superior organization, extraordinary resources and state-of-the-art media artillery. On the other side were defenders of the democratic Republic, a tattered band armed mostly with a belief that an unrestrained Executive was anathema to all that Americans had fought and bled for since an earlier generation of patriots confronted the forces of King George III on Lexington Green and at Concord Bridge.

◆◆◆

Part of the challenge that Americans faced at the start of 2006 was the cognitive dissonance that came from five years of the President and his team making statements routinely at variance with the truth. Much as a legal system would break down if too many people committed perjury, a democratic political system couldn't function if key leaders lied with abandon, especially if the opposition party and the news media shied away from correcting the record.

For Bush's part, his dysfunctional relationship with the truth seemed to be shaped by two complementary factors – a personal compulsion to say whatever made him look good at that moment and a permissive environment throughout his life that rarely held him accountable for his lies. That pattern was on display again in his New Year's Day comments to reporters in San Antonio, Texas. In that session, as Bush denied misleading the public, he twice again misled the public.

Bush launched into a defense of his honesty by denying that he had lied when he told a crowd in Buffalo, New York, in 2004 that "by the way, any time you hear the United States government talking about

---

[*] Cheney apparently was referring to his counsel David Addington

wiretap, it requires – a wiretap requires a court order." Two years before that statement, Bush had approved rules that freed the National Security Agency to use warrantless wiretaps on communications originating in the United States without a court order. But Bush still told that Buffalo audience, "Nothing has changed, by the way."

On New Year's Day 2006, Bush sought to explain those misleading comments by contending, "I was talking about roving wiretaps, I believe, involved in the Patriot Act. This is different from the NSA program." However, the context of Bush's 2004 statement was clear. He broke away from a discussion of the USA Patriot Act to note "by the way" that "any time" a wiretap is needed a court order must be obtained. He was not confining his remarks to "roving wiretaps" under the Patriot Act.

Bush further misled the public on New Year's Day by insisting that his warrantless wiretaps only involved communications from suspicious individuals abroad who were contacting people in the United States, a policy that would be legal. Bush said the eavesdropping was "limited to calls from outside the United States to calls within the United States."

But Bush's explanation was at odds with what his own administration had previously admitted to journalists – that the wiretaps also covered calls originating in the United States, which should have required warrants from the FISA court. The White House soon "clarified" Bush's remarks to acknowledge that his warrantless wiretaps did, indeed, involve communications originating in the United States.[6]

Other revelations about Bush's secret warrantless wiretaps indicated that the Bush administration had misled *The New York Times* during Campaign 2004 to keep the lid on the wiretapping program. Explaining why the *Times* spiked its exclusive wiretap story for a year, executive editor Bill Keller said U.S. officials "assured senior editors of the *Times* that a variety of legal checks had been imposed that satisfied everyone involved that the program raised no legal questions."

But the Bush administration was concealing an important fact – that a number of senior officials had protested the legality of the operation. In the months after the *Times* agreed to hold the story, the newspaper "developed a fuller picture of the concerns and misgivings that had been expressed during the life of the program," Keller said. "It became clear those questions loomed larger within the government than we had previously understood."

In March 2004, Deputy Attorney General James B. Comey refused to sign a recertification of the wiretap program, the *Times* learned. Comey's objection caused White House chief of staff Andrew Card and Bush's counsel Alberto Gonzales to pay a hospital visit on then-Attorney General John Ashcroft, who was hospitalized for gallbladder surgery. But

Ashcroft also balked at the continuation of the program, which was temporarily suspended while new arrangements were made.[7]

◆◆◆

Even as the Iraq War disaster and the Katrina debacle were eroding American public confidence in President Bush, he was busy putting the final bricks in the wall for the crypt to entomb the old Republic. On January 9, 2006, Nat Parry described this moment in a *Consortiumnews.com* article, which began:

"The U.S. Supreme Court nomination of Samuel Alito may represent a point of no return not only on the issue of abortion and other longtime conservative political targets but on the checks and balances that have been the cornerstone of American democracy. With Alito's confirmation to fill the swing-vote seat of Sandra Day O'Connor, George W. Bush could well consolidate a majority on the high court to endorse his expansive interpretation of presidential authority, including his insistence that his Commander-in-Chief powers are virtually unlimited throughout the indefinite 'war on terror.'"[8]

After the Supreme Court nomination of Bush's White House counsel Harriet Miers failed because of conservative opposition, the President sent up the name of right-wing favorite Alito. The nomination came in the midst of disputes over Bush's warrantless wiretaps of Americans; his use of "extraordinary rendition" of terrorist suspects kidnapped and shipped to countries that practice torture; the CIA's network of secret prisons where people were jailed without charge; the practice of subjecting U.S. detainees to abusive and degrading treatment; and privacy concerns regarding the USA Patriot Act, all of which related to Bush's unprecedented view of presidential power.

"Recent events overlap with some of the beliefs and behavior of Mr. Alito that are of greatest concern," Senator Ted Kennedy, the Massachusetts Democrat, wrote in an e-mail to supporters. "We have a President who unilaterally orders wiretaps on American citizens without judicial oversight – and he has given us a Supreme Court nominee whose record indicates a belief that the Executive Branch operates above the law, including the power to ignore prohibitions on torture."

Alito was not just a run-of-the-mill conservative jurist; he was a leading advocate for the Imperial Presidency. While a legal counsel in the Reagan administration, Alito had promoted the concept of the "unitary executive," which holds that Congress lacks constitutional authority to put law enforcement power in the hands of regulatory agencies, such as the Securities and Exchange Commission, that are not directly accountable to the President. At a Federalist Society symposium in 2001, Alito recalled that when he was in Ronald Reagan's Office of Legal Counsel, "we were strong proponents of the theory of the unitary executive, that all federal executive power is vested by the Constitution in the President."

In 1986, Alito further advanced his theory of expanded presidential power by proposing "interpretive signing statements" from presidents to counter the court's traditional reliance on congressional intent in assessing the meaning of federal law. While other presidents periodically had issued comments about laws at signings, George W. Bush had taken Alito's idea to new heights.

Bush's "signing statements" amounted to rejection of legal restrictions especially as they would bear on presidential powers. In December 2005, for instance, Bush used a signing statement to blunt the impact of a law banning cruel, inhuman and degrading treatment of detainees in U.S. custody. When Bush signed the law, he reserved the right to bypass it under his Commander-in-Chief powers.

"The Executive Branch shall construe [the torture ban] in a manner consistent with the constitutional authority of the President ... as Commander in Chief," the signing statement read. In other words, since Bush considered his Commander-in-Chief authorities boundless, he was asserting his right to waive the torture ban whenever he wanted.

"The signing statement is saying 'I will only comply with this law when I want to, and if something arises in the war on terrorism where I think it's important to torture or engage in cruel, inhuman, and degrading conduct, I have the authority to do so and nothing in this law is going to stop me,'" said New York University law professor David Golove.[9]

◆◆◆

Besides the idea of the "unitary executive," the Alito nomination brought into focus another concept of a President's authority, his "plenary" powers as Commander in Chief. "Plenary" in this context meant "full, absolute, unqualified." Under this theory, the President during a time of war had what amounted to dictatorial powers; at least in relation to fighting a war, the President could do pretty much whatever he wanted.

But, given the vague nature of the "war on terror" – where the battlefield was everywhere and when the conflict would last forever – the President's "plenary" powers would apply endlessly to Americans in their cities and towns as well as to foreigners around the world. So, when Alito testified before the Senate Judiciary Committee that no one, not even the President, is "above the law," that palliative had little meaning since under the "unitary" and "plenary" theories favored by Alito the President *was* the law or, put differently, the law could be overridden whenever the Commander in Chief decided that was needed.

In earlier speeches, Alito even argued that a powerful Executive was what the Founders intended. In a speech in 2000, he said that when the U.S. Constitution was drafted in 1787, the Framers "saw the unitary executive as necessary to balance the huge power of the legislature and the factions that may gain control of it."

Scholars, however, disputed Alito's historical argument, noting that the framers worried most about excessive executive powers, like those of a king, and devised a complex system of checks and balances, putting the Legislature in the preeminent position to limit the President's powers.[10]

Still, whatever the scholars thought would mean little if Bush could build a U.S. Supreme Court majority that would endorse the notion of "unitary" and "plenary" presidential powers. With Alito's nomination, Bush was putting himself with reach of that goal.

Chief Justice John Roberts was a longtime supporter of the "unitary executive." More support for the theory was likely to come from Justice Antonin Scalia, considered the court's leading right-wing thinker. He had been associated with the drive to expand presidential powers since the mid-1970s when he headed President Gerald Ford's Office of Legal Counsel and served as assistant attorney general. Justice Clarence Thomas would appear to be a reliable fourth vote, having cited the theory of the "unitary executive" in arguing in 2004 that the Supreme Court had no right to intervene in granting legal protections to detainees at Guantanamo Bay.

So, that would leave the court's balance on the issue of an all-powerful President up to Justice Anthony Kennedy, a loyal Republican who drafted the opinion in the *Bush v. Gore* case that handed the White House to George W. Bush, but who was considered a less ideological conservative than Scalia, Thomas, Roberts and Alito.

What was happening around Bush's assertion of presidential power and in the Alito nomination was monumental and historic. Every American school child was taught that in the United States, people had "unalienable rights," heralded by the Declaration of Independence and enshrined in the U.S. Constitution and Bill of Rights.

Supposedly, these liberties could never be taken away, but – if one followed the logic of Bush's vision of his own powers – those rights were gone, replaced by what Bush's followers believed were the exigencies of an existential struggle, the endless "war on terror." Americans no longer had the rights that the Founders had recognized as "unalienable." Their rights existed only at George W. Bush's forbearance.

Perhaps because Bush's assertion of power was so extraordinary and so audacious, almost no one dared connect the dots. After a 230-year run, the "unalienable rights" – as enunciated by Thomas Jefferson, James Madison and the other Founders – were history.

The Justice Department spelled out Bush's latest rationale for his new powers in a 42-page legal analysis defending Bush's right to wiretap Americans without a warrant. Bush's lawyers said the congressional authorization to use force against the perpetrators of the 9/11 attacks "places the President at the zenith of his powers" and lets him use that authority domestically as well as overseas.

According to the analysis, the "zenith of his powers" allowed Bush to override both the requirements of the Fourth Amendment, which protects against searches and seizures without court orders, and the 1978 Foreign Intelligence Surveillance Act, which created a special secret court to approve spying warrants inside the United States.[11]

In its legal analysis, the Justice Department added, "The President has made clear that he will exercise all authority available to him, consistent with the Constitution, to protect the people of the United States." While the phrase "consistent with the Constitution" sounded comforting to many Americans, what it meant in this case was that Bush believed he had unlimited powers as Commander in Chief to do whatever he deemed necessary to fight the "war on terror."

For a time, some Americans might have thought that Bush's Commander-in-Chief powers applied only to foreigners linked to al-Qaeda and to the occasional American who collaborated with a foreign terrorist group. So they didn't mind much when Jose Padilla was arrested in Chicago and locked up without charge as an "enemy combatant."

At the end of 2005 and early 2006, however, with the disclosures of warrantless spying, Americans learned that Bush's unlimited powers extended to a much broader category of citizens. By authorizing the National Security Agency to scoop up a large number of calls and e-mails, Bush made the operation so expansive that it not only violated the rights of American citizens but generated a flood of useless tips.

"Virtually all of [the tips], current and former officials say, led to dead ends or innocent Americans," *The New York Times* reported. "FBI officials repeatedly complained to the spy agency that the unfiltered information was swamping investigators. ... Some FBI officials and prosecutors also thought the checks, which sometimes involved interviews by agents, were pointless intrusions on Americans' privacy."[12]

◆◆◆

Bush, meanwhile, was demonstrating how angry America's new "unitary executive" could get when critics of the Iraq War accused him of lying or having ulterior motives. In a speech to the Veterans of Foreign Wars, Bush marked out the parameters for what he regarded as an acceptable Iraq War debate. That, he said, excluded those who "claim that we acted in Iraq because of oil, or because of Israel, or because we misled the American people." On the other hand, Bush said it was permissible to "question the way the war is being prosecuted."

But that safe zone wasn't exactly safe either. People, such as Representative John Murtha, a Pennsylvania Democrat who favored a prompt withdrawal of American troops from Iraq, came under ugly personal attacks from Bush's surrogates. In a smear reminiscent of Campaign 2004 when Republicans mocked Senator John Kerry's war wounds, a right-wing news outlet, Cybercast News Service, publicized accusations that Murtha misrepresented wounds he suffered during combat in Vietnam for which he received two Purple Hearts.

Cybercast, formerly the Conservative News Service, said the criticism of Murtha's war record was justified "because the congressman has really put himself in the forefront of the antiwar movement," said Cybercast editor David Thibault. Cybercast was part of the conservative Media Research Center run by L. Brent Bozell III, a longtime right-wing operative in Washington who has been funded by conservative foundations to denounce journalists as "liberal" and pressure them to write stories more to the liking of conservatives.[13]

Like Campaign 2004 – when Bush balked at specifically repudiating the smears against Kerry's war record – Bush issued no clear guidance to his supporters about the propriety of questioning Murtha's bravery.

In November 2005, Murtha, who was in the Marine Corps for 38 years and fought in both the Korean and Vietnam wars, had called for repositioning U.S. troops outside Iraq. White House spokesman Scott McClellan accused the congressman – long considered one of the most pro-military members of Congress – of advocating "surrender to the terrorists" and associated him with "Michael Moore and the extreme liberal wing of the Democratic Party."

Bush later softened the White House tone by calling Murtha "a fine man." But the President made clear that war critics who continued raising questions outside his parameters could expect to pay a price. "We must remember there is a difference between responsible and irresponsible debate – and it's even more important to conduct this debate responsibly when American troops are risking their lives overseas," Bush said.

On January 11, 2006, in another speech, Bush repeated one of his favorite canards about the Iraq War, that Saddam Hussein brought the war on himself by refusing to let United Nations weapons inspectors search the country. Speaking to a friendly "town hall" audience in Louisville, Kentucky, Bush told a folksy tale.

"I went to the United Nations," he said. "Some of you were probably concerned here in Kentucky that it seemed like the President was spending a little too much time in the United Nations. But I felt it was important to say to the world that this international body, that we want to be effective, spoke loud and clear not once, but 15 odd times to Saddam Hussein – said, 'disarm, get rid of your weapons, don't be the threat that you are, or face serious consequences.'

"That's what the international body said. And my view is, is that in order for the world to be effective, when it says something, it must mean it. We gave the opportunity to Saddam Hussein to open his country up. It was his choice. He chose war, and he got war."

Bush's listeners warmly applauded this fictional account of the run-up to war in Iraq.

◆◆◆

Despite Bush's extraordinary assertion of power, few American politicians were willing to sound the alarm, nor was the national news media giving the story – the end of America's inalienable rights – the front-page treatment that such an historic development would seem to merit. One of the exceptions again was former Vice President Al Gore, who addressed the constitutional issue in a speech on January 16, 2006, the holiday honoring Martin Luther King Jr.

"The American values we hold most dear have been placed at serious risk by the unprecedented claims of the administration to a truly breathtaking expansion of executive power," Gore said in a speech to an enthusiastic crowd at Constitution Hall in Washington. "The Executive Branch of our government has been caught eavesdropping on huge numbers of American citizens and has brazenly declared that it has the unilateral right to continue without regard to the established law enacted by Congress to prevent such abuses. It is imperative that respect for the rule of law be restored. ...

"On this particular Martin Luther King Day, it is especially important to recall that for the last several years of his life, Dr. King was illegally wiretapped – one of hundreds of thousands of Americans whose private communications were intercepted by the U.S. government during this period. The FBI privately called King the 'most dangerous and effective Negro leader in the country' and vowed to 'take him off his pedestal.' The government even attempted to destroy his marriage and blackmail him into committing suicide. This campaign continued until Dr. King's murder.

"The discovery that the FBI conducted a long-running and extensive campaign of secret electronic surveillance designed to infiltrate the inner workings of the Southern Christian Leadership Conference, and to learn the most intimate details of Dr. King's life, helped to convince Congress to enact restrictions on wiretapping. The result was the Foreign Intelligence and Surveillance Act (FISA), which was enacted expressly to ensure that foreign intelligence surveillance would be presented to an impartial judge to verify that there is a sufficient cause for the surveillance. ...

"Yet, just one month ago, Americans awoke to the shocking news that in spite of this long settled law, the Executive Branch has been secretly spying on large numbers of Americans for the last four years and eavesdropping on 'large volumes of telephone calls, e-mail messages, and other Internet traffic inside the United States.' ...

"During the period when this eavesdropping was still secret, the President went out of his way to reassure the American people on more than one occasion that, of course, judicial permission is required for any government spying on American citizens and that, of course, these constitutional safeguards were still in place. But surprisingly, the President's soothing statements turned out to be false. Moreover, as soon as this massive domestic spying program was uncovered by the press, the President not only confirmed that the story was true, but also declared that he has no intention of bringing these wholesale invasions of privacy to an end. ...

"A President who breaks the law is a threat to the very structure of our government. Our Founding Fathers were adamant that they had established a government of laws and not men. Indeed, they recognized that the structure of government they had enshrined in our Constitution – our system of checks and balances – was designed with a central purpose of ensuring that it would govern through the rule of law. As John Adams said: 'The Executive shall never exercise the legislative and judicial powers, or either of them, to the end that it may be a government of laws and not of men.'

"An Executive who arrogates to himself the power to ignore the legitimate legislative directives of the Congress or to act free of the check of the Judiciary becomes the central threat that the Founders sought to nullify in the Constitution – an all-powerful Executive too reminiscent of the King from whom they had broken free."

Gore continued: "The President has also declared that he has a heretofore unrecognized inherent power to seize and imprison any

American citizen that he alone determines to be a threat to our nation, and that, notwithstanding his American citizenship, the person imprisoned has no right to talk with a lawyer – even to argue that the President or his appointees have made a mistake and imprisoned the wrong person. The President claims that he can imprison American citizens indefinitely for the rest of their lives without an arrest warrant, without notifying them about what charges have been filed against them, and without informing their families that they have been imprisoned.

"At the same time, the Executive Branch has claimed a previously unrecognized authority to mistreat prisoners in its custody in ways that plainly constitute torture in a pattern that has now been documented in U.S. facilities located in several countries around the world. Over 100 of these captives have reportedly died while being tortured by Executive Branch interrogators and many more have been broken and humiliated.

"In the notorious Abu Ghraib prison, investigators who documented the pattern of torture estimated that more than 90 percent of the victims were innocent of any charges. This shameful exercise of power overturns a set of principles that our nation has observed since General Washington first enunciated them during our Revolutionary War and has been observed by every President since then – until now. These practices violate the Geneva Conventions and the International Convention Against Torture, not to mention our own laws against torture.

"The President has also claimed that he has the authority to kidnap individuals in foreign countries and deliver them for imprisonment and interrogation on our behalf by autocratic regimes in nations that are infamous for the cruelty of their techniques for torture. Some of our traditional allies have been shocked by these new practices on the part of our nation. The British Ambassador to Uzbekistan – one of those nations with the worst reputations for torture in its prisons – registered a complaint to his home office about the senselessness and cruelty of the new U.S. practice: 'This material is useless – we are selling our souls for dross. It is in fact positively harmful.'

"Can it be true that any President really has such powers under our Constitution? If the answer is 'yes' then under the theory by which these acts are committed, are there any acts that can on their face be prohibited? If the President has the inherent authority to eavesdrop, imprison citizens on his own declaration, kidnap and torture, then what can't he do?"

Gore continued: "Don't misunderstand me: the threat of additional terror strikes is all too real and their concerted efforts to acquire weapons of mass destruction does create a real imperative to exercise the powers of the Executive Branch with swiftness and agility. Moreover, there is in fact an inherent power that is conferred by the Constitution to the

President to take unilateral action to protect the nation from a sudden and immediate threat, but it is simply not possible to precisely define in legalistic terms exactly when that power is appropriate and when it is not. But the existence of that inherent power cannot be used to justify a gross and excessive power grab lasting for years that produces a serious imbalance in the relationship between the Executive and the other two branches of government. ...

"But there is yet another Constitutional player whose pulse must be taken and whose role must be examined in order to understand the dangerous imbalance that has emerged with the efforts by the Executive Branch to dominate our constitutional system. We the people are – collectively – still the key to the survival of America's democracy. We – as Lincoln put it, 'even we here' – must examine our own role as citizens in allowing and not preventing the shocking decay and degradation of our democracy."

Except for citizen Gore, however, few national leaders or news commentators dared to draw the hard conclusions about Bush's authoritarian tendencies.

◆ ◆ ◆

In late January 2006, the Senate Democratic leaders had enough no votes on Samuel Alito – 42 – to sustain a filibuster and force Bush to come up with a more moderate candidate. But the Democratic leaders wanted to avoid a showdown with the President and the Republican majority.

The Republicans had threatened the so-called "nuclear option" – a rule change that would eliminate filibusters altogether and thus let the Senate act with simple majorities. To save the principle of extended debate, a bipartisan group of 14 centrist senators had banded together in an agreement to oppose filibusters on judicial nominees except in "extraordinary circumstances."

The "Group of 14" decided that Alito's Supreme Court nomination did not meet that standard, so a last-minute filibuster mounted by Senator John Kerry was defeated. Many Democrats collaborated in this humiliation of their 2004 standard-bearer even after Republicans mocked him as a "Swiss Miss" for first urging the filibuster while he was attending an economic conference in Davos, Switzerland.

Presidential spokesman Scott McClellan piled on Kerry at a White House press briefing. "I think even for a senator, it takes some pretty serious yodeling to call for a filibuster from a five-star ski resort in the Swiss Alps," McClellan joked.

Kerry and his close ally, Senator Ted Kennedy, didn't help their cause either when they failed to concentrate on Alito's authoritarian theories about presidential power. Instead, Kerry and Kennedy built their anti-Alito argument on what sounded like a checklist of favorite causes from liberal single-issue groups, giving the exercise an appearance of politics as usual.

The threat that Alito represented to constitutional checks and balances – and thus the liberties of all Americans – was treated as an after-thought, even though the only real hope to stop Alito was to convince the American people and senators that his nomination threatened the survival of the Republic.

Kerry mustered 25 votes to support his filibuster, while the Republicans amassed 72 votes for cloture – a dozen more than the 60 needed to shut off debate. Those votes included 19 Democrats who had been freed from party discipline by Senate Minority Leader Harry Reid of Nevada. On the final confirmation vote, however, Alito was approved by a much smaller margin, 58-42, meaning that he could have been kept off the Supreme Court if all those who considered him a poor choice had backed the filibuster.

The Alito capitulation by many Senate Democrats infuriated much of the Democratic "base," which recognized the constitutional stakes of putting another supporter of the "unitary executive" on the Supreme Court. That split was on display again on January 31, 2006, as a triumphant Bush, fresh from his Alito victory, went to Capitol Hill to give his State of the Union Address.

Anti-war protesters rallied outside as Democratic members of Congress assembled indoors. Before Bush arrived, Capitol police arrested Gold Star mother Cindy Sheehan when she sat down in the gallery and removed her coat to show a shirt noting the number of American soldiers, including her son Casey, killed in Iraq. Sheehan was dragged from the gallery after a policeman spotted her shirt reading, "2245 Dead. How Many More?"

Despite the fuss, most Democratic members of Congress joined in giving Bush standing ovations when he read his applause lines. The Democrats did show some spunk by putting up a mock cheer as Bush mentioned his failed plan to partially privative Social Security – and some sat silently when Republicans cheered Bush's plans for more tax cuts.

29

A Last Stand

As a congressional election year, 2006 stood out as a key test both for President George W. Bush and for those who opposed his consolidation of executive power. The stakes amounted to what kind of nation the United States would be: the old Republic with its "unalienable rights," checks and balances and rule of law or a new-age autocratic state organized around security, run by an all-powerful Commander in Chief and ever fearful of some devastating terrorist attack.

Though President Bush insisted that his policies were designed only to protect Americans from terrorists, he continued to build what looked to critics like a framework for an authoritarian system that could take shape quickly in the event of some future emergency or attack. Even as the Democratic "base" grew more determined to resist Bush's vision and as a few Democrats in Congress began to find their voice, the Republican congressional majority stayed firmly behind Bush and his "we'll-do-whatever-is-necessary" formulation.

On February 21, 2006, in a *Consortiumnews.com* article entitled "Bush's Mysterious 'New Programs,'" Nat Parry wrote: "Not that George W. Bush needs much encouragement, but Senator Lindsey Graham suggested to Attorney General Alberto Gonzales a new target for the administration's domestic operations – Fifth Columnists, supposedly disloyal Americans who sympathize and collaborate with the enemy."

"The administration has not only the right, but the duty, in my opinion, to pursue Fifth Column movements," Graham, Republican of South Carolina, said during Senate Judiciary Committee hearings on February 6, 2006.

"I stand by this President's ability, inherent to being Commander in Chief, to find out about Fifth Column movements, and I don't think you need a warrant to do that," Graham added, offering to work with the administration to draft guidelines for how to neutralize this alleged threat.

"Senator," a smiling Gonzales responded, "the President already said we'd be happy to listen to your ideas."

"In less paranoid times," Nat Parry observed, "Graham's comments might be viewed by many Americans as a Republican trying to have it both ways – ingratiating himself to an administration of his own party while seeking some credit from Washington centrists for suggesting Congress should have at least a tiny say in how Bush runs the 'war on terror.'

"But recent developments suggest that the Bush administration may already be contemplating what to do with Americans who are deemed insufficiently loyal or who disseminate information that may be considered helpful to the enemy. Top U.S. officials have cited the need to challenge news that undercuts Bush's actions as a key front in defeating the terrorists, who are aided by 'news informers' in the words of Defense Secretary Donald Rumsfeld.

"Plus, there was that curious development in January when the Army Corps of Engineers awarded Halliburton subsidiary Kellogg Brown & Root a $385 million contract to construct detention centers somewhere in the United States, to deal with 'an emergency influx of immigrants into the U.S., or to support the rapid development of new programs,' KBR said. "[1]

The New York Times reported later that "KBR would build the centers for the Homeland Security Department for an unexpected influx of immigrants, to house people in the event of a natural disaster or for new programs that require additional detention space." Like most news stories on the KBR contract, the *Times* focused on concerns about Halliburton's reputation for bilking U.S. taxpayers by overcharging for sub-par services.

"It's hard to believe that the administration has decided to entrust Halliburton with even more taxpayer dollars," remarked Representative Henry Waxman, a California Democrat, about the giant corporation that Vice President Cheney once ran.[2]

Less attention centered on the phrase "rapid development of new programs" and what kind of programs would require a major expansion of detention centers, each capable of holding 5,000 people. Jamie Zuieback, a spokeswoman for Immigration and Customs Enforcement, declined to elaborate on what these "new programs" might be. Only a few independent journalists, such as Peter Dale Scott and Maureen Farrell, pursued what the Bush administration might actually be thinking.

Scott speculated that the "detention centers could be used to detain American citizens if the Bush administration were to declare martial law." He recalled that during the Reagan administration, National Security Council aide Oliver North organized Rex-84 "readiness exercise," which contemplated the Federal Emergency Management Agency rounding up and detaining 400,000 "refugees," in the event of "uncontrolled population movements" over the Mexican border into the United States.

Farrell pointed out that because "another terror attack is all but certain, it seems far more likely that the centers would be used for post-9/11-type detentions of immigrants rather than a sudden deluge" of immigrants flooding across the border. Vietnam-era whistleblower Daniel Ellsberg said, "Almost certainly this is preparation for a roundup after the next 9/11 for

Mid-Easterners, Muslims and possibly dissenters. They've already done this on a smaller scale, with the 'special registration' detentions of immigrant men from Muslim countries, and with Guantanamo."

The government's list of terrorist suspects also kept swelling. *The Washington Post* reported on February 15, 2006, that the National Counterterrorism Center's central repository held the names of 325,000 terrorist suspects, a four-fold increase since the fall of 2003. Asked whether the names in the repository were collected through the NSA's domestic surveillance program, an NCTC official told the *Post*, "Our database includes names of known and suspected international terrorists provided by all intelligence community organizations, including NSA."

As the administration scooped up more and more names, members of Congress questioned the elasticity of Bush's definitions for words like terrorist "affiliates," used to justify wiretapping Americans allegedly in contact with such people or entities. During the Senate Judiciary Committee's hearing on the wiretap program, Senator Dianne Feinstein, a California Democrat, complained that the House and Senate Intelligence Committees "have not been briefed on the scope and nature of the program." Feinstein added that, therefore, the committees "have not been able to explore what is a link or an affiliate to al-Qaeda or what minimization procedures [for purging the names of innocent people] are in place."

The Defense Department also seemed to be moving toward legitimizing the use of propaganda domestically, as part of its overall war strategy. A secret Pentagon "Information Operations Roadmap," approved by Defense Secretary Rumsfeld in October 2003, called for "full spectrum" information operations and noted that "information intended for foreign audiences, including public diplomacy and PSYOP, increasingly is consumed by our domestic audience and vice-versa. ... PSYOPS messages will often be replayed by the news media for much larger audiences, including the American public."

The Pentagon plan also included a strategy for taking over the Internet and controlling the flow of information, viewing the Web as a potential military adversary. The "roadmap" spoke of "fighting the net," and implied that the Internet was the equivalent of "an enemy weapons system."

In a speech on February 17 to the Council on Foreign Relations, Rumsfeld elaborated on the administration's perception that the battle over information would be a crucial front in the "war on terror," or as Rumsfeld called it, "the Long War."

"Let there be no doubt, the longer it takes to put a strategic communication framework into place, the more we can be certain that the vacuum will be filled by the enemy and by news informers that most assuredly will not paint an accurate picture of what is actually taking place, " Rumsfeld said.

Nat Parry's article concluded, "In such extraordinary circumstances, the American people might legitimately ask exactly what the Bush administration means by the 'rapid development of new programs,' which might require the construction of a new network of detention camps."[3]

◆◆◆

While laying the physical and legal foundations for a potential authoritarian system, the Bush administration pushed the limits, too, on the abuse of language. As Robert Parry wrote at *Consortiumnews.com* on March 3, 2006, "Even Kafka and Orwell, masters at dissecting the cruel absurdities of totalitarian state power, might be at a loss for words in the face of George W. Bush's latest legal and rhetorical formulations on torture.

"Bush, of course, insists that the United States does not torture despite extensive evidence that detainees in the Iraq War and the 'war on terror' have been subjected to simulated drowning by 'water-boarding,' beatings to death, suffocations, coffin-like confinements, painful stress positions, naked exposure to heat and cold, anal rape, sleep deprivation, dog bites, and psychological ploys involving sexual and religious humiliation. But Bush says none of this amounts to torture, even as his protection of abusive practices now ventures beyond word games into mind-bending legal rationalizations.

"Bush's lawyers went into federal court in Washington on March 2 and argued that a new law that specifically prohibits cruel, inhuman and degrading treatment of detainees – known as the McCain Amendment after its sponsor, Senator John McCain – can't be enforced at Guantanamo Bay because another clause of the law grants these prisoners only limited access to U.S. courts.

"In other words, the Bush administration is contending that the McCain Amendment might make it illegal to abuse the Guantanamo prisoners, but that the inmates have no legal recourse to enforce the law by going to court and getting an order for the abuses to end. With the courts removed from the picture, the administration's legal reasoning holds that only Bush can act. He, after all, asserts that he is the nation's 'unitary executive,' meaning that he and he alone decides what U.S. laws to enforce.

"But, in this case, Bush also is the ultimate authority behind the criminal behavior. Bush and his top advisers, such as Defense Secretary Donald Rumsfeld, were the ones who ordered 'the gloves off' in the treatment of prisoners seized in both the worldwide 'war on terror' and the resistance to the U.S. military occupation of Iraq. ...

"In effect, Bush is calling on the Executive Branch, the Congress and the Judiciary to collude in a charade that lets the U.S. government publicly condemn torture and other mistreatment of detainees, but then permits this criminal behavior to continue unabated while barring the victims any legal recourse to justice.

"Bush's legal arguments turn the 'rule of law' inside out, essentially making all branches of the U.S. government complicit in a criminal conspiracy that is perpetuated even as U.S. anti-torture laws are held up as shining examples of the American commitment to humanitarian principles. It's a case that would leave Kafka and Orwell either scratching their heads or contemplating how to incorporate these twisted legal absurdities into a new book."[4]

◆ ◆ ◆

Over the previous five years, President Bush's success in manipulating information would not have been possible without the collaboration and/or incompetence of the major U.S. news media. However, that cozy relationship began to shift in spring 2006 as the bloody war in Iraq dragged on and the U.S. public grew restless over the steady rise in the death toll. Even some of the war's early cheerleaders, like *Washington Post* columnist Richard Cohen, admitted to second thoughts.

"Those of us who once advocated this war [in Iraq] are humbled," Cohen wrote. "It's not just that we grossly underestimated the enemy. We vastly overestimated the Bush administration." Primarily, however, Cohen faulted the President, citing "his embrace of incompetents, not to mention his own incompetence" and the lack of accountability.

"Rummy still runs the Pentagon. The only generals who have been penalized are those who spoke the truth," Cohen wrote. "Victory in Iraq is now three years or so overdue and a bit over budget. Lives have been lost for no good reason – never mind the money – and now Bush suggests that his successor may still have to keep troops in Iraq."[5]

Yet, these tactical retreats by "humbled" pro-war columnists focused on U.S. ineptness in waging the war, not on the illegality, immorality and insanity of invading a major Arab country that wasn't threatening the United States. By failing to expand the criticism of Bush beyond success or failure, the mainstream U.S. news media continued to embrace implicitly Bush's assertion of a special American right to attack wherever and whenever the President says.

It was still out of bounds to discuss how the Iraq invasion violated the Nuremberg principle against aggressive war and the United Nations Charter, which bars attacking another country except in cases of self-defense or with the approval of the U.N. Security Council. To one extent or another, nearly all major U.S. news outlets had bought into the imperial neoconservative vision of an all-powerful United States that operates outside of international law.

That perspective could be found among the loudmouths at Fox News but also in the more tempered columns by Thomas Friedman of *The New York Times*. Despite growing mainstream U.S. doubts about whether the Iraq War was "worth it," there were almost no second thoughts about whether it was a war crime.

Big-name journalists bristled, too, when comedian Stephen Colbert held up a mirror to the media's courtier culture. On April 29, 2006, at the annual White House Correspondents' Association dinner – a time for politicians, journalists and some invited celebrities to dress up in formal wear and rub shoulders – Colbert outraged the gathering with a withering satire of the press corps. As the keynote entertainer, Colbert performed in character as the self-absorbed right-wing acolyte of President Bush that Colbert created for his Comedy Central program, "The Colbert Report," pronounced with silent T's.

Earlier in the evening, the assembled journalists had laughed and applauded at Bush's own comedy routine, which featured a Bush double, Steve Bridges, who voiced Bush's private contempt for the news media while the real Bush expressed his insincere respect. The scene had the look of eager employees laughing at the boss' joke even when they were the butt of it.

Two years earlier, at a similar dinner, journalists had laughed and clapped when Bush put on a slide show of himself searching under Oval Office furniture for Iraq's non-existent weapons of mass destruction. Rather than shock over Bush's tasteless humor – amid the growing carnage in Iraq and the media's own guilt in falling for the WMD deceptions – the press corps played both the part of good straight man and appreciative audience.

But the journalists got their backs up over Colbert. His monologue struck too close to home as he poked fun at the journalists for letting the country down by not asking tough questions before the Iraq War. Colbert explained to the journalists their proper role: "The President makes decisions; he's the decider. The press secretary announces those decisions, and you people of the press type those decisions down.

"Make, announce, type. Put them through a spell check and go home. Get to know your family again. Make love to your wife. Write that novel you got kicking around in your head. You know, the one about the intrepid Washington reporter with the courage to stand up to the administration. You know – fiction."

Many Americans watching the performance at home got the joke, but the journalists in the room mostly acted as if someone had released a foul odor. *The Washington Post*'s Dana Milbank appeared on MSNBC on May 1 to sum up the consensus and pronounce Colbert's spoof "not funny," while praising the President's skit as a humorous hit.

Columnist Richard Cohen weighed in with a similar review on May 4. "Colbert was not just a failure as a comedian but rude," Cohen wrote.

"Rudeness means taking advantage of the other person's sense of decorum or tradition or civility that keeps that other person from striking back or, worse, rising in a huff and leaving. The other night, that person was George W. Bush."

According to Cohen, Colbert was so boorish that he not only criticized Bush's policies to the President's face, but the comedian mocked the Washington journalists who had invited Colbert to be the night's lead entertainer.

"Colbert took a swipe at Bush's Iraq policy, at domestic eavesdropping, and he took a shot at the news corps for purportedly being nothing more than stenographers recording what the Bush White House said," Cohen wrote. "Colbert was more than rude. He was a bully."[6]

Even as the number of U.S. soldiers killed in Iraq passed 2,400 and the toll of Iraqi dead – attributed directly and indirectly to the war – soared possibly into the hundreds of thousands, Cohen and other journalistic insiders were more concerned about Washington decorum. The American people may have once considered the national press corps their watchdogs on the federal government, but the modern U.S. news media mostly had turned into lap dogs wagging their tails, licking the faces of administration officials and hoping for some morsel of reward.

Around the country, however, a whiff of rebellion was in the air. On May 4, in Atlanta, Defense Secretary Rumsfeld spoke before a crowd of international affairs experts and appealed for civility and renewed faith in the President's honesty. But he was greeted with shouts from citizens outraged over government lies.

"You know, that charge [of lying] is frequently leveled against the President for one reason or another, and it's so wrong and so unfair and so destructive of a free system, where people need to trust each other and government," Rumsfeld said.

That position retained broad sympathy within the national press corps, which still held to the view that Bush didn't willfully lie, only was misled by mistaken intelligence. But in Atlanta, Rumsfeld encountered sterner resistance than he had come to expect from the Washington media.

After Rumsfeld bemoaned the harm done by calling Bush a liar, former CIA analyst Ray McGovern rose to ask several pointed questions. "Why did you lie to get us into a war that was not necessary and that has caused these kinds of casualties? Why?" asked McGovern.

"Well, first of all, I – I haven't lied. I did not lie then," Rumsfeld said before falling back on the argument that the problem was simply bad intelligence. "I'm not in the intelligence business. They gave the world their honest opinion. It appears that there were not weapons of mass destruction there."

Persisting in his questions, however, McGovern cited Rumsfeld's earlier certainty about where Iraq's WMD caches were hidden. McGovern also noted the administration's discredited claims that Saddam Hussein's government had ties to al-Qaeda terrorists.

Rumsfeld responded first by falsely denying that he had said what McGovern said he said about the WMD caches. The Defense Secretary then pulled out an old canard that supposedly proved a Hussein-al-Qaeda connection by noting that Jordanian terrorist Abu Musab al-Zarqawi had spent time in Baghdad.

"Zarqawi was in Baghdad during the prewar period," Rumsfeld said. "That is a fact."

Some news coverage of the Atlanta confrontation, such as the clip on NBC's Nightly News, ended with that Rumsfeld statement, leaving his Zarqawi point unchallenged. However, CNN and other news outlets carried a fuller version, in which McGovern put Rumsfeld's claim in context: "Zarqawi? He was in the north of Iraq in a place where Saddam Hussein had no rule. That's also ..."

"He was also in Baghdad," Rumsfeld interjected.

"Yes," McGovern said, "when he needed to go to the hospital. Come on, these people aren't idiots. They know the story."

◆◆◆

As the American public and even some elements of the U.S. news media slowly shook off years of timidity, the Bush administration reminded them that there might be a price to be paid. On May 21, 2006, Attorney General Alberto Gonzales told ABC's "This Week" that news organizations like *The New York Times* could be prosecuted for publishing classified information about the "war on terror," such as the disclosure of Bush's secret program of warrantless wiretapping inside the United States.

"We are engaged now in an investigation about what would be the appropriate course of action in that particular case, so I'm not going to talk about it specifically," Gonzales said. But he cited "some statutes on the book which, if you read the language carefully, would seem to indicate that that is a possibility."

Though Gonzales did not mention a specific statute, he apparently was referring to the Espionage Act, which was passed in 1917 during World War I and barred an unauthorized person from receiving defense information and passing it on to others. The rarely used statute generally has been interpreted as applying to spies for other nations.

Besides the *Times* wiretap story in December 2005, administration officials also complained about a *Washington Post* story on secret overseas CIA prisons where suspected terrorists were allegedly tortured and about a *USA Today* story on a Bush-approved plan to build a vast database of phone calls in the United States.

While some experts doubted the administration would bring Espionage Act charges against journalists, it appeared the Justice Department at least would examine phone records of reporters involved in the stories as part of investigations to identify government leakers. Even if not prosecuted directly, journalists could face jail time if they were hauled before grand juries and refused to identify their sources.

In the ABC-TV interview, Gonzales also made clear that the administration believed government secrecy superceded the First Amendment. "I understand very much the role that the press plays in our society, the protection under the First Amendment we want to promote and respect," Gonzales said, "but it can't be the case that that right trumps over the right that Americans would like to see, the ability of the federal government to go after criminal activity. ... We have an obligation to enforce the law and to prosecute those who engage in criminal activity."

Gonzales's message to government whistleblowers and the press corps was hard to miss. If you disclose misconduct by the Bush administration in areas of national security, you will be hunted down and punished.

◆◆◆

By early summer 2006, George W. Bush found himself on the defensive on another front, when Anthony Kennedy and four other justices on the U.S. Supreme Court rejected a key feature of Bush's imperial presidency. By a narrow majority, the court stopped proceedings by Bush-created military tribunals that had stripped Guantanamo Bay detainees of basic legal protections. In the ruling on June 29, the five justices made clear that they were not prepared to endorse Bush's vision of his "war powers" as limitless and beyond challenge.

But it was equally noteworthy that only five of the nine justices believed that Bush's powers should be constrained by the rule of law and constitutional limits. Four justices – Antonin Scalia, Clarence Thomas, Samuel Alito and John Roberts – made clear that they were prepared to endorse pretty much any judgment that Bush made.

In dissenting opinions on the tribunal case, Scalia, Thomas and Alito embraced legal arguments that bowed before Bush's imperial presidency. Chief Justice Roberts would surely have joined them, except that he had already ruled in Bush's favor in the case while sitting on the U.S. Appeals Court and thus was forced to recuse himself.

The one-vote fragility of the Supreme Court's embrace of constitutional principles over one-man rule was further underscored by the fact that the landmark ruling was written by Justice John Paul Stevens, a decorated World War II veteran who was 86. Another justice, Ruth Bader Ginsburg, was known to have battled health problems.

In the ruling, the Supreme Court majority also rebuffed Bush's long-held contention that the Geneva Conventions did not apply to detainees in the "war on terror." The justices repudiated, too, Bush's tribunal rules that allowed a defendant to be excluded from his own trial and permitted hearsay evidence, unsworn testimony and evidence secured through coercive means.

"The Executive is bound to comply with the rule of law that prevails in this jurisdiction," Stevens wrote in the majority opinion. "The Court's conclusion ultimately rests upon a single ground," added Justice Stephen Breyer. "Congress has not issued the Executive a blank check."

In demanding reasonable legal safeguards for the Guantanamo detainees, the Supreme Court majority asserted that other human beings who share the planet with Bush have rights, too. The Court's ruling meant that Bush would have to go to the Republican-controlled Congress and negotiate new standards to try some of the 450 detainees held at Guantanamo.

◆ ◆ ◆

Despite a few policy setbacks and declining approval ratings, President Bush remained an icon to a large segment of the American population and to many of the major pundits. Especially at moments like the fifth anniversary of 9/11, Bush's supporters recalled him as an almost mythical leader who exuded manly powers and possessed a farsighted vision for saving the world. In one of those paeans to Bush, conservative *New York Times* columnist David Brooks wrote on September 14, 2006:

"A leader's first job is to project authority, and George Bush certainly does that. In a 90-minute interview with a few columnists in the Oval Office on Tuesday, Bush swallowed up the room, crouching forward to energetically make a point or spreading his arms wide to illustrate the scope of his ideas – always projecting confidence and intensity. He opened the session by declaring, 'Let me just first tell you that I've never been more convinced that the decisions I made are the right decisions,' and he grew more self-assured from there.

"I interview politicians for a living, and every time I brush against Bush I'm reminded that this guy is different. There's none of that hunger for approval that is common in the breed. This is the most inner-directed man on the globe. The other striking feature of his conversation is that he possesses an unusual perception of time. Washington, and modern life in general, encourages people to think in the short term. But Bush, who stands aloof, thinks in long durations."

Brooks's example of Bush's visionary quality was the President's assertion that he had gotten into politics because of his "campaign against the instant gratifications of the 1960s counterculture," which helped qualify him "to think about the war on terror as a generations-long struggle."[7]

In his awe-struck account, Brooks made no mention of Bush's own extensive dabbling in "instant gratifications" from his playboy life-style that included evading military service in Vietnam, heavy drinking (at least until his 40th birthday), and illicit drug use (which he implicitly acknowledged during Campaign 2000).

Like other Bush enthusiasts, Brooks also failed to consider the dangers from an autocratic leader who both was "inner-directed" and possessed a messianic view of the world. "Inner-directed" could be defined as impervious to outside criticism, advice or even reality. Many of the history's most dangerous dictators were "inner-directed."

Brooks's only criticism was that Bush didn't act aggressively enough in implementing his visionary programs. "The sad truth is, there has been a gap between Bush's visions and the means his administration has devoted to realize them. And when tactics do not adjust to fit the strategy, then the strategy gets diminished to fit the tactics," Brooks wrote.[8]

◆ ◆ ◆

On September 19, when Bush gave his annual speech to the U.N. General Assembly, his soaring rhetoric about American idealism was back, even though it left many world leaders shaking their heads at the separation between Bush's words and reality. Bush framed his speech in the context of the U.N.'s 1948 Universal Declaration of Human Rights. "The words of the Universal Declaration are as true today as they were when they were written," Bush declared.

But it was hard to believe that Bush had the faintest idea what principles he was embracing – or perhaps he had grown so cocky about his immunity from challenge that he felt he could say anything he wanted, no matter how misleading. Among the 30 rights proclaimed in the Universal Declaration of Human Rights were these:

> Everyone has the right to life, liberty and security of person ... No one shall be subjected to torture or to cruel, inhuman or degrading treatment or punishment. ... Everyone has the right to recognition everywhere as a person before the law... No one shall be subjected to arbitrary arrest, detention or exile. ... Everyone is entitled in full equality to a fair and public hearing by an independent and impartial tribunal, in the determination of his rights and obligations and of any criminal charge against him. ... Everyone charged with a penal offence has the right to be presumed innocent until proved guilty according to law in a public trial at which he has had all the guarantees necessary for his defense. ... No one shall be subjected to arbitrary interference with his privacy, family, home or correspondence. ... Everyone has the right to freedom of opinion and expression; this right includes freedom to hold opinions

without interference and to seek, receive and impart information and ideas through any media and regardless of frontiers.

Though Bush was arguably in violation of many if not all these human rights tenets, he unblushingly cited the Universal Declaration as the foundation for his international policies, from the invasion of Iraq to his handling of the "war on terror." He did so even as he was working with the Republican-controlled Congress to codify his concept of military tribunals that would trample many of the principles he had hailed.

◆◆◆

On October 17, George W. Bush signed legislation that could be read as the obituary for the Republic. On one level, the law gave congressional sanction to a system of tribunals similar to what Bush had sought to create on his own authority before his approach was rejected by a narrow majority of the U.S. Supreme Court. In some ways, however, the cobbled-together congressional version was even more draconian than Bush's original plan and granted the President more power.

At *Consortiumnews.com*, Robert Parry wrote, "History should record October 17, 2006, as the reverse of July 4, 1776. From the noble American ideal of each human being possessing 'unalienable rights' as declared by the Founders 230 years ago amid the ringing of bells in Philadelphia, the United States effectively rescinded that concept on a dreary fall day in Washington. At a crimped ceremony in the East Room of the White House, President George W. Bush signed the Military Commissions Act of 2006 while sitting behind a sign reading 'Protecting America.'

"On the surface, the law sets standards for harsh interrogations, prosecutions and executions of supposed terrorists and other 'unlawful combatants,' including al-Qaeda members who allegedly conspired to murder nearly 3,000 people on September 11, 2001. 'It is a rare occasion when a President can sign a bill he knows will save American lives,' Bush said. 'I have that privilege this morning.'

"But the new law does much more. In effect, it creates a parallel 'star chamber' system of criminal justice for anyone, including an American citizen, who is suspected of engaging in, contributing to or acting in support of violent acts directed against the U.S. government … anywhere on earth.

"The law strips 'unlawful combatants' and their alleged fellow-travelers of the fundamental right of *habeas corpus*, meaning that they can't challenge their imprisonment in civilian courts, at least not until after they are brought before a military tribunal, tried under special secrecy rules and then sentenced. One of the catches, however, is that with *habeas corpus* suspended these suspects have no guarantee of a swift trial and can theoretically be jailed indefinitely at the President's discretion. Given the endless nature of the 'global war on terror,' suspects could disappear forever into the dark hole of unlimited executive authority, their fate hidden even from their families.

"While incarcerated, the 'unlawful combatants' and their cohorts can be subjected to coercive interrogations with their words used against them if and when they are brought to trial as long as a military judge approves. The military tribunals also could use secret evidence to prosecute a wide range of 'disloyal' American citizens as well as anti-American non-citizens."

Robert Parry's article continued, "When Congress was debating the military tribunal law in September, some Americans were reassured to hear that the law would apply only to non-U.S. citizens, such as legal resident aliens and foreigners. Indeed, the law does specify that 'illegal enemy combatants' must be aliens who allegedly have attacked U.S. targets. ...

"But the law goes much further when it addresses what can happen to people alleged to have given aid and comfort to America's enemies. According to the law's language, even American citizens who are accused of helping terrorists can be shunted into the military tribunal system where they could languish indefinitely without constitutional protections."[9]

The language of the law states: "**Any person** is punishable as a principal under this chapter who commits an offense punishable by this chapter, or aids, abets, counsels, commands, or procures its commission. ..... **Any person** subject to this chapter who, **in breach of an allegiance or duty to the United States**, knowingly and intentionally aids an enemy of the United States ... shall be punished **as a military commission ... may direct. ...**

"**Any person** subject to this chapter who with intent or reason to believe that it is to be used to the injury of the United States or to the advantage of a foreign power, collects or attempts to collect information by clandestine means or while acting under false pretenses, for the purpose of conveying such information to an enemy of the United States ... **shall be punished by death or such other punishment as a military commission ... may direct.**" [Emphases added]

In other words, a wide variety of alleged crimes, including some specifically targeted at "any person" with "an allegiance or duty to the United States," would be transferred from civilian courts to military tribunals, where *habeas corpus* and other constitutional rights would, in effect, be suspended or have limited application. While this "allegiance" phrasing would not cover Osama bin Laden, it would seem to drop a legal net over many American citizens.

Once inside the tribunal system, secrecy would dominate these curious trials. Under the new law, a judge "may close to the public all or a portion of the proceedings" if he deems that the evidence must be kept secret for national security reasons. Those concerns could be conveyed to the judge through *ex parte* – or one-sided – communications from the prosecutor or a government representative.

The judge also could exclude the accused from the trial if there were safety concerns or if the defendant were disruptive. Plus, the judge could admit evidence obtained through coercion if he determined it "possesses sufficient probative value" and "the interests of justice would best be served by admission of the statement into evidence."

The law permited, too, the introduction of secret evidence "while protecting from disclosure the sources, methods, or activities by which the United States acquired the evidence if the military judge finds that ... the evidence is reliable." During trial, the prosecutor would have the additional right to assert a "national security privilege" that could stop "the examination of any witness," presumably by the defense if the questioning touched on any sensitive matter.

The prosecution also would retain the right to appeal any adverse ruling by the military judge to the U.S. Court of Appeals in the District of Columbia. For the defense, however, the law states that "no court, justice, or judge shall have jurisdiction to hear or consider any claim or cause of action **whatsoever** ... relating to the prosecution, trial, or judgment of a military commission under this chapter, including challenges to the lawfulness of procedures of military commissions."

By putting detainees, potentially including American citizens outside the U.S. civilian judicial process, the tribunal system made a mockery of the Sixth Amendment in particular. It reads: "In all criminal prosecutions, the accused shall enjoy the right to a speedy and public trial, by an impartial jury of the State and district wherein the crime shall have been committed ... and to be informed of the nature and cause of the accusation; to be confronted with the witnesses against him; [and] to have compulsory process for obtaining witnesses." None of those rights would be countenanced by the military tribunals.

Further, the tribunal law states "no person may invoke the Geneva Conventions or any protocols thereto in any *habeas corpus* or other civil action or proceeding to which the United States, or a current or former officer, employee, member of the Armed Forces, or other agent of the United States is a party as a source of rights in any court of the United States or its States or territories."

In effect, that provision amounted to a broad amnesty for all U.S. officials, including President Bush and other senior executives who may have authorized torture, murder or other violations of human rights. Beyond that amnesty provision, the law granted the President the authority "to interpret the meaning and the application of the Geneva Conventions."

The new law also appeared to put traditional crimes, such as espionage, under the tribunal system. The law states that the U.S. government could jail "any person" who "collects or attempts to collect information by clandestine means or while acting under false pretenses, for the purpose of conveying such information to an enemy of the United States."

Since the Bush administration and its political allies often accused U.S. news organizations of collecting and publishing information, from confidential sources, that was helpful to U.S. enemies – for instance, *The New York Times'* stories about Bush's secret wiretapping program – this provision arguably could apply to American journalists. The "spying" provision not only put alleged offenders into Bush's special legal system but could result in the offenders being sentenced to death.

In signing the Military Commissions Act of 2006, Bush remarked that "one of the terrorists believed to have planned the 9/11 attacks said he hoped the attacks would be the beginning of the end of America." Pausing for dramatic effect, Bush added, "He didn't get his wish."

Or, perhaps, the terrorist did.

◆◆◆

Despite Bush's legislative victories, fall 2006 was not a happy time for the President. More and more Americans were tuning out his appeals to fear about terrorism. The public was beginning to reset its priorities, recognizing other growing threats to the safety of the nation and the world.

As the scientific consensus built around the reality of global warming and its likely disastrous consequences, many American saw Bush's stubborn resistance to the danger as head-in-the-sand stupidity. In effect, the American populace was aligning itself with the views of Al Gore and much of the international community, against President Bush.

Bush found himself more isolated on the Iraq War, too, as the public registered rising discontent over the lack of noticeable progress and the lengthening death toll. Though Americans were divided over what to do next, they surely weren't confident that the Commander in Chief knew best.

As Bush hit the political hustings to stump for Republican congressional candidates he acted with a growing desperation, frantic to reconnect with his once adoring public. He behaved like a spurned lover determined to win back an old flame by repeating the same lines that once had worked, but now failed to do the trick, though uttered more loudly and with extra arm-waving.

The magic was gone. On Election Day 2006, the voters threw out the Republican majorities in the House and Senate, albeit by relatively narrow margins. In the Senate, the Democrats held the majority by a single vote, dependent on two Independents, leftist Bernie Sanders of Vermont and neoconservative icon Joseph Lieberman of Connecticut.

Though it appeared Bush's political wave finally had crested, it was still unclear how far the new Democratic majorities could or would go in reversing Bush's policies, whether in Iraq, the "war on terror," the environment, tax cuts, budget deficits, and perhaps most importantly, the notion of an all-powerful President.

Conclusion:

End of the Republic?

The audacity and devastation of the 9/11 attacks shook the American psyche, provoking anger and instilling fear, mixing some reasonable concerns for safety with an irrationality that often made matters worse. While some retaliation – not to mention revenge – was justified, how the U.S. government settled on the scope and the targets of the reprisals could have varied widely. If the United States had a different set of leaders at the time – and assuming the attacks were still not averted – the nation's response would surely have had similarities to what was done but also many differences.

As it turned out, the interests of the neoconservatives who surrounded George W. Bush meshed with the political opportunities that the anger and fear from 9/11 laid open. So, instead of finishing off Osama bin Laden and al-Qaeda, the government's focus strayed to other alleged threats that had nothing to do with 9/11, even to bin Laden's enemies, such as the leaders of Iraq and Iran.

A frightened American public was unable to make the necessary distinctions, especially in the face of widespread disinformation from the Bush administration and its media allies – and additionally given the failure of the mainstream American press corps and the Democratic opposition to ask tough questions and demand real answers.

Bush also convinced many Americans that the U.S. government had no greater responsibility than protecting them from danger, even if that required the people surrendering some of their liberties. This assertion played well with self-absorbed Americans who saw their personal safety, comfort and convenience as preeminent. Sacrificing some civil rights seemed like a trivial price to pay in the face of the 9/11 tragedy and the President's warnings of worse dangers ahead.

But the idea that there was no more important task for the U.S. government than physically protecting Americans represented an historic divergence from the nation's traditions and principles. Indeed, time and time again, previous generations of Americans had traded safety for liberty. From the Lexington Green to the Normandy beaches, from the Sons of Liberty to the Freedom Riders, it had been part of the American narrative that risks were taken to expand freedom, not freedoms sacrificed to avoid risk.

The Founders challenged the most powerful military on earth, the British army, all the while knowing that defeat would send them to the gallows. The American colonists spurned their relative comfort as British subjects for a chance to be citizens of a Republic dedicated to the vision that some rights are "unalienable" and that no man should be king. Since then, despite some ups and downs, the course of the American nation has been to advance those ideals and broaden those freedoms.

In the early years of the Republic, African-American slaves resisted their bondage, often aided by white Abolitionists who defied unjust laws on runaways and pressed the government to restrict slave states and ultimately to eliminate slavery. With the Civil War and Abraham Lincoln's emancipation of the slaves, the United States underwent a painful rebirth that reaffirmed the nation's original commitment to the principle that "all men are created equal." Again, the cause of freedom trumped safety, a choice for which Lincoln and tens of thousands of brave soldiers gave their lives.

In the latter half of the 19th century and into the 20th, the Suffragettes demanded and fought for extension of basic American rights to female citizens. These women risked their reputations and their personal security to gain the right to vote and other legal guarantees for women. When fascist totalitarianism threatened the world in the 1930s and 1940s, American soldiers turned back the tide of repression in Europe and Asia, laying down their lives in battlefields from Normandy to Iwo Jima.

The march of freedom continued in the United States in the 1950s and 1960s, as the Rev. Martin Luther King Jr. and other civil rights fighters – both black and white – risked and sometimes lost their lives to tear down the walls of racial segregation. For two centuries, the expansion of freedom came with dangers and sacrifices. Yet, despite temporary reversals – the Cold War's McCarthy era, for example – the trend has been to expand liberty even when that meant taking on risks.

Only in this generation has the march taken what could become a permanent reversal, with the Executive claiming unlimited powers for what looks like an endless war. Instead of swapping safety for liberty, many Americans – traumatized by the 9/11 attacks and under the leadership of George W. Bush – have chosen to trade liberties for safety. Instead of Patrick Henry's stirring Revolutionary War cry of "give me liberty or give me death," this era has Senator Pat Roberts's instant-classic expression of self over nation. "You have no civil liberties if you are dead," the Kansas Republican said.

Roberts's dictum echoed through the U.S. media where it was embraced as a pithy expression of homespun common sense. But the commentators missed how Roberts's preference for life over liberty was the antithesis of Henry's option of liberty or death.

Roberts's statement also represented a betrayal of two centuries of bravery by American patriots who gave their own lives so others could be free. After all, it would follow logically that if "you have no civil liberties if you are dead," then all those Americans who died for liberty were basically fools. Roberts's adage reflected a self-centeredness, which would shame the millions of Americans who came before and who put principle and the "interests of posterity" ahead of themselves.

If Roberts were right, the Minutemen who died at Lexington Green and at Bunker Hill had no liberty; the African-Americans who enlisted in the Union Army and died in Civil War battles had no liberty; the GIs who died on the Normandy beaches or the Marines who died at Iwo Jima had no liberty; Martin Luther King Jr. and other civil rights heroes who gave their lives had no liberty.

If Senator Roberts were right, they had no liberties because they died in the fight for liberty. In Roberts's view – which apparently represented the dominant opinion of the Bush administration and many of its supporters – personal safety for the individual topped the principles of freedom for mankind.

This security-over-everything notion emerged as the key justification for stripping the American people of what the Founders called their "unalienable rights," liberties that were promised them in the Declaration of Independence and enshrined in the Constitution and the Bill of Rights. In this era, however, the American people were told that the President could exercise "plenary" – or unlimited – powers as long as the indefinite "war on terror" continued.

In claiming these "plenary" powers as Commander in Chief and arguing that the United States was part of the battlefield, Bush asserted that all rights were his. Bush and his successors would get to decide which rights the American people still had and which ones had been taken from them. Like before the Declaration of Independence, the American people found themselves as "subjects" reliant for their rights on the generosity of a leader, rather than "citizens" possessing rights that couldn't be denied.

As a tradeoff for accepting Bush's unlimited powers, Bush told the American people that he would make them a little safer and that there was no higher priority for a U.S. government official than protecting them from danger. However, the oath for Presidents and other federal officers says nothing about shielding the public from danger; rather it's a vow to "preserve, protect, and defend the Constitution of the United States."

Since George Washington first took the oath, it has been the Constitution that was paramount, because it guaranteed the liberties that defined America. Within that presidential oath and the nation's historic commitment to freedom, there was no assurance against risk or danger.

Indeed, it has been assumed by previous generations of Americans –
dating back to the beginning of the Republic – that risk and danger were part
of the price for maintaining and expanding freedom. The choice that faces
this generation of Americans is whether that tradition will be maintained or
abandoned. President Bush has favored putting the goal of safety ahead of
liberty, but public resistance to this tradeoff has continued to mount, with
more and more Americans voicing their preference for the historic American
vision that makes freedom the foremost priority.

◆ ◆ ◆

Yet, besides the swap of liberty for safety, there was the question of whether
Bush's policies had actually made Americans safer. By late 2006, more than
3,000 American soldiers had died in the Iraq War, along with Iraqi dead
attributed to the war estimated at possibly half a million, and many more
victims were horribly maimed.

With the Iraq War showing no signs of ending, anti-Americanism only
grew more and more widespread around the globe and especially in the
Islamic world. U.S. intelligence agencies discovered that al-Qaeda appeared
to be on the rebound, flush with thousands of new recruits and again plotting
spectacular terrorist attacks. Except in the propaganda bubble that
surrounded President Bush and among his shrinking cult of followers, there
was a sense that something had gone terribly wrong in America.

Yet, the truth was that while Bush and his cohorts might deserve the
bulk of the blame, the problem was bigger than those individuals. The crisis
could be traced to a systemic failure in Washington, with fault reaching from
the White House to congressional Republicans and Democrats, from an
insular national news media to Inside-the-Beltway think tanks and pundits.

The Bush administration could get away with its excesses after 9/11
because of conditions that had been building for more than a quarter century,
a collision of mutually reinforcing political elements. This perfect storm
included aggressive Republicans, triangulating Democrats, careerist
journalists, bullying cable-TV and talk-radio personalities, hard-hitting and
well-funded think tanks on the Right versus ineffectual and marginalized
groups on the Left.

This combination of forces had allowed the "tough-guy-ism" of
Washington's armchair Rambos to become the capital's controlling ideology,
a dominance that was reinforced by the national trauma from the 9/11 terror
attacks when many Americans were desperate for a protector.

In a way, the resulting Iraq War and the excesses of the "war on terror"
emerged from a *macho* parlor game of one-upmanship gone mad, with very
few in political and media circles daring to stop it and run the risk of being
called unmanly or "un-American." The few who tried to say no lost their
standing in the Washington community and, in some cases, lost their jobs

and livelihoods. For the majority who stayed to play the game, there seemed to be endless rewards of status, money and power.

For the politicians, the think-tankers and the opinion leaders who pushed the Iraq invasion, the war was a win-win-win. Not only did they enhance their standing and influence, they had the vicarious thrill of dispatching armies into battle. Plus, under the cover of national security secrecy, their friends and business associates lined up for the gravy train of war profits. There was the chance to buy up oil fields, too. While cashing in politically and financially, most insiders knew that the human price of this lucrative game of *macho* would be paid by other people's children and the dollar costs would be passed to future generations.

Even though many in Washington understood the grave risks behind Bush's invasion, it made more sense for them to join the pro-war herd. That was true of journalists as well as politicians and pundits. Even if the invasion of Iraq went badly, there would be very little danger of career-threatening recriminations because too many important people were in the same position. The worst that might happen would be the need to issue a muted *mea culpa* a few years later while shifting the blame onto someone – say, Donald Rumsfeld – for his incompetent execution of the plan.

By contrast, there was a serious personal risk if you stood up to Bush's pro-war juggernaut in 2002-2003. You'd get called ugly names; your career would suffer; you'd be treated like a pariah. Just ask the Dixie Chicks, former weapons inspector Scott Ritter and Al Gore.

Though fear of ostracism didn't compare with the dangers faced by the troops at war, it was noteworthy how few Washington insiders dared ask the tough questions – and how few of those who helped mislead the nation paid any serious price. Even the most notorious Iraq War screw-ups – former CIA Director George Tenet, Gen. Tommy Franks and pro-consul Paul Bremer – got Medals of Freedom, the highest civilian honor that can be bestowed by the President.

Most pink slips went to officials who were not sufficiently enthusiastic about the Iraq War, from early skeptics like Treasury Secretary Paul O'Neill to later doubters like Secretary of State Colin Powell. Whatever the later excuses from the Democrats who supported Bush's war resolution, the most powerful motive behind their decision was the consultant-driven advice that a yes vote was the safest political choice. A no vote was viewed by many Democratic consultants as political suicide for their clients.

If anything, the national news media experienced even less accountability for running with the pro-Bush herd. With the exception of *New York Times* reporter Judith Miller whose career imploded over her WMD credulity and *Washington Post* columnist Michael Kelly who died in a vehicle accident in Iraq, the disastrous Iraq War caused little shake-up in the line-up of national pundits and top journalists.

One could even argue that the wrongheaded Washington columnists and editors were more deeply entrenched in 2007 than they were when the invasion was launched on March 19, 2003. The revised "smart" position on Iraq was to have supported the invasion but then complain about poor follow-through. Indeed, in the up-is-down world of Washington, it was considered an act of courage to have been part of the pro-war herd; conformity was independence; limited second thoughts about the war became a sign of wisdom.

The national news media also underwent very little structural change in those years. The Right continued to pour hundreds of millions – even billions – of dollars into building media outlets and creating pro-Bush content, from print to radio to TV to the Internet. The investment gave the Right a huge advantage in defining issues and setting the agenda.

Meanwhile, American liberals and progressives still resisted making anything close to that kind of commitment in terms of a countervailing media infrastructure. In 2006, one of the few liberal broadcast initiatives, Air America Radio, sought protection under the bankruptcy laws although it later emerged under new management. Progressive Internet sites mostly had to fend for themselves.

Yet what made sense for Washington insiders didn't match up with what was best for the broader American public and especially military families. For those who were sent to war and for their families, the balance sheet was different. They suffered the casualties, the uncertainty, the heartbreak.

But these two groups – the war's architects and its enablers on one side and the troops and their families on the other – rarely crossed paths, representing two disparate social classes. While American soldiers and their loved ones worried about actual death, what mattered most in Washington was political and career self-preservation.

By spring 2007, however, a change could be detected in public awareness of the national crisis. Perhaps the most hopeful sign was that many Americans had come to understand how little the Washington insiders – whether in political office or in the news media – deserved to be trusted. That skepticism, if it were ever combined with serious demands for reform, could be the start of a rebirth for the American Republic.

NOTES

Introduction

[1] See Dan Gilgoff, "The Yale Men," *U.S. News & World Report* (December 21, 2003)

Chapter One

[1] *The Washington Post* (November 2, 1998)
[2] Ibid.

Chapter Two

[3] See Kevin Phillips, *American Dynasty: Aristocracy, Fortune, and the Politics of Deceit* (New York: Penguin Group, 2004), pp. 21-23
[4] See Kitty Kelley, *The Family: The Real Story of the Bush Dynasty* (New York: Random House, 2004), pp. 17-19
[5] Associated Press (May 9, 2006)
[6] Phillips, *American Dynasty*, pp. 24-25
[7] Phillips, *American Dynasty*, p. 39
[8] Ibid.
[9] See Sam Parry, "The Bush Family Oil-igarchy, " *Consortiumnews.com* (Aug. 14, 2000)
[10] See Herbert S. Parmet, *George Bush: The Life of a Lone Star Yankee* (New Brunswick: Transaction Publishers, 2001), p. 82
[11] Ibid., p. 83
[12] Ibid., p. 85
[13] Ibid.
[14] For details, see Robert Parry's *Secrecy & Privilege*
[15] See *The New York Times* (July 11, 2000)
[16] Associated Press (July 5, 1999)
[17] See *The Dallas Morning News* (September 28, 1999); *The Washington Post* (September 21, 1999)
[18] See *The Boston Globe* (May 23, 2000)
[19] Reuters (September 29, 2004)
[20] See Bill Minutaglio, *First Son: George W. Bush and the Bush Family Dynasty* (New York: Three Rivers Press, 1999), pp. 147-8
[21] See *The Washington Post* (July 30, 1999) and *Harper's Magazine*'s "The George W. Bush Success Story: A heartwarming tale about baseball, $1.7 billion, and a lot of swell friends," Joe Conason (February 2000)

[22] *The Washington Post* (July 30, 1999)

[23] *The Washington Post* (July 30, 1999)

[24] *The Washington Post* (July 30, 1999)

[25] *The Washington Post* (July 30, 1999)

[26] See *Harper's Magazine* (February 2000)

[27] *The Washington Post* (July 30, 1999)

[28] *Harper's Magazine* (February 2000)

[29] *The Washington Post* (July 30, 1999)

[30] *Harper's Magazine* (February 2000)

[31] *Harper's Magazine* (February 2000)

[32] See *The Wall Street Journal* (December 6, 1991)

[33] *Harper's Magazine* (February 2000)

[34] *Harper's Magazine* (February 2000)

[35] See Sam Parry, "Bush's Life of Deception," *Consortiumnews.com* (November 4, 2002)

[36] See *The Boston Globe* (October 30, 2002) and *The Washington Post* (November 1, 2002)

[37] Sam Parry, "Bush's Life of Deception," *Consortiumnews.com* (November 4, 2002)

[38] Minutaglio, *First Son*, p. 322

[39] Minutaglio, *First Son*, p. 216

[40] *GQ* (September 2003)

[41] Minutaglio, *First Son*, p. 217

[42] See Ken Silverstein, "The Polluters' President," *Sierra Magazine* (November/December 1999)

[43] Ibid.

[44] Associated Press (April 3, 2000)

[45] Ken Silverstein, "The Polluters' President," *Sierra Magazine* (November/December 1999)

[46] *Austin Chronicle* (June 1, 1999)

[47] Ken Silverstein, "The Polluters' President," *Sierra Magazine* (November/December 1999)

[48] See Richard A. Fineberg, "'Shocking?' Evidence Mounts from Alaska and Elsewhere that BP's Inadequate North Slope Performance Should Have Been No Surprise to Public Officials or Monitors," Alaska Forum for Environmental Responsibility (September 3, 2006)

[49] See <http://www.veco.com/Locations/default.asp>

[50] See *The Austin Chronicle* (March 17, 2000)

[51] See Cox News (May 10, 2000)

[52] See *The Boston Globe* (October 3, 1999)

[53] EPA TRI data, 1997

[54] Associated Press (April 3, 2000)

[55] Center for Public Integrity, "George W. Bush: Top 25 Career Patrons," *The Buying of the President 2000*

Chapter Three

[1] Associated Press (October 26, 1999)

[2] See *The New York Times* (July 24, 1999)

[3] *Report of the Congressional Committees Investigating the Iran-Contra Affair* (November 1987), p. 437

[4] Associated Press (July 26, 2000)

[5] See Halliburton's Annual Report (March 2000)

[6] See Halliburton's filings with the Securities and Exchange Commission

[7] Associated Press (July 26, 2000)

[8] See *The New York Times* (August 12, 2000)

[9] See The New York Times (August 19, 2000)

[10] See Jim Motavalli, "Scorched Earth Policy," *E Magazine* (May-June, 2001)

[11] Associated Press (September 28, 2000)

[12] See Department of Energy, "Long Term World Oil Supply," www.eia.doe.gov

Chapter Four

[1] See *The Washington Post* (December 1, 1999)

[2] *Hardball*, CNBC (December 1, 1999)

[3] See *The Washington Post* (December 2, 1999)

[4] Associated Press (December 14, 1999)

[5] See *The Boston Globe* (December 26, 1999)

[6] Associated Press (December 14, 1999)

[7] *Lancaster New Era* (December 9, 1999)

[8] See *The Milwaukee Journal Sentinel* (December 12, 1999)

[9] See *National Journal* (December 18, 1999)

[10] See *The Providence Journal* (December 23, 1999)

[11] *The Washington Times* (January 7, 2000)

[12] *The New York Times* (December 14, 1997)

[13] *The Boston Herald,* (December 5, 1999)

[14] Associated Press (March 11, 1999)

[15] See *The Daily Howler* (December 14, 1999)

[16] *The Daily Howler* (January 13, 2000)

Chapter Five

[1] *Bloomberg News* (October 6, 2000)

[2] See Sam Parry, "Protecting Bush-Cheney," *Consortiumnews.com* (Oct. 16, 2000)

[3] NPR's Morning Edition, (October 11, 2000)

[4] Sierra Club, "Bush Debate Environmental Fiction Vs. Facts," Press Release (October 12, 2000)

[5] Ibid.

[6] NBC News (October 6, 2000)

[7] New Democracy Project, http://www.newdemocracyproject.org/publications/info_manip_ii.cfm

[8] *The New York Times* (October 15, 2000)

[9] *The New York Times* (October 27, 2000)

[10] *The Washington Post* (October 19, 2000)

[11] See Oliver L. North and William Novak, *Under Fire: An American Story* (New York: HarperPaperbacks, 1991), p. 306
[12] *The New York Times* (February 4-5, 2001)
[13] Ibid.
[14] Ibid.
[15] Ibid.
[16] Ibid.
[17] *The New York Times* (September 7, 1999)
[18] *The New York Times* (October 27, 2000)

Chapter Six

[1] See *The New York Daily News* (November 1, 2000)
[2] *The New York Daily News* (November 1, 2000)
[3] *The New York Daily News* (November 1, 2000)
[4] *The New York Daily News* (November 1, 2000)
[5] See *The Boston Herald* (November 3, 2000)
[6] *The Boston Herald* (November 3, 2000)
[7] John Ellis, Inside.com via Associated Press (December 12, 2000)
[8] Ibid.
[9] Ibid.
[10] Ibid.
[11] The National Archives historic vote tallies
[12] National Archives, election records
[13] See *The New York Times* (November 21, 2000)
[14] *The New York Times* (November 21, 2000)
[15] *The New York Times* (November 24 2000)
[16] See Jake Tapper, *Down and Dirty: The Plot to Steal the Presidency* (New York: Little, Brown and Company, 2001), p. 264
[17] Tapper, *Down and Dirty*, p. 265
[18] Tapper, *Down and Dirty*, p. 266
[19] See *The Washington Post* (November 27, 2000)
[20] See *The Wall Street Journal* (November 27, 2000)
[21] Ibid.
[22] Ibid.
[23] Tapper, *Down and Dirty*, p. 260
[24] *The Wall Street Journal* (November 27, 2000)
[25] See *The Miami Herald* (July 14, 2002)
[26] See *The Washington Post* (November 24, 2000)

Chapter Seven

[1] See *The New York Times* (December 5, 2000)
[2] See *The Orlando Sentinel* (November 12, 2001)
[3] See Robert Parry, "A Dark Cloud," Consortiumnews.com (December 10, 2000)
[4] See Mollie Dickenson, "Supreme Court Intrigue," *Consortiumnews.com* (December 11, 2000)

[5] See Mollie Dickenson, "Supreme Ambitions," *Consortiumnews.com* (January 7, 2001)

[6] See *USA Today* (January 22, 2001)

[7] Ibid.

[8] Ibid.

[9] Ibid.

[10] See *The Washington Post* (January 19, 2001)

Chapter Eight

[1] Iran-Contra Depositions, Appendix B, Vol. 27, p. 45

[2] See John Dinges, *Our Man in Panama: How General Noriega Used the United States – and Made Millions in Drugs and Arms* (New York: Random House, 1990), p. 161

[3] Iran-Contra Depositions, Appendix B, Vol. 21, p. 228

[4] Iran-Contra Depositions, Appendix B, Vol. 21, pp. 229-230

[5] Iran-Contra Depositions, Appendix B, Vol. 21, p. 241

[6] Iran-Contra Depositions, Appendix B, Vol. 21, p. 273

[7] Iran-Contra Depositions, Appendix B, Vol. 27, p. 22

[8] Iran-Contra Depositions, Appendix B, Vol. 27, pp. 652-653

[9] Iran-Contra Depositions, Appendix B, Vol. 25, p. 557

[10] Iran-Contra Depositions, Appendix B, Vol. 25, pp. 564-565

[11] Iran-Contra Depositions, Appendix B, Vol. 24, p. 82

[12] Iran-Contra Depositions, Appendix B, Vol. 2, p. 1093

[13] Iran-Contra Depositions, Appendix B, Vol. 16, p. 568

[14] Iran-Contra Depositions, Appendix B, Vol. 16, p. 582

[15] Iran-Contra Depositions, Appendix B, Vol. 16, p. 585

[16] Iran-Contra Depositions, Vol. 11

[17] Iran-Contra Depositions, Appendix B, Vol. 2, p. 721

[18] Ibid., p. 102

[19] Ibid., p. 168

[20] Ibid.

[21] Ibid., p. 171

[22] See Bob Woodward, *Shadow: Five Presidents and the Legacy of Watergate* (New York: Simon & Schuster, 1999), p. 186

[23] See H. Norman Schwarzkopf and Peter Petre, *It Doesn't Take a Hero: The Autobiography* (New York: Bantam Books, 1992), p. 514

[24] Ibid., pp. 511-512

[25] Woodward, *Shadow*, p. 186

[26] *The Washington Post* (February 25, 1991)

[27] See George Bush [Sr.] and Brent Scowcroft "Why We Didn't Remove Saddam," *Time* (March 2, 1998)

[28] See *Time* (March 13, 1995)

[29] See *Time* (August 28, 1995)

[30] *The Washington Post* (September 13, 1995)

[31] See *Rolling Stone* (November 16, 1995)

[32] See *The New Republic* (April 17, 1995)

[33] *The Washington Post* (April 10, 1995)

[34] *The New York Times* (November 9, 1995)

[35] *The New York Times* (November 10, 1995)

[36] *The New York Times* (November 11, 1995)

Chapter Nine

[1] *The Washington Post* (February 25, 2001)

[2] *The Wall Street Journal* (April 10, 2001)

[3] *The New York Times* (April 4, 2001)

[4] *The Seattle Post-Intelligencer* (March 28, 2001)

[5] *The Washington Post* (March 25, 2001)

[6] *The New York Times* (April 1, 2001)

[7] *The Washington Post* (March 31, 2001)

[8] *The Washington Post* (April 24, 2001)

[9] See Ron Suskind, *The Price of Loyalty: George W. Bush, the White House, and the Education of Paul O'Neill* (New York: Simon & Schuster, 2004), p. 71

[10] Ibid., p. 72

[11] Ibid., p. 96

[12] See *The New Yorker* (February 16, 2004)

[13] *The New York Times* (May 3, 2001)

[14] See *Energy Daily* (May 16, 2002)

[15] *The Washington Post* (May 7, 2002)

[16] *The Washington Post* (January 26, 2002)

[17] *The New York Times* (May 25, 2001)

[18] *The San Francisco Chronicle* (January 30, 2002)

[19] *The Los Angeles Times* (April 19, 2001)

[20] *The Los Angeles Times* (May 30, 2001)

[21] *The Los Angeles Times* (June 19, 2001)

[22] *The New York Times* (May 9, 2002)

[23] Associated Press, (January 31, 2002)

Chapter Ten

[1] *The Washington Post* (June 8, 2001)

[2] Ibid.

[3] Ibid.

[4] *The Washington Post* (May 31 and June 1, 2001)

[5] *The Los Angeles Times* (May 21, 2001)

[6] *The Los Angeles Times* (May 21, 2001)

[7] *The Washington Post* (July 5, 2001)

[8] *The Los Angeles Times* (July 5, 2001)

[9] *The Wall Street Journal* (June 25, 2001)

[10] See *The 9/11 Commission Report: Final Report of the National Commission on Terrorist Attacks Upon the United States* (New York: W.W. Norton & Company), pp. 58-59

[11] Ibid., pp. 62-63

[12] "Jihad Against Jews and Crusaders," World Islamic Front Statement, 23 February 1998, http://www.fas.org/irp/world/para/docs/980223-fatwa.htm

[13] *The 9/11 Commission Report*, pp. 69-70

[14] Ibid., pp. 116-117

[15] Associated Press (April 18, 2002)

[16] Ibid.

[17] *The 9/11 Commission Report*, pp. 177-179

[18] Ibid., p. 190

[19] Ibid., p. 191

[20] Ibid.

[21] See Harold Evans, "What We Knew: Warning Given...Story Missed," *Columbia Journalism Review* (November/December, 2001)

[22] Ibid.

[23] See Lawrence Wright, "The Counter-Terrorist," *The New Yorker* (January 14, 2002)

[24] *The Washington Post* (May 17, 2002)

[25] See George Tenet, *At the Center of the Storm: My Years at the CIA* (New York: HarperCollins Publishers, 2007) p. 151-158

[26] CNN (July 10, 2001)

[27] *The 9/11 Commission Report*, p. 259

[28] Ibid., p. 260

[29] Ibid., p. 262

[30] See Ron Suskind, *The One Percent Doctrine: Deep Inside America's Pursuit of Its Enemies Since 9/11* (New York: Simon & Schuster, 2006), p. 2

[31] CNN's "Larry King Live" (March 24, 2004)

[32] Tenet, *At the Center of the Storm*, p. 159

Chapter Eleven

[1] *The New York Times* (September 16, 2001)

[2] Ibid.

[3] Ibid.

[4] *The New York Times* (September 22, 2001)

[5] See Ron Suskind, "Why Are These Men Laughing?" *Esquire* (January 2003)

[6] Robert Parry, *Lost History*, pp. 14-26

[7] Ibid.

[8] *The Washington Post* (October 16, 2001)

[9] *Financial Times* (October 15, 2001)

[10] Ron Suskind, *The One Percent Doctrine*, pp. 74-75

Chapter Twelve

[1] See Nat Parry, "Bush's Return to Unilateralism," *Consortiumnews.com* (February 18, 2002)

[2] *The Independent* (January 19, 2002)

[3] See Michael Isikoff , "Double Standards?," *Newsweek* (May 25, 2004)

[4] See Michael Isikoff, "Memos Reveal War Crimes Warnings," *Newsweek* (May 17, 2004)

[5] Ibid.

[6] *The Washington Post,* http://www.washingtonpost.com/wp-dyn/articles/A62516-2004Jun22.html (June 23, 2004)

[7] Ibid.

[8] See Bob Woodward, *Bush at War* (New York: Simon & Schuster, 2002), p. 342

[9] See Sam Parry, "Bush's Endless War," *Consortiumnews.com* (March 8, 2002)

[10] See David Hoffman, "Beyond Public Diplomacy," *Foreign Affairs* (March/April 2002)

[11] *Agence France-Presse* (February 27, 2002)

[12] *The Washington Post* (September 20, 2001)

[13] *The Washington Post* (March 7, 2002)

[14] See Nat Parry, "Bush's Grim Vision," *Consortiumnews.com* (June 21, 2002)

[15] See Ian Williams, "The U.S. Hit List at the United Nations," *Foreign Policy in Focus* (April 30, 2002)

[16] Ibid.

[17] *The Independent* (April 20, 2002)

[18] See Ian Williams, "The U.S. Hit List at the United Nations," *Foreign Policy in Focus* (April 30, 2002)

[19] *Christian Science Monitor* (April 24, 2002)

[20] See Ian Williams, "The U.S. Hit List at the United Nations," *Foreign Policy in Focus* (April 30, 2002)

[21] See John R. Bolton, "Letter to UN Secretary General Kofi Annan," U.S. State Department Web site, http://www.state.gov/r/pa/prs/ps/2002/9968.htm

[22] "U.S.: 'Hague Invasion Act' Becomes Law," Human Rights Watch, http://www.hrw.org/press/2002/08/aspa080302.htm (August 3, 2002)

[23] See Eric Boehlert, "The Dragnet Comes Up Empty," *Salon.com* (June 19, 2002)

[24] *The Washington Post* (June 13, 2002)

[25] BBC (June 12, 2002)

[26] *The Washington Post* (May 17, 2002)

Chapter Thirteen

[1] See Richard Sale's summary of the CIA-Hussein relationship, UPI (April 10, 2003)

[2] See Jerry Meldon, "A CIA Officer's Calamitous Choices," *Consortiumnews.com* (May 15, 2003)

[3] See John J. Mearsheimer and Stephen Walt, "An Unnecessary War," *Foreign Policy* (January/February 2003)

[4] "Haig's Top Secret 'Talking Points' on 1981 Trip to Mideast," http://www.consortiumnews.com/2003/haig-docs.html

[5] Ibid.

[6] See Christopher Dickey and Evan Thomas, "How Saddam Happened," *Newsweek* (September 23, 2002)

[7] See Murray Waas and Craig Unger, "In the Loop: Bush's Secret Mission," *The New Yorker* (November 2, 1992)

[8] *The New York Times* (January 3, 2003)

[9] *The McLaughlin Group*, taped on August 10, 1990
[10] *The Washington Post* (August 16, 1990)
[11] *The Washington Post* (March 22, 1991)
[12] Robert Parry, *Secrecy & Privilege*, pp. 52-55
[13] See Stefan Halper and Jonathan Clarke, *America Alone: The Neo-Conservatives and the Global Order* (Cambridge: Cambridge University Press, 2004), p. 14
[14] Ibid., p. 33
[15] Ibid., p. 14
[16] Robert Parry, *Secrecy & Privilege*, p. 184-187
[17] See Seymour Hersh, "Selective Intelligence," *The New Yorker* (May 12, 2003)
[18] See Karen Kwiatkowski, "The New Pentagon Papers," *Salon.com* (March 10, 2004)

Chapter Fourteen

[1] Associated Press (September 3, 2002)
[2] See Bob Woodward, *Plan of Attack* (New York, Simon and Schuster, 2004), p. 421
[3] Ibid.
[4] *The Washington Post* (February 13, 2002)
[5] *The New York Times* (March 27, 2006)
[6] *The Los Angeles Times* (June 15, 2005)
[7] *The London Sunday Times* (June 12, 2005)
[8] CNN, *Dead Wrong* (August 21, 2005)
[9] *The New York Times* (September 7, 2002)
[10] Ibid.
[11] *The New York Times* (September 25, 2002)
[12] *The New York Times* (October 10, 2002)
[13] CNN, *Dead Wrong* (August 21, 2005)
[14] Ibid.
[15] Ibid.
[16] *The New York Times* (October 12, 2002)
[17] *The New York Times* (October 13, 2002)
[18] *The New York Times* (October 12, 2002)
[19] *The Washington Post* (September 24, 2002)
[20] *The Washington Post* (September 25, 2002)
[21] *The Washington Post* (September 27, 2002)
[22] *The Wall Street Journal* (September 26, 2002)
[23] Sam Parry, "The Politics of Preemption," *Consortiumnews.com*, Oct. 8, 2002

Chapter Fifteen

[1] For the history of how the CIA's analytical division was politicized, see Robert Parry's *Secrecy & Privilege*.
[2] Select Senate Committee on Intelligence, "Postwar Findings About Iraq's WMD Programs and Links to Terrorism and How they Compare with Prewar Assessments," INC Volume (September 8, 2006), p. 8
[3] Ibid., pp. 21-22

[4] Ibid., pp. 24-25

[5] Ibid., pp. 25-26

[6] Ibid., pp. 30-32

[7] Ibid., p. 32

[8] Ibid., p. 40

[9] Ibid., p. 42

[10] See Douglas McCollam, "How Chalabi Played the Press," *Columbia Journalism Review* (July/August 2004)

[11] Ibid.

[12] Ibid.

[13] Select Senate Committee on Intelligence, "Postwar Findings About Iraq's WMD Programs and Links to Terrorism and How they Compare with Prewar Assessments," INC Volume (September 8, 2006), p. 88

[14] Ibid., pp. 44-45

[15] Ibid., pp. 51-52

[16] Ibid., pp. 58-65

[17] Ibid., pp. 103-104

[18] *The Los Angeles Times* (April 2, 2005)

[19] CIA-DIA report, "Iraqi Mobile Biological Warfare Agent Production Plants" (May 16, 2003)

[20] Select Senate Committee on Intelligence, "Postwar Findings About Iraq's WMD Programs and Links to Terrorism and How they Compare with Prewar Assessments," INC Volume (September 8, 2006), p. 106

[21] Ibid., pp. 106-108

[22] Ibid., p. 113

[23] Ibid., pp. 52-59

[24] Ibid., pp. 60-61

[25] Suskind, *The One Percent Doctrine*, p. 62

[26] Ibid.

[27] Ibid., pp. 62-64

[28] Ibid., pp. 65-66

[29] Ibid. p. 72

[30] Ibid., pp. 76-78

[31] Ibid.

[32] Ibid., p. 77

[33] Ibid. pp. 79-80

[34] Ibid., p. 81

[35] Ibid., p. 106

[36] Ibid., pp. 90-91

[37] Ibid., pp. 109-111

Chapter Sixteen

[1] *The Guardian* (October 9, 2002)

[2] *Knight-Ridder* (October 8, 2002)

[3] *The Los Angeles Times* (October 11, 2002)

[4] *The New York Times* (October 10, 2002)

[5] *The* [UK] *Times* (November. 22, 2002)
[6] *The Washington Post* (November 19, 2002)
[7] *The Independent* (February 26, 2004)
[8] *The Guardian* (February 28, 2004)
[9] CNN, *Dead Wrong* (August 21, 2005)
[10] Ibid.
[11] See Chapter Eight: The Legend.
[12] CBS News (February 4, 2004)
[13] CNN, *Dead Wrong* (August 21, 2005)
[14] *The Washington Post* (March 18, 2003)
[15] CBS, *60 Minutes* (May 14, 2006)

Chapter Seventeen

[1] *The Guardian* (November 24, 2002)
[2] *The Washington Post* (December 26, 2002)
[3] *The Wall Street Journal* (April 11, 2003)
[4] *The Washington Post* (April 15, 2003)
[5] *The New York Times* (April 14, 2003)
[6] See Ann Scott Tyson, "US troops' anguish: Killing outmatched foes," *Christian Science Monitor* (April 11, 2003)
[7] *The New York Times* (April 14, 2003)
[8] See Patrick Buchanan, "Whose War?" *The American Conservative* (March 24, 2003)
[9] See Howard Dean, "Bush: It's Not Just His Doctrine That's Wrong," *CommonDreams.org* (April 17, 2003)
[10] *The Independent* (April 13, 2003)
[11] *The New York Times* (April 17, 2003)
[12] *The New York Times* (April 20, 2003)
[13] Ibid.

Chapter Eighteen

[1] See Fairness and Accuracy in Reporting, "The Final Word Is Hooray!" http://www.fair.org/index.php?page=2842 (March 15, 2006); also, see Norman Solomon, "War-Loving Pundits," *Fair.org* (March 16, 2006)
[2] *The Wall Street Journal* (April 21, 2003)
[3] *The Independent* (April 23, 2003)
[4] NBC Nightly News (April 25, 2003)
[5] *The New York Times* (May 6, 2003)
[6] See Fairness and Accuracy in Reporting, "The Final Word Is Hooray!" http://www.fair.org/index.php?page=2842 (March 15, 2006); also, see Norman Solomon, "War-Loving Pundits," *Fair.org* (March 16, 2006)
[7] *The New York Times* (May 16, 2003)
[8] MSNBC (May 8, 2003)
[9] *The Independent* (May 29, 2003)
[10] BBC News (May 29, 2003)

[11] *The Washington Post* (May 31, 2003)

[12] See Robert Parry, "America's Matrix," *Consortiumnews.com* (June 2, 2003)

[13] *The New York Times* (June 7, 2003)

[14] *The Observer* (June 8, 2003)

[15] See Nat Parry, "Bush & the End of Reason," *Consortiumnews.com* (June 17, 2003)

[16] "Meet the Press," NBC (June 8, 2003)

[17] *The New York Times* (June 22, 2003)

[18] See Robert Parry, "Bush's Iraqi Albatross," *Consortiumnews.com* (June 25, 2003)

Chapter Nineteen

[1] See Joseph Wilson, *The Politics of Truth: Inside the Lies that Put the White House on Trial and Betrayed My Wife's CIA Identity* (New York: Carroll & Graff Publishers, 2005),p. 5

[2] *The New York Times* (July 16, 2005)

[3] *The New York Times* (October 25, 2005)

[4] *The Los Angeles Times* (February 13, 2007)

[5] *The New York Times* (October 25, 2005)

[6] *The Washington Post* (September 14, 2006)

[7] *The New York Times* (July 16, 2005)

[8] *The Washington Post* (January 30, 2007)

[9] *The New York Times* (October 16, 2005)

[10] *The Washington Post* (September 14, 2006)

[11] See Timothy M. Phelps and Knut Royce, "Columnist Blows CIA Agent's Cover," *Newsday.com* (July 22, 2003)

[12] *The Washington Post* (January 30, 2007)

[13] See John Dickerson, "Where's My Subpoena?," *Slate* (February 7, 2006)

[14] See Michael Isikoff, "Matt Cooper's Source," *Newsweek* (July 18, 2005)

[15] *The New York Times* (October 16, 2005)

[16] *The Washington Post* (September 28, 2003)

Chapter Twenty

[1] *The Washington Post* (October 1, 2004)

[2] See Nat Parry, "Bush's Floundering Doctrine," *Consortiumnews.com* (September 3, 2003)

[3] *The New York Times* (December 7, 2003)

[4] *Newsday* (December 8, 2003)

Chapter Twenty-One

[1] See Ron Suskind, *The Price of Loyalty: George W. Bush, the White House, and the Education of Paul O'Neill* (New York: Simon & Schuster, 2004), p. 122

[2] For the chronological list of rollbacks see the Natural Resources Defense Council Web site at http://www.nrdc.org/bushrecord/.

[3] See Robert F. Kennedy Jr., "Crimes Against Nature," *Rolling Stone* (December 11, 2003)

[4] See David Stipp, "The Pentagon's Weather Nightmare," *Fortune* (February 9, 2004)
[5] Suskind, *The Price of Loyalty*, p. 306
[6] See Ron Suskind, "Faith, Certainty and the Presidency of George W. Bush," *New York Times Magazine* (October 17, 2004)
[7] Ibid.
[8] *USA Today* (May 3, 2004)
[9] See Nat Parry, "Apocalypse Again," *Consortiumnews.com* (May 4, 2004)
[10] *The Wall Street Journal* (June 7, 2004)
[11] Convention (II) for the Amelioration of the Condition of Wounded, Sick and Shipwrecked Members of Armed Forces at Sea. Geneva, 12 August 1949, <http://www.icrc.org/ihl.nsf/COM/370-580006?OpenDocument>

Chapter Twenty-Two

[1] See Duane Clarridge, *A Spy for All Seasons: My Life in the CIA* (New York: Simon and Schuster, 1997), p. 245
[2] Robert Parry's *Lost History*,
[3] Robert Parry, *Lost History*, p. 237
[4] Robert Parry, *Lost History*, p. 231
[5] *The Washington Post* (August 12, 2004)
[6] ABC News Nightline (October 14, 2004)

Chapter Twenty-Three

[1] *The Washington Post* (October 26, 2004)
[2] *The Plain Dealer* (September 16, 2003)
[3] Suskind, *The One Percent Doctrine*, p. 336
[4] See Bill Sammon, *Strategery: How George W. Bush is Defeating Terrorists, Outwitting Democrats, and Confounding the Mainstream Media* (Washington, DC: Regnery Publishing, 2006), p. 184
[5] Ibid.
[6] *The New York Times* (November 5, 2004)
[7] *The Hill* (November 8, 2004)
[8] See Sam Parry, "Bush's 'Incredible' Vote Tallies," *Consortiumnews.com* (November 9, 2004)
[9] Nat Parry, "Bush Victory's Lesson to the World, *Consortiumnews.com* (November 11, 2004)
[10] Robert Parry, "Evidence of a Second Bush Coup," *Consortiumnews.com* (November 6, 2004)
[11] *The Washington Post* (November 4, 2004)
[12] *The Washington Post* (December 30, 2004)

Chapter Twenty-Four

[1] *The Washington Post* (January 16, 2005)
[2] See Jane Mayer, "Outsourcing Torture," *The New Yorker* (February 14, 2005)

[3] *The Washington Post* (January 21, 2005)
[4] Ibid.
[5] See Anonymous, *Imperial Hubris: Why the West is Losing the War on Terror* (Washington, DC: Brassey's, Inc., 2004), p. 15
[6] Ibid., p. 17
[7] *The Washington Times* (January 19, 2005)
[8] *The New York Times* (February 3, 2005)
[9] Ibid.
[10] See Robert Parry, "Sinking in Deeper," *Consortiumnews.com* (February 3, 2005)
[11] *The New York Times* (February 27, 2005)
[12] *The New York Times* (March 1, 2005)
[13] *The Washington Post* (March 1, 2005)
[14] Ibid.
[15] *The Washington Post* (March 2, 2005)
[16] *The New York Times* (March 3, 2005)
[17] *The Washington Post* (March 4, 2005)
[18] *The Boston Globe* (March 1, 2005)
[19] See Sam Parry, "Terry Schiavo & the Right-Wing Machine," *Consortiumnews.com* (April 1, 2005)
[20] *The Washington Post* (April 25, 2005)
[21] *The Washington Post* (June 12, 2005)
[22] *The Washington Post* (June 17, 2005)
[23] *Reuters* (June 22, 2005)

Chapter Twenty-Five

[1] See Robert Parry, "Braveheart, Edward I & George W. Bush," *Consortiumnews.com* (August 10, 2005)
[2] See Robert Parry, "Lessons of the London Bombings," *Consortiumnews.com* (July 9, 2005)
[3] *The Washington Post* (July 19, 2005)
[4] *The New York Times* (August 16, 2004)
[5] See Nat Parry, "Bush's Grimmer Vision," *Consortiumnews.com* (July 21, 2005)
[6] *The Washington Post* (August 14, 2005)
[7] See Robert Parry, "Iraq & the Logic of Withdrawal," *Consortiumnews.com* (August 17, 2005)

Chapter Twenty-Six

[1] See Will Bunch, "Did New Orleans Catastrophe Have to Happen?" *Editor & Publisher* (August 31, 2005)
[2] See Evan Thomas, "How Bush Blew It," *Newsweek* (September 18, 2005)
[3] Ibid.
[4] See Robert Parry, "After Katrina, America's Political Crisis," *Consortiumnews.com* (September 9, 2005)
[5] *The New York Times* (September 18, 2005)
[6] *The New York Times* (September 21, 2005)

[7] Ibid.

[8] See Nat Parry, "Roberts & the 'Apex of Presidential Power,'" *Consortiumnews.com* (September 6, 2005)

[9] *The New York Times* (September 28, 2005)

[1] *The New York Times* (November 29, 2005)

[2] See Robert Parry, *Lost History*

[3] *The New York Times* (May 26, 2004)

Chapter Twenty-Eight

[1] *The New York Times* (December 16, 2005)

[2] *The Washington Post* (November 27, 2005)

[3] *The Washington Post* (December 19, 2005)

[4] *The New York Times* (December 21, 2005)

[5] Ibid.

[6] *The New York Times* (January 2, 2006)

[7] *The New York Times* (January 1, 2006)

[8] See Nat Parry, "Alito & the Point of No Return," *Consortiumnews.com* (January 9, 2006)

[9] Pacifica Radio (January 5, 2006)

[10] *The Wall Street Journal* (January 5, 2006)

[11] *The New York Times* (January 20, 2006)

[12] *The New York Times* (January 17, 2006)

[13] *The Washington Post* (January 14, 2006)

Chapter Twenty-Nine

[1] *Market Watch* (January 26, 2006)

[2] *The New York Times* (February 4, 2006)

[3] See Nat Parry, "Bush's Mysterious 'New Programs,'" *Consortiumnews.com* (February 21, 2006)

[4] See Robert Parry, "Bush Flummoxes Kafka, Orwell," *Consortiumnews.com* (March 3, 2006)

[5] *The Washington Post* (April 4, 2006)

[6] *The Washington Post* (May 4, 2006)

[7] *The New York Times* (September 14, 2006)

[8] Ibid.

[9] See Robert Parry, "Shame on Us All," *Consortiumnews.com* (October 18, 2006)

INDEX

ABOUT THE AUTHORS

Award-winning reporter Robert Parry, a 30-year veteran of Washington journalism, broke many of the stories now known as the Iran-Contra Affair while working for *The Associated Press* and *Newsweek* in the 1980s. He is the author of several books, including *Lost History* and *Secrecy & Privilege.* In 1995, he founded the investigative Web site, *Consortiumnews.com* and has served as its editor since. He lives in Arlington, Virginia.

Sam Parry, managing editor of the Consortium for Independent Journalism, worked for the Sierra Club from 1997 to 2003, and currently works for Environmental Defense. In 1995, he was instrumental in designing and launching *Consortiumnews.com*, billed as "the Internet's first investigative 'zine." He lives in Arlington, Virginia with his wife and two young children.

Nat Parry has worked for the Organization for Security and Cooperation in Europe, Public Citizen, and the American Constitution Society. His articles on foreign policy and human rights have appeared in *Foreign Policy in Focus, In These Times*, and *Consortiumnews.com.* In 2006, he received a Project Censored award for "outstanding investigative journalism." He has a Master's degree in political science from George Mason University.